Revolution in the Echo Chamber

Revolution in the Echo Chamber
Audio Drama's Past, Present and Future

By Leslie Grace McMurtry

intellect Bristol, UK / Chicago, USA

First published in the UK in 2019 by
Intellect, The Mill, Parnall Road, Fishponds, Bristol, BS16 3JG, UK

First published in the USA in 2019 by
Intellect, The University of Chicago Press, 1427 E. 60th Street,
Chicago, IL 60637, USA

Copyright © 2019 Intellect Ltd

All rights reserved. No part of this publication may be reproduced, stored in a retrieval system, or transmitted, in any form or by any means, electronic, mechanical, photocopying, recording, or otherwise, without written permission.

A catalogue record for this book is available from the British Library.

Copy-editor: MPS Technologies
Cover designer: Aleksandra Szumlas
Production manager: Naomi Curston
Typesetting: Contentra Technologies

Print ISBN: 978-1-78320-982-8
ePDF ISBN: 978-1-78938-044-6
ePUB ISBN: 978-1-78938-043-9

Printed and bound by Gomer, UK.

In memory of Nigel Jenkins (1949–2014) and Laurence Raw (1959–2018)
To listeners of audio drama everywhere

Radio 'turns the psyche and society into a single echo chamber'.
– Marshall McLuhan (1964)

Contents

Acknowledgements		xiii
Introduction: Why Bother with Audio Drama?		1
Section I:	**Audio Drama in Context**	**11**
Chapter 1:	**Audio Drama in the Context of the Literary Canon**	**13**
	How to treat radio drama	16
	Radio drama as high and low art	18
	A deluge of dirt?	20
	Against the Storm (1939-42)	23
	The Country and the City and *The Archers* in Middle England	26
	The radio western	29
	Conclusion	32
Chapter 2:	**Audio Drama and Listening**	**33**
	Listening is centripetal	36
	One and many	38
	Modes of listening	39
	Understanding listening	41
	Conclusion	42
Chapter 3:	**Audio Drama Techniques and Effects**	**45**
	How is audio drama made?	47
	The role of the actor in audio drama	51
	The role of the director and producer in audio drama	53
	Creating a soundscape	54
	The architecture of time	58

	Previously unheard worlds	58
	Painting a picture	60
	Dialect	60
	Heightened language	62
	Audiopositioning	63
	When we might like earlids	64
	Sex and violence on air	65
	Conclusion	67
Section II:	**History (1919–2010)**	**69**
Chapter 4:	British Radio Drama (1919–60)	71
	The birth of broadcasting (1895–1918)	73
	The British Broadcasting Company (1922–26)	76
	The BBC: Ambition and control (1927–39)	80
	Europe at war (1939–45)	85
	Post-war content (1945–55)	87
	The 1950s: The Golden Age of British radio drama	89
	Conclusion	90
Chapter 5:	US Radio Drama (1919–60)	93
	Spies, detectives, crime-fighters and victims	96
	Tinkering (1901–20)	97
	The Radio Act of 1927 (1920–27)	99
	Early advertising (1927–30)	99
	The Columbia Workshop and art vs. commodity (1935–40)	102
	Genre and audience (1940–55)	105
	Post-war radio trends (1945–55)	109
	Conclusion	111
Chapter 6:	Why US Audio Drama Died and British Audio Drama Survived	113
	Commercial advertising and control in the United States	116
	US network executives shape policy	117
	Censorship and TV	119
	The BBC and US radio policy	121
	Let's pretend: Was there any US radio drama 1948–58 that could have saved the genre?	124

Chapter 7:	The Ascendance of the Background Medium: Drama on US and British Radio (1960–2010)	129
	Radio drama in Britain (1960–2010)	131
	Radio drama in the United States (1960–2010)	138
	Conclusion	147
Section III:	**Audio Drama Today**	**149**
Chapter 8:	Current British Audio Drama	151
	Structure and strands	154
	BBC radio drama, body of work: Statistics	157
	BBC radio drama: Range of work	158
	Range of work: Anecdotal evidence	158
	Audiences	162
	iPlayer	163
	The gamechanger and *Life and Fate*	165
	Alternatives to the BBC	168
	Conclusion	171
Chapter 9:	Current US Audio Drama	173
	A tyranny of choice	177
	Serial	178
	What does public service broadcasting mean in the United States?	179
	Audiobooks	182
	Performatory OTR recreations	182
	Satellite audio drama	183
	Audio drama podcasts	187
	Conclusion	190
Section IV:	**The Future of Audio Drama**	**193**
Chapter 10:	Listening Now	195
	Shrimp sale at the Crab Crib: Advertising in podcasting paradise?	198
	Serial's sophomore slump	203
	Serial's audience: Those who don't listen	208
	Conclusion	211

Chapter 11: The Post-*Serial* World and Listeners of the Future	213
Throw us your pennies and we'll make you a kingdom	216
A rewrite of US communications legislation	221
Where do we go from here?	222
Audio drama in the political landscape	224
Conclusion: We're Listening	**227**
Appendices	**233**
Appendix 1 – Methodology: Statistics on BBC Radio Drama 2012	235
Appendix 2 – British winners of the Prix Italia and Prix Europa in Radio Drama since 1949	239
Appendix 3 – Panel of experts for *Radio Times* survey	245
Appendix 4 – Audio drama awards	246
References	**251**
Index	**289**

Acknowledgements

'On the other hand, if I want to intrigue my interlocutor, I say, I write and produce cultural programs for public radio.' This works unless the questioner is in professional sports or commercial broadcasting, or a Republican. I never tell them outright that I make radio plays because the quizzical looks I get depress me. Lately, 'I make audiobooks' often leads to further pleasant chat.
– Yuri Rasovsky, 'What exactly does a producer do?'

This book had a long gestation period. I would like to thank the following for their guidance and help throughout the process of bringing it to birth. Many thanks to my supervisors, David Britton and Richard Robinson, for their help during the period this project was conceived as my Ph.D. thesis. I am also indebted to Alan Bilton and Laurence Raw. Thanks are also necessary to those at the BBC who answered my questions: Alison Hindell, Caroline Raphael and Sharon Terry. As I spent a substantial amount of time in the British Library, St Pancras, thanks to all the staff there and particularly Ian Rawes and the Listening and Viewing Services. I am grateful to those who allowed me to interview them for the book: Kip Allen, Rick Huff, Linda López-McAlister, Wil Moore, John Pilkington and Fiona Thraille. Further thanks go to the organisers of In the Dark, Dorota Babilas, Alec Badenoch, Rick Coste, Kevin Curran, Andrew Dubber, Isabel Ermida, Nele Haise, Donna Halpern, Mary Traynor, Neil Jones, Leonard Kuffert, Denis Lachapelle, Jason Loviglio, Jamie Medhurst, Janne Nielsen, Andrew Ó'Baoill, Robert Ready, Seán Street, Heidi Svømmekjær and Hans-Ulrich Wagner. For ideas, inspiration, and critique, I am especially indebted to Hugh Chignell, Danielle Hancock, Nora Patterson, Alison Plant, Emma Rodero, Jennifer Stoever, Jack J. Ward and Frederick Greenhalgh. Special thanks to Mr Greenhalgh for permission to use his photos. As I completed this book as a lecturer at the University of Salford, I am grateful to my colleagues on the BA in Television and Radio for their insights and support. I also want to thank the staff at Intellect for their professionalism and their patience while developing this book, including Tim Mitchell, Jelena Stanovnik, Alex Szumlas and especially Naomi Curston.

A number of people had to put up with me during the eight or so years of this book's conception and development. I would like to thank Aya Vandenbusscche and Juha Niesniemi for their contributions. I am also indebted to my better half, Jamie Beckwith, who read drafts of this book in its every iteration (though I've not yet converted him to a podcast-listener). My family's unwavering support was invaluable to me, so big thanks to Christina Young, Illene Renfro, Sally Renfro and Lura Renfro. And last but never least, to my parents, Carol Renfro and Larry McMurtry, who have always believed in me.

Introduction

Why Bother with Audio Drama?

Radio-drama is in fact such an extraordinarily personal and private matter that it may be difficult to avoid appearing egotistical in writing about it.

– Lance Sieveking (1934)

'Why bother with audio drama?' In a world that seems so predisposed towards the visual, sound is often relegated to second-best.[1] As several sound theorists have pointed out, in Aristotle's parable of the cave of ignorance, it is the light not the sound that leads the lost person to safety. Paradoxically, sound is often felt to be so omnipresent as to be insignificant background noise. Jo Ann Tacchi has described radio's central yet invisible position as being as ubiquitous as brushing your teeth (1997: 106). Furthermore, sound studies are underdeveloped compared to other media studies (Attali 2013: 25). Hugh Chignell's *Key Concepts in Radio Studies* in 2009 was the first book to have the words 'radio studies' in the title, a signal of increasing scholarly interest in radio generally. Yet radio remains underresearched (Crook 1999a: 3), including radio drama. In addition to being underresearched, there is another challenge facing audio drama: its state on the margins of many people's experiences, in comparison to more widely recognized forms of audio-visual media like film and television. Radio drama is frequently on young people's peripheries. Guy Starkey noted:

> A common reaction to the proposition that they should produce drama, among students working with radio early in their careers, is surprise that anyone should even contemplate such an activity. Although inevitably exposed to various short forms of drama in their own listening, in, for example, radio advertisements […] they do not always perceive radio's potential for longer works of 90 minutes or more.
>
> (2004: 180)

Although the popularity of podcasts is making in-roads in perceptions of audio drama, for the majority of Americans at least, radio drama died in the 1960s – or, for many British people, it is vaguely experienced in passing, something for old people. So why bother with it?

But is radio what these young people think it is? What *is* radio? This may seem a naïve question, but it remains extremely relevant. In 2018, Dr Janey Gordon at the University of Bedfordshire asked this very question to the Radio-Studies JISC Mail e-mail newsgroup (Gordon 2018). For many observers, digital radio itself remains the barometer of radio's elasticity of form, 'increasingly the preferred platform for the continuity and modernization' of radio's 'languages, narratives, practices and, [sic] identities' (Fernández-Quijada 2017: 77). Podcasting, too, has significantly changed the audio landscape. In their introduction to the 2016 special edition of *The Radio Journal* on podcasts, editors Mia Lindgren and Michele Hilmes noted, '[i]t's timely to focus an issue of a journal dedicated to studies of radio and audio media on podcasting, as the field of sound production continues to grow and the power of audio is increasingly discussed in mainstream media' (2016: 3). As yet, however, the study of audio drama itself remains both fragmented and sparse. Indeed, Hilmes would suggest that ephemerality is the key to the lack of previous radio studies (2013: 45).

'Contemporary culture', as Simon Malpas puts it, 'moves at an almost incomprehensible speed' (2005: 1). Listening habits have always been in flux, though perhaps the recent speeding up of technological change has made an accelerated impact. Shortening of attention span is cited as evidence of this. While evidence regarding attention spans and their shortening is contradictory, some research has demonstrated that personality-trait narcissism has risen since the early 1980s among US college students and that media technology may in part be responsible for this (Konrath 2013, 2015; Konrath et al. 2014). From the computer to the tablet and smartphone, a great deal of media consumption is now situated on a screen. The concept of convergence – the melting of technologies into one device – has absolutely come to pass – Henry Jenkins' 'Black Box Fallacy' notwithstanding (Jenkins 2008). This has relevance for radio and listening habits, too, as the binge-watch culture and the breakdown of a monolithic concept of public service broadcasting (PSB) in the United States and the United Kingdom has implications for the consumption of radio.

In this changing environment, it is still critical that we pay attention to the past and present of audio drama in order to divine its future. This book explores the idea that audio drama can exist as both high and low art, and likewise tries to explore and ultimately bridge the gap between existing audio drama and a larger potential audience. Increasingly, what Tiziano Bonini (2011) refers to as 'the game' – when savvy listeners of drama intellectually understand that an aural work is fiction, yet their emotional investment causes them to almost 'forget' and believe in the 'truthfulness of what they are hearing' – has assumed real importance. *Serial* (2014–present) and the post-*Serial* drama podcasts have, as I argue in Chapter 9, made this mode of storytelling difficult to ignore.

Why bother with audio drama? Because it is an important art form that we need to invest in. In order to do so, we have to be honest with ourselves and learn from the lessons of the past and our current experiences. A world without audio drama is not one I want to experience, and yet many young people in the United States and the United Kingdom are not aware that they are missing out. I hope to provide some reasons in the next section for why they *should* bother with audio drama, and I hope, by the end of this book, to posit some strategies for continuing their enjoyment once hooked. Furthermore, this book identifies other audiences who have traditionally not engaged with audio drama: audiences who are less educated and non-white, as well as elderly audiences who specifically do not engage with the podcasting technology through which much audio drama is now transmitted. The function of the book is in part to identify these audiences and see what can be done by audio drama to engage them.

Introduction

Reasons to exist

Radio drama's defiance of its often-forecast death knell may seem remarkable. Even virtuosi of the genre predicted its demise. For example, BBC radio dramatist Lance Sieveking claimed as early as 1934, '[p]erhaps, and it is more than likely, this present decade will be the only decade in the history of the human race which will know the radio-play', comparing audio drama's short life to that of the silent film (1934: 28).

Critics continue to suggest that in our age of visual supremacy, audio drama is at best superfluous and at worst, aesthetically bankrupt and commercially bereft. 'So is radio drama dying, as Equity warned us?' *The Guardian* asked in 2010. 'Not yet, not while the BBC still exists', it concluded (Benedictus 2010). Annie Caulfield sarcastically remarked, '[p]eople could stop listening to radio. The sky might fall' (2009: 17). There are, in fact, far more than Sieveking's 'handful of reasons' for believing strongly that humanity should bother with audio drama. They include access; value for money; portability and ease; dramatic potential for social education beyond that of radio journalism; the bringing together of a multifaceted audience; its sweep and its intimacy; its ability to simulate reality and its unparalleled capacity to prompt our brains to construct mental imagery.

For the maker of radio and audio drama, these forms represent, in many ways, a very accessible art form, something they share in common with podcasting more generally. Podcasting has been identified with a grassroots, non-corporate veneer, 'content that could not have come into existence another way' (Lombardo 2008: 217, 226). Indeed, as Hancock and McMurtry note, in the 'shared voices, stories and forum-comments' of horror drama podcasts in particular, 'speakers and listeners may engage with one another, if not face-to-face, then mouth-to-ear-to-eye' (2017: 5). Looking at radio in the Internet age, Fiona Thraille argued against the prescriptiveness and elitism of stage theatre, contrasting it with the freedom to tell stories without commercial pressure. 'Anyone with a computer and access to the Internet can write, mix and distribute audio drama using free programs and resources', Thraille argued (2014). For her, 'satellite radio drama' is the most liberating of forms of dramatic expression because 'there is no need to be in the same geographical area as other group members' with fewer financial constraints (Thraille 2014). Some would also argue that traditional broadcast radio shared some of these aspects. Indeed, as Caulfield has argued, '[t]here is no radio equivalent of the studio or upstairs theatre, where beginners are tucked away to try their early works' (2009: 13). Geoffrey Heptonstall has described radio as 'potentially the most enriching, and the most democratic, of media' (2009: 204). Frances Berrigan has characterized audio drama's appeal to people 'with no group categorization' because the focus is on the human voice rather than visual identification (1977: 166), a quality noticed by DJs at London's Desi Radio Southall: 'Fortunately, on radio, they never see you. They don't see your colour or your caste' (cited in Coyer 2007b: 121).

Professionally, radio drama is arguably easier to break into for writers than the more heavily regulated film, television and print industries (e.g. Caulfield 2009: 13). The continued strong response to BBC Writersroom and the ever-growing free audio drama industry would seem to suggest this (BBC 2014a). Radio drama can also be categorized as an appropriate training ground for other media, as David Hendy has argued, with Radio 4 programmes including drama setting standards of technical and editorial quality that were a yardstick for the whole of British broadcasting (2007: 273). As one example, writer Joe White, who was chosen as one of the 2014 BBC Writersroom winners, had a drama, *Temples,* broadcast on Radio 3 that year and went on to win the Channel 4 Playwriting Award (formerly Pearson Award) and in 2015, he was the Writer in Residence of Pentabus Theatre Company. This is one way in which audio drama is accessible.

In the earliest days of radio, drama was characterized by a different kind of unprecedented access. It opened doors for not only producers but also for listeners, especially those in rural areas, in geographical ranges as dissimilar as rural Scotland and the American South, to the kind of theatre these listeners would not be able to access in their remote locations (cf. Walker 2011; Barfield 1996). Malcolm Usrey recalled that in the United States during the Great Depression, 'many rural people never saw the inside of a library, never read a newspaper, never read a magazine. But nearly everyone had a radio' (cited in Barfield 1996: 22).

All of this highlights two of audio drama's very commercially important elements and excellent reasons to pursue it: the relatively negligible constraints in time and money to produce it. As Tim Crook has put it, 'the narrative long shot in radio could establish with a few words and within a few seconds a fictional reality that would be financially prohibitive in any other medium' (1999b). Writer Angela Carter was also quick to recognize the expressive potentials of audio drama versus its cost, writing in 1985 that its collage and montage effects were 'beyond the means of any film-maker', not just financially 'but also because the eye takes longer to register images than does the ear' (1985: 7). Nicholas Briggs, co-producer of the successful Big Finish imprint, said, 'you can do amazing things that would be hellishly expensive to do otherwise in a visual form' (2013: 33).

More convenient and less expensive to make, more portable and technologically accessible, audio drama has progressed from reels of hand-bladed tape to cassette tapes to CD tracks to MP3 files, which are relatively small and therefore instantly portable. 'The podcast liberates' the audio drama experience, 'allowing listeners to alter any space at any time' (Hancock and McMurtry 2017: 3). Moreover, the great virtue of radio – which is why it continues to feature in developing countries – is its ability to reach many people in a much cheaper form than other types of broadcasting and media (Nwaerondu and Thompson 1999; Mark 2009). Without venturing into the issues regarding whether radio is a primary or a secondary medium (see Chapter 2), it is enough to note that radio has become absolutely integrated into daily life (Tacchi 1997: 106). This quality is impossible to ignore and highlights audio drama's versatility in an increasingly frenetic modern life. It can be listened to while 'travelling, exercising, doing the housework' (Thraille 2013).

Radio drama also offers dramatic potential for education beyond that of radio journalism. As Heptonstall put it, 'programming of sincere, good intentions can be dull', while 'intelligent radio of the spoken word is inclined by nature toward the style and substance of literature' (2009: 204). Perhaps the reason that this is true is what Kenneth Burke hinted at in 1941 in calling popular culture 'proverbs writ large'. If the literary text must, in William Touponce's words, 'invoke and at the same time problematize, question, and even negate reader's expectations' (1998: 21), the dramatic potential in audio drama to tackle issues that might be dull or proselytizing in journalism is demonstrably closer to entertainment and therefore more generally palatable.

As Carter recognized in the previously cited example, the radio montage – used equally effectively in radio documentary as in fictional drama – appears uniquely radiogenic. In this way, audio drama makes use of radio's hybridization of 'several trades and expressive registers' (Verma 2012: 5). Nicholas Briggs, who won the 2014 Best Online or Non-Broadcast Audio Drama at the BBC Audio Drama Awards for *Doctor Who: Dark Eyes* (2012), underlines how new aesthetic techniques can be pioneered or can best be used to full effect on audio. Discussing his play *Embrace the Darkness* (2002), he said:

> when Charley realizes that the person has no eyes I was really quite proud of that. I think actually that seeing that would have been so horrible it would have been distracting in a way.
> (Briggs 2013: 33)

The ability of audio drama to reach mass audiences and while at the same time addressing the individual ear is one of its greatest assets, what Dermot Rattigan calls audio's macro and micro scale (2002: 13). 'Radio puts its dispersed listeners under the spell of a shared event', Evan Eisenberg wrote (1987: 31), echoing the memories of thousands of Americans who grew up and immortalized, some might say fetishized, radio dramas like *The Lone Ranger* (1933–54, MBS/ABC). *The Lone Ranger* was an impressively persuasive shared experience of the 1930s and 1940s. Frances Gray captures the social element of audio drama's vast sweep when discussing the BBC's *Dick Barton, Special Agent* (1946–51) and *It's That Man Again* (*ITMA*) (1939–49): a 'true collective response when discussed the next day in the workplace, or when their catchphrases or distinctive voices passed into common currency' (2004: 252). With audio drama, *you* 'shadow the Shadow', as Verma put it (2012: 60). Both Michael Socolow (2004) and Alexander Russo (2009) determined in their analyses of radio advertising encroachments on an American listening public of the 1940s and 1950s that listeners' personal space can be violated by sound in a way other methods cannot. Michael Bull (2013b) has performed work on the more current practice of headphone listening, particularly iPod culture, which has argued for the way listeners can transform their landscapes.

The intimacy and trust occasioned by the listening experience comments on the nature of reality, what Carter called 'that magical and enigmatic margin, that space of the invisible, which must be filled in by the imagination of the listener' (1985: 7). Audio drama continues to engage listeners in 'the game', as mentioned earlier in this chapter, with listeners suspecting a narrative is fictional but enjoying playing along as if it were non-fiction. Seán Street suggests that 'radio can add the weapon of blurring reality to its armoury of imaginative devices' (2012: 30). The blurring of reality and fiction in audio drama, which is accomplished with such consummate skill, taps into the core of human nature, the desire to be complicit in a deception and to debate about the nature of reality itself. BBC plays of the early 1920s exploited this conceit, as did French and German plays like *Marémoto* (1924) and *Hörspiel–S.O.S….rao rao…Foyn. 'Krassin' rettet 'Italia'* (1929). However, deceiving people on a grand scale, whether intentionally or unconsciously, began to be subsumed by more subtle explorations that challenged listeners to 'make-believe' deliberately. The dramatized trials of Louis XVI, of Danton and of Charlotte Corday made on French radio in the 1930s were considered 'better than live theatre' (Brochand 1974: 379). This tradition continues, with Italian radio's *Amnèsia* (2008–09, RAI Radio 2), and with post-*Serial* podcast fiction such as *The Black Tapes* (2015–present), *TANIS* (2015–present), *Archive 81* (2016–present), *The Message* (2015–present), and even BBC radio drama, such as *That Was Then* (2018) (Hancock and McMurtry 2018).

Davia Nelson, a producer of Peabody Award-winning radio documentaries, compares radio production to food: 'You spend hours, days, months gathering the ingredients, cutting and mixing – making it cook. The minute it hits the air/table, it's gone' (Nelson and Silva 2010: 36). For all this ephemeral quality, it is audio's images that endure in the imagination and the memory, something that critics as disparate as Valeri V. Prosorov in Russia (2012) and Garrison Keillor in the United States (2005) have noticed. 'Twiddle the dial', Keillor wrote, 'and in the midst of the clamor and blare and rackety commercials you find a human being speaking to you in a way that intrigues you and lifts your spirits' (2005: 38). As Frances Gray noticed, audio can create 'Ancient Rome or the planet Mars simply by mentioning them, and the listener can be transported from one to the other in seconds' (2009: 268).

This superb visual extrapolation from sound clues remains poorly understood. 'By imagining the missing visual component', the listener embarks 'on an instinctual search for sense, order, security' (Marc 1996: 180). Yet this journey is different for each listener. And it is difficult to quantify and understand the components that mentally create such pictures. However, cognitive theory offers some clues. Stephen Kosslyn's research beginning in 1983 was pioneering. 'That people differ in their abilities to use mental images', Kosslyn wrote, 'has been known almost since the birth of scientific psychology' (1983: 194). Intriguingly, people can imagine things that never existed in nature and therefore they never would have seen. This, says Kosslyn, is 'hallmark' of mental events (1983: 91). Research in this field (such as that of Emma Rodero at the Universitat de Pompeu Fabra in Barcelona and Charlotte Russell at King's College London) continues to work to demystify this process; yet the effects of it remain undeniable.

To summarize, audio drama's remarkable longevity is paralleled only by its adaptability. This quality is most likely to ensure its success through the next century. Radio drama, then, is an excellent medium in terms of access, value-for-money for those who invest in making it, its portability and ease of dissemination; its dramatic potential for education beyond that of radio journalism and its ability to combine elements from other media to make something unique are not to be discounted. Furthermore, its most potent weapons are its dichotomy of vast sweep and intimacy; its ability to simulate reality and the unparalleled ability for our brains to construct our own images.

To return to our opening question, 'what is radio?' Tacchi (2012) argues that radio-like media still perform the same roles as radio. Dubber suggests that radio is best defined *by what people call radio*, and with that in mind, this book often uses 'radio drama' and 'audio drama' interchangeably. 'A podcast remains radio', Chignell asserts, 'because of the way it is produced. A film, after all, is still a film even when it is shot using a digital video camera and watched on a television set' (2009: 1). This work's title suggests that it will examine audio drama's past, present and future, which is indeed the overarching method. This book professes a transnational approach similar to Michele Hilmes' in *Network Nations: A Transnational History of British and American Broadcasting* (2012), that is, focusing on the interplay between US and British radio, though this work focuses to a much deeper level on drama particularly. While it would be satisfying to deal with *all* Anglophone national traditions of audio drama (including those of Canada, Australia, New Zealand and South Africa), unfortunately the scope of the present work cannot cover these countries in any detail, nor still can it examine European traditions of radio drama. The field is open for such studies to be attempted in the future.

This book is a history and a celebration of audio drama, though not an uncritical one. Audio drama has the potential to be many things to many people, but it needs to work to continue reaching listeners; it cannot afford to narrow its definitions or its audiences. We begin in Section I investigating in Chapter 1 some aesthetic and sociocultural elements of radio and audio drama, particularly the contentious place of radio drama as high art or low commodity. In so doing, we use Kenneth Burke's 'proverbs writ large' theory in the context of soap operas and radio westerns, ultimately arguing that audio drama is everywhere on this cultural/literary continuum, a unique feature that should be highlighted, not scorned or ignored. In Chapter 2, we examine the available literature on mental imagery generation during audio drama listening and how this has (and sometimes hasn't) informed audio drama's reception and production. In Chapter 3, we continue the theme of producing drama, tying theory and practice together. Section II provides a sociohistorical survey of radio drama in the United Kingdom and the United States between 1919 and 2010, noting the way radio regulation influenced form and content, comparing similarities and differences in genres and techniques, and examining the dialogue between the two countries' radio output.

Section III presents an overview of audio drama today in the United States and the United Kingdom, examining current structure and strands on BBC Radio as well as British independents, and presents the many aspects of US PSB radio as well as detailing the proliferation of audio drama online, including in podcast and audiobook forms. Section IV attempts to synthesize trends from the current audio drama environment, including the influence of *Serial,* to formulate how people listen to audio drama today and how they might listen in the future. Chapter 11 focuses specifically on how to harness the passion and innovation of the multifaceted US audio drama scene and create a sustainable environment for long-lived audio drama.

Note

1 Though some sound scholars warn against a possible oversimplification of pitting sound vs. sight, cf. Crisell (1994: 7), Sterne (2003: 16–19) and Supper (2016: 72).

Section I

Audio Drama in Context

Chapter 1

Audio Drama in the Context of the Literary Canon

> Why is it worse to be a robot than an automaton, worse to imagine oneself a phonograph than a music box?
>
> – Evan Eisenberg (1987: 231)

As Val Gielgud, BBC head of radio drama 1922–56, implied, radio is often thought of as the Ugly Stepsister, and 'Television Drama snatched the glass slipper, and married the Prince' (1957: 7). This notion is in some degree responsible for an incomplete critical history for radio and for radio drama specifically. As Hugh Chignell wrote in 2009, radio studies has only been recently organized as an area of study. Indeed, the historical record of radio drama is somewhat better served than radio drama's place in terms of aesthetics. Can there be said to exist an audio drama canon? With an incomplete degree of accuracy and consensus, an audio drama literary canon sketchily begins to emerge from disparate sources. A radio drama canon would be seen as second-best to a stage-based one, much in the way television studies followed much later in the wake of film studies. Val Gielgud himself is in no small measure responsible for engendering this artificial hierarchy, championing radio drama that was most like its stage cousin. In practical terms, too, radio drama fares worse than its stage counterpart (due to the poor availability of scripts, which are rarely published) and other creative forms like film, prose fiction and television.

The central point of contention examined in this chapter is radio drama's place within the high or low art debate. As a very simplistic definition, high art in this context refers to what has generally been perceived as art forms that only those with the most cultivated taste can appreciate, while low art is accessible to anyone. It is almost impossible to say radio drama is high or low art as a body of work; indeed, my ultimate argument is that it encompasses the entire spectrum between the two, and that this is no bad thing. Ironically, in periods when radio drama has been alleged to be morally bankrupt and artistically bereft, such criticisms have helped it to achieve its most complex creations (such as the late 1930s on US network radio). Furthermore, it should be recognized that the high/low art debate has a gendered aspect, which also has roots in radio production and can be traced through the radio soap opera (serial). The radio soap opera has, by definition, been almost universally sneered at as the 'lowest' form of radio drama. Nevertheless, by using Kenneth Burke's idea about parables, as well as John G. Cawelti's approaches to popular culture critique, even the radio soap can aspire to the literary canon. While framing errors (defined below) are not unique to soap operas or to radio drama, they seem to be an enduring part of the appeal and aesthetics of radio drama. Indeed, it is framing errors themselves that we find emblematic of radio drama's high/low art qualities, because it is impossible to draw the line where the artist is following convention and where he or she is innovating. This chapter expands upon the above contentions and seeks to place audio drama within the literary canon, and the chapter is strongly characterized by an approach that critiques representations of gender and ethnicity in popular media.

How to treat radio drama

There are a number of difficulties that face those seeking to identify a radio drama canon. These converge on categorization, definition, theoretical framework, and lack of meaningful, analytic archives. How do we 'treat' radio drama? How do we work with radio drama theory? Can radio drama be treated like a literary text, like a film, like poetry, like stage drama? In short, what we lack is what Dan Lander calls 'an autonomous theory of sound' (1994: 11). There is no consensus in the way there is for film (Chignell 2009: 2).

It should be obvious by now from my interchangeable (and perhaps not wholly satisfying) use of 'radio' and 'audio' drama that we are without a meaningful term for the genre itself. This was made abundantly clear at the 2014 *Audiodrama Conference* at the University of Copenhagen, which assembled international scholars, all of whom agreed in the difficulty of a correct and 'catch-all' term. In English, we have terms like radio drama, radio play, audio drama and the theatre of the imagination, among others; in French, there is *théâtre-radiophonique, radio-théâtre, art radiophonique, scène radiophonique* and *roman radiophonique* ('radiophonic novel'). Later Francophone radio scholars made the distinction between *théâtre radiophoné* (that is to say, an adaptation from another medium) and *théâtre radiophonique* ('newly written'). This is an interesting distinction, but we lack something similar in English. In the German tradition, the radio play is known as *hörspiel,* which has a meaning of 'audio game'.

Without a 'theoretical framework' of our own, we are left groping as we cannot do a 'close reading' or a shot-by-shot analysis (Rudin 2011: 60). Indeed, our lack of vocabulary sees us adopting terms like 'shot-by-shot' from film and 'close reading' from print literature. A radio producer can be likened to a chemist or a chef, or in Tim Crook's phrase, a 'sound *philosophe*' (2012: 121), mixing a variety of ingredients from a variety of disciplines, treating his creative endeavour like a musical score at times, at other times invoking the vocabulary of poetry to describe its repetition, rhythm, rhyme and stanzas (James 1994: 4). Indeed, a quality that pervades radio is one of ambiguity:

> Because radio has no universal equivalent to the quotation mark, auditors could easily misinterpret whether a character was speaking to us in the present, subsequent to the main action, or to another character in the past during that action.
>
> (Verma 2012: 61)

This assertion highlights the difficulty in understanding sound generally through written language. A music-based vocabulary has developed for some aspects of sound studies, such as film sound. However, as Martin Shingler has noted, '[t]he English language lacks an adequate vocabulary to define sounds and the speaking voice' (Shingler 2006), and therefore analysing performance in radio has traditionally proven challenging.

Along with a lack of universal framework for textual analysis of radio drama, we are also dealing with a body of work that is both colossal and elusive. It is true that until recently, much radio drama has been inaccessible for study, far more so than many other forms of literature such as novels, stage plays and film (as noted by Crook 1999a: 3). There are several reasons for this. The first is that older plays were broadcast live and often never recorded. Playwright Tyrone Guthrie alluded to this, feeling the structure he composed was 'solid', but 'it melted as you looked and listened, and, like so much moonshine, it disappeared forever' (1931: 24). Davia Nelson of the Kitchen Sisters alluded to the impermanence of radio in a kitchen metaphor (as noted in the introduction), and broadcaster Kip Allen writes of music radio, 'a loaf of bread may be baked beautifully, but until it is eaten, it is of little use' (Allen 2013c). As noted by Rudin (2011: 61), this ephemeral quality makes long-term study challenging.

While technology has played its part – no one could have recorded the earliest broadcast plays, even had they wanted to, as the technology did not exist – it is just as often industry or listening public indifference that sealed the lost radio's fate. Even during the first half of the twentieth century, those who worked in radio seemed to be aware of this failing. Seymour and Martin in 1938 rather sadly noted that the price of making a career out of writing radio was being consigned to ephemera, doomed with 'the knowledge that [one's] work will be heard once and lost forever' (1938: 304). Sometimes elements of industry and production disastrously decided that the work was not worth saving, as S. Meltem Ahıska (2000) noted as regards Turkish national radio. To further frustrate the radio researcher, copyright issues often mean that broadcasts are not available for public and even scholarly access, and while some radio scripts, particularly older ones, have been published in book format, they are rarely catalogued within a subject heading of radio drama in libraries – they are usually found as part of the general fictional oeuvre of the author (Rudin 2011: 61), meaning researchers must first be aware of writers for radio before they can access many scripts. There is a dismissive critical attitude to those who write 'plays to hoover to' (as John Scotney intimated that the BBC Afternoon Play was informally subtitled) – in short, filler material (cited in Wade 1981: 228). Interesting, the new generation of audio writers and producers working outside the large broadcasters, creating works for podcast and online rather than broadcast, are often unpaid non-professionals – yet a freely available, text transcript for audio drama is becoming more and more important (Thraille 2018).

Finally, one of radio drama's erstwhile strengths, its sheer volume, can be a challenge to the researcher. Most restrain their research body to one country's output or a certain genre or time period. When broadcast historians do try to give an overview of radio, audio drama is usually lost in the vast ocean of material. This is not surprising. It would be inconceivable for a film scholar to write a single volume in any depth about every US feature film, documentary, short or cartoon, in every genre made between 1926 and 1960. John Dunning's *On the Air* (1998) does just that for radio, and Lord Asa Briggs' multi-volume *History of Broadcasting in the United Kingdom* (1961–79) was unable, by sheer volume, to examine *drama* in any depth.

Why, then, has radio drama not been preserved for study? The most obvious answer is that it was not considered particularly valuable, except in rare cases (usually when the playwright was a success in other media such as stage plays or film). Why was the average radio drama writer's output, then, not considered valuable? Pre-eminent radio scholar Andrew Crisell famously wrote about radio's quality of blindness in *Understanding Radio* in 1986, subsequently reiterated in a revised edition of the book (1994: 3), and throughout Crisell's writings (2004: 10). It is evidence of this statement's controversy, despite Crisell's assertion that '[w]*hat strikes everyone*, broadcasters and listeners alike, as significant about radio' (1994: 3, emphasis added), that subsequent radio scholars have questioned it (for an overview of the debate, see Chignell 2009: 66–68). Shingler and Wieringa have suggested that radio's 'invisibility' might be a more apt description (1998: 137), Hand and Traynor propose that 'darkness' characterizes radio (2011: 33, 35–36), and writers such as Tim Crook (1999a: 62–64) and Andrew Dubber (2013: 11, 13) reject the idea of blindness out of hand. Indeed, Dubber quite rightly points out that what appears to be significant to one individual about radio may not be universal (2013: 11). In sound studies, there is a recognized continuum between what is considered 'good sound' and 'bad noise', and perhaps in some ways radio's reputation as a background medium has equated it with 'noise' rather than 'sound':

> Most radio producers recognise an essentially distracted listenership and, with only a few exceptions (e.g. drama, news, and features), much of mainstream radio broadcasting is designed not only to accommodate listening as a secondary activity but positively to exploit the advantages of a semi-attentive audience.
>
> (Shingler and Wieringa 1998: xi)

If radio is characterized (as it has been many times, in a largely pejorative sense) as a secondary medium, then it is perhaps unsurprising that it has not been considered worthy of extensive study. The dichotomy between radio as compelling and radio as 'wallpaper' (Dubber 2013: 12) is explored in the next section.

Radio drama as high and low art

From the earliest radio dramas in the 1920s, there was a sharp divide among practitioners between those who considered what they were making to be high art and those who considered it to be entertainment, a job to be done – at worst, ephemera to be dismissed as consumer-based commodity. Verma's research has shown that those who worked in early

US radio drama were of the latter persuasion, tending to think of their work as 'show business' (Verma 2012: 5). As Robert Louis Shayon noted about station WOR,

> Our ambition was to get paid. There was no avenue in theater. The movies were too far away. The natural thing was to drift into radio, which was wide open at that time […] At WOR we did everything. We were producers and writers and directors.
>
> (cited in Balk 2006: 127)

Robert L. Mott, without a trace of malice, gives an amusing anecdote about Orson Welles trying to create the evocative sound of sand in a drama set in the Saharan desert. Mott and his fellow sound effects artists wanted the effects work to be left to them, as was the convention, while Welles wanted the actors to take their own steps in the sand. To achieve this, Welles arranged for a truck to dump sand into the studio. This created problems for the engineer, as the microphone levels were inconsistent for picking up the subtlety of the sand footsteps and the dialogue for a live production. 'Later that day when everyone returned from lunch, no one in the cast and certainly neither of the sound effects artists was really surprised to find the sand in the studio gone' (Mott 2014: 76). Mott's playful anecdote highlights the tension (if not full-blown hypocrisy) between an emerging auteur like Welles (who, nevertheless, was earning a living by playing the Shadow in popular, rather than 'art' radio) and the reality of the radio drama production schedule.

Who then decides whether radio drama is high art or not?

The 1920s were an era for early artistic experiment in radio drama. Almost as soon as plays began to be broadcast, dissenting voices began to argue about the respective merits of a 'pure' radio art (which could come about only through original, conceived-for-the-ear material) and the artistic value of radio adaptations of canonical texts. Some practitioners in Europe considered the integrity of the text soiled by adaptation into radio. Both Cécile Méadel and Hélène Eck have commented on the way French radio in the 1930s combined several genres, including stage theatre ('which is the most obvious transplant') but also the novel, the cinema, music, 'sometimes even painting' (Méadel 1994: 297). Eck noticed the ever-present pull between high art and mass culture, noting that for a long time, the elite regarded radio as merely a 'mediocre "music box"' (2006: 243).

In the United States, we need look no further than the writings of Theodor Adorno and Max Horkheimer and the Frankfurt School to discover the attitude of many critics, then as now, to the notion of radio in the spectrum of high and low art. Adorno's main concern was that an aficionado of culture – a true amateur in the etymological sense of the word – was being driven to *consume* culture and pay for the privilege. 'The delight of the moment and the gay façade', he wrote in 1938,

> becomes an excuse for absolving the listener from the thought of the whole, whose claim is comprised in proper listening. The listener is converted, along his line of least resistance, into the acquiescent purchaser.
>
> (2013: 5)

Adorno disdained *ether flâneurs*[1] for having no investment, personal or political, in content:

> it is irrelevant to him [the *ether flâneur*] what he hears or even how he hears; he is only interested in the fact that he hears and succeeds in inserting himself, with his private equipment, into the public mechanism, without exerting even the slightest influence on it.
>
> (2013: 21)

Not only were Adorno and other cultural critics disgusted with the state of radio, US radio network executives as early as 1936 were also concerned about the quality of artistic content. Some argued that 'radio, overall, never reached the high [a]esthetic plane many felt it should' (MacDonald 1979: 2). Still, we know from Verma's and Blue's scholarship that sometimes the best artistic drama was fostered when doubts were raised about the networks' highbrow or lowbrow status, such as the fabled works produced in 1936 and 1937 on CBS.

As it appears that radio producers and writers could not agree amongst themselves as to whether making radio drama was an art or the business of entertainment, what tools are at the disposal of textual analysis for meaningfully resolving this issue? In the following section, I look at the example of the consistently reviled soap opera and examine whether its rehabilitation can tell us anything about the place of radio drama in the literary canon.

A deluge of dirt?

In Kenneth Burke's 1941 'Literature as equipment for living', he suggests that 'proverbs are *strategies* for dealing with *situations*', which I would argue is one way of accounting for radio soaps (1941: 296, original emphasis). He uses, however, an acknowledged work of (prose) literature, *Madame Bovary* (1857), to illustrate his theory (though he says later in the essay that he could equally apply it to the works of Shakespeare, Dashiell Hammett or Marie Corelli). *Madame Bovary* relates a situation that is 'sufficiently representative of our social structure, that recurs sufficiently often *mutandis mutatis*, for people to "need a word for it" and to adopt an attitude toward it' (1941: 300). As in Raymond Williams' discussion regarding drama later in this chapter, Burke is treating each work of art as an entry in a dictionary, moving seamlessly between the categories of convention and invention. He suggests that the high level of abstraction of Aesop's Fables means their specificity/simplicity is actually an invitation for timeless reinterpretation. In writing of his 'proverbs writ large' theory, he says critics have already objected because it offends good taste. Nevertheless, he advocates a 'reintegrative point of view' instead of the inertia of good taste (Burke 1941: 304). Ien Ang continues this approach with the TV soap opera *Dallas* (1978–91), noting that its metaphors 'derive [their] strength from a *lack* of originality and uniqueness: precisely because it constantly recurs in all sorts of popular narratives, it takes on for viewers a direct comprehensibility and recognizability' (1985: 65, original emphasis). Soaps are then, perhaps, a heighted form of ultra-reality, mirroring problems in 'concave mirrors', according to Alice Reinhart, a US radio soap opera star (cited in MacDonald 1979: 234).

Studying soap operas for their cultural and aesthetic merits is no longer taboo (Hobson 2002; Geraghty and Weissmann 2016), in part through a recognition of their importance in gender studies. However, most scholarship has focused on the television soap opera while generally ignoring the genre's origins in radio. Indeed, many radio historians still have little time for soap operas (as summarized by Chignell 2009: 49). The term itself is especially charged, fecund with an argument about high and low art: the name 'soap opera' was never given by the producers to their own product; when soaps emerged, they were properly called serials. Indeed, the tension inherent in the term continues today, with modern TV soaps in the United Kingdom being referred to by those who make them as 'continuing drama'. But before the end of the 1930s, trade journals were labelling these dramas as 'washboard weepers', 'sudsers' and 'soap operas'. Val Gielgud, unsurprisingly, labelled soap opera as 'cheap and nasty' (Crook 1999b). Soap opera puts us at the nexus of popular commodity versus high art debate and adds the element of gender, which has featured in the history of radio drama. For example, Baughman has summarized the Frankfurt School's disdain for the US soap opera, with such cultural commentators suggesting that soap operas represented female listeners at their worst, 'listening in a state of excessive susceptibility defined by animalistic lust for products and lack of critical judgement' (2007: 123). Such analyses did not leave room for the possibility that radio soaps were popular with women listeners because they were accessible, featuring aspirational female characters and dealing with everyday issues, providing strategies for dealing with situations.

Soap operas seem to have been created out of a perception that real-life women needed identifiable characters to represent them. In this sense, the soap opera seems to share some attributes with modern fan fiction that has traditionally been, in Abigail Derecho's words, the 'literature of the subordinate' responding to an underrepresentation of women in media (2006: 73). Radio soaps certainly seem to have been a precursor to the precepts of chick lit and romance narrative (Driscoll 2006: 81). While the uses and gratifications theory (cf. Katz et al. 1974: 21–22; Tulloch 1990: 196–97) was never particularly applied to radio, it is tempting to ponder what female audiences of Old Time Radio (OTR) soap operas 'got' from them.

For example, what to make of aspirational figures like female radio detectives, news anchors and cops? In the late 1940s, this was a short-lived but pervasive genre, with shows such as *Candy Matson, Yukon 28209* (1949–51, NBC), *Meet Miss Sherlock* (1946, CBS) and *The Affairs of Anne Scotland* (1946–47, ABC). *Policewoman* (1946–47, ABC), which followed events in the career of real-life Sergeant Mary Sullivan of the NYPD, was more in the docudrama vein and perhaps the most relevant and realistic. *Wendy Warren and the News* (1947–58, CBS) was popular with male as well as female listeners. It began each episode with a three-minute capsule of each weekday's headlines delivered by newscaster Douglas Edwards followed by a one-minute dispatch of 'news from the women's world' by a fictitious female radio journalist. Then the serial began, with

Wendy's life as a reporter. Wendy's life advanced one day for each episode, a predecessor of the television programme *24* (2001–10).

Kate Lacey emphasizes that 'there is a hint that the melodramatic mode' (i.e. soaps) 'was at least in some measure translated into a broadcast form for women' (1996: 79). Such cautiously positive attitudes towards radio soaps are uncommon, even from women researchers. Hilmes (2014: 120) is an exception; 'for some the soap is a critical example of what radio does best, the creation of the intimate, often feminized, everyday world' (Chignell 2009: 49). For others, such as Susan Douglas, the soap is 'something of an irrelevance' (Chignell 2009: 49). Early US radio soap operas met with great hostility by some moralists and 'arbiters of taste'. Marion Dickerman, education director of the American Arbitration Association, called them a 'deluge of dirt' and accused them of being without morals (cited in MacDonald 1979: 232). The radio networks believed that US radio soaps appealed to women of lower income and education. They were profitable and inexpensive to produce, financed through commercial sponsorship. A study made at Kansas State College noted that in the average fifteen-minute (soap) serial, 17.8 per cent of the time was spent advertising (MacDonald 1979: 223). This was two-and-a-half times the amount spent for hour-long evening shows.

In the minds of many, then, the low art/mindless consumerist product, the soap opera deserved censure for being an instrument of blatant commercialism – *never* artistic expression. The 'alleged pathology of female soap listeners' connected 'with the commercial constraints and programme mediocrity' in many critics' minds in the 1940s (Boddy 2004: 51). It is, indeed, then a gendered fault line, with US soaps demonized due to their appeal to women, the fact that they were frequently populated by female-centric casts and because many were written by women for women, such as the prolific and outspoken Irna Phillips (Hilmes 2014: 109–11). The elite citizen, as Hilmes writes, 'is imagined as masculine, leaving women in particular out of the analysis' (2012: 14). Even in imagining the potentialities of television, many (male) writers, including Charles A. Siepmann in *Radio's Second Chance* (1947), defined the female audience with 'offhand and disdainful references to daytime radio soap opera listening' (Boddy 2004: 49). In the United Kingdom, where radio soaps did not have the same history as in the United States, *Housewives' Choice* (1945–67), argues Stephen Barnard, reinforced gender roles (1989: 141) and had a potent, long-lived influence on perceptions of women as listeners and women as broadcasters. 'Sexism within radio runs deep', Barnard wrote in 1989, influencing the way women were treated as broadcasters both on the BBC and commercial radio (1989: 142). Radio, Caroline Mitchell argues, 'has been described as a medium that is particularly accessible and pertinent to women', but until the last two decades of the twentieth century, it would seem 'radio was a very male domain in which to work' (Mitchell 2001: 159).

It can be argued that the centrality of the female leads and the relative weakness of the male characters in soaps are reasons for their popularity with female listeners. Douglas has made a convincing case for Depression-era male comics in positions of weakened authority reflecting what real men and women of the time were feeling. Jack Benny in particular 'spoke to men who blamed themselves and blamed the system, and to women who blamed their unemployed husbands yet couldn't blame them at all' (Douglas [1999] 2004: 117). While we recognize that there are a finite number of story archetypes, we do not suppose that there is one-size-fits-all. Therefore, excluding radio soap from analysis or even from acknowledgement seems at best short-sighted and at worst patronizing. Just as radio drama could encompass everything on the spectrum from high art to low art, it could arguably be said that some programmes could encompass all of this in and of themselves.

Against the Storm (1939–42)

Against the Storm was a US network soap from the 1940s and does, I would argue, encompass aspects of high and low art. Ang, in discussing TV soap *Dallas*, notes that it possessed multiple identification – 'viewers cannot simply identify with one character in order to understand and judge all the developments from that character's point of view', contrasting it with an action/adventure story (Ang 1985: 88). Indeed, in Sandra Michael's *Against the Storm,* multiple identification is one of the elements that situates the serial within the soap opera tradition – others are its focus on female characters and its paratexts and packaging – whereas other elements of its construction situate it within a more literary tradition. Despite this, *Against the Storm* would seem to disprove the tension 'between interpretations of soaps that stress their feminist, liberalising qualities and those which see them as reinforcing a woman's domestic role' (Chignell 2009: 50). *Against the Storm* is mentioned in radio histories, if it is mentioned at all, for its Peabody Award, the only daytime soap coming from US network radio to receive such an award. MacDonald praised its 'maturity', calling its 'warm, poetic world' powerful and 'capable of great idealism as well as powerful invective' (1979: 258).

From an interview made between 1979 and 1980 with radio drama director Axel Gruenberg, we know that *Against the Storm*'s author Sandra Michael was Danish-born, 'so was particularly moved when the Germans took that country, and I think that's what prompted her to go the route against the evils of Nazism', said Gruenberg (1998: 61). Latvian-born Gruenberg, one of the founding members of the Radio Directors Guild, began directing at WWJ Detroit and moved to Chicago and NBC in 1939, 'because Chicago was doing most of the so-called soap operas […] I think of them as continuous stories, or daytime dramas' (1998: 59). During a summer series when writer Jane Crusinberry was on vacation, Sandra Michael filled in on soap *The Story of Mary Marlin* (1934–45). Michael 'was a very, very talented writer' (Gruenberg 1998: 59). Michael's Danishness is almost as important to *Against the Storm* as her American-ness, as hinted by Gruenberg above. Without sufficient evidence, it is impossible to prove, but I suggest that Michael's quest for a more intelligent soap opera may have been part of the Danish pedagogical tradition.[2] Denmark's radio policy was categorized by strong political polarization, resulting in a state broadcasting monopoly between 1925 and 1983. Denmark's 'government all but forbade the networking of syndicated radio programmes completely up until 1997' (Hendy 2007: 45).

In 1940, Gruenberg was offered the job of directing *Against the Storm* by the producer, John Gibbs, who was also Sandra Michael's husband. Gruenberg remembered in interview that 'the thing about *Storm* was that it was beautifully written. It was an outstanding show. Everybody, all the actors in New York, wanted to be on it' (1998: 61). *Against the Storm* was set originally in a fictional university town called Hawthorne. The main characters were Professor Jason McKinley Allen and his family. The show quickly acquired other characters and other locales as 'after we joined the war against Germany, Sandra turned to a theme that involved the war, particularly in Europe' (1998: 61). Indeed, as MacDonald has remarked, production was 'almost contemporaneous with the outbreak of hostilities in Europe in September 1939' (1979: 257).

As a daily serial, *Against the Storm* would have produced around 260 fifteen-minute episodes each year; as far as can be ascertained, only sixteen have survived. As a hallmark of the success of soaps, it is possible to listen to these remaining programmes and build up an understanding and even an empathy with fictional characters from 80 years ago. One is able to connect the dots; 'soap opera directors adapted well to listeners expecting spatial texture because their work was always defined by pace' (Verma 2012: 29). *Against the Storm* was sponsored by Procter and Gamble who advertised extensively for Ivory Soap during each broadcast of the serial, using a variety of techniques. They appealed often to mothers' sense of duty (using Ivory Flakes to wash 'baby's sensitive skin'), thriftiness and fashion (running a promotion for silk stockings 'with a doll finish'), and running contests ('Finish this sentence: "I like Ivory Flakes because …"' to enter in a contest to win a Pontiac). 'Radio programs often integrated their sponsor's message right into the narrative of the drama', Hilmes has found (2012: 70). The commercial sponsors, it seemed, had the final word: when Michael wanted to expand her episodes to 30 minutes each, the sponsors reacted by cancelling *Against the Storm,* despite the programme having won the Peabody Award.

Despite the intensive sponsorship and normalization of gender roles, many scenarios in *Against the Storm* seem to play against convention. In one of the most interesting surviving episodes of *Against the Storm* (broadcast 15 May 1940), the character Reed Wilson is hesitating over proposing to Kathy Reimer. Reed is a journalist, Kathy is the daughter of Dr Reimer who knows Professor Allen's family in Hawthorne; Kathy has immigrated to the United States from Europe, perhaps central Europe (Czechoslovakia?). During a warm night in New York City, Reed imagines three situations in which he proposes to Kathy, which makes fascinating use of Hills' 'endlessly deferred narrative' (2002: 128). However, it hardly makes Reed a decisive, strong silent type in the tradition of coded masculinity; Kathy Reimer, on the other hand, is represented as a strong, iconoclastic woman, who is enthusiastic to have a career outside the home.

While the gender norms of *Against the Storm* may be inverted, this is as much a result of the structure of soap operas as it is evidence of *Against the Storm*'s unusual qualities.

Unfortunately, the two most celebrated literary moments in the serial's history – the long-wave reading by British Poet Laureate John Masefield and the reading by Edgar Lee Masters from the *Spoon River Anthology* (1915) incorporated into one of Professor Allen's classroom scenes – do not survive.

Although the surviving episodes of *Against the Storm* often give the impression that Kathy or Reed are the main characters, the character who carries the most consistently through all the episodes is Professor Allen, an unusual hero for a soap, a man in his 60s. Thus the serial is concerned with portraying intellectualism in a positive light, although other characters have their poetic moments. Finally, as suggested by Gruenberg, a good deal of *Against the Storm* was taken up by the allegorical (and sometimes not-so-allegorical) discussion of the war in Europe. In an episode that does not seem to survive, a character remarked to a refugee – probably Kathy – that Hitler had done a lot of good for Germany. The response included the polemical lines,

> I can tell you what he did for the German people! […] Suppose he had built the most wonderful national order ever conceived, would you say it was justified if the ground of his nation were soaked with the blood of innocent people? And that maniac did not try to build a great nation. He built a slave state whose purpose is the destruction of all free states everywhere.
>
> (cited in MacDonald 1979: 259, from the *Radio and Television Mirror*, December 1942)

The reason (we assume, not having heard her side of the story) that Kathy refused to marry Reed is because she is still in love with Manuel, who she knew before she emigrated. Kathy feels a great deal of guilt having escaped to America.

KATHY: Should I not have stayed and –
REED: And what? Gotten in the same fix as they are?
KATHY: I feel so shamefully useless here.
REED: There's nothing you can do.

The most famous episode of *Against the Storm* was the one broadcast on Memorial Day 1941, in which Professor Allen explained that his pacifism had stemmed from a young age, from witnessing Mr Mason, a Civil War veteran, break down in response to battle trauma, and his childhood friend Porky being killed on a battlefield in Belgium during the First World War. This highly praised, lyrical episode demonstrates the equivocal nature of Michael's polemic, in which she seems to be questioning the effects of war despite one of the serial's ostensible goals to bring the United States into the Second World War.

Radio soap operas like *Against the Storm* remain a critically embattled and highly gendered space. Theoretical perspectives like Burke's provide a way of evaluating a genre that has traditionally been ignored or disdained, highlighting its palimpsest nature. Arguing for subversion and reinforcement of convention within forms like the radio soap opera puts radio drama squarely in the high/low art debate and provides a microcosm of the way radio drama has been approached in the literary canon. In the next section, I suggest a literary technique that has flourished within the radio soap genre.

The Country and the City and *The Archers* in Middle England

The Archers (1951–present, BBC) is the world's longest-running soap opera. I have defined the term 'framing errors' to represent 'the tension between fiction and reality' (McMurtry 2015c: 7). In this section, *The Archers*' framing errors show that for some fans, the programme represents a way of dipping back into a rural environment, and the nostalgia of this imagined rural environment has become unreal in some senses. This provides a very different way of using radio soap operas than as represented in *Against the Storm*.

S. Meltem Ahıska, looking at the listeners of early Turkish radio soaps, determined that listeners committed 'framing errors', using 'fantasy as a means of representing and safeguarding the national truth' (2000: 222). Taking Ahıska's definition one step further, we can use it to define when the audience is unable to tell fiction from reality in a broadcast. As noted earlier in the chapter, radio requires signposting for contextual reasons, inherent in the form itself. Indeed, Tim Crook has highlighted this with social science experiments, which suggest that signposting is a very important factor in the way sound is perceived and contextualized (1999a: 54–60, 68–69). Obviously, framing errors are not unique to soap operas or to audio drama, but they seem to be an enduring part of the appeal and aesthetics of radio drama.

The fact that audio drama has cultivated such close encounters between fact, fiction, actuality, adaptation and artifice suggests its own awareness of this powerful creative asset. Taken out of context, a novel could be read as nonfiction and vice versa (cf. Nunes 2011; Ferrara 1998). A fictional film, if stumbled upon midway through on television, may be mistaken for dramatized documentary and vice versa again. While, as Aldana Reyes (2015) would argue, the found footage phenomenon in film is a technique not a genre, McRobert makes strong points regarding found footage as a kind of framing error, by using representation codes and aesthetics 'more typically associated with amateur and non-fiction media' (2015: 139). Yet most illusions of this nature are 'exposed', whereas radio framing errors have the power to galvanize segments of entire populations, as in *War of the Worlds* (1938), and with a command of time that is unknown in other media. As John Frow points out, Jacques Derrida has said that a text never *belongs* to a genre, it can only participate in several genres. 'The judgement we make ("is it like this, or is it more like that?") is as much pragmatic as it is conceptual' (Frow 2006: 54). As I discovered during the broadcast of BBC's *Life and Fate* (2011), in September 2011, there is no such disclaimer broadcast 'either before or after the vast majority of radio dramas which also pretend to portray "real" life' (Starkey 2004: 202).

Sound, indeed, has been described as a temporal medium, and while Sterne (2003: 16–19) would caution against emphasizing sound's temporality against its spatiality, time seems an important concept to highlight here. In theoretical terms, Raymond Williams' *The Country and the City* (1973) may be a useful place to start when looking at sound and temporality. This work imbues the country with 'the idea of a natural way of life: of peace, innocence, and simple virtue' (1973: 1). Nothing in the present, Williams argues, is ever like it was in the good old days. What he describes is an escalator effect in tracing back a notion of a time when things were infinitely better than in the present. He uses historical sources for each period to try to pinpoint when this escalator started. When was this 'golden age'? The 1750s? The 1620s? 1516? The 1370s? 'Where indeed shall we go, before the escalator stops?' (1973: 11). I would argue in the section below that *The Archers* is very much in line with Williams' ideas of the country and 'the good old days'.

The Archers, a British soap opera, fits within its context. In contrast to US networks, the BBC was very cautious about introducing radio serials. Its late adoption of the soap opera genre, in serials such as *Front Line Family* (1941–48)*, Mrs Dale's Diary* (1948–69) and *Life with the Lyons* (1950–61), was a delayed response to popular demand. During the Second World War, series of these kinds had flourished, originally on the Forces Network. Programmes of this type were considered improper imports from US commercial radio. The BBC's cold-shouldering of the kinds of programming available on the Continent, particularly Radio Luxembourg, and its Reithian disdain for America's 'Mammon'-obsessed commercial writing engendered distrust for 'radio soaps that showed ordinary […] people, linked to their regions, certain of their values, attached to their traditions' (Sabbagh 1995: 74). As Remonté put it, 'soap operas gripped the public and kept them loyal to their weekly rendez-vous' (1989: 31).

Quite differently to US soap opera serials, *The Archers* began as a fictional way of getting across important farming information to Britain's Midlands during post-war shortages: 'if the farmers' wives started to listen, then the husbands would have to listen' (Smethurst 1996: 13). Written 'to reflect every aspect of farming in a Midlands village', *The Archers* had by 1952 gained 8 million listeners in Britain (Smethurst 1996: 14). *The Archers*' educational content, especially in its original brief, has been a salient part of its function. 'Stories of passion, betrayal, and sabotage were mixed up with dramas about dirt tare on sugarbeet, and problems with cows' milk butterfat content: things nobody would ever *make up*' (Smethurst 1996: 38, original emphasis). More recent farming issues integrated into drama include organic vs GM farming (1984), bovine tuberculosis (1994), foot-and-mouth disease (2001) and the floods of 2015 (Miller 2015).

With an apparent commitment to treating current issues, how does *The Archers* link up with Williams' idea of the country? Almost immediately, *The Archers* engendered an intense radio community, one that seemed invested in the 'reality' of its vision. Godfrey Baseley, creator of *The Archers,* actively cultivated such investment. Just before Christmas 1950, Baseley interviewed the cast in character, using an improvised format.

He assumed that Borchester was a real town, and Brookfield a real farm […] and that he, Godfrey Baseley, a well-known BBC Midlands agricultural reporter, was able to go there with his OB unit […] and talk to the inhabitants.

(Smethurst 1996: 23)

Broadcast on 28 December 1950, *Announcing the Archers* made an impact, doubling the audience to 4 million. Baseley had helped craft an appealing programme that delighted listeners, whether they 'believed' in it or not. A woman overheard *Archers* actor John Franklin speaking and said, 'You are Mike Daly in *The Archers,* aren't you? Oh, I am pleased to meet you. All my family said you were fiction, but I know you must be real' (cited in Smethurst 1996: 40).

Nick Couldry notes television soaps' 'complex intertextuality', saying we cannot be sure 'that different viewers would necessarily agree about how a particular programme should be watched' (2000: 72). Devotees of *The Archers* manifest their interest in different ways. For example, *The Archers* Anarchists began as a reaction against 'castism', i.e. people who promote impostors (i.e. actors) who claim to be characters from Ambridge and persist in this self-aware illusion. The way *The Archers* is interpreted among its fans clearly resonates beyond a mere radio entertainment. Internationally, *The Archers* is represented in countries like Poland where rural or urban soaps[3] with great community investment formed a perpetual, and perpetually welcoming, to its fans, sunny, time-warped environment, a refuge both in reality and from reality. Temporality, community and framing errors are important factors in radio soaps, particularly to *The Archers*.

If the major criticisms against US soaps at the time were that they were trashy and vacuous fare for women who lacked discerning judgment, and Burke's 'proverbs writ large' theory, previously discussed, notes that there must surely be a place for radio soaps, Williams' theory on nostalgia and the value of the country implies that *The Archers'* hyperdiegetic universe provides strategies for dealing with situations that listeners still find relevant. The notion of the country embodied in *The Archers* may represent, both to fans and to the world at large, a bygone way of life, but wrapped up in this are still 'proverbs writ large' from which listeners derive satisfaction. To that end, then, we could argue that the twin poles of high and low art are noticeably at work in *The Archers*. The bygone way of life here invoked is inherent within the framing errors; the programme is both 'a fixture of popular entertainment and utterly familiar escapism' (Hendy 2007: 107). Critics have, in an indistinct way, recognized the tension between modern and old-fashioned in *The Archers*. Richard Kelner, columnist for *The Independent,* described *The Archers* in 2012 as 'homely, anachronistic', serving 'only to perpetuate myths and prejudices about life in the British countryside', finally adding, '[l]ong may it continue!' (Kelner 2012). It is nevertheless deceptive to imagine that *The Archers* has been immune to change. *The Archers* has 'tackled sex, drugs, abortion, homosexuality and the local vicar marrying a Hindu' (Singh 2011). Accusations of sensationalist storylines emerged after the hiring of Sean O'Connor (former producer of BBC TV soap *EastEnders*) as editor in 2015 (Miller 2015: 159). In April 2011, the BBC launched *Ambridge Extra* on Radio 4 Extra, to follow *The Archers* during broadcast on Radio 4. The show was designed to highlight younger characters and was dubbed 'Low Fat *Archers* for Young People' by some fans, according to *The Daily Telegraph* (Anon. 2011). The two storylines, in *Ambridge Extra* and *The Archers* proper, would run parallel, and did so, until the series was 'rested' in 2013.

As the Archers Academics prepare to convene their second academic conference in 2018, it is clear that beyond popular appeal, *The Archers* demonstrates radiogenic elements. Formula and repetition when tempered by varied forms of content and format, is one of the keys to BBC radio drama's success, and never is this writ so large than with *The Archers*. Writer Sally Wainwright has said that the best thing about *The Archers* is that 'it never ends' (cited in Miller 2015: 121).

The radio western

This chapter has dealt in part with genres or formats that in radio have been deplored for their vacuousness and formulaity, examples of which critics could supposedly point out and describe as the dregs of radio. The western genre was, at the height of its popularity, less frequently derided for its focus on convention rather than innovation than the radio soap, yet has suffered a lack of subsequent critical engagement. Thus, this final section of the chapter deals with the radio western's fall from grace and how its evolution successfully illustrates Burke's argument for the palimpsest quality of moving seamlessly between the categories of convention and invention. The US radio western of the 1930s–60s was a unique cultural text, related to but separate from its filmic, prose and television counterparts. I suggest that the radio western is emblematic of the nexus of high and low art, gendered radio and subversion and confirmation of radio drama conventions. Radio westerns are emblematic of radio drama's high/low art qualities because it is impossible to draw the line where the artist is following convention and where he or she is innovating. This claim will be examined as regards the progression of aural depictions of Native Americans in radio westerns.

We begin with another theoretical vantage point provided by Raymond Williams' 1968 study of modern drama: 'The individual genius and the particular conventions through which it is expressed are or seem inseparable' (Williams 1968: 12). Williams noted the interplay between the individual and the 'authentic communities', between literature and the theatre, and common acceptance that creates convention (1968: 8). To take Williams at face value, we can perhaps explain why one of US radio's most popular genres in the first half of the twentieth century has all but disappeared from the airwaves, though its influence upon culture and literature remains undeniable. The radio western has perhaps not disappeared as such, but like its filmic and television counterparts has changed to suit audience demands, frequently migrating into science fiction. Cawelti has recorded that in the United States in 1958, westerns constituted 10.76 per cent of all works of fiction and 1.76 per cent of all books published. At least 54 feature film westerns were made in 1958 in Hollywood. In 1959, eight of the top ten programmes on US television were westerns (Cawelti 1984: 3). Although, as suggested above, it is true that the western in radio drama migrated to the science-fiction vista, it is difficult now to find any original western audio drama series with the reach and impact of these programmes in the days of OTR. Couldry suggests that Raymond Williams recognized this revaluation of different cultural forms as a 'tension' (2000: 23). 'Williams is not simply arguing that we pay more attention to "popular" culture at the expense of elite culture', Couldry continues (2000: 25). Cawelti allows that westerns permitted writers to explore new social values and definitions (1984: 4). However, I would argue this process happened slowly and with the specific mechanism of Williams' formulation of conventions and invention.

There are many ways of charting this process. However, I choose below to highlight the depiction of the 'Indian' on the radio western as emblematic of this process. There were Native Americans visually represented as Other from the nineteenth century in popular visual art and in silent film. How was the Indian depicted on radio? To answer this, let us allow Hilmes to pose a further question: 'How could one be sure a person belonged to his or her purported racial or ethnic group over the radio' in the early years of the twentieth century on US radio? (Hilmes 1997: 359) The solution, Hilmes argues, was through carefully selected aural context, language and dialect use, with stereotypical dialects and accents being carried over from the realm of vaudeville and the minstrel show (1997: 359). Radio westerns responded to the established precepts of the genre by including Native American and Hispanic characters, and the 'Othering' of the West on radio quickly took hold, audibly so with the Lone Ranger's 'kemo sabe'[4] Tonto. Tonto, a Potawatomi, was created by Fran Striker for WXYZ Detroit in 1933, as the Lone Ranger's loyal sidekick, a role borrowed from films. MacDonald contends Tonto was portrayed as a 'strong character whose intelligence and dedication often placed him in strategic operations without which the Lone Ranger could not have brought law and order to the West' (1979: 199). Nevertheless, by audio convention, Tonto's dialect (which marked him as 'Indian') reduced him to linguistic sub-normality. Whereas Douglas has argued that programmes such as *Amos 'n' Andy* (1926–55) showcased linguistic rebellion from minority groups ([1999] 2004: 208), Tonto, like later Striker sidekick Kato in *The Green Hornet* (1936–52, MBS), spoke in pidgin English (this despite the Asian Kato being a university graduate and a master chemist, as Russo [2002: 261] has noted). Indeed, as Hilmes suggests, a certain form of nationalized, homogenized English in America was promoted as 'the norm', and anyone who deviated from this 'proper, uninflected' English was not only different, 'but not as good' (1997: 357).

As *Amos 'n' Andy* and other dramatic programmes featured white actors playing black characters, it was evidently unthinkable on network radio that a Native American actor should play the most famous Native American character ever heard on the airwaves. Indeed, despite Native American cultural diversity and population diffusion, prior to the 1970s, no radio existed to serve Native peoples' needs or even to entertain them (Keith 1995: 3). Even so, eventually, the Tonto talk/pidgin English dialect solution was subverted. Cawelti contends that giving 'the Indian' a more complex role than that assigned to him in traditional westerns would increase the moral ambiguity of the story, an extra effort at dislocation and destabilization that most writers, producers and commercial sponsors on network US radio would not have attempted. Furthermore, it would be far more difficult, Cawelti continues, to resolve the average western with reaffirmation of the values of (white) American society if the Native peoples were given a more complex role. Nevertheless, series emerged from OTR which did just that.

For example, in the debut episode of the short-lived sustaining programme *Dr Sixgun* (1954–55, CBS), a wagon train of white settlers at Frenchman's Creek are the villains and the local Mescalero Apache the victims, with the heroic Dr Sixgun saving Chief Tall Horse's son and preventing bloodshed. The Apache in this story are aurally depicted with Hispanic accents, presumably due to the group's original homelands in the southwestern United States, but do not speak pidgin English.

'An egalitarian impulse' seemed to motivate heroes like Dr Sixgun and the Lone Ranger, who did good for its own sake (MacDonald 1979: 209). The highlight of the radio cowboy was his code of ethics, which, for most of these characters, was similar to the B-western, musical cowboy of the films. In 1958, however, in *Frontier Gentleman* (CBS), despite a production that remained determinedly neutral about events during the Indian Wars of the 1870s in South Dakota, 'Indian' characters were still depicted using pidgin English.

The Lone Ranger's idealism, however well-intentioned, had no place in the post-war westerns, which, like their detective story counterparts, had become more interested in realism, social apathy and personal greed. *Gunsmoke* (1954–57) was CBS' most successful experiment in this vein, a sustaining programme for eighteen months until a commercial sponsor was found. *Gunsmoke,* also taking place during the 1870s Indian Wars, was characterized by a certain cynicism alongside hard-bitten Sheriff Matt Dillon's refusal to compromise on matters of justice and morality. In the 1955 episode 'Indian White', a young man, Dennis, disrupts societal norms in frontier town of Dodge due to the way he dresses and acts (like an Indian, including speaking in pidgin English and referring to himself in the third person). Recovered from the Cheyenne by the US Army and returned to a woman who lost a son his age to raids previously, Dennis rebels linguistically as well as behaviourally.

The innovative programme *You Are There* (1947–48, CBS) capitalized on CBS' post-war reputation for news reporting excellence, and reported on events in history as if radio news crews had been there. In the 2 May 1948 episode, 'The Surrender of Sitting Bull', the news crews visited 'one of the most shameful events in American history' in 1881. In its commitment to factual accuracy, this episode presented historical characters such as Sitting Bull (Tatanka Iyotanka) speaking in Lakota and not in English, his words interpreted by other English-speaking characters such as reporter Ken Roberts who, as part of the fantasy of the programme, spoke Lakota. Chief Crazy Bull, grandson of Sitting Bull, played Chief Gall and was consultant to the production. This aural landscape depicting Native Americans played by Native Americans at last returns to audio drama in a meaningful way in Akpik Theatre/

Travis Mercredi and Reneltta Arkluk's 2012 adaptation of a Richard Van Camp story. Van Camp, a critically acclaimed Tłįchǫ/Dogrib author, has published a number of short stories, of which *I Count Myself Among Them* (2012) is one. The adapted drama (2012), available on Soundcloud, epitomizes agency for indigenous peoples, as it is written, acted and produced by a Northwest Territories indigenous community. Naturally, there is no recourse to Tonto talk here.

'In an artistic construction', Cawelti writes, events 'take their meaning from the whole structure' and the way conventions are 'used, abused, or subverted contribute to the piece's meaning' (1984: 54). The aural depiction of Native Americans in radio westerns illustrates this idea, as conventions established in *The Lone Ranger* (1933–54) inform later radio westerns, at last being subverted and discarded with *You Are There* and *I Count Myself Among Them*. Radio westerns are emblematic of radio drama's high/low art qualities because it is impossible to draw the line where the artist is following convention and where he or she is innovating. In conclusion, audio drama's 'slipperiness' as a text is an asset. Audio drama's historically popular modes of expression, epitomized by Cawelti's 'mystery literature' and including the rather unique genre of westerns, are also highly slippery and mark a Williams-ian axis between convention and invention. This explains both their perennial popularity and their lack of critical attention.

Conclusion

This chapter has tried to argue for a place in the literary canon for audio drama, still troubled by unresolved questions of its status in high/low art. We can conclude that audio drama can be both, historically and contemporaneously, if we accept the theoretical perspectives of Burke, Williams and Cawelti. In rejecting previous hidebound categorizations of audio drama, particularly soap operas and westerns, we can enjoy the vast catalogue of audio drama while recognizing its many facets of interpretation, its Williams-ian formulation of conventions and invention.

Notes

1. This term was coined by historian Dieter Daniels.
2. Cf. Janne Nielsen's work on Danish educational broadcasting and Heidi Svømmekjær's work on *The Hansen Family* (1929–49).
3. *The Matysiak Family* (1956–present) and *Jezioany* (1960–present); cf. McMurtry 2015a.
4. It is suggested that this is a phonetic rendering of *giimoozaabi* from Ojibwe, which may indeed have also meant 'scout' (i.e. 'one who sneaks').

Chapter 2

Audio Drama and Listening

Sound Radio offers me
not poems I can't read, plays I cannot see,
but calms and tempests of a thousand voices
in which the inward eye, as the outer ear rejoices.

– R.C. Scriven (1974: 153)

David Marc stated confidently in 1996 that 'computer programmers and hamburger flippers do not watch the same TV shows' (1996: xxx). Will a computer programmer and a hamburger flipper listen to the same programmes on radio or to the same podcasts? Can we convincingly state that the millennial generation will even listen to produced dramatic audio content? Can we commit to a pedagogical ideal that people, once given the choice to listen to what is (more) culturally elite, will do so, will enjoy it, will appreciate it, even if they have to be coaxed into doing it?

In spring 2016, Professor Hugh Chignell of Bournemouth University helped me to set up a unique experiment at Corfe Hills School in Dorset. Eleven teenaged students of this school (and their teachers) were participating in a distinctive audio programme I had devised. Over a period of six hours, the students listened collectively and in the dark to nine short audio dramas, ranging from a 1947 episode of *You Are There* (1947–48) to BBC shorts from the '*Ten Lessons in Love*' (2011) *Afternoon Drama* to an episode of Jonathan Mitchell's *The Truth* podcast (2009–present). The object was to refute a frequent assertion, that due to shortening attention spans, young people could not attend to and would not enjoy audio drama, especially if they were unfamiliar with the form. Furthermore, the experiment sought to understand imagery generation, in the manner of experiments performed primarily by psychologists using radio advertisements, and furthered by the work of Emma Rodero.

The results of the 'listening day' were published in *The Journal of Radio and Audio Media* in 2017. Surprising though some of the results were, generally they were positive, suggesting more such experiments should take place. 'It is unlikely that seventeen-year-olds will suddenly be attracted to radio drama in droves', Annie Caulfield wrote (2009: 9), but the research suggests that exposure can create listeners. The research underlined the fact that '[h]umans find it useful – in fact, highly pleasurable – to use our brains to create our own images' (Douglas [1999] 2004: 26). And many of us are also very good at this process.

In this chapter, by examining the fundamental act of listening to audio drama, we focus on three major areas that showcase both audio drama's mystique and areas that require further study. That radio has been known to function as both a background medium and as companionship for listeners has figured in the radio experience since the 1920s. Furthermore, as many observers have recognized (Douglas [1999] 2004: 30; Caulfield 2009: 9; Kendall et al. 2011), our lack of earlids makes us more vulnerable to aural assaults. Finally, the creation of soundscapes is considered. Soundscape, a term borrowed from acoustic ecology, denotes the world created by sound alone in aural dramatic presentation, which nevertheless appeals strongly to other senses. By interrogating these three important areas of listening, we highlight the importance of performing further research and establish some of the elements that make audio drama worth studying. By doing so, we contribute in concrete terms to the continued value of the audio drama form and work towards a refined understanding of the factors that will dispose people to continue listening.

No matter the genre of the audio drama, there is one thing that each successful drama shares. It is at the heart of 'framing errors' and underlines, too, the success of *War of the Worlds* (1938, CBS). Every critic and enthusiast[1] has his or her own favourite phrase to label the listening experience described by Neil Verma in *Theater of the Mind* (2012). For Susan Douglas, it's the radio audiences' use of 'their supple, agile, bygone imaginations' ([1999] 2004: 4). For Stan Freberg, 'it stretches the imagination' (Freberg et al. 1965). For David Marc, it's 'a kind of cyber-image on an internal screen (or what in quainter times was called the imagination)' (1996: 180). For Jean Shepherd it was children's radio announcer Pierre André who 'could get more out of just numbers than Orson Welles was able to squeeze out of *King Lear*' (2000: 52). Perhaps the most potent example is the one Howard Blue reports, a US policeman in the 1920s who, 'hearing the screaming [from a radio] through an open window, was so convinced by its realism that he came bursting into the house to stop the "assault"' (2002: 2).

As Verma has insisted, radio drama presented not *a* theatre of the mind, but *the* theatre of the mind (2012: 1). Few have tried to systematically define why this should be true. One of radio's greatest assets is also paradoxically one of its least explored. Some current research is making advances, such as the studies of Rodero, Paul Bolls and others. What cognitive science has told us so far is that listening facilitates storytelling. The mind devises outcomes based on sound combinations. Without this ability, radio storytelling would be meaningless. Therefore, as Rattigan has suggested, 'it would be impossible to substantiate a claim that radio *is* "all things" to all people, but through its polymorphic nature it philosophically *could* be' (2002: 20, original emphasis).

Listening is centripetal

Martyn Bond reminds us that underneath the umbrella title of 'radio' or 'audio' drama remains 'a kind of loose confederation of diverse offerings whose only points in common are that they are usually in the form of dialogue' (1970: 218). Andréa Baker puts it nicely, calling radio 'increasingly elastic' (2012: 3). Dubber stresses the problematic side of this lack of definition, describing 'radio' as an idea that 'perpetually sidesteps the question of definition' (2013: 10), even going as far as to say that 'in a very important sense, radio may not, in fact, even exist' (2013: 10–12). Returning to Bond, the implication is that even if we can't define it, we still like it – whatever *it* is exactly. I am opposed to passing radio's power off as a semi-mystical throwback to oral culture, as Marshall McLuhan has done (1964: 297). Nevertheless, there is truth to Douglas' contention that radio listening is centripetal – it pulls you in. This simple statement perhaps explains why the experiment that began this chapter was successful – audio drama will find an audience as long as there are still open ears and imaginations to be tapped.

Rudolf Arnheim had presciently captured this side of radio's power in *Radio: An Art of Sound*, including its macro-micro scale (1971: 259), intimacy (1971: 211), and its potential for reaching wide audiences, which he called 'a spiritual event of primary importance' (1971: 226). Marinetti and Masnata more militantly claimed anarchic powers for radio, that it 'begins where theater cinema and narrative end', representing 'the immensification of space' and an amplification of 'wordless noise-states' (1933). Khlebnikov was also assured of radio's principle of centripetal unification to the point of making other media redundant (1921). These early theorists, particularly Khlebnikov and the Italian Futurists, saw the avant-garde possibilities of radio as a medium. Actual events bore out less the agit-prop qualities of radio and depicted more eloquently its centripetal qualities. Cantril's 1940 study, *The Invasion from Mars: A Study in the Psychology of Panic*, estimated that 6 million people heard the initial broadcast of War of the Worlds (*WotW*). Of 1,700,000 listeners who potentially took the broadcast to be real, 1,200,000 were upset (not every respondent may have been truthful, so that number might actually be higher). Roger Wood suggests that the people who panicked 'were the people who had no knowledge of radio drama', though this is difficult to authenticate (2008: 96). No matter what people thought or how they acted, they listened. The centripetal force pulled them in.

It should be recalled that listening doesn't involve merely ears and brain. As John M. Picker noted, the increasingly deaf Thomas Edison was well-documented as having to 'listen' to sound through vibrations, usually through his teeth. His household piano was covered with his teeth marks from when pianists came to play, and he absorbed their playing through his teeth (Picker 2013: 32–33). His phonographs, too, bore teethmarks (Sterne 2003: 41). There is comparatively little written on the 'feeling' of sound:

> Sound, once heard, is absorbed through the human body, its tissues, central nervous system, neurological system etc. Therefore any sound, but in particular 'invisible' sound such as radio sound, touches a remote primate response in the human once it is heard.
> (Rattigan 2002: 14)

Consequently, '[f]og does not have a sound, but on radio – although we cannot see it', we can hear it (Street 2012: 5), maybe even *feel* it.

One and many

Many aspects of radio generally are contained in what Rattigan calls the broadcaster–solo listener relationship. In my interview with broadcaster Kip Allen (2013a), we talked about why radio as a medium seems so intimate, as if a voice on radio actually seems to be addressing an audience of one – *you* – while in reality the voice is addressing a massed, perhaps unquantifiable audience. This broadcaster–solo relationship gave a 'fillip' to Maurice Gorham (1949: 119), and he described it as one of the unique selling points of radio, despite his investment in television development. 'Television', he wrote, 'cannot transcend frontiers as sound broadcasting has done' (1949: 120). Tim Crook was likewise interested in interior consciousness as touched by radio. 'Intimate emotion and mental turmoil', he wrote, 'can communicate to the listener with ease' (1999b). David Hendy in his *Noise: A Human History* project gives this idea historical perspective. 'In a very real sense, being within earshot of a sound was what made you a citizen or a subject. With radio, the distances involved were dramatically transformed' (2013a: 283).

Audio drama may move a listener great distances outward in space and time, but it also moves listeners into deep inward spaces. During a postgraduate conference at Swansea University in 2012, Alison Plant played a recording of the sound of <<a cup clinking,>> which, as she said, became the *sign* for a real-world cup. Along with the physical cup itself, it was also indexically linked to the making of hot drinks, and suggests a subjective location based on listeners' lived experiences (Plant 2012). As Mark Sadoski and Allan Paivio determined, neither the printed word nor the pronunciation of an object link in any meaningful way to the object itself. 'Hence the word *cup* can stand for all cups in the abstract without referring to any particular one' (2013: 69, original emphasis). Plant encouraged the audience to imagine and 'see' the cup that represented <<a cup clinking.>>. For each person, the cup was bound to be different; <<a cup clinking>> 'comes loaded with associations, resonances, meanings, and metaphorical potential' (Hall 2010: 101). Plant argued that the apparently unemotional <<cup clinking>> might be a comforting sound for those who associated it with a warm and familiar kitchen. For Hand and Traynor, this was one of the most impressive elements of audio drama. One constructs one's personal response to sound 'with reference to all my knowledge and experiences, meaning that my interpretation of the work is widely informed, but is unique and personal to me' (Hand and Traynor 2011: 66). Similar conclusions were reached during the experiment with the high school students in 2016; the students generated some strikingly vivid and personal imagery while listening to the short dramas, such as '[t]all trees, a starless night, the only light coming from the cars headlights as it rambled down the unkempt road' (McMurtry 2017: 278).

Neuroscientist Stephen Kosslyn has examined visual imagination in stroke victims who suffer from unilateral visual neglect (their brain ignores one side of their vision). 'Unlike words, images are not arbitrarily associated with what they stand for. Thus images provide a means for thinking about something when it is not there' (1983: 75). Plant performed a few informal experiments during her paper presentation that resonate with Kosslyn's findings.

She played <<waves crashing,>> <<fire crackling>> and <<a playground>> without telling the audience what the sound was and then asked what the individual interpretation was. <<Waves crashing>> did not always indexically link to the seaside, nor did <<fire crackling>> cause everyone to think of a hearth. It is impossible to verify how each person interprets nonverbal images (Kosslyn 1983: 37).

Keynote sounds, a term with its origins in acoustic ecology (Schafer 1994: 101), which Verma uses in his analyses, have become clichés in audio drama-making. However, Plant's examples above show that we should not take such processes for granted. The cry of a seagull is called by Gielgud 'the most effective of all "effects"' (1957: 43), 'instant shorthand', as James puts it, 'for a sea setting' (1994: 22) – an *earcon*, the aural equivalent of the *icon* (Blesser and Salter 2012). The soundscape 'is both a world and a culture constructed to make sense of that world' (Thompson 2004: 1). We can relate this to Barthes' configuration that the *symbol* as 'the representation is analogical and inadequate', and in the *sign*, 'the relation is unmotivated and exact' (1979: 38). 'One can say, for instance, that a certain sweater means *long autumn walks in the woods*', just as the cry of the seagull has, through convention, come to mean *seaside* (1979: 43, original emphasis). Imagery based on aural cues is therefore absolutely unique to each listener, yet broad assumptions have been put into place based on conventional practice.

Modes of listening

Examinations of how people listen are full of apparent contradictions. As Tacchi has observed, 'radio is personal and experiential, rarely talked about, and deeply naturalised' (1997: 2). Almost as often as radio drama has been said to demand 'more' of a listener than TV does of a viewer, it has also been called a background medium (as discussed previously). Why does radio specifically work well in the background and for what reason do people use it that way? Douglas frames radio as providing 'a sense of security that silence does not' ([1999] 2004: 8). This is surely why many people put the television on while engaging in conversation or performing other rote tasks, not looking at or even listening to the device, and why we have entered an era of 'second screens'.[2] People use radio to help ease feelings of loneliness, for example 60 per cent of rural Russians surveyed by Valeri Prosorov in 2012. This is neither new nor perhaps a conscious process. In a 1935 article from *Radio Pictorial*, titled 'The bachelor woman's good-bye to loneliness!', Rosalind Wade writes, 'What does the radio mean to the bachelor woman? Well, in my opinion it means just the difference between solitude and loneliness' (1935: 10). Many scholars have noted the sense of personal companionship created by radio (Crisell 1994: 10; Arnheim 1971: 235; Chignell 2009: 74–78).

Jody Berland has argued that radio as a background medium is part of a further (urban) conditioning 'to ignore the soundscape, including radio' (1994: 88). This is why, presumably, one of the objects of Kip Allen's career as programming director of KHFM

Albuquerque was to, every once in a while, 'pierce' through listeners' 'self-protective layer of unfocused hearing', and use music to *move* them, what he saw as a different process than absorbing facts (Allen 2013c). So what we choose to hear brings us closer to radio's intimacy (Street 2012: 46). To what extent, then, is listening to a radio play a choice? As both Michael Socolow (2004) and Alexander Russo (2009) determined in their analyses of radio advertising, listeners' personal space can be violated by sound in a way no other medium can. A US court upheld that 'a physiological fact, the inability to prevent sound waves from reaching one's ears' argues 'that sound could compel attention in a way that visual stimuli could not' (Russo 2009: 12). To paraphrase Douglas ([1999] 2004), as infants, when we are still focusing our eyes, we are much more soothed/startled/scared by sounds than sights. A sound as outwardly minute as a drop of water in a vast hall 'can provide a clue to the imagination that unlocks the possibility of a potent set of images, expectations and ideas' (Street 2012: 32). A key question of audio drama for many years has been where to situate the drama being created: is it expected that the audience will be a distracted one using the radio or podcast as a secondary medium, or will all attention be focused there, using it as primary medium? Both approaches have been successfully pursued thousands of times. Yet as argued previously, audio storytelling focuses on narrative. Is it a naïve question to ask how exactly this works?

It would seem self-evident that one hears an audio drama and one pieces together the action through listening to the clues. But how does this actually work, and why should it work at all? Is it a consequence of the postmodern condition? In the First World War, soldiers became dependent on sound, sometimes to the extent of confusing the order of action (a gun firing) with effect (the sound of the gun firing) (Stedman 2017).

> One historian has described these trenches [in the First World War] as a troglodyte world, largely sightless, because it was simply too dangerous to put your head above the parapet. It was your ears that were the connection with what was happening above.
>
> (Hendy 2013d)

In a type of video game, known as first-person shooter (FPS), something similar seems to be occurring when a gunshot is 'heard some time after a muzzle flash is seen, but the firing is perceived as one event' (Grimshaw 2012: 347). Although Grimshaw is talking about a time delay between a seen event and its co-existent audio, there is a delay (though only of milliseconds) between a sound being produced in reality, our 'hearing' it and our interpreting it:

> In using the continuous past form of the verb 'to hear' it is understood that all sound heard by an individual is post-impulse sound. The sound has been caused to happen and is metaphorically dying, decaying or dead, before our brains have identified or perceived what the sound is meant to be.
>
> (Rattigan 2002: 124)

The example Rattigan gives is of <<tires screeching>> + <<scream>>-<<bang>>-<<breaking glass>>, which is interpreted as a car crash. Truax suggests that there must be a survival instinct that has instructed humans on how to piece disparate sound elements together (2001: 21). Rattigan suggests that, once heard, a sound sequence like the one signifying 'car crash' is enough to prompt the brain to recognize, when the first sound is heard, the completed image in the brain, assuming that the rest of the sequence will follow. This is presumably why radiogenic comedy like that of *The Goons* (1951–60) and *Fibber McGee and Molly* (1938–53) works well, both setting up expectations (the overstuffed closet that elicits laughter as soon as it's mentioned, like a Pavlovian response) and subverting them (the comedy of *The Goons* works in part because none of the sound sequences they created are sensible).

Understanding listening

Douglas lamented that there is virtually no collaborative work between media historians and cognitive scientists; therefore, 'our knowledge of how we extract and *use* acoustic information seems quite limited' ([1999] 2004: 26, original emphasis). Unfortunately, little has changed since she originally wrote that in 1999. In 2012, Rodero published a study in the *Journal of Radio & Audio Media* which proved the hypothesis that 'a radio story with a dramatised presentation structure will achieve a greater level of stimulation of the imagination than a radio story with a narrated presentation structure' (2012a: 45). Such a hypothesis seems at first glance startlingly simplistic, but the truth is, 90 years after the origination of radio drama, it is still necessary to conduct such experiments because few formal investigations have been done into the cognitive science of radio drama. There could be better organization, communication and cooperation between radio enthusiasts, historians and scientists. There is forward momentum – consider the studies by McMurtry (2017), Rodero (2012a, 2012b, 2014), Forsslund (2014), Bolls (2002, 2006), Potter and Choi (2006), Potter et al. (1997), Babin and Burns (1998), Bolls and Potter (1998) – but progress is slow, as there is considerably less interest in such experimentation as would seem warranted. Another difficulty with experiments on aural dramatic stimulation and storytelling is that they cannot replicate actual listening conditions, as acknowledged by Bolls (2006). Listeners may be more predisposed to respond to what they think the researchers want than they would be listening on their own.

Much of the existing research on listening, emotion, narrative and mental imagery generation has come to us from psychology and advertising research (McMurtry 2017: 1). We know that structurally complex audio messages seem to invoke greater use of resource allocation in the brain. As specifically regards audio drama, the use of dramatic technique – what Rodero calls *sound effects* and *sound shots* – brings more listener interaction and better imagery generation (Rodero 2012b: 462). Questions remain:

- While the ear is 'tremendously sensitive to distortion and levels of semantic implication' (Truax 2001: 34), our ability to put faces to characters in audio drama may lag behind our visual ability. We can recognize and remember visually up to 10,000 faces, but we do not seem to have the same ability to voices unlinked with faces (Beck 1997: 97). How do we imagine a face in audio drama? Moreover, how do we visualize a character in his or her entirety? Where does this information come from? Is it related merely to memory, as Moulton and Kosslyn (2009) would conclude? Is it a case less of what is 'seen' than what is perceived or understood, as Patterson (2016) would have it?
- Hearing is, as Michel Chion puts it, 'omnidirectional' (1999: 17); others have written about the immersive qualities of hearing and listening (Bull 2000, 2007), while still others have challenged this conception of the ear's abilities (Sterne 2003: 15).

While we are not yet in a position to answer these questions, it is true that we still encounter mental imagery on a day-to-day basis (Kosslyn 1983: 1). Kosslyn has suggested that the fact we can instantly imagine a horse jumping over a house – even though we have never seen this in real life – supposes we generate images, not retrieve them. Writing more than 20 years later, however, Kosslyn seems to conclude that the primary function of mental imagery, 'is to allow us to generate specific predictions based on past experience' (Moulton and Kosslyn 2009: 1274). However, if this is the case, why do we use mental imagery in listening to audio drama? It seems unlikely that we are generating specific predictions that will help us functionally live our lives, but rather that imagery generation based on aural clues in a storytelling situation may help us enjoy the story more fully, by engaging with all our senses, as the chapter epigraph from blind and deaf playwright R.C. Scriven suggests.

Conclusion

Clearly, there is still a great deal of work to be done in these areas of sound studies. Rodero and Bolls are, at the time of writing, working on further studies that are more broadly concerned with sound and imagery generation, particularly as relates to Alzheimer's patients. While the anecdotal feelings that listeners have reported for 90 years on the way listening affects them, either on the micro scale or the macro scale, is interesting, we are well overdue for an understanding of the neurological underpinnings of these processes. For the continued survival of audio drama as a form, it is necessary to make a more codified study rather than blundering around in the dark. There have been many happy accidents that have occurred through that approach, but we need to employ serious scientific study. This requires a new generation of enquiring minds and the ability to fund this research beyond studies that primarily benefit the radio advertising industry. Perhaps, as some have suggested, radio advertising storytelling should be absorbed into the study of radio drama.

There remains an intriguing mystery regarding mental imagery generation and listening, especially to radio, dismissed as a background medium, which hinges on the fact that images remain so personal and cannot be expressed verbally. While, naturally, radio and audio drama cannot lay exclusive claim to this strikingly intimate relationship, this phenomenon does go some way in justifying the broadcaster–solo relationship that gives such a 'fillip' to radio listeners.

Notes

1 Though Patterson (2016) claims that visual imagery generation in audio drama is neither universal nor as important as previously argued.
2 'There are certain people who have maintained that the American housewife would turn television on early in the morning just as she does the radio, and leave it on throughout the day and most of the night. [...] That, of course, is hardly so, because the benefits of television can be derived only when you are looking at it directly and not doing anything else. The housewife will not very long remain a housewife who attempts to watch television programs all afternoon and evening instead of cooking or darning socks' (Samuel Cuff, general manager, WABD, 1946, cited in Boddy 2004: 51).

Chapter 3

Audio Drama Techniques and Effects

> Every radio work I approach with the same kind of expectations – does it make creative use of the medium, and how does it tell its story?
> – Laurence Raw (cited in Hand and Traynor 2011: 113)

Even those who know little about radio have heard of *War of the Worlds* (1938, CBS). Just as its infamy ensures it has remained a household name even now, radio scholars interpret the programme in many ways, each with his or her own theoretical hobbyhorse to ride. For some, it's to show the power of the imagination when partnered with radio; for others, it's a classic example of mass hysteria; for others, it's evidence of Orson Welles' genius or vainglorious attitude; for still others, it's an opportunity to mock the credulousness of our forebears. But if listeners believed, *why* did they believe? Beyond the obvious answers (the escalating tensions in Europe providing the possibility of invasion by a foreign power; the fact that many listeners tuned in midway through broadcast and therefore missed the token assurances that the broadcast was fictional), we have the centripetal power of radio to thank (as described in the previous chapter) – skilfully and knowingly manipulated by Welles and his team.

If the cognitive studies interrogating audio drama are still in their infancy, then we are still pondering the *why* of audio drama's cognitive and emotional effects on audiences. Dubber, noting the discontinuity of media theory as regards radio (2013: 16), has coined the term *techné* from Greek to describe the crafts and aesthetics of radio (2013: 21), which nicely sidesteps the need to characterize it as a highbrow medium (the 'art' of radio) or a lowbrow medium (the 'craft' of radio). This chapter, then, discusses the *techné* of radio drama, illuminating some of the approaches towards making a 'theatre of the mind', as well as what they tell us about audiences. It will also provide examples of where to continue our studies and forge links with audio drama's place in the literary canon, one of the goals established in Chapter 1.

How is audio drama made?

As noted in Chapter 1, there is arguably no unanimous vocabulary for theorizing about the components of audio drama. Nevertheless, that has not stopped the writing of technical manuals on audio drama, from 1926 to the present day. We thus return to the dichotomy introduced in Chapter 1 regarding the high and low art debate and audio drama's place within it. Is the mode of audio drama production more related to ideological, auteur-like decisions on behalf of impresarios or to practical, workaday reasons? As Challis et al. noted, during the mass production of radio 'shockers' on US network radio in the 1940s, sometimes only four or five hours elapsed between the writing of a script and its broadcast (2014: 255). It would have been difficult, though not impossible, to use an auteur-like approach to such drama-making (as demonstrated in Mott's anecdote in Chapter 1). Perhaps complicating this issue is the fact that the production side of audio drama is missing from most works on radio drama history and theory, and theory is necessarily sidelined in most published works on production. In the next chapter, these questions become important as we explore the ways in which audio drama is made, production techniques resulting both from cerebral ponderings on the art form and as practical workaday production of a piece of entertainment.

The first radio drama, of course, went out live and was dictated by the confines of the studio. The studio could contain actors, musicians, directors and special effects men (almost always men) and could keep out intrusive noise. Studio-based drama is still the preferred mode for many audio drama-makers, including the BBC, whose studios have become expertly equipped for staging any imaginable scene. Frederick Greenhalgh, host emeritus of the *Radio Drama Revival* podcast (2007–present) and showrunner of epic science-fiction drama *The Cleansed* (2011–present), suggests the benefits of this approach include 'consistent voice tracks' for manipulation in post-production (2008). Effects are mixed in post-production, but a clean recording with acoustic hints of environment is usually desired. However, studio recording can be as basic as cramming a performer into a newsreader's booth, as described by Richard Shannon (2014a) in his early LBC efforts (see Chapter 7).

Greenhalgh, working from the perspective of a satellite audio drama producer, is aware that many of those discovering audio drama for the first time through the Internet have not had the advantage of access to consistently scheduled, public service broadcasting (PSB)-broadcast radio drama (like the BBC). Therefore, to him, one of the disadvantages of the studio system is its expense.[1] Without the infrastructure, experience and equipment that such institutions have built up over the decades, access to studio environments is not realistic for the amateur or satellite audio drama-maker – where well-equipped radio studios can cost around £50,000 to outfit. Greenhalgh (2008) also cites as disadvantage the practice of creating an atmosphere for a drama in post-production, rather than through natural ambience during performance. Reasonable ambience *can* be created without overreliance on post-production, in a BBC studio by virtue of different screens, acoustics and material constructions of recording rooms, though, of course, post-production effects are added to scenes, including 'atmos' (the reverb in a cathedral or outdoor sounds for a jogging scene, for example).

Greenhalgh himself seems to prefer what he calls the Indie Film Way, or on-location recording. The emphasis on actuality and on-location recording is one borrowed from news and journalistic recording. As with film location shooting, the difficulties stem from unpredictability. On the other hand, this method offers 'sonic verisimilitude' (Greenhalgh

Figure 1: In-studio recording. Courtesy of Fred Greenhalgh.

2008). Greenhalgh's *The Cleansed* is recorded in this way, and photos show that the practical microphone set-up most closely resembles film recording.

Greenhalgh also describes a third mode which he calls the Brave New Way, but a more accepted name is *satellite audio drama*. The term was originated by Jack J. Ward of the *Sonic Society* (Paterson 2008). In approximately ten years of practice, satellite audio drama has steadily benefited from refinements and the increasing availability of technology with which to make the drama. It has therefore developed its own production practices, which begin with the scriptwriter/producer, who posts an audition call on a variety of online media, such as Audio Drama Talk Forum, Slack or social media platforms like Facebook or Twitter (Golding and Thraille 2017). The actors (who range from professional voice-over actors to non-professional enthusiasts) record their lines in isolation, frequently in bedroom studios, with a range of recording equipment. The producer mixes the performances as well as sound effects (frequently sourced from Freesound.org) and music (again, potentially sourced from free sites like Kevin MacLeod's Incompetech) on Digital Audio Workstations (DAWs) such as Freeware Audacity or industry-standard such as Adobe Audition (or at the highest end,

Figure 2: Final Rune Productions recording audio drama on location with a Rode T4 mic and a Marantz PMD-660. Courtesy of Fred Greenhalgh.

ProTools). Some recording in this mode is done *en masse* in the studio, but frequently the performers never meet face-to-face.

The drawbacks, according to Greenhalgh, include 'a lot of post-production work to assemble the voice tracks', and this is usually almost single-handedly the work of the producer (2008). Greenhalgh suggests it also creates 'inconsistency in quality/room timbre', though as actors' home studios become more sophisticated, this has become less of a problem (Greenhalgh 2008). Actors who cannot physically interact and sometimes do not even hear one another as they play their scenes suffer from a lack of what Greenhalgh calls 'the special sumthin' sumthin' when actors act in a scene together' (Greenhalgh 2008). However, increasingly, the satellite audio drama mode is the preferred one for freelance audio drama distributed online, for practical as well as ideological reasons. It is, or has been until the monetization of the podcast, relatively rare to find any of the proponents of satellite audio drama offering their work for sale. This mode of production simultaneously balances an attempt for high-quality production with a democratic access policy. At its best, this means, to quote Fiona Thraille, a voice artist and one-time co-host of the *Audio Drama Production Podcast* (2015–present), 'a very large number of people are able to tell their stories and find an audience without any commercial pressure' (2013).

Whether an audio drama is created using traditional BBC-style studio-based techniques or by Greenhalgh's newer approaches, one of the audio director's primary tasks is to bring out the best possible performances from the actors. To paraphrase Evan Eisenberg, a good audio drama actor will create the belief that the drama is happening somewhere between the earphones and your brain, or even more intimately, the drama is happening *inside* you. The actors' lips are in effect next to your ears, directing you to feel their inner anguish, to laugh at their comic moments, and, if pitched correctly, you will feel swept up in the drama.

The role of the actor in audio drama

Though the technology surrounding radio and now audio drama has changed significantly since the 1920s, the part that the actor has to play in the process, and how his or her technique and practice must necessarily differ from stage, film and other types of visual acting, remains crucial. Edwin Duerr's words from 1950 in *Radio and Television Acting: Criticism, Theory, Practice* are still a good guide to the craft practised today, whether in the traditional studio arrangement or in satellite audio drama. The actor's main role is 'to try in so far as he is an artist, to assist the playwright in communicating his perceptions, his qualities' (Duerr 1950: 4). It is a perhaps hard truth for the dramatist to assimilate that whether or not his or her drama will be taken seriously will hinge in large part on the level of convincing and professional performances from the actors. Thraille corroborates that 'the listeners' focus [is] on the voice alone and the intimacy and sheer sensitivity of a microphone make accuracy and control essential' (2014).

Not only meaning and emotion, but also accent 'and related background nationality or ethnicity; age; class; implied physique; speech impediments, etc.' must come from the performance (Thraille 2014). For example, although not, strictly speaking, a radio drama, Hugh Quarshie's performance in a reading of Chester Himes' *Cotton Comes to Harlem* (1965) in a BBC Radio 4 production from 2012 provides superb directive for one actor creating a multiplicity of voices, all conveyed through Alan Beck's formulation of dialect (see below). 'A well-defined portrayal of characters in radio drama', Rodero et al. noted, 'includes personal, physical, psychological, social and cultural data' (2014: 173). Himes' gritty detective potboilers set in 1960s Harlem feature American black inner city detectives, Coffin Ed and Grave Digger Jones, as well as a variety of other voices. Clearly here, as Beck notes, '[d]ialects are always changing and no one speaker in real life conforms to the group norm' (1997: 109). Quarshie effectively differentiated between the speakers by voice modulation, acid-scarred Coffin Ed's rough, gravelly, smoker's voice contrasting with Grave Digger's slower, deeper, more deliberate dialect.

Duerr believed that the key to creating a successful performance was two-fold. The physical component was in avoiding 'voices that are thin, harsh, bleak, monotonous, and completely lacking in individual color or warmth' (1950: 31). As MacArthur and Miller suggest, '[m]onotone performance is – at least acoustically – quite uninformative for the brain' (2016). Mentally, the actor's performance finds and expresses meaning. BBC Radio actor John Aubrey captures this triumph of the imagination: 'Looking back through twenty years of radio work, I don't see Studio B10 or whatever. I see backstreets, a large house, Vietnam. And I see my fellow actors in costume. I can see the sky and everything' (cited in Beck 1997: 79). Success in visualization therefore 'depends on the actor's knowing the full meaning of what he says', despite the brevity of time actors have with their scripts (Duerr 1950: 97). Richard Shannon characterizes audio drama acting as 'instinctual' (2014a). Rehearsals are likewise brief – in BBC studio drama, two days is usual for the rehearsal and recording of a 45-minute play – and, as US radio actor Wil Moore noted, rather than acting to an audience, the radio actor acts to the mic (2014). Radio acting also means reading from a script and no memorization, and there is also (usually) little to no physical contact with the other actors (Shannon 2014a).

Yet it should not be assumed that an audio actor picks up a script and simply reads it. Both Thraille (2014) and BBC actor John Gibbs (2006) point out the importance of smiling and using facial expressions in audio drama; actors use different parts of the body to resonate the sound, such as head, nose and chest, 'to make the voice sound reedier, more nasal, broader and stronger' (Thraille 2014). 'Your voice and how your voice works can be affected by how you move, how you breathe, how you're sitting', Erika Sanderson of the *NoSleep* podcast notes (cited in Golding and Thraille 2017). When done well, audio acting can be enthralling for the audience and enjoyable for the actor. It's a chance for actors to stretch themselves. As Richard J. Hand notes, classic Hollywood stars frequently performed horror roles in Old Time Radio (OTR), with radio's 'invisibility' allowing leading men and women to try more sinister roles than they would be able to play on-screen (2006: 47). 'It is conceivable', notes Gibbs (2006), 'that a 25-stone 55-year-old man can play the dashing romantic lead or an Indian grandmother can play a schoolboy!' As actor Samuel West put it, 'it's easier [on radio] to get great actors for small roles', and 'it's harder to be typecast' (2007). Besides the enjoyment of stretching their acting prowess, actors often find that they can easily fit radio drama into their schedules, with weekend and day work suiting availability, especially if the actor is in a stage run (Beck 1997: 5). 'Actors love radio drama' Caulfield confirmed (2009: 5).

Nor should it be assumed that a television actor can necessarily excel at the kind of delivery and nuance required of the audio drama actor. This can sometimes become painfully obvious when entertainment 'stars' are cast as leads in BBC radio drama only to have marked difficulty creating the kind of performance needed for the medium. In light of the 2014 debacle of BBC TV's *Jamaica Inn*, which lost one quarter of its viewing audience after the first episode, the pursuit of overly naturalistic styles of acting on television can lead to an undervaluing of the careful craft of speech acting. Some viewers of *Jamaica Inn* complained that they could not hear the actors, their Cornish accents 'impenetrable' (Boyle 2014).[2] This highlights a long-standing debate regarding clarity of expression and meaning on an axis between enunciated, performed elocution and relaxed, informal, regionalized speech. For example, Duerr had no time for 1950s Method Acting, noting, 'if that is the way people actually converse [with ums and ahs] it is not the way they should converse in acting' (1950: 187). Whether this means pitching the drama to a 'tone higher on the scale of reality', as actor Peter Egan (Richardson et al. 2013) commented, or simply maintaining a standard of diction, audio drama acting remains vocally demanding.

The role of the director and producer in audio drama

'Radio directors seem to have less individual renown' than film and stage directors (Beck 1997: 34). Yet their role is vital. Duerr saw the role of the director in radio drama to advise 'about such structural matters as change of beat, contrast, pace, picking up cues, pointing a line, reversals, rhythm, subordination, style, or pictorial composition' (1950: 371). Duerr and Hand and Traynor agree that the director should help the actor give the best interpretive reading, 'the unique sound and skill of each of them' (Duerr 1950: 372). Directors have individualized systems for giving actors notes; BBC actor Anna Gilbert explained, '[t]he director has to notice the slightest thing I do off beam, like something not in line with accent or a word mispronounced or stressed wrongly' (cited in Beck 1997: 39). This was echoed by Yuri Rasovsky (see Chapter 9), who wrote that without a director, '[d]ialogue is devoid of subtext, and structure is amorphous. Tension is absent or misplaced. Climaxes are in the wrong place, if they're present at all' (2001a).

The director should help the cast work as a team. Inheriting rehearsal aesthetics from both stage and post-single camera location television (Hewett 2015), radio dramas can be recorded in studio with individual scenes rehearsed and then recorded or rehearsed all the way through and recorded. In the studio recording system, the process begins with a read-through. In the read-through, directors 'discover how this cast sounds working together', and some actors present a nearly complete performance in read-through (Beck 1997: 41). Furthermore, with adaptations, the director has to 'define and interpret creatively the conventions and period style of both the script and the original work; as well as dealing with larger and more starry [sic] casts' (Beck 1997: 35). The playwright is sometimes in studio as well, and writer Wally K. Daly warned that it is also the director's role to moderate between a dogmatic, inexperienced author and the cast. Director Martin Jenkins told Daly during the recording of his first play, '[y]ou are the skeleton and you have to allow the studio to put on the flesh' (cited in Beck 1997: 43).

The producer of an audio drama should deal with the practical aspects of the drama.

> Producers do a great deal of preparation before actually recording the play. The script must be written, the characters cast and decisions made on the recording locations and

technical requirements. Detailed schedules have to be prepared so that the play can be produced within the budget and with the resources available.

(Hand and Traynor 2011: 161)

Yuri Rasovsky waxed his normal lyrical and puckish self in the early noughties when describing his role as producer for both audio drama and audiobooks:

> The producer normally hires the cast, director, engineer, composer – oversees the whole process […] In America, we have many auteur audio dramatists who write and direct as well, such as the legendary Norman Corwin and the not so legendary me. […] The publishers of audiobooks do things differently. Some only hire narrators who have their own recording equipment and who can therefore produce, voice and edit their assignments. Some freelancers make a living offering package deals, recording, directing and editing performances on their own equipment and in their own facilities. Many of the smaller publishers are producer owned and operated. […] When I make audio plays, […] I am firmly in control. When I make audiobooks I often think no one's in control. At any rate, the definition of a good job changes with the publisher and doesn't seem to have much to do with artistic quality.
>
> (Rasovsky 2002)

Creating a soundscape

In spring 2014, Audible, Amazon's arm of 'talking books' (see Chapter 11), mounted an aggressive public campaign in London's transport system. The heart of the campaign suggested that commuting Londoners would find themselves immersed in worlds far more exciting than the 9-to-5 grind by putting on headphones. Visually, they would continue to connect with the reality around them, but through their aural senses engaged by the talking book mediated through headphones, they would find themselves (1) 'Travelling with a Killer', advertising a woman listening to a thriller by Thomas Harris; (2) 'Off to a Distant Galaxy' in Douglas Adams' universe in *The Hitchhiker's Guide to the Galaxy* (1979). Most saliently, one of the London commuters 'became' the character within the audiobook by transforming into a First World War soldier while listening to Sebastian Faulks' novel *Birdsong* (1993) (see Figures 3 and 4).

Audiobooks, occupying a liminal existence between 'pure' audio drama and readings, have nevertheless risen to some prominence (see Chapter 9). Indeed, Audible's campaign further refined itself in 2016 with advertisements that whispered into listener's ears ('Come Closer') or posed that horror listeners might enjoy the furry legs of a tarantula crawling out of their ear-buds (see Figures 5 and 6). The message from the advertising campaigns is clear: the listener could sustain two realities, the mundane, predictable visual one, and the more intimate, adventurous aural/cognitive one, at the same time.

Figure 3: London Overground advertisement as part of Audible's campaign for audiobooks, 2014. Photo: Leslie McMurtry.

Figure 4: London Overground advertisement for Audible, 2014. Photo: J. Beckwith.

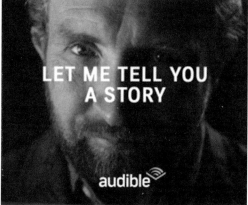

Figure 5: Online advertisement for Audible featuring Juliet Stevenson, 2017.

Figure 6: Online advertisement for Audible featuring Eddie Marsan, 2017.

Indeed, drama-makers themselves are aware of this possibility. If a particular story matches the listener's real-life setting (e.g. a story about a security guard in a haunted building being listened to by an actual security guard alone in a building), the overlap between fiction and reality can be particularly unnerving (David Cummings cited in O'Donoghue 2016).

Theorists have long been aware of the absorption of headphone-wearing, personal stereo consumption, originally with Walkmans and naturally continuing with iPods. Indeed, Michael Bull is the authority on this. Walkman users, he wrote, 'consistently claim to be "somewhere else"' while using personal stereos (2000: 73). Users look and do not look (Bull 2000: 74). Sound overwhelmingly envelopes them (Bull 2000: 78). More recently, he has noted that geographical space becomes 'recessed' yet is more charged with the user's mood

(2007: 41, 84). More damningly, he comments that listeners can become locked into their own interiority (2007: 29).

Whether the absorbing effect of iPod listening in an urban environment is positive or negative is a moot point for us here; we are interested in the nature of the effect itself. An actor reading an audiobook can *tell* the listener that the story is taking place on the Moon or in a German town at midnight in the early twentieth century, but a convincing aural soundscape can make this seem more real and effortless. Hand and Traynor suggest that the constituent parts of radio drama are:

- Words
- Sounds
- Music
- Silence

(2011: 40)

All of these elements are used to create a soundscape. 'A soundscape', Mary Louise James has found, 'can be confusing if heard in isolation' (1994: 23). The soundscape is therefore a carefully constructed setting composed of contributions from the actor, the writer (explicit and implicit clues about time, date, place and situation), acoustics, music and special effects. The audio drama writer and director must be implicitly aware of the potential for confusion and therefore must strive hard for clarity (Ward 2017a).

A soundscape can be established with surprisingly little sensory information. Don Haworth's 1975 BBC drama *On a Day in Summer in a Garden* was perfect for the radio medium for two reasons: its pastoral opening and dialogue between two men and a boy suggested a very mundane story, only for that to be turned on its head when it was revealed the voices embodied dock plants, not humans; and because if this had been played out on stage or film, it ran the risk of being absurd to the point that the humour and then pathos could not be appreciated. The audio medium helped suspend disbelief, and the skill of the writing created convincing dock plant 'personalities' as well as characters we could, as humans, relate to:

>   DICK: You're dusty, Jim, from cowering against that wall. You're asymmetric.
>   JACK (*making the peace*): But he's quite tall, grandad [sic].
>   JIM: Considerably taller than your grandad.
>   DICK: He's got next to no leaf.
>   JIM (*ironically*): And your grandad, Jack, has some lovely broad fronds.
>   DICK: I do at least look like a dock plant, not crawling up the wallside like the nettles.
>   JIM (*laughs, ridiculing*): You look like a clump of rhubarb.
>   DICK (*angry*): I what? I what?
>   JACK (*distressed*): Uncle Jim. Grandad, please –
>
> (Haworth 1976: 109)

The further irony was that the human characters in the play were oafish, destructive buffoons who couldn't even speak intelligibly.

On a Day in Summer in a Garden also uses pauses, or silences, to great advantage. 'Pause, whether slight or dramatically long, exhibits the entire human mechanism actively at work, lets the audience share in that process' and reinforces meaning through suspense (Duerr 1950: 125). Therefore, it is important to acknowledge that the soundscape can also be composed of silence. Seán Street reminds us that 'on the air', 'air time', 'dead air' – all broadcasting terms – connote a sense of mystery and expectation. Silence in audio drama can suggest 'a moment of terror, the possibility of its existence being broken by some unseen, threatening presence or act' (Street 2012: 39). To paraphrase Allen Weiss, characters can exist in audio drama who are only indicated by their names being spoken; if they are silent characters and speak no dialogue, there is a certain strangeness about their invisibility, or inaudibility (Weiss 1995: 62). In the context of *On a Day in Summer in a Garden,* the dock plants Dick (Granddad), Jack and Uncle Jim are not the only plants in the garden, but as the only ones given voice, they have to report second-hand on the activities of any other plants.

The vast majority of science-fiction audio dramas, while often taking place in the vacuum of space, do not take place in a silent void.[3] Some, however, have come close, for example, Jonathan Mitchell's *Moon Graffiti* (2010). A short play that begins with an authorial intrusion telling us that it is a 'what if?', this play is a dramatization of Nixon's 1969 speech written by William Safire that would salve the failure of the Apollo 11 mission. With two actors in the near-silence of space using their last two hours of life to reflect on the human condition, the silence contributed to a feeling of sparseness and poignancy.

A soundscape created effectively seeks to solve issues of listener confusion. For example, *Dracula* the stage play (1897) and how subsequent radio adaptations have tried to resolve visualization and confusion issues is an area worth examining in detail (McMurtry 2015b). *Dracula* on stage was originally conceived as a five-hour dramatic reading with fifteen actors in May 1897. As *Dracula* expert David Skal points out, certain scenes during the reading would have made no sense unless the action was somehow described or acted out (1997: 377), in particular one of the most dramatic moments of the early part of the book, when imprisoned hero Jonathan Harker looks out the castle window and sees Dracula climbing up the steep vertical stone face. In terms of how radio adaptations have handled this particular moment, two BBC radio *Dracula* 'spin-offs', *The Voyage of the Demeter* (2008) and *Sherlock Holmes vs Dracula* (1981), have excised the scene from their scripts as a matter of perspective: with the narrative taking place away from Harker, it is not necessary to insert the scene. In the 1991–92 seven-part full-cast BBC adaptation, Jonathan Harker in monologue merely describes the action of Dracula crawling up the castle wall. While this may, on the surface, seem an unsatisfying attempt to recreate a key visual moment in the novel, it fits in perfectly with this adaptation's ethos. Harker's experiences during the first 70 pages of the novel are compressed into about twelve scenes in this adaptation. The actor playing Jonathan's personal turmoil, as manifest in his vocal performance, is enough to convey his horror of viewing Dracula climbing, and if the listener has been at all invested in the story so far, his or her aural imagination will do the rest.

The architecture of time

If, as the old adage goes, a picture is worth a thousand words, a snatch of music in audio drama is worth a thousand lines of description. More than almost any other element, music can ground and set the soundscape for an audio drama with precision and can touch the audience emotionally. It can be elegant and explicit at the same time. Also, it is bound up inextricably with paratexts. If a drama begins with the Beatles' 'Twist and Shout' (1964) or Bach's 'Aria on the Goldberg Variations' on period instruments, the listener is left with an immediate impression of the era of the drama and the setting itself. This first judgement may not always be correct, and indeed, some dramas capitalize on the ironic disconnect between the expectations raised by the music and the reality of the drama's setting. Verma likens music to 'fertile seeds of information' by supplying short cuts by playing on a 'network of pre-existing associations and understandings' (2012: 33). A 2014 BBC *15 Minute Drama* adaptation of *Modesty Blaise* capitalized on this concept by commissioning Will Gregory of contemporary group Goldfrapp to give the adaptation its distinctive sound. The music, so indelibly saturated with the era it attempts to recreate, that of the 1960s (not in reality but the 1960s of the James Bond film), becomes almost a character in its own right. Eisenberg rightly calls music 'the architecture of time' (1987: 27).

Hand and Traynor characterize music used in audio drama in four different functions: music as link; 'mood' music; music as stylized sound effect and music as indexical function (2011: 50). As with film, there is also the distinction between the diegetic (within the universe of the story) and the non-diegetic (outside the universe of the story). In many audio dramas, the split between the two is not always explicit, and a great deal of amusement or enjoyment can come from acknowledging this within the universe of the drama. Throughout the 2011 award-winning BBC Radio 3 drama *Kafka the Musical!* by Murray Gold, the listeners are informed that, despite his protests, Franz Kafka's life is being turned into a musical, to be enjoyed on the Berlin stage. It is only in the last third of the 90-minute play that characters actually begin singing, including Kafka's gruff father who shows his vulnerable side through song. However, only Kafka seems to be able to hear him. Later, rehearsals on stage merge into reality and back again as Kafka struggles with illness, both physical and mental, to the point where the (listening) audience is never quite sure whether what it's hearing has actually occurred or is just in Kafka's head. A validation of sorts occurs in the last scene wherein Kafka at last adds his own voice to the chorus, though once again it is unclear whether this is occurring diegetically or non-diegetically.

Previously unheard worlds

Sound effects are eloquent in audio drama. 'Noises like the ticking of a clock, the dulcet tones of the deep-voiced announcer, and the moaning of the air-raid siren make persuasive arguments to us' (Goodale 2011: 4). Beyond the practical application of sound effects, in theoretical terms we find ourselves borrowing much from cinema. The term *acousmatic*, meaning sound with no visible source, originated with Chion (1994: 71–73). Grimshaw (2012), therefore borrows from cinematic terms for the genre of first-person shooter (FPS) sound, as we sometimes do to describe radio drama, using the term 'acousmatic sound' to describe 'off-screen' sound, a sound that emanates from an object not 'seen' on the screen of the FPS vision. We can therefore use acousmatic in radio drama terms, as well as another cinematic term, 'close-up'. In terms of the radio 'close-up', as Douglas has discovered, some sound effects are often better than hearing the real thing. 'A single shot' from a gun, as Val Gielgud puts it, or 'a solitary slammed door, will have all the dramatic value of a film close-up' (1957: 90).[4]

The eloquence, and indeed necessity of sound effects to the audio drama soundscape, cannot be underestimated. During the recording of the BBC's *Life and Fate* (2011), I experienced first-hand in the BBC studio the rehearsal and recording process. I learned that much effort was made to preserve authenticity in the use of sound effects that were period-specific. This ranged from the right telephone handset on which Viktor answers the call from Stalin, to the use of a fountain pen for Viktor to use to sign his recantation. Mark Burman personally recorded authentic tank sounds for *Novikov's Story* (2011) at the Tank Museum in Bovington, Dorset, using one of their Soviet T-34 tanks. Another of the *Life and Fate* dramas in which sound effects made an interesting contribution was '*Abarchuk*' (2011), a *15 Minute Drama* set in a prison camp. In script and in studio, the story ended with the sinister sound of a knife being drawn. However, it appears that in post-production, the sound wasn't convincing enough, so the broadcast version ends with the last line of dialogue – the sound of the knife is gone.

Radio fantasy and science fiction have existed since the 1920s, and with them, the desire for appropriate sound effects. To that end, what is the authentic sound for things that do not exist? Rattigan wonders 'what is the point of spending time and human resources in creating the sounds of giant boulders cracking open and turning into space ships?' (2002: 76). A good sound effect for something that doesn't exist can ensure a listener's immersion within the soundscape, guaranteeing the success of that drama for them, and furthering human creativity as a whole. British writer Angela Carter scripted challenging plays that had to be interpreted by her BBC producer, Bruce Young. Carter's imagination created sounds and concepts that could not be seen and were an interesting challenge in *Come Unto These Yellow Sands* (1979) and *Puss in Boots* (1982). In the former, the direction 'the beginning of a rustling and tittering, the sounds of the stirring of a horrid, goblin crowd' was far more faithfully created in the broadcast version than the direction 'the music hiccups and begins to repeat itself', proving that even excellent audio drama producers are not necessarily as good as the stage directions imagined in one's own head (Carter 1985: 22, 43). To illustrate the previously unheard (or at least uncommon) world of *Puss in Boots*, Carter gave Puss, as played by Andrew Sachs, a dramatic monologue that gave him a narrative reason to describe his cat-like features while he retained a colourful and eloquent voice that, luckily for us, spoke English. Lance Sieveking was aware of this potential in the 1920s, writing,

> the funniest things can happen intentionally also, when the sounds are deliberately divorced from their expected nature, when the hippopotamus sings like a lark, or the steam tractor speaks with the voice of a country vicar.
>
> (1934: 67)

'What is the authentic sound', Grimshaw wonders, 'of the zombies in *Left 4 Dead* (Valve Corporation 2008)? What is the authentic sound of the BFG in *Quake III Arena* (id Software 1999) and the various imaginary monsters in *Half-Life 2* (Valve Software 2004)?' (2012: 361). One might also ask what the sound of a petulant teenage robot going into 'French Avenger mode' would be, or the sound of Murgala the leader of the Graspatron troops vaporizing (or perhaps liquidizing?) one of his minions? Certainly, Tim Gambrell and Andrew Hyde's approach in their independently produced play *Turbo Tina 3* (2009) is one answer among infinite variation. This substantiates that, as effective as the BBC studio system has proven in creating previously unheard worlds, successful SFX can help suspend disbelief in any production.

Painting a picture

Guy Starkey makes an important point when he writes 'everyone who speaks displays demographic characteristics inherent in themselves' (2004: 190). How does an audience build up an aural picture of characters in radio drama? As Greg Goodale, paraphrasing Shai Burstyn, suggests, '[v]oices "paint" character on the radio' (2011: 10). Beck writes at length on the actor's arsenal in creating character on audio drama, suggesting that the audio drama actor must work much more quickly in establishing character:

> Your first lines tell the listener of your character's dialect […] and identity. This information could be later adjusted or confirmed, but you have to be sure of these signals when recording because you stick by them. The difference with radio is that the revealing of character must be gradual and progressive, whatever the signalling you do with your first lines. Stage and screen give a complete display of body, costume, and face.
> (1997: 108)

In terms of choosing actors to paint these aural pictures, BBC dramas are cast from a producer's specialist knowledge, from discussion with colleagues, from listening to drama, going to the theatre, watching films and TV. Very occasionally there is an open audition or a targeted audition if an unusual role is being sought. Independent audio drama and its (often) freelance actors use the resource of the Internet and podcasts to listen to and practise accents (Golding and Thraille 2017).

Dialect

Accents have an overwhelming importance in audio drama, especially via the BBC, given that accent as an index of class is a fundamentally British characteristic. Director Hilary

Norrish notes: 'Choosing accents and regional accents is a deeply political act on radio' (cited in Beck 1997: 111). Beck says that actors must convey geographical region, social class, gender, age, style and subgroup through dialect (1997: 108). One useful example of the importance of dialect is of D.J. Britton's BBC Radio 4 *Classic Serial* adaptation of James Fenimore Cooper's *The Spy,* broadcast in 2012. Cooper's novel retraces the complicated loyalties during the American Revolution. Because this is a radio adaptation, audience-generated judgements of characters, which in visual or prose media can be made based on a number of markers like physical appearance and costume, had to be based on accents and vocal tones. Using a cast primarily of British extraction but including US-born actors, the director, Sasha Yevtushenko, had to make decisions regarding accent standardization. As we know, interesting, individual voices are necessary in audio drama to avoid what Beck calls 'clustering', and for that reason, dialects more distinctive than required in Cooper's prose were a necessity in the *Classic Serial* '*Spy*'. Performing dialect in a less-than-convincing way can damn the drama to inauthenticity or even ridicule.

In *The Spy,* since there were characters with (a) regional variations; (b) loyalties to the rebels and loyalties to Mother England; (c) obviously heroic and villainous characters as well as a few of whom we are unsure at first; (d) a historical divide of 200 years, care had to be taken to make the most of a few seconds' dialogue. The Wharton family, for example, use a muted, 'mid-Atlantic' accent, effectively neither 'British' nor stridently 'American' with short vowels, which underlines their position as 'trapped' in neutrality. British officers like Colonel Wellemere speak standard neutral English (a modified form of received pronunciation). Certainly, one cannot help being reminded that 'a well-educated British accent', in US films at least, 'had come to serve as a sufficient shorthand for villainy' (Glancy 2005: 537). Contrast this, however, with the villainous Skinners in the adaptation, who have a much more colloquial and regionalized accent, suggesting back-country or even the American rural South with undertones of Jim Crow and segregation. Their accent, which seems to ooze with nastiness, suggests they are villains not only morally, but through blood and breeding. In a case such as this, while historical accuracy is not to be flouted, it is more important that today's audience is satisfied that they know enough demographic information about each character to understand them, as much as possible, and can integrate them immediately within the framework of the story.

If we take Laurence Raw's expectations of good audio drama from the chapter epigraph to heart, an inappropriate radio voice or dialect can bring listeners out of the drama and suspend their immersion. Andy Cartwright of the University of Sunderland acknowledged as much at the 2014 *Audiodrama Conference,* emphasizing that poor performances doomed otherwise solid work (2014). Intentionally deployed, however, such disjunctions between expected dialect within context can be particularly hilarious. Such was the case in a 1987 episode of the BBC comedy *Radio Active,* in which spoof radio DJ Martin Brown's high-pitched, nervous, oscillating voice contrasted tellingly with the real-life, famously terse and low-key DJ John Peel.

Heightened language

Despite the beliefs of BBC Radio 4's core group of letter-writing, disapproving listeners in the 1970s (Hendy 2007: 243), dialogue in radio drama is not naturalistic. Mary Louise James describes it as 'a heightened form of language' (1994: 16). Angela Carter describes the 'rich textures of radio' that are 'capable of stating ambiguities with a dexterity over and above that of the printed word' (1985: 10). Almost any form of drama needs to use such language – it cannot depend on naturalism to get a story across – but James' point is that in radio drama, dialogue has to be highly concentrated, using the 'full range of connotation' (1994: 17). Just as there is room for a great deal of nuance in performance, 'there appears to be a playful enthusiasm on the part of radio communicators to test the assumptions and expectations of their listening audiences' (Crook 2012: 133).

As discussed earlier, in character terms, Haworth made the audience in *On a Day in Summer in a Garden* believe that not only were we listening to the private dialogue of three dock plants, they also sounded just like northern English people (relatable characters for its author, who grew up in Lancashire). Haworth did not choose to characterize other plants in the garden, but he used their graphic deaths by insecticide spray as portents of impending doom for Dick, Jack and Uncle Jim. Through their silence they were denied the chance to speak for themselves; using heightened language, Haworth vividly highlighted their helpless plight in just two lines:

> JIM: They're rising up in the sky like contorted worms, they're swelling like melons.
> JACK: Oh, grandad [*sic*].
>
> (Haworth 1976: 125)

R.C. Scriven, the deaf and blind playwright, produced a body of work characterized by the richness of its heightened language, often moving fluidly between blank verse and prose. *Seasons of the Blind* (1968), was one of the most emphatically poetic of his works:

> NIGHT: I, the flower of darkness,
> petal on petal shall fold upon your eyes,
> closing all other flowers, all other colours
> within my own
> denying you delight
> when summer lightfall is as autumn nightfall
> and skies of spring are the same as autumn skies.
>
> (1974: 152)

In *Seasons of the Blind,* the seasons, Night, Frost and Persephone appeared alongside real people (performed by such star actors as Edith Evans and Robert Donat). Allegory and imagery remained mainstays of his poetic, dramatic writing.

Audiopositioning

In studio recording in the first half of the twentieth century, cramped quarters, lack of microphones and tight scheduling often did not permit full blocking of scenes, which occasionally impacted the degree of verisimilitude in a play. For example, in the *I Love a Mystery* (1936–50, NBC/CBS) serial 'The Thing that Cries in the Night' (1949), the setting is almost exclusively a Los Angeles mansion with at least four storeys. While the special effects producers (perhaps aided by the actors) created spot effects by using props to foster the illusion of characters climbing up and down stairs, the actors themselves never seem out of breath. Thus in some ways the illusion is weakened. However, in BBC radio drama studios today, a wide variety of environments can be accommodated within a studio floor (or foley area), and blocking is often worked out to the smallest detail. 'A live studio like this offers seven basic areas', with a flight of stairs 'in triplicate because side-by-side lie carpet, wooden and concrete surfaces' (Beck 1997: 11). In practice, this means that, for example, during the recording of Mark Lawson's *Afternoon Drama* 'Expand This' (2007), two actors playing journalists used a pavement-type floor, one of many options in the well-equipped Cardiff studio, and created the illusion that they were running after the object of a news story by running in place as if holding microphones. Certainly the actors did not *need* to run in place, nor did they need to walk upon a pavement-type floor. However, a more complete suspension of disbelief is achieved by adding these touches.

Due to the size of the pavement-type floor and the positioning of the microphones in the Cardiff studio for '*Expand This*', the actors could not jog in a linear or circular motion – they would have appeared to have been running *away* from the object of their search, or running around him. By staying in one place for the microphone but simulating moving in space, their audioposition always followed the man whom they pursued – with whom the audience was identifying – as if the audience were riding around in the man's lapel. Verma sees the roots of this in 1930s radio. He points out that you rode with Tom Mix but you couldn't keep up with the Lone Ranger (2012: 37). This is due to the specific kind of heroic mould in which the Lone Ranger was cast, as being conveyed from adventure to adventure on a fleet-footed steed by the name of Silver. The Lone Ranger by definition conveyed mythic proportions; thus, how could the mere mortals, the listeners, keep up?

Surround-sound, or spatially aware sound, in combination with blocking 'can actually locate characters very precisely in relation to one another' (James 1994: 24). Verma described Edward R. Murrow using the concept in his Blitz broadcasts in 1940, refusing 'to divulge his location, yet' triangulating 'his listener in imaginary exterior space' (Verma 2012: 31). *I Love a Mystery* often had very complex spatial blocking in order to depict settings often not drawn from normal everyday experience; 'seven characters climbing rope ladders above a bottomless pit beneath a lost Cambodian wat hidden behind waterfalls while pursued by werewolf priests' were not something the average listener would encounter in reality (Verma 2012: 36). Binaural sound, infrequently used in most audio drama, lends a further crisp spatiality to drama, which some producers are now framing as 'close to virtual reality audiobooks as you can get!' (The Owl Field n.d.).

When we might like earlids

As suggested in the previous chapter, we do not have earlids and cannot block out disturbing content the way we can with visual stimuli. Besides radio drama's unique tap into the imagination, many writers and listeners over the years have noticed a rather eerie quality of disconnect in the midst of connection.[5] This is displayed when the airwaves were originally known as the ether. As Anthony Enns explains, the ether was 'an invisible yet material' substance that 'permeated the universe, which allowed the movement of all vibrations, including light, sound, and electricity' (2013: 346). It was believed to be the vehicle for radio transmissions and potentially also for supernatural communications. Sir Oliver Lodge's theories of the ether as a medium for ghostly voices as well as living ones were largely based on the writings of Isaac Newton, and physicist James Clerk Maxwell eventually used these theories to understand the way electromagnetic radiation works.

Douglas, among others ([1999] 2004: 52–55), has noted that early radio broadcasting was deeply connected to a revival of spiritualism in the 1920s. After the First World War, people were grasping meaning from such indiscriminate carnage. Verma called this 'paranormal hokum' with evangelists using 'radio to heal the sick' (2012: 100). Spiritualists, as John Durham Peters has observed, performed a '*danse macabre* of the telegraph', linking the 'realm of the immortals' from the 'remembered dead to the recorded and transmitted dead' (2013: 362). *The Edison Cylinders* (2013) by Mike Walker capitalized on a recent trend for the transformation of nonsonic data into audible sound, as described by Jonathan Sterne and Mitchell Akiyama's 'The recording that never wanted to be heard and other stories of sonification' (2012). As John M. Picker suggests, the Victorian phonograph was used to speak to 'concerns over issues ranging from the domestic to the imperial' (2013: 12). Certainly the recording in *The Edison Cylinders* wanted to be heard, but hearing it was to cause untold damage. A great deal of vicarious enjoyment is had through *The Edison Cylinders* as an imaginary set of wax cylinders, the diary of a chauvinist, imperialist scientist dating to the end of the nineteenth century, are found and commissioned to be played through a computer software. Part of the jeopardy of *The Edison Cylinders* is that 'we do not know if we have heard a series of *sounds* or else *the idea of sounds* within a character's mind' (Verma 2012: 112, original emphasis). The protagonist has had a history of mental breakdown so only when another character confirms that the scientist's voice is not behaving like a recording do we feel justified in sharing their peril. As G.E. Lessing has hypothesized, when we experience fear in drama, it is a result of the similarity of our position to the sufferer, which is much easier to achieve in audio drama than other media (cited in Verma 2012: 38). Interestingly, when Sterne and Akiyama note that we can listen to sound and recognize patterns and anomalies without necessarily devoting our full attention to listening (2012: 550), this anticipates how the protagonist of *The Edison Cylinders* becomes aware that something out of the ordinary is happening.

Many radio drama writers have exploited this spiritual connection and that of the telephone. 'Strangulation is a very common form of murder in old radio, a removal of life that is also a removal of voice' (Verma 2012: 117). Michel Chion corroborates this, suggesting that the telephone 'serves in separation and disjunction; the voice travels through space, bodies stay where they are' (1999: 63). Furthermore, Verma found in his broad analysis that US plays of the 1940s were structured around 'a character performing some great feat of aural perception' (2012: 124). Carleton E. Morse, in writing 'The Thing that Cries in the Night', was very conscious of the conventions of suspense on radio drama at the time. The three freelance investigators, Jack Packard, Doc Long and Reggie York, take on a case in a rambling California villa where strange things are happening, most of them aural. They hear a baby crying that no one else can hear, prompting Doc Long to suggest it's a 'ghost baby'. The explanation, far more mundane and a wicked jab at a credulous listening audience, is, as in all the best mysteries, staring us (or blaring at us) right in the face from the second episode. Angela Carter has described radio as 'the medium for the depiction of madness; for the exploration of the private worlds of the old, the alienated, the lonely', a description that makes perfect sense in light of 'The Thing That Cries in the Night' (Carter 1985: 8).

If Mike Walker's play exploited a noughties vogue for recreating sound that was 'never meant to be heard', Jonathan Mitchell's *Tape Delay* (2012) takes Starkey's observation that 'next to the telephone, radio is the most intimate form of broadcasting' to a purely twenty-first century conclusion (Starkey 2004: 96). It's difficult to imagine such a play being written, or indeed being produced with such effortless naturalism, at the last millennium. *Tape Delay*, recorded on location in New York City, explores themes of technology, relationships and perception and makes one empathize both with its 'victim' and with its 'perpetrator'.[6] In a nod to twenty-first century noise/glitch (Krapp 2011), protagonists Ben and Erica, meeting for a first date, are presented to the listener only through a mobile phone conversation, only for Erica to break off the date before they even speak face-to-face. Ben (accidentally) records their conversation and finds himself, afterwards, piecing it together, cutting it up and re-editing it through computer software, in an attempt to figure out what went wrong. After an unspecified amount of time during which Ben has a fantasy relationship with Erica's recording, he calls her back, only to learn that she is at least as culpable as he in 'selective memory'. *My One and Only* (2012) by Dawn King on BBC Radio 4 pursued many of the same paths as *Tape Delay*, though its characters were less innocent than Mitchell's and the play purported to use 'found footage' (mobile phone messages, the audio tracks of webcam conversations) to tell its story. Jonathan Myerson took this thematic motif even further in 2018 with *That Was Then*, a story told entirely through the sound recordings of a neurotic vicar, via her mobile phone.

Sex and violence on air

Radio is still tasked with governing the areas of tact, decency and privacy and the legal constraints on depiction of sex, violence and racial prejudice – audio drama available through other means is perhaps less constricted. Perhaps the ultimate manifestation of when we would like earlids is during the *Life and Fate* dramatization 'Journey' (2011). In 'Journey', Sofya Levinton, a Jewish doctor in her fifties, finds herself on the way to the gas chambers. The sounds during the final moments of Sofya's life are more arresting than any televisual representation. This was a sentiment echoed by Tom Meltzer: 'the sound effects are unpleasantly perfect [...] the horror of the gas chambers evoked with unspecified crunches and cracks' (2011: 24). The meticulously researched BBC First World War drama, *Tommies* (2014–18), brought particularly excruciating and violent soundscapes to the ear; in the 9 June 1916 episode, for example, the listener hears a group of three men get buried up to their necks in chalky mud after tripping a land mine, and one man presses an enemy's eyeballs into his skull in an attempt to kill him.

By contrast, Allen Weiss feels that all spoken sounds 'have a primarily libidinal value', because 'rhythm, harmony, euphony, even dissonance and cacophony have a passionate, often erotic, quality' (2001: 24). Despite, or perhaps because of this, sex is surprisingly unappealing on audio. 'A kiss and a sigh and a rustle of crinoline could mean something – or nothing', as Hendy has pointed out; 'the action really was in the ear of the beholder' (2007: 102). Lee Hall and Angela Carter have combined sex and violence on radio in a way that is designed to make the listener uncomfortable. Carter's characters Henri Blot and Mr Beane in *Vampirella* (1976), a necrophagic incestuous anthropophagus and a necrophiliac respectively, prove themselves much more monstrous than the vampire with their lurid monologues. Peter, a paraplegic, in Hall's *Bollocks* (broadcast as *Gristle* on BBC Radio 4 in 1997), combines rage and the libidinous in a purely confrontational way:

> [...] All I see is a sea of cocks and cunts and arseholes all getting fucked, all cumming all over. And at first it was sexy – feeling turned on all the time, but then it gets horrible, all these apertures disconnected from bodies.
>
> (Hall 2002: 69)

By receiving this onslaught aurally, the listener can feel assaulted. However, Carter in *Puss in Boots,* following in the *commedia dell'arte* tradition, celebrates the sexual in a way that uses the audio medium to the fullest.

> UNDERTAKER: Why, a handsome young couple naked as nature intended, stretched out on the carpet and at it hammer and tongs!
> Hurrah!
> Magnificent!
> *Cheers and applause*
> *The mutes applaud and make enthusiastic, if inarticulate, cries; torrent of applause and cheers; fade in climax of Tchaikovsky's 1812 Overture, with cannons; shattering climax, thunderous applause.*
>
> (Carter 1985: 157)

Without the humour and allegorical framework of works like *Puss in Boots,* even relatively innocuous contact like passionate kissing can sound lewd and unsatisfactory on audio. On the other hand, using our theory of heightened language, sentences that might seem melodramatic or awkward on film can take on a much more passionate meaning if uttered in context on audio. 'Tell me you love me with your lips', Cathy begs Heathcliff in KFI Los Angeles' 1948 adaptation of *Wuthering Heights* (1848) in *Favorite Story*. 'Tell me with your lips, but not with your words'. Several writers have pointed out that pornographic audio drama has been surprisingly absent on the whole (Dueker 2008; Trandafir 2013); perhaps in the future, audio drama-makers will utilize sexual content differently in the *techné* of audio drama.

Conclusion

The challenge, then, for audio drama-makers, is to keep the listener interested. The listener must feel personally addressed and emotionally involved. Using her imagination, she must be able to cognitively 'see' the action of the drama, however mundane or fantastic. This may seem simple, and perhaps, thinking in terms of Kosslyn's observation in the last chapter that we are instantly able to conjure up images that we have never seen in real life, it is. However, to sustain this and not put the listener out of her cocoon of disbelief – this is the challenge for audio drama. Audio drama-makers address the challenge by creating a soundscape. They populate this soundscape with evocative music, precise, interesting or even amusing special effects. They employ actors who in turn use their imaginations to present as whole a picture of a character as is possible, using vocal techniques to 'show' dialect. The playwright's prose uses heightened language to help with the scene-setting. The director uses audiopositioning to add to the illusion. This, in Dubber's formulation of the term, is the *techné* of audio drama. As suggested, the *techné* combines the art and craft of audio drama, capable of producing both high art and less elevated 'entertainment'.

In the next section, we move away from analysis of the *techné* of radio and into the history of the last century of broadcast radio drama and audio drama diffusion.

Notes

1 In *The Radio Drama Handbook,* Hand and Traynor also have characterized three modes of audio drama recording based on how extensive the set-up is for their studios (2011: 129–32).
2 However, it should be noted that more recent allegations of low-volume levels on BBC primetime viewing may have had as much to do with poor sound quality as with what is termed 'Familiar Talker Advantage'. Cf. Lauren Ward (2017).

3 Though, as Quinton et al. (2016) note, space is not a total vacuum so sound waves can travel through space. Space would still be a very quiet place.
4 Though this does not always achieve what the dramatists desire. 'According to *Time*, one test subject reacted positively to a villain just because she appreciated that he always closed the door quietly' (Verma 2012: 120).
5 Sterne (2003) thinks that this link is perhaps overstated but acknowledges its long history (289–92).
6 The play was heard on *The Truth* (2009–present), as part of *This American Life* (1995–present) as produced by Ira Glass, an irregular slot for short audio drama. See Chapter 7.

Section II

History (1919-2010)

Chapter 4

British Radio Drama (1919-60)

> The transmitter itself, by virtue of its role, was an object of awe, a symbol of the material world reaching into the air.
>
> – Seán Street (2012: 26)

In examining all aspects of audio drama, this book has begun by noting aesthetic and technical aspects. In this section, I present a historical analysis, emphasizing the interplay between the US and the British national systems and how this affected radio drama. The decisions affecting a broadcasting body's content, format and philosophy are made in reaction to its national and international environment. This chapter establishes the development of radio following the First World War as this stage of expansion influenced the kind of content that was produced and the attitudes listeners and regulators had in terms of content as well as the medium itself. This chapter, while arranged chronologically, is also arranged topically, touching on some of the most important genres and developments in British radio drama between 1919 and 1960. While audio drama pre-dating radio has been occasionally explored (Crook 1999a: 4, 15–20, 33–36; Hanrahan 2014), radio drama as a form appeared on the British airwaves gradually, from 1922, and was at first predicated mainly around adaptations from other media. When radiogenic plays and children's drama programming appeared in the mid-1920s, they were swiftly followed by more technically sophisticated programming and a clear influence from stage drama, due in large part to Val Gielgud's leadership of BBC Radio Drama. The 1930s and 1940s also gave way to lighter programming on the BBC – partly due to competition from commercially sponsored English-language programming like Radio Luxembourg – including some influential radio comedies and US-influenced suspense and horror programmes. It is safe to say that the 1950s brought a strong crop of uniquely British, uniquely radiogenic drama associated with the prestigious Third Programme.

The birth of broadcasting (1895–1918)

'If sound-reproduction technologies changed the way we hear', Sterne writes, 'where did they come from?' (2003: 1). While acknowledging the long lineage of influences that led to the technological uptake of radio, the story has to start somewhere. And we start with post–First World War anxieties about radio's eavesdropping capabilities. Following its early uses in military and maritime communications, the potential of radio as a means of mass communication emerged slowly but surely in Europe during the first 25 years of the twentieth century.

A 2017 episode of the BBC First World War serial drama *Tommies* (2014–18) demonstrates well the wartime origins of the concept of 'listening in':

CAPTAIN MICKEY BLISS: And Grüder, you know that he was lying?
GANNION: You signallers. Lying is your job.
MICKEY: The one thing we know for a fact is Fritz can hear us.
GANNION: You know he's listening, so you have to choose what to tell him.
MICKEY: That's about the top and bottom of it.

('10 April 1917' 2017)

The awareness of an enemy potentially party to everything transmitted over telephone cable became a concern that unidentified 'lurkers' could eavesdrop on wireless communications. While such is the concern of *Tommies* during the First World War, history shows that it was an important anxiety in the post-war world. Immediately post-war, former members of the signal corps (*Zentralfunkleitung*) in Germany seized control (Gilfillan 2009: 30). The heyday of the radio amateur broadcaster (and unlicenced, non-paying listeners) was indeed short within both the German and the US aural landscapes. Fears of 'unsanctioned eavesdropping by *Zaungäste,* or lurkers, illegally tuning into the airwaves' affected both countries (Gilfillan 2009: 34). Although interested in the methods employed by the United States and the United Kingdom, German officials were hesitant, wishing to guide the medium away from lurkers and towards paying subscribers.

This early concern with the question of who owns the airwaves has strong resonance. DXers (see page 98) were radio enthusiasts who tried to tune their receivers as far away from themselves geographically as possible, with the ultimate goal of hearing radio from all over the world. They usually did this at night, when the signal could reach further. Thus, they were often more interested in testing the bounds of their signalling equipment than heeding any actual content on radio. The British system was unique and was based on pre-existing legislation. The British government had exercised strict control over emerging technology since 1869. The Post Office, through the Telegraphy Act of 1869, had had the exclusive right to transmit telegrams. It was a natural progression for such control to continue to new technology. The Telegraphy Act was extended in 1904, giving the Postmaster General supervision of wireless telegraphy and then telephony. At this stage, Britain was primarily interested in the strategic communication possibilities of radio creating speedy links with its colonies. It continued to impose control over telephony throughout the First World War. In the opinions of 'private enthusiasts who had already built their own receivers and were keen to have something to listen to', a central control was chafing (Crisell 2002: 13). The Post Office was slow to respond to agitated enthusiasts who ached for the kind of DXing – weather reports, news and music – going on across the Atlantic.

The Marconi Company, which manufactured radio receivers, took advantage of this uncertainty in 1920, when it was given permission to make broadcasts from its transmitter at Writtle near Chelmsford (2MT). Further, commercially funded transmitter stations blossomed, such as a London station (2LO) owned by Marconi, 2WP by Western Electric, 51T in Birmingham and 2ZY by Metropolitan Vickers in Manchester. Later came Aberdeen (2BD), Belfast (2BE), Bournemouth (6BM), Cardiff (5WA), Glasgow (5SC) and Newcastle (5NO). 2MT was the brainchild of engineer Peter Eckersley who himself became a radio announcer. 2MT's 1922 inaugural broadcast was an extract of the play *Cyrano de Bergerac* (1898). The first radio drama sound effects may have been used here, with RTB Wynn recalling in 1946 that his job in that first dramatic broadcast was rustling some leaves (Wood 2008: 35). Certainly, a sense of informality seemed to reign on 2MT Writtle that has been virtually forgotten in the wake of the Reithian BBC. Eckersley chatted informally to his radio audience, sang 'grand opera', and signed off to his listeners with an early version of a theme tune:

> Dearest, the concert's ended, sad wails the heterodyne.
> You must switch off your valves, I must switch off mine.
> Write back and say you heard me, your 'hook up' and where and how,
> Quick! For the engine's failing, goodbye, you old low-brow.
>
> (Briggs 1995a: 21)

Crisell identifies this as a parody of a popular Tosti ballad, which would explain the amusing and surprising classification of the listening audience as an 'old low-brow', an affectionate and individual epithet one could hardly contemplate on the BBC Radio of the 1930s (2002: 13). Eckersley would go on to work for the BBC until dismissed by Reith on moral grounds (2002: 18).

Maurice Gorham characterizes the working force at the newly formed BBC as a mixture of those with no particular interest in broadcasting, and 'pioneers' (1948: 16). Indeed, Street typifies this era by its the strong sense of experiment, fun and excitement (2005: 32). Many of these employees were ex-Service (Gorham 1948: 16). Hendy has linked this concept to a widespread desire for silence after the aurally experienced cacophony of the First World War (2013g). Given that shellshock was experienced in flashbacks through sound, soldiers in the First World War developed what Hendy calls 'listening-in-readiness': discerning 'different and distinct sounds amid the din', they made 'sense of what they heard to work out what might be happening around them' (Hendy 2013d: 272).

Who was tuning into Eckersley and his radio ballad? Shaun Moores has produced work on the 'hidden history' of early British radio by engaging in oral history interviews with elderly people from northern England. They recalled for him that early radio sets were large and occasionally dangerous, disrupting domestic space. Crystal sets came with two pairs of earphones and were assembled from kits. One of Moores' witnesses recalled,

> Only one of us could listen-in and that was my husband. The rest of us were sat like mummies. We used to row over it when we were courting. I used to say, 'I'm not coming down to your house just to sit around like a stupid fool'.
>
> (2001: 119)

Valve wireless sets, introduced in 1923 in the United Kingdom, replaced crystal sets by the 1930s. As suggested by Moores' speaker, early radio listening was gendered towards mainly male enthusiasts – 'women perceived [radio] as an ugly box and an imposed silence' (2000: 47). However, this seems to have changed after the popularity of the valve set. Since women 'assumed the main responsibility for "making the home look nice"' manufacturers would have soon learned to 'design aesthetically pleasing sets' (Crisell 2002: 17). 'Radio in Britain began to fit itself into the repetitive rhythm of quotidian culture' (Moores 2000: 53). Yet, by no means was radio listening ubiquitous in the 1920s. Maurice Gorham reported in 1948 that he had never owned a radio until years after he started working for the BBC.

In 1923, the English transmitter stations were joined by outlets in the other constituent countries of the United Kingdom, as noted above. 5SC Glasgow's staff of five struggled, according to David Pat Walker, to keep two days ahead of their output. 5SC had a troupe of amateur stage players at its disposal, and drama soon emerged on the Scottish stations. R.E. Jeffrey gave excerpts in 1923 from Sir Walter Scott's *Rob Roy* (1817), with music provided by the band of the 1st Royal Scots Fusiliers and the choir of Glasgow's Lyric Club. 'Effects were used frequently – the noises being made by whoever was free at the time' (Walker 2011: 30). Relay simultaneous broadcast technology meant that London was able to hear a rebroadcast of *Rob Roy*.

The British Broadcasting Company (1922–26)

In the early 1920s, the British Post Office invited leading British wireless manufacturers – including Marconi Wireless and seven other companies – to form a broadcasting syndicate (Crisell 2002: 13). Young engineer J.C.W. Reith, who had spent time in the United States during the war, represented the sentiments that shaped and moulded policy at this early stage, his 'familiarity with the United States and its emerging broadcasting' to prove 'invaluable' (Baker and Dessart 1998: 36). He was appointed general manager in December 1922 (Street 2005: 28). As Wood (2008) points out, the selection of Reith, at 33, appointed with neither qualifications nor experience 'to a position of total dominance within an autonomous department of a national monopoly' might have raised eyebrows. 'At the time, though, it was the norm' (69).

Major General Sir Frederick Sykes, who headed the 1922 committee, rejected advertising as a possible source of revenue because he feared 'it would lower standards' (Crisell 2002:16). However, he was also concerned that the 'precious natural resource' should not be an unrestricted monopoly (Crisell 2002: 14). Transmissions by the British Broadcasting Company began on 14 November 1922 offering mainly music and talks.

In the United Kingdom, enough transmitters had been built by 1925 to reach 80 per cent of the population. A policy of centralization had begun after the regional centres in Birmingham, Manchester and Glasgow. Within five years, this policy had totally eliminated 'genuinely local radio' (Crisell 2002: 15). By 1923, there were 80,000 listeners in Britain. By the following year, the number had reached 1 million. Crisell believes the official reports represent only a fraction of total listenership. After 1928, there could have been up to 15 million listeners. One reason for the inaccuracy of the figures is due to relay exchange, a central receiver that was cabled to individual homes in return for a modest weekly rent. They were termed 'wired wireless', and the BBC disliked them because they could carry foreign stations. This concern, as well as the issue of enthusiasts building their own radio sets that were unlicensed, led to the convening of another government committee in 1925, this time under the Earl of Crawford (Street 2005: 30). The outcome of this committee's decision was that 'monopolistic control' of British airwaves was still strongly approved of, but in the hands of a public corporate acting as a trustee – the British Broadcasting Corporation.

The *Classic Serial*

Excerpts of drama were broadcast from British stations (2MT Writtle and 5SC Glasgow) from the very beginning of radio, as we have just seen. The first substantial dramatic broadcasts in Britain of an English work were scenes from Shakespeare, including scenes from *Julius Caesar* (1599)*, Henry VIII* (1613) and *Much Ado About Nothing* (1598–99)*,* presented by the British Broadcasting Company's organizer of programmes, Cecil Lewis. Val Gielgud notes that arbiters of culture in the United Kingdom had to be convinced that '[d]rama Could be Broadcast; that Drama was Worth Broadcasting' (1957: 18). He also suggests that listeners needed to be taught how to listen to radio drama, how to understand its functions, to respect its strengths and work around its limitations. Perhaps unsurprisingly, British broadcast drama clung at first to adaptations of 'classic literature' and stage drama.

As Shingler notes, 'classic literary and theatrical adaptations proved much more popular' than experimental or original content (2000: 202). Shakespeare's *Twelfth Night* was the first full-length piece produced by the British Broadcasting Company in 1923, with its star Cathleen Nesbitt not only playing Viola but producing from Marconi House in a room 'draped about with a perfect spider's web of thin black cables, attached to microphones with quasi-telephone mouthpieces' (Gielgud 1957: 19). It was, at first, difficult for producers, writers and actors to appreciate that they were not playing on stage – and understandably so. Martyn Bond reports that the first radio play performed in Germany was Schiller's *Wallenstein* (1799) in 1924, and that the actors wore stage costuming for 'the sake of realistic sound effects, the clank of armour, the clash of swords' (1970: 1). Finding theatrical conventions difficult to discard, as late as 1926, British plays of longer length were regularly prefaced with five minutes of musical stage overture. Enterprising adapters even took microphones to live stage plays, concealing the microphones in props (Gielgud 1957: 19, 32).

Though few of the early radio plays survive in script form, let alone in recording, the 'gamechangers' of the era have been recorded in memoirs. For example, the 1927 BBC adaptation of Conrad's *Lord Jim* (1899–1900) by Cecil Lewis introduced the narrator as a device in radio drama for the first time in English. Mary Louise James calls it a breakthrough 'compromise' between 'story' and 'play' (1994: 41). Wood points out that no one at the time considered serializing such pieces, giving them in their entirety in chunks of 60 or 100 minutes. Crook has suggested that narration was not an obvious storytelling device, given that it has not been an important device in cinema or in western theatre. 'Narration marked the natural and elegant symbiosis between radio playwriting and literary prose' (Crook 1999c).

The importance of adaptation in British radio drama history cannot be overstated. The British *Classic Serial* is a cultural institution and a quality yardstick by which all that followed it could be held up (including the long BBC television tradition of 'costume drama'). Thousands of titles have been adapted by the BBC, whether from stage plays, novels or short stories. It is true that, particularly in the BBC tradition, some of these same titles are remade three or more times over successive periods and regimes. Although *Westward Ho!* (1855) was the first novel to be adapted on English radio in 1925, it has not captured the imaginations of producers or listeners the way Dickens, Dumas, Trollope, Balzac, the Brontës and Jane Austen have.

'A classic', wrote Gielgud, 'must have entertainment possibilities over and above a storied reputation' (1957: 26). The first British Dickens adaptation was a melange of scenes in 1924, the first full serial being *Pickwick Papers* (1836) in 1939. Despite the predominance of authors such as Thackeray, Hardy, Collins, Dumas, Tolstoy, Stendhal, Verne, Flaubert, Dostoevsky, Elizabeth Gaskell, George Eliot, John Galsworthy, P.G. Wodehouse, H.G. Wells and Arnold Bennett, BBC radio was also capable from the earliest days of surprising radio adaptations. For example, Karel Capek's *R.U.R.* (1920) and the Eric Maschwitz adaptation of Compton MacKenzie's *Carnival* (1912), 'one of the most imaginative of these early attempts at transferring novels to the air' (Wood 2008: 72). For a nine-part serialization of *The Prisoner of Zenda* (1894) in 1939, the producers wanted to print a plan of the castle in the *Radio Times*, but this was deemed too complicated. Audiences were listening to pieces such as *The Spirit of Poland* (1939) and *The English Pageant* (1939–40), Louis MacNeice's *Christopher Columbus* (1942), Alice Duer Miller's *White Cliffs of Dover* (1942) and US-influenced programmes like *The Experimental Hour* (1937), inspired by CBS' *Workshop* (1956–57), and *Saturday Night Theatre* (1943). By 1930, the BBC was producing nearly 200 plays per year.

Original drama

With our lack of recordings of early British radio drama, the paucity of published scripts and the internal politics that have made archiving BBC radio drama problematic, it is difficult to depict trends and innovation within the genre with much certainty or detail. Nevertheless, we can identify some clusters of modes, beginning with 'danger' plays in the early 1920s (a Europe-wide theme, in fact), as well as particularly radiogenic topical drama dealing with the First World War and post-war life. Although fleetingly documented, children's drama here also becomes significant.

BBC Radio Drama, as far as Humphrey Carpenter was concerned, 'was far more adventurous than the West End' in the 1930s (1996: 4). 'Their gear was primitive, their difficulties were great', Gielgud wrote of radio actors, who had to be enthusiastic, versatile and immune to the scorn of their stage colleagues, who believed 'there was nothing in broadcasting but script-reading and the equivalent of cigarette-money' (1957: 25). Britain had caught the mood of the early 1920s with one of the first entries in the 'danger' genre – an international rash of 'danger' plays that force the audience into paying attention due to extreme and present peril. *Five Birds in a Cage,* a one-act comedy from 1915 in which different social classes get stuck in a Tube lift shaft, was broadcast on 2LO in 1922 (Wood 2008: 39). *Danger* by Richard Hughes, the first acknowledged original British play for radio, was broadcast in 1924. In it, a group of middle-class sightseers are trapped in a mine. Despite poor characterization, *Danger* tapped into a Europe-wide trend, typified by *Marémoto* (1924) and *S.O.S. …* (1929), French and German plays, respectively, which dealt with early radio and telegraph communication during emergency conditions. These first original radio dramas were uniquely radiogenic, set in a sight-deprived coal mine, or down the radio waves of doomed communication between sailors and the shore. In 1924, without recorded effects and performing live, 'the difficulties were immense' (Wood 2008: 42). Tim Crook suggested that listeners to *Danger* on original broadcast turned off the lights and listened to it in the dark (1999c).

R.E. Jeffrey, Gielgud's predecessor within British radio drama, was more experimental than the stage-bound Gielgud. Jeffrey 'encouraged radio's first *auteurs*', Lawrence DuGarde Peach and Reginald Berkeley, 'to exploit the uniquely personal engagement of broadcast drama with the listener in plays of ideas' while with his colleagues Lance Sieveking and Tyrone Guthrie, 'he created experimental radio dramatic art as extreme as anything being suggested by European theorists of the avant-garde' (Wood 2008: 48). Peach's play, *Light and Shade* (1924), another in the series of 'danger' plays, Wood believes to be the same as the mysteriously retitled *Switched* (1927), whose in-joke is 'that the threatening voice they [the protagonists] hear is actually a play on the radio' (2008: 48).

The British Broadcasting Company broadcast its first full-length original, adult radio play, *The White Château* by Reginald Berkeley, in 1925. *The White Château* challenged the persistent doubt that radio drama any longer than 30 minutes would prove unlistenable. Set between 1914 and 1919, *The White Château* had an unprecedented scale, with its characters numbering 43 and its actors seventeen. As talented as Berkeley clearly was, his play *Machines*, written in 1927, was banned from British broadcast for advocating workers' rights, an especially sensitive issue less than eighteen months after the 1926 General Strike. As Wood has pointed out, the 1925 BBC on which *The White Château* was broadcast was very different from the 1927 for which he had written *Machines*. It is not difficult to see that the play's radical political content would have concerned the BBC, yet its ambition and radiogenics remain noteworthy. Written the same year as *Metropolis* (1927), in *Machines* is 'clearly realised the unequalled ability of radio to convey the indescribably huge' (Wood 2008: 56).

Tyrone Guthrie's *The Flowers Are Not For You to Pick* (1930) and *Squirrel's Cage* (1929) are most often cited as his best work in early radio drama. However, his *Matrimonial News* (1930) was also experimental and moving. An early radio event in stream-of-consciousness, it follows Florence, meeting a man in a tea room with whom she has corresponded by taking out an ad in *Matrimonial News*. Her mother, who wouldn't have approved, constantly invades Florence's thoughts. 'You needn't try to keep *me* out of your thoughts, you *can't* you know' (Guthrie 1931: 90, original emphasis). The result is wonderfully rhythmic prose that jumps off the page, influenced by the modernist techniques of Virginia Woolf and James Joyce. The technique is later embellished upon in *The Flowers Are Not For You to Pick,* when the hapless clergyman learns that his beloved has married someone else. Mary Louise James has highlighted the literary prowess of *The Flowers Are Not for You to Pick*, which begins and ends with the clergyman drowning, between which all is flashback. Its rich language painted vivid pictures in words of people and scenes, and its 'pauses convey the subtext' (1994: 58). Both James and Wood recognize Guthrie's work as prescient of Samuel Beckett's.

Children's programming was not entirely composed of drama but often included it. The British *Kiddies Corner* (1922–24) was broadcast from Manchester in 1922, quickly followed by *Children's Hour* (1923–24) from Birmingham, which Moores describes as using radio 'aunts' and 'uncles' to keep children amused while their mothers prepared dinner (2001: 122). *Children's Hour* began broadcasting from London in December 1923 (Dolan 2003: 329). *The Truth about Father Christmas,* the first original drama written specifically for British radio, was broadcast on Christmas Eve 1923 out of Newcastle. It was written by one of the 'aunties', Phyllis M. Twigg (Wood 2008: 36). An interview with Ruth Field, chief of Midland Regional *Children's Hour* in *Radio Pictorial* in 1935, stressed the programme's importance. On air she played 'Aunt Judy'. 'I try to make all the talks as informal and exciting as possible, while at the same time convey a certain amount of information' (Anon. 1935: 17). She also noted that plays and dialogue had 'strong appeal' for children (Anon. 1935: 17).

The BBC did not have a monopoly on children's programmes. The BBC's *Children's Hour* was broadcast weekdays between 5.15 p.m. and 6 p.m. at the same time as Radio-Normandie's and Radio Luxembourg's *Horlicks Tea Hour* (1936–39) and *The Ovaltineys* (1934–39, 1945–57). While the BBC seemed to dislike the tradition of radio 'aunts' and 'uncles', eventually abolishing them for something more scholarly and less informal, David Pat Walker was in no doubt that 'being *Children's Hour* Organiser was probably one of the most difficult jobs in broadcasting' (2011: 103). This was at least partially because presenters had to fit their children's broadcasts around existing station duties. In Wales, the children's serial *Galw Gari Tryfan* (c. 1950–55) 'convinced many of those in their young teens who were on the fringes of Welsh-speaking Wales that Welsh – and indeed Wales – had something to offer them' (Davies 1994: 271).

The BBC: Ambition and control (1927–39)

The British Broadcasting Company became the British Broadcasting Corporation, in effect, from 1927. Britain's policy-makers had seen the effect of chaotic airwaves in the United States and had feared its own brand of lurkers. British radio as an institution began to be shaped. Drama productions grew more sophisticated as the 1930s and 1940s wore on, disrupted, naturally enough, by the advent of war and further shaped by the post-war period. The BBC as an institution has become both celebrated and infamous, and many of the seeds of its current aspects were sown during this period. Furthermore, such tensions spill over into evaluations of the state of radio drama during this period, which requires researchers to approach contemporary accounts with caution.

Baker and Dessart put it succinctly: 'the British opted for a monopoly, but in the hands of a public trust' (1998: 38). Parliament's unusual choice of a royal charter granted the BBC a certain independence from the government. The General Strike, between 3 and 12 May 1926, was the emerging BBC's proving ground. Unless this broadcasting entity – in transition from company to public corporation – 'was seen as neutral by people of all opinions it would be unable to realize its aim to be an institution above politics and commanding universal trust' (Crisell 2002: 19). In the opinions of most, the BBC's balanced news coverage justified its existence, and the British Broadcasting Corporation began broadcast on 1 January 1927, from Savoy Hill, which remained its home until 1932.

The BBC as a corporation was fully under the aesthetic and moral guidance of J.C.W. Reith. Ien Ang has identified many of the traits that contributed to Reith's BBC. The emphasis was on classical music, talks and drama. Genres such as 'comedy, popular music, and variety were also included, but in a manner, context and style that revealed an upper-middle-class approach and orientation' (Ang 1991: 108). Reith himself was influenced by educator and essayist Matthew Arnold and by the desire for silence and order after the cacophony of the First World War (Hendy 2013c). Berkeley's *The White Château,* for example, has the sound aesthetic of war written into it, as when he describes the 'whoo-bong' of shells, the 'tut-tut-tut' of machine gunfire. During this post-war period, the emerging study of psychology said that minds were susceptible; a righteous guide was needed. Reith believed he could and should do this. As 'tempting' as it is to see Reith's 'religious effusiveness and moral rigidity as compensatory symptoms of a deep, residually Victorian ethical doubt', he also proved himself a 'brilliant' administrator (Avery 2006: 22, 25).

A style of listening was cultivated, which hinted at 'appointment' listening, not using the radio as background noise. To assist listeners the *Radio Times* was created in 1926.[1] Listeners would therefore know in advance what programmes to tune into. BBC presenters, who were predominantly male and educated, upper middle class, used a style of speaking related to received pronunciation or RP, in dialect a southern English style. It would not be until the 1930s that other regional voices began to be heard. Pegg (1983: 160) suggests that the broadcasting voice had little effect on the way real people spoke, although the influence of broadcasting upon accent homogenization is debatable. In 1933, a woman, Sheila Borrett, broadcast on the BBC, to a deluge of complaints from women listeners (Hodgson 2014: 183). (It should, however, be noted that Seán Street's research into private radio during this period has shown that the spoken word on channels like English-speaking Radio Luxembourg used much the same accents.)

Nor was the picture of a unified BBC approach completely accurate; from the beginning, as Street and Gorham have suggested, there was dissension in the ranks. Street cites David

Cleghorn Thompson in 1937 saying, '[h]e [Reith] is clearly the dominating force in a ship which is not yet a happy ship' (2006: 19). Gorham, writing in 1948 and 1949, emerged from his BBC experience essentially bitter and disillusioned, so his writing must be weighed carefully. Nevertheless, his observations on the BBC as a workplace are striking, particularly in light of more recent scandals. 'I never knew an office where sex played so large a part',[2] or more pertinently, 'tremendous confusion of values reigned' (Gorham 1948: 20). Gorham may have been notorious for not saying 'Sir' to Lord Reith (he cultivated his image around this), but it was D.G. Bridson who conjured up a telling image of Reith:

> As [E.A.] Harding recalled it later, Sir John Reith had been magisterial. 'I think you'd be better up in the North, where you can't do so much damage'. In which opinion we see clearly how little was known about the North in Portland Place during the Depression years.
>
> (1971: 22)

Wood cites the work of Tim Crook in highlighting the unreliable nature of Gielgud's professional reminiscences in *British Radio Drama 1922–1956* (Gielgud 1957), due to several factors including a selective memory, a desire for validation of viewpoint and Gielgud sometimes writing on periods of history about which he actually had little precise knowledge. Wood draws attention to the *Caesar's Mistress* (1948) corruption scandal at the BBC. *Caesar's Mistress*, written by Labour MP Wing Commander Geoffrey Cooper, exposed and derided corruption within the BBC. It did not specifically mention Gielgud,[3] but the producer's 'disproportionate' response did not go unnoticed (Wood 2008: 15, 163).

This incident also foregrounded the chief conflict in drama at the BBC, which is one that, in some ways, continues to this day. Wood has called it the pro-Gielgud and anti-Gielgud camps, similar but not analogous to our earlier nexus of high and low art. Gielgud's viewpoint was that stage-based drama held supreme, with some very small windows for radio experiment. 'Experimental programmes had to be found a place in normal programme hours', he wrote, while they were '"tried out" upon a patient, but necessarily largely uncomprehending public' (1957: 26). It is clear that Gielgud also enjoyed his commissioning freedom, boasting that, unlike works for the stage theatre of the time, the plays he commissioned never had to be approved by the Lord Chamberlain. He betrayed a certain amount of exasperation with the listening (and potential playwriting) audience, who 'were, by a large majority, dyed-in-the-wool conservatives', yet he was reluctant to rise to challenging them too much (1957: 68). Gielgud also felt that the Research Section, founded in 1928, and comprised of Lance Sieveking, E.A. Harding, E.J. Bull-King and Mary Hope Allen, engendered jealousy rather than cooperation: the researchers being 'envied their freedom from the tyranny of the stopwatch and ordinary departmental duties' (1957: 27). Gielgud had many allies at the BBC who believed, alongside him, that stage drama was the pre-eminent form and that radio drama should be used to bring the stage to life.

He created the policy by which plays were selected (and in the early days selected them personally), he controlled the studios in which they were produced, selected the producers and, certainly during the war years, selected the actors who could play in the repertory.

(Wood 2008: 68)

By contrast, W.O. Mitchell, a Canadian dramatist and Gielgud's contemporary, disliked what he saw as a culture of adaptations, writing an article called 'Radio drama is not theatre' (Kuffert 2013b).

The anti-Gielgud camp can generally be defined as the more experimental writers and producers either employed by or who freelanced for the BBC, perhaps best exemplified by Lance Sieveking. Sieveking was deeply influenced by Soviet film director Vsevolod Pudovkin, cinema theory and Shakespeare. Montage, created by Soviet filmmakers of the 1920s, influenced German *hörspiel* producers in the late 1920s, who in turn influenced experimental features producers at the BBC – and Sieveking's drama. Montage, according to Pudovkin, should be used for contrast, parallel action, simile and simultaneity in film (2006b: 62). Sieveking, like Gielgud, was a contentious figure, described as 'grandiose and loquacious' by Scannell and Cardiff (1991: 135). As no recordings of Sieveking's work survive, it is difficult to do his approach justice. His most ambitious project was *The End of Savoy Hill* (1932), which covered ten years of radio history in two-and-a-half hours.

Sieveking's surviving radio drama scripts display a delightfully zany sense of humour. However, if Gielgud was an elitist champion of stage drama, Sieveking was evidently an Orson Welles-in-the-making. Kate Whitehead's history of the Third Programme records that in 1949, Sieveking decided to stop giving out copies of *Drama Notes* for potential writers because these new voices (who would never make the grade, in his opinion), were wasting his time. Four years later the dearth of radio scripts was so severe, the BBC's Board of Governors decided to investigate. Out of 250–300 unsolicited plays received each month, only around 2 per cent were accepted. The report by Charles Lefeaux (acting script editor for sound drama) 'shows a fairly jaundiced view of the quality of those scripts received, which was perhaps understandable' (Whitehead 1989: 83). While the Third Programme would continue to look for new talent in the 1950s, Whitehead here suggests the crux of the matter: 'there was a fundamental difference of opinion about the amount of undiscovered talent waiting to be found by Drama Department' (Whitehead 1989: 85).

Features and regions

BBC Radio Drama ran parallel to the Radio Features Department. Radio features were a specific kind of documentary, with much emphasis on political leftism. D.G. Bridson is the best-known early British feature-maker, deeply impressed by E.A. Harding's politics and ethos and by England's northern region, 'the Manchester in which I then grew up' in the

1920s, 'a grimy and despondent city' (1971: 30). Encouraged by Harding to pursue a policy of engaging people to express their own views rather than giving them spokesmen, and coming from a background of writing poetry for documentary films, he migrated into BBC Radio in the North Region around 1934. Bridson's drama *Prometheus the Engineer* (1934) was banned because it depicted 'a revolt of the workers' (Bridson 1971: 40). (T.S. Eliot, however, published the script in *The Criterion*.) Other northern writers, such as Maurice Horspool, used humour to gently satirize what they saw as the London-centric BBC. His *Julius and the Bront* (1937), a *'Hyperbolic Anachronism'*, cast the Romans under Julius Caesar in 54 BC 'or thereabouts' as contemporary southern English intelligentsia and the Brigantes as contemporary northern English people:

> TRIPPA: Let's dig a deep dyke right across the north country, then it can't get out!
> WONK: Brilliant idea! Especially as the north country's *always* getting out.
>
> (1939: 19, original emphasis)

During his career as a features writer, Bridson continued to write what could also be termed dramas, including *The Christmas Child* (1948). Though included in a printed edition that was described by its author as 'spoken poetry', *The Christmas Child* is a radio drama reworking of the Nativity story set in 'the grim North' of England, in the shadow of not only 'the fells' but also the bomb. It was notably performed in northern dialect by Marjorie Westbury and Wilfred Pickles, performances Bridson found 'moving' upon broadcast (1950: 240). As suggested earlier, there was a great deal of potential for crossover between strictly defined drama and feature. Bridson's process for recording features was unconventional for the BBC of the period: he went to people's homes, took notes, scripted them, returned to the subject with a portable microphone and recorded them reading back their own words (Shapley 2001: 29). As noted by Crook, even Bridson's features were not as spontaneous as they first appeared, 'documentary production and "talks" were heavily censored, allowing them a heavily scripted existence analogous to drama' (Crook 1999b).

The North was not the only region of Britain looked down upon by BBC London. Developed in 1936, the Welsh service lost its localized content to London programming in the late 1930s. When it was pointed out to Gielgud that there were existing drama societies in Wales that could fulfil roles in radio drama, Gielgud wrote, '[r]adio drama from Cardiff is inconsiderable' (Davies 1994: 98). As Wood has pointed out, such 'glib oneliners' were given to most regional initiatives, 'in no sense constructive and meant to hurt' (2008: 104). As Pegg observes, '[l]ocal broadcasting was a technical limitation which actually ran counter to the avowed BBC policy to provide a full national service, based upon the terms of the monopoly granted to it by the Post Office' (1983: 18). However, Welsh-language dramas provided more scope for disguised militancy, as with Swansea University lecturer Saunders Lewis, appointed by Owen Parry to write a play for St David's Day 1937 (Davies 1994: 71). Parry did not tell London that Lewis had been convicted and would serve a year in jail for burning a school as protest against the lack of recognition for the Welsh language. Davies praises Lewis' subsequent play, *Buchedd Garmon* (*The Vita of St Germanus*) (1937), and Lewis went on to write a great deal of Welsh-language content for radio.

Despite the lack of consideration shown by the BBC to the output of its regions, it could not afford to ignore European English-language radio, to which its listeners illicitly strayed. The radio broadcasts that crossed national borders in Europe originated with innovators like Captain Plugge. The eccentric, English-born Plugge organized the first packaged tours of the Continent. He made commercial broadcasts from Fécamp in Normandy. Radio Normandie broadcast to England every night between 12 and 3 a.m. 90 per cent of the output was popular dance music. Plugge's ally/competitor was the International Broadcasting Company with stations in Toulouse, Lyon and Paris. Radio Luxembourg began tests in 1933. *Advertiser's Weekly* in England proclaimed the first programmes available for British listeners would be on 4 June. Continental programming was generally in a lighter vein, and presenters spoke less formally to their audiences (Nichols 1983: 30). With an emphasis on popular music, it is hardly surprising that Radio Luxembourg produced little drama of its own – 'sometimes simply airing transcriptions of American programs' (Hilmes 2012: 60).

Europe at war (1939–45)

Radio drama, like many other aspects of British life, changed irrevocably during the Second World War. The supplementary issue of the *Radio Times* from 4 September 1939 attempts to reassure the British public, after the declaration of war, there will be plenty on the BBC to keep their minds occupied. In the article 'Your radio theatre', BBC Features and Drama Departments reported they had 330 play scripts and 200 features ready to be produced and broadcast. Among them, *Shipwreck* (1939) 'a newspaper play for broadcasting' by Robert Barr, produced by Laurence Gilliam, and *The Last Crusade* (1939), a narrative of the Spanish Armada by Stephen Potter and Igor Vinogradoff. The BBC's prescience paid off: with the theatres and cinemas closed in the early blackouts,

> Literally thousands of listeners who had never bothered to give serious attention to that type of radio programme which must demand from the audience both attention and imagination found themselves making these necessary contributions to their own enjoyment because they had little or no alternative.
>
> (Gielgud 1957: 84)

Features and Drama were evacuated from London to Evesham in Worcestershire, and at the end of 1939 the departments moved again to Manchester. Drama productions included *The Spirit of Poland* and *The Saviours* (1942). Features included *Aaron's Field* (1939), *Go For It!* (1939) and *We Speak For Ourselves* (1941). Although, as Starkey notes, 'rarely can the discourse presented in radio drama be ideologically neutral' (2004: 204), in the realm of news reporting, the BBC 'took the policy decision to tell the truth, as far as the truth could be ascertained', which Crisell considers 'perhaps the wisest decision it [the BBC] has ever taken' (2002: 56). Indeed, Krishan Kumar characterizes the BBC during this period as standing for Britain, 'the most representative of national institutions' (2003: 237–38). In 1941, Manchester was bombed, so the departments again left for London. Bridson began producing features for overseas, 48 of which were made in 1941. These included *We Love This Land* (1941), *Hail Freedom!* (1941), *East by North* (1941), *Arms for Russia* (1942), *Stalingrad* and *Christmas Among the Allies* (1941).

The BBC quickly realized it had to approach broadcasting in a different way when audience research suggested that fighting men would need less formal, more upbeat programming. They created a new network, the Forces Programme, which proved extraordinarily popular. In 1942, 50 per cent of the civilian population was listening to the Forces Programme. In 1944, the General Forces Programme was created and would lead, eventually, to the Light Programme and then to Radio 2. It used new forms of syntax and vocabulary for news bulletins, which could command 43–50 per cent of the population at 9 a.m.. The BBC also began, perhaps not surprisingly, to invest in comedy programming. *It's That Man Again* (*ITMA*) (1939–49), which took its title from a *Daily Express* headline about Hitler, ran to 310 episodes. Produced by Francis Warsley and written by Ted Kavanagh, *ITMA* like *Fibber McGee and Molly* (1938–53) and *The Jack Benny Program* (1932–58) (see Chapter 5) celebrated routine and anticipation. Comedian Tommy Handley 'was visited by a motley sequence of characters' (Crisell 2002: 58). Like *Fibber McGee and Molly*, *ITMA*'s star sound effect prop was a door. Like the door, the microphone 'itself was often part of the play' (Briggs 1995b: 512). Absurdist sound comedy seemed to resonate, as *ITMA* had been preceded by *Band Waggon* (1938–39) in which, 'on one occasion a grand piano was heard slipping down the back of their settee' (Crisell 2002: 57). *ITMA* was extremely popular, 'the most successful and best-loved of the war-time light entertainment shows', and 'one day in 1949 there was a sharp drop in the number of people who said they were dissatisfied with the BBC'. It was the day when the news was announced of the sudden death of Tommy Handley (Silvey 1974: 99).

The war also imported US-style thrillers, specifically *Appointment with Fear* (1943–48), written by John Dickson Carr, frequently adapted from previous *Suspense* (CBS) scripts. Herbert Farjeon was one voice of dissension, claiming that *Appointment with Fear* appealed to the lowest common denominator; he wrote in 1944 in *The Listener*,

> the B.B.C., our One-and-Only-and-Practically-National-Theatre, competes with the columns of the less reputable Sunday newspapers by dwelling with bald relish on realistic details connected with the ritual of the electric chair.
>
> (cited in Hand 2014: 97)

Appointment with Fear also introduced the British Man in Black, a radio horror institution whose influence extends into the twenty-first century. *Appointment with Fear* was a 'once weekly cathartic thrill in a world of daily, all-too-real [wartime] horrors' (Hand 2014: 66).

Post-war content (1945–55)

Immediately post-war, according to BBC audience research, the audience for light entertainment was 20–24% (of the whole population), plays and features 15–30%, symphony concerts 5–10% (Silvey 1974: 125). The BBC planned for post-war broadcasting in 1943, with what would eventually become the Light Programme (the old Forces Programme), the Home Service and the Third Programme (the cultural strand), to 'provide for popular tastes without abandoning the old Reithian seriousness of purpose' (Crisell 2002: 62). In 1944 the new Director-General William Haley had to 'sell' the new tripartite system, the cultural pyramid, to the BBC Governors. Haley, a workaholic with no university education, had been a wireless operator in the First World War and 'was a compulsive self-educator' (Carpenter 1996: 7). In fact, there would soon be more crossover between Light and Home than at first expected; indeed, they differed more in tone than in substance. The Light Programme aired *Family Favourites* and *Housewives' Choice* (1945–67), which was, in Stephen Barnard's view, 'designed as a kind of recognition of or even reward to the female populace for giving up their wartime occupations […] and returning to an almost wholly domestic role' (2000: 126). According to Hilmes, Haley's role was to 'return the BBC to its most British roots, rejecting American influence and re-dedicating the organisation to national public service' (2012: 186).

As a testament to its aesthetics in a Reithian BBC, 'Bertrand Russell was allowed to question the existence of God' on the Third Programme (Crisell 2002: 64). Also on the Third Programme, R.C. Scriven's first radio drama was broadcast, *A Single Taper* (1948), 'an account of an eye operation' during which the patient had to remain unanaesthetized (Wood 2008: 147). Bridson noted that more of his own work was heard on the Third Programme after its creation than on the other two strands. 'In terms of pure prestige, there can be no doubt at all that the Third Programme paid off handsomely' (Bridson 1971: 180). Bridson especially seems to have enjoyed the drama broadcast early in the Third Programme's history: *The Compleat Angler* (1946), 'Swift and Sterne and Rabelais and Aristophanes', and *Trimalchio's Feast* (1948, with Wilfred Pickles and Dylan Thomas) (1971: 185). Lord Asa Briggs also comments favourably on the number of foreign plays that were broadcast 'often – but not exclusively' on the Third Programme (1995c: 633). Despite the fact that much of his work found an audience on the Third Programme, as he himself admitted, Bridson also had praise for the Home Service, which broadcast drama such as *Wilfred Pilgrim's Progress* (1957). In this 'lively piece of virtuosity', Pickles played all fourteen male parts, 'which new tape-editing techniques made thoroughly convincing' (Bridson 1971: 228).

In Wales, Cardiff was very proud of its Third Programme output. Gwyn Thomas' *Gazooka* (1953) and *Vive l'Oompa* (1955) and R.S. Thomas' *The Minister* (1952) were all heard nationally on the Third Programme. *Welsh Rarebit* (1938–49), a comedy, became known throughout the United Kingdom and included a cast mostly from Monmouthshire. It was written by Mai Jones, a musician from Newport who joined Cardiff BBC's Light Entertainment division in 1941, despite management concerns about whether a woman could do the job.

Welsh Rarebit achieved a 59 per cent Listener Barometer Record in 1948. Welsh comedy was heard much more often than drama (Davies 1994: 185). Welsh-language playwrights such as Leyshon Thomas and Idris Williams were popular; Williams' *The Rescuers* (1949), starring Richard Burton, received an appreciation index of 85 in Wales. There were also ambitious Welsh-language translations of Sophocles, Aristophanes, Shakespeare, Molière, Ibsen and T. S. Eliot, and in 1949 five Welsh language plays by Saunders Lewis, though in general this was felt by Welsh speakers to be too highbrow. Preceding *The Archers* (1951–present, see page 127), *Teulu Tŷ Coch* was 'a daily serial portraying the life of a Swansea Valley schoolmaster and his family' (Davies 1994: 198). It ran between 1951 and 1954.

As we have seen, radio comedy during wartime was very popular on the BBC. There had not been, however, a soap opera on the BBC until one was created for external broadcasting for US servicemen stationed in Britain. Gielgud reveals why: 'brutal phrases such as "Daily Dope for the Lunatic Fringe" have been coined to describe' serials like the adventure series *Dick Barton, Special Agent* (1946–51) (Gielgud 1957: 71). However, the situation had been different in Scotland. In 1947 Scotland's Variety department created *The McFlannels*. It hit its peak early in 1948, attracting nearly half the listening audience in Scotland. It had finished its run by the time *The Archers* debuted in 1951, but by that time author Helen W. Pryde had written 252 scripts. Perhaps most remarkably, 'already within sight of middle age and the product of an extremely puritanical upbringing', Pryde 'had never been to a theatre, far less a pantomime in her life' (Walker 2011: 169). As for other serials, on the Light Programme, *Mrs Dale's Diary* (1948–69) was a story about a suburban doctor and his wife. Reportedly the Queen Mother used the serial to understand what life was really like in middle-class families; 'it was mocked by critics and satirised for its cut glass accents and bourgeois pretensions' (McNicholas n.d.).

Despite images of 'austerity Britain', post-war BBC Radio was also exemplified by the presence of *The Goons* (1951–60), which Crisell characterizes as 'fundamentally a joke about the possibilities and limitations of radio itself' (1994: 179).

> Having spent the bulk of their adult lives so far wondering whether they were going to die today, the demob generation faced peacetime with confidence, ambition, and determination. They were going to live a world of their own design – and that included comedy.
>
> (Coward 2003: 8)

The Goons demonstrated, among its other qualities, 'its wholesale departure from ordinary logic, and almost hysterical determination to laugh at everything that should not be laughed at' (Coward 2003: 9). Its radiogenic character has often been remarked upon, Crisell noting 'if we can go to East Cheam [in *Hancock's Half Hour*] merely by saying so, then why not to the South Pole, the moon, or even up somebody's trouser-leg?' (Crisell 1994: 171). Furthermore, by the time writer Spike Milligan had 'finished rummaging in the effects man's cupboard, he had virtually created a new sound language' (Coward 2003: 39). It was followed by *Hancock's Half Hour* (1954–61), which Coward calls the first modern sitcom, in 1954 (2003: 10).

The 1950s: The Golden Age of British radio drama

For the radio writers of the 1950s (particularly those pitching to the cerebral Third Programme), the Prix Italia was the pinnacle of achievement. The Prix Italia was established in 1949 originally for radio art forms only. The oldest and most prestigious of the radio drama competitions, the Prix Italia differs from the Prix Europa, in that its selection is not limited to European countries, accepting entries from over 90 public and private broadcasting entities, including those from Canada, Australia, Japan and the United States. RAI (the Italian state broadcaster) presents the competition. International juries are made up of expert judges selected on a rotating basis from a variety of countries, and the competition includes public debate. The BBC's stature in terms of objective critical acclaim for drama began to be formed in the 1950s. Indeed, Hand and Traynor would go so far as to say that the 'naissance of *radio drama* as distinct from *theatre for radio* [in the United Kingdom] was not fully achieved' until this period (2011: 33, original emphasis). Many of the radio playwrights of the 1950s continue to be studied whereas their modern counterparts are, for the most part, ignored. These famous dramas had their debut on the then-Third Programme and are associated with a group of personnel, including then-Assistant Head of Drama and producer, Donald McWhinnie. Original radio drama's progression into the 1950s may appear unadventurous, 'but it certainly did not seem so at the time, either to its admirers or to its critics' (Briggs 1995b: 631). Citing the poetic work of Louis MacNeice and Dylan Thomas in the post-war period, Tim Crook declares that it 'would be wrong to condemn the work of Radio Drama as pedestrian and ineffective' (1999b).

Giles Cooper, whose work embodies this kind of Third Programme experimentation, has suffered critical neglect – until now. In a happy demonstration of the renewed interest in radio studies, Cooper is returning to public attention with Hugh Chignell's work on this writer's disturbing dramas of repression and bleak humour (2016). In 1949, Cooper met Lance Sieveking who encouraged him to write his first radio drama, *Fools Rush In* (Chignell 2016). A dramatization of William Golding's *Lord of the Flies* followed in 1955, produced by Cooper's brother-in-law, multi-Prix Italia-winning Douglas Cleverdon (Wood 2008: 194). Cooper went on to contribute what are considered classic examples of British radio drama, including *Mathry Beacon* (1956), *The Disagreeable Oyster* (1957) and *Under the Loofah Tree* (1958) – in which one man's fantasy life fades in and out of his bath-time – which Mary Louise James considers to anticipate Dennis Potter's approach to 'multi-genre […] dramatic presentation' (1994: 189). Cooper wrote 31 original plays, nine of which were broadcast on the Third Programme, as well as adaptations – Kate Whitehead has noted the mutability and variety of his work (1989: 37–41).

Wood considers another 1950s writer, Henry Reed, 'too uncommercial for the stage and too cerebral for the Home Service' (2008: 172). Reed's most important piece is considered to be *The Streets of Pompeii* (1952)[4] although Savage cites Reed's work as the creator of Hilda Tablet as one of his most significant contributions (1981: 158). Dylan Thomas' *Under*

Milk Wood (1953) was also considered a triumph of this era,[5] both in critical terms and in popular terms (its audience appreciation indices were in the 80s), though it was anomalous by both Thomas' and the Third Programme's standards, in part because it was produced by the Features Department. The influential playwright Samuel Beckett's contribution to BBC radio drama, particularly on the Third Programme, should not be overlooked. Beckett contributed five dramas written-for-radio, including *All That Fall* (1957) and *Embers* (1959). Beckett's radio works are particularly radiogenic and represent 'some of the most aurally challenging and intellectually demanding' BBC radio drama of the 1950s, if not of all time (Chignell 2015: 11).

The fact that works by Cooper, Reed, Thomas and Beckett originated from the Third Programme has added to that now-defunct channel's elite mystique. When the Third Programme became Radio 3 in 1967, as Carpenter reports, many employees continued to feel that making Radio 4 the more speech-based and giving Radio 3 classical music content was a mistake (1996: 286). *The Dock Brief* (1957) by John Mortimer was among the last of the Third Programme dramas to win at the Prix Italia. Tom Stoppard's first radio script *The Dissolution of Dominic Boot* had been accepted by the BBC in 1963; he won a 1968 Prix Italia for *Albert's Bridge* (1968). Another era in British radio drama history was ending, and a new one was beginning.

Conclusion

In conclusion, British radio drama arose through the formation of the British Broadcasting Corporation, created from an ethos of control and a post-war desire for quiet. Radio drama was at first modelled closely on the stage, eventually developing its own aesthetic and conventions, such as the *Classic Serial,* and in part rejecting populist/commercialist drama like that associated with US soap opera serials. The Arnoldian philosophy of J.C.W. Reith informed the BBC's programming with a desire to expose listeners to a variety of content, though a didactic and improving tone was always manifest. This tone mellowed in the 1950s, a decade that saw a 'demob generation' producing off-the-wall comedy and cerebral Prix Italia award-winning drama. The BBC produced a large body of radio drama during the first half of the twentieth century, much of it highly acclaimed. We will now examine the same period in US radio drama history and observe areas of influence between the BBC and the US network radio system.

Notes

1   Hilmes describes the *Radio Times,* the *Listener* and *World Radio* as 'an ancillary business' for the BBC (2012: 52).

2 Olive Shapley described getting pregnant by someone in senior management in the early 1930s, and how he gave her the necessary money for a dangerous and painful abortion (Shapley 2001: 31–32).
3 Hodgson takes a different tack with Gielgud, holding him responsible for discovering writer Joe Orton, in her rather rose-tinted portrayal of Reith, Gielgud and Louis MacNeice as iconoclastic anti-establishment figures whose daring genius could not exist in today's world of cost-cutting measures (2014: 31).
4 It won the 1953 RAI prize for literary or dramatic programmes in the Prix Italia.
5 It won the 1954 Prix Italia for literary or dramatic programmes.

Chapter 5

US Radio Drama (1919-60)

Who knows what evil lurks in the hearts of men? ... The Shadow knows .... The Shadow, Lamont Cranston, a man of wealth, a student of science, and a master of other people's minds, devotes his life to righting wrongs, protecting the innocent, and punishing the guilty. Using advanced methods that may ultimately become available to all law enforcement agencies, Cranston is known to the underworld as the Shadow – never seen, only heard ...

– *The Shadow*

Another tale well-calculated to leave you in ... Suspense.

– *Suspense*

Ladies and gentlemen: the story you are about to hear is true. Only the names have been changed to protect the innocent.

– *Dragnet*

Yours truly, Johnny Dollar.

– *Yours Truly, Johnny Dollar*

A delicate balance existed from the beginning of US radio between control/government and freedom/anarchy. Radio policy is not made in a vacuum. The United States, the United Kingdom and Europe existed in a crucible of broadcasting cause-and-effect. In the following chapter, more pieces of the puzzle of the past begin to fall into place. While the radio landscape in the United States is currently dominated by commercial format radio, we need to understand how US broadcasting got there in the first place. It was never preordained. What the following chapter reveals are the factors that shaped the decisions America's policy-makers ultimately made in terms of who could access the airwaves, who could broadcast and who could regulate. Once these policies were established – though not always uniformly and not always without protest – they dictated content, and dramatic content itself began to emerge, as in Britain and Europe, in the mid-1920s. The early 1920s were characterized by a chaotic free-for-all; when US radio fell under federal regulation, a predominantly commercial environment arose, into which a variety of dramatic content survived and sometimes thrived. Those who listened, when and under what circumstances were interpreted by the commercial system.

Neil Verma, in *Theater of the Mind: Imagination, Aesthetics, and American Radio Drama* (2012), has considered why the critical response to the history of US radio drama has been so meagre. He suggests that it is difficult for one writer to decide which genres, slots and programmes to focus on to get a fair account of the broad and vast data sets available. His personal solution to this challenge was to tackle the subject via depth rather than breadth, by listening to between four and 650 episodes of each of the 70 primary programmes he examined, and between one and three of the 90 secondary programmes, totalling, by his tally, around 16,000 unique broadcasts. My method in this chapter is somewhat less intensive, presenting a narrative overview of the period, to be more fully analysed and critiqued in later chapters. While acknowledging that the splitting of eras of radio drama into discrete, photon-like packets is somewhat artificial, the structure of the chapter attempts to restore a measure of fluidity by providing small case studies of the emblematic programmes identified in the chapter epigraphs throughout.

Spies, detectives, crime-fighters and victims

John Cawelti calls it 'mystery literature', a phrase that encompasses Gothic, detective, crime thriller and spy stories (2004: 340). Arguably, mystery literature had a strong presence in British radio drama, but where it was particularly visible was in US radio. Some of early US network radio's most influential characters have been spies, detectives or crime-fighters. While the importance of the western hero in US radio culture has already been discussed, as has that of soap operas, and while the impact of radio comedy will be shown to have a major influence as well, the mystery literature phenomenon on US network radio in the twentieth century cannot be overstated. For all the eras of mystery literature traced by Cawelti – from conservative detectives of the 1910s and 1920s heavily influenced by Sherlock Homes, to the cynical film noir post-war detective or lawman – there were dozens of examples in radio. Verma has argued that the prevailing critical attitude towards US Old Time Radio (OTR) has been a search for gold nuggets submerged by commercial shlock (2012: 18). While British scholar Roger Wood is more neutral in tone, there is a pejorative edge when he suggests that OTR relied predominantly on the serial form for its drama, rather than the original, standalone play (which was more common in British broadcasting of the period). For example, the first known standalone radio drama broadcast in the United States, *The Wolf* (1922), is an adaptation mounted by the Masque Theatre Group of Eugene Walter's then-current stage melodrama of the Canadian wilderness from 1908. The stage play's length was reduced to 40 minutes, as Kolin Hager, manager of WGY, 'presumed that a lack of visual stimuli reduced the listener's attention span' (Wood 2008: 34). Wood was unable to determine whether WLW Cincinnati's broadcast of *When Love Awakens* in April 1923 was an adaptation or the first original play written for radio in the United States (2008: 35). Crook also posits that an opera-only station, KYW in Chicago in 1921, can lay claim to the earliest dramatic broadcasts (1999a: 5).

Contemporary events profoundly affected US radio drama of the late 1920s, when public interest in gangsters caused US network radio's programmers – who were socially conservative and supporters of the system of law and order – to invest heavily in programmes that de-glamorized gangsters and ennobled law enforcement. The US show *Gangbusters* (originally *G-Men*, 1935–57, NBC/CBS/MBS) had one of radio's most boisterous openings – so much so that it created its own slang term, something 'is coming in like gangbusters'. There were many variations on the precedent set by *The FBI in Peace and War* (1944–58, CBS). Like its close rival *This Is Your FBI* (1945–53, NBC), 'both were sold as completely "authentic"' (Dunning 1998: 245).

Cawelti has found that the detective story in particular offers a place for writers to 'explore new social values and definitions and push against the traditional boundaries' (1984: 281), much as we suggested in Chapter 1 regarding westerns. The following chapter playfully interrogates Wood's contention that genre formatting (such as the serial) played a more important part in developing US radio drama than the somewhat more serious, standalone plays that developed from the BBC system. Though in this chapter and elsewhere, other important genres have been discussed – soap opera serials, comedy, westerns – by looking at four types of mystery literature on US radio in the first half of the twentieth century, typified by four different, popular titles, we can create a strategy to mirror Verma's intensive efforts that attempts a broader thematic picture.

Tinkering (1901–20)

At the turn of the twentieth century in the United States, radio 'made being a nerd almost glamorous' (Douglas [1999] 2004: 99). The distinction between the way the amateur tinkerers responded to and used radio (Douglas 1987: 191) and the way later listeners consumed entertainment via radio cannot be overemphasized. 'Not everyone can play an instrument or sing a harmony part', Evan Eisenberg has noted, 'but anyone can play a record' (1987: 178); therefore, amateurs – using Eisenberg's complimentary rather than pejorative term – could be identified with tinkerers during the earliest civilian use of radio. North America, lacking the curiously specific communications policy of Britain – governed by the Post Office – in the early years of the twentieth century, seemed to reward individual inventors and entrepreneurs in their pursuit of radio technological advances. Nerds were at the forefront of radio's development (Douglas 1987: 187): Canadian inventor Reginald A. Fessenden linked telephone components, a 'spark-gap' transmitter and an electrolytic 'detector' for signals from his base at Cobbs Island, Maryland in 1901. By December 1906, he had alerted passing ships to listen to his Christmas Eve broadcast, which included music and speech. Other inventors such as Lee DeForest and Charles D. Herrold were among the first to broadcast musical concerts over short range. Indeed, Westinghouse had begun to produce wireless sets before the First World War, but the wartime ban on amateur radio killed the demand (Shingler and Wieringa 1998: 16).

Douglas highlights the often-mystical nature of early tinkering; however, in mundane reality, most radio amateurs were male, white and middle class ([1999] 2004: 59). Early crystal sets clarified signals, but no one could explain why or how. Even as local, community stations began to form, an uncertainty about radio's origin and use caused the rise of DXing (when local broadcasters shut down so people could try tuning in to distant stations, surfing channels to tune in as far afield as one possibly could). As evidence of the widespread nature of this practice, local stations held 'silent nights', usually scheduled once a week, so listeners could DX. Content in this sense was 'irrelevant' to DXers ([1999] 2004: 73).

The practice of DXing did not really survive due to two factors: the US government's role in regulation, and the rise of advertising. The Wireless Ship Act in 1910 attempted to address DXing's ability to speak to anyone. In one case, a single wireless operator was credited with saving the lives of 1200 people, preventing a shipping accident by keeping in wireless contact. However, radio silence for calamities was not sufficiently maintained to prevent the *Titanic* disaster. The US Radio Act of 1912 introduced broadcasting licenses. During the First World War, the US Navy requisitioned Marconi's and other companies' and countries' transoceanic stations. The extensive use of this technology by the government, as well as the push to improve it, 'spectacularly advanced' radio technology (Balk 2006: 31).

From this point on, listening freedom was ultimately limited by consensus and commercial enterprise. Douglas, among others, has noted the cultural elements inherent in America of the 1920s, including race riots, a nostalgia for life as people saw it in the 'Gay Nineties', and a 300 per cent increase in recreational spending. Public pleasures began to be relinquished for private ones, and there was a shift in the desire for 'the security, ease, and privacy of the home during leisure hours' (Douglas [1999] 2004: 65). Ownership of radios among the middle class was highest from the start, and with that came, arguably, middle-class values. Though radio at this stage was serving as a forum for local amateur singers and musicians, a quality that was mocked and parodied, advertisers began to realize the selling potential of regularly scheduled programming.

William Baker and George Dessart have offered the example of Westinghouse, a manufacturer of radio sets, which inaugurated its public station, KDKA, during a US Election Day broadcast at 8 p.m. on 2 November 1920. KDKA quickly began distributing typewritten schedules to newspapers, then created its own listing publication, *Radio Broadcasting News*. In 1921, RCA, headed by its highly ambitious director David Sarnoff, added Westinghouse to its holdings, including station KDKA. That year, 32 wireless stations were licensed. Westinghouse, at least in part, influenced radio policy and the shift from DXing to content and advertising.

Other commercial ventures quickly followed Westinghouse's lead; as James Baughman has noted, many radio stations began to be owned by newspapers, regarding 'a broadcast license as more of a public trust than would be the case later in the century' (2007: 21), and contrasting tellingly with the British experience, where newspapers regarded radio as a dangerous rival. Telecommunications company AT&T proposed using their telephone properties as a toll-paying rental charge version of a station, WEAF, beginning in 1922. Congress did not believe this was a proper use of radio technology, accusing AT&T of monopoly, and upon the Federal Trade Commission (FTC) inquiry, AT&T ended its toll-paying service. WEAF continued, but as a radio station in the sense we understand it now.

The Radio Act of 1927 (1920–27)

The involvement of the FTC ushers in the next development in early US radio policy. A no-man's broadcasting-land seemed to exist in the United States in the early 1920s, to which Baker and Dessart have referred to as 'aural bedlam' (1998: 72) and which Douglas characterizes as 'etheric hell' ([1999] 2004: 63). Revisionist accounts such as Jesse Walker's (2004) paint a slightly different picture; early programming was 'energetic and diverse' and the chaotic nature described by previous historians has been exaggerated (2004: 300). Nevertheless, in 1925, the United States had 571 radio stations, but only six of them maintained constant frequencies. So many people had applied for licences that the Secretary of Commerce, Herbert Hoover, stopped issuing them in 1927. Even the aggressively capitalist David Sarnoff, newly appointed head of RCA, offered an uncharacteristic regulation model, a licence fee system based on Britain's, as David Marc has outlined. In Sarnoff's model, General Electric (GE), Westinghouse and RCA would allocate 2 per cent of radio sales revenues to operate a nationwide network (Marc 1996: 175). Initially, Hoover also favoured a system like the one in Britain, quoted as saying in a 1924 radio conference that direct advertising would destroy broadcasting (Balk 2006: 62).

It is unclear what changed the minds of both Sarnoff and Hoover, but the consequences were far-reaching. Hoover's relationship with regulating radio was complex, as he seems to have disdained direct intervention, believing that 'the regulation of culture was best left to academics and clerics' (Marc 1996: 176). Yet he was horrified at the thought of direct advertisers being allowed to shape culture. In creating the Radio Act of 1927, he maintained that the US government owned the airwaves. Through this, he established the Federal Radio Commission (FRC), later the Federal Communications Commission (FCC). Critics of today lacerate Hoover's self-regulation policy, with Marc claiming 'this failure of American intellectuals to take an early activist interest in the aesthetic formulation and cultural impact of radio broadcasting would be repeated thirty years later with television' (1996: 177).

Early advertising (1927–30)

In 1926, the first advertising jingles were heard on US radio, and many stations adopted slogans that boasted of their regional location. US radio developed two strategies towards show production. The *sponsored programme* was paid for by the commercial sponsor, which was usually some kind of tangible product (soap, coal, breakfast cereal, etc.). These sponsors sometimes incorporated their business into the names of the programmes, for example, *The A& P Gypsies*,[1] *The Ponds Players*,[2] *The Atwater Kent Hour*,[3] and *The Camel Caravan*.[4] Later, sponsored programmes mentioned the business names during the short 'soft sell' monologues; a salient example is Blue Coal and Goodrich Tires during *The Shadow* (1937–54). By contrast, the *sustaining programme* did not have a commercial sponsor and was produced through the aegis of the station where it was made. Needless to say, sponsored programmes were more abundant and better-funded, but there was still a demand for sustaining programmes. A writer's manual from 1938 admitted that fees for sustaining programmes were 'low', whereas the national sponsor for a half-hour drama paid $150–$200 for each script. A sponsored five-time-a-week radio serial would pay between $125 and $250 per week (Seymour and Martin 1938: 304). Nevertheless, large stations did employ creative specialists for sustaining modest-budget unsponsored shows. As Douglas put it, 'networks didn't produce radio shows, ad agencies did' ([1999] 2004: 100). Radio would be further commodified at the end of the 1920s due to a new design in radio sets, making them both more practical and more aesthetically pleasing.

Sarnoff's idea for a national network survived in some sense in the idea of 'chain' broadcasting, something that had initially been tried in 1921 with AT&T's WEAF station. Networking provided a symbiotic relationship with advertising sponsors, 'web-linked outlets' providing more 'sophisticated fare' that usually 'originated at a trio of New York-based flagships' (Cox 2009: 4). In this context, 'chain' broadcasting should be understood to mean several stations all broadcasting at once the same content, beamed from one station where it was being simultaneously produced; in this way, large areas could be covered that were beyond the reach of a single station. Network should be taken to mean the corporate body that owned one or more stations and presided over the content and decision-making of each of its stations.

Despite the received wisdom, commercial broadcasting was not an unqualified success. Some listeners distrusted chain broadcasting to the extent that they felt it contributed to the Great Depression. Marc has highlighted the most aggressive aspects of corporate capitalist methods within media by demonstrating how the radio networks' manipulation of the FCC barred movie studios and unaffiliated technology companies from 'entering the telecast business' (1996: xxvi). Baker and Dessart have charted network dissent among listeners, beginning with Joy Elmer Moran who established the National Committee on Education by Radio (NCER),[5] which demanded that 15 per cent of broadcasting frequencies be allocated to schools and colleges as opposed to commercial networks.

Robert McChesney notes that resistance to advertising saturation reached a peak in the early 1930s, with huge public outcry, that crossed political bounds (2013: 146; 2008: 198). Indeed, inventor Lee DeForest detested advertising so much that he tried to invent a device that would automatically mute ads (McChesney 2013: 146). Resistance and the reform movement culminated in the Wagner–Hatfield Amendment in 1934. Father John B. Harney, a Paulist Father, became embroiled in a disagreement with the FRC, who wrested his radio station, WLWL, away in favour of a commercial venture, Starlight Amusement Park, which was sharing the same frequency in New York (McChesney 2003: 44). Harney saw the FRC's actions as 'a clear endorsement of the private, commercial development of the airwaves' (McChesney 2003: 44). By 1933, Harney had entered the Congressional arena to fight for WLWL. Only two senators voted for the Harney-sponsored amendment to further commercialization, Democrat Robert Wagner of New York and Republican Henry Hatfield of West Virginia. However, in spring 1934, further proposed legislation, led by Harney and called the Wagner–Hatfield Amendment, was debated in the Senate. Harney's impassioned defence of the Amendment suggested that to repel education from an opportunity on the airwaves would make one 'a laughing stock of the American public'; nevertheless, the Amendment lost 42–23 (McChesney 2003: 53). Furthermore, reformers were hindered because no one wanted or thought possible a BBC-like system but favoured a subscription-based system like the licence fee (McChesney 2008: 199–200).

Eventually, advertising won the radio broadcast battle, by the late 1930s reformers had given up, and advertisers have continued to consolidate their position ever since. Many of today's television broadcasters began as radio networks, such as the National Broadcasting Company (NBC), which began in 1922 as a New York station, WEAF. In 1926, AT&T sold WEAF to the Radio Group for $1 million. It was then bought by RCA's network, NBC. Quickly, NBC announced a second network, NBC Blue, would begin operations in 1927. The original network would be called NBC Red (Cox 2009: 22). (The reason for this choice of colour-coding is not recorded.) The NBC launch in November 1926 was a special broadcast from the Waldorf-Astoria Hotel in New York City and included chain broadcasting with a dozen outlets from Washington DC to Buffalo, New York, to Kansas City, Missouri to Springfield, Illinois (Balk 2006: 37). NBC Red established a reputation for sporting events while NBC Blue had many more sustaining programmes. It was also common for shows to debut on Blue, then move to Red – *The Jack Benny Program* (1932–58) and *The Bob Hope Show* (1935–55) are just two examples. NBC, with owner David Sarnoff's drive and RCA's financial backing, established a ratings leadership that 'had less to do with show business wizardry than with its strong chain of affiliates' (Baughman 2007: 83). By 1937, 33 Blue, 30 Red and 48 independent stations carried one or more Red or Blue shows. The networks achieved a peak of 225 stations in 1941 – 92 Blue, 74 Red and 59 independents that carried the programming. One of NBC's most enduring contributions was the comic programme *Amos 'n' Andy* (1926–55), which began on WGN Chicago in 1926. The two actors, Freeman Gosden and Charles Correll, were white but portrayed the two black leads (as well as all the other characters). Between the hours of 7:00 and 7:15 p.m., 'no one visited, made plans, or was robbed' – historian John Dunning called it 'the most popular radio show of all time' (1998: 32).

CBS was another television broadcaster that started in radio. Columbia Phonograph Record merged with UIB in 1927 and was renamed as CBS (Columbia Broadcasting System). At the forefront of the network's fortunes was prodigy Bill Paley, a cigar salesman whose sponsored programme, *The LaPalina Smoker* (1927–30), achieved such impressive sales due to his sponsorship on the network that he invested heavily and became David Sarnoff's only real competition. Consequently, CBS was soon offering its affiliate stations twenty hours of programming a week. In 1928, it boasted seventeen affiliates, or 4 per cent of all stations then in operation. By 1939, it ran a total of 113 stations. Where CBS really excelled, however, was drama. Among its offerings were *Lux Radio Theater* (1935–54), *The Columbia Workshop* (1936–47), *The Mercury Theater on the Air* (1938, 1946) and *The CBS Radio Workshop* (1956–57). It was also the home of the influential western, *Gunsmoke* (1952–61), which successfully transferred to TV in 1955. CBS was also considered the most politically tolerant of the national chains.

By the early 1930s, the serial had established itself as the major continuing dramatic form on US radio, epitomized by *The Shadow*.

The Shadow

The Shadow, originating on MBS (see below), was one of US OTR's most radiogenic programmes, despite its close association with print pulp fiction. In spite of his clearly upper crust-background, Lamont Cranston as the Shadow shared some characteristics with the hard-boiled detective, 'a plebeian with distinctly subversive undertones' (Cawelti 1984: 278). Dunning has noted that 'it is difficult to overstate the impact of this program on the children of the 1940s' (1998: 609). The Shadow's relatively straightforward morality nevertheless 'emerged through vigilante processes' (MacDonald 1979: 175). He demonstrated the hero as an individual assuming responsibility and bringing justice to his community. He was an 'Old Testament avenger, a ruthless slayer of the wicked' (Steinbrunner 1979: i). Despite the fact that 'scarcely any story in all those broadcast years fully made sense', (Barfield 2010: 690) what *The Shadow* contributed was tone.

It seems obvious that a character like the Shadow should thrive on radio where his 'invisibility' could be imagined in the most efficacious way possible. The Shadow's acousmatic laugh was 'a laugh of menace, of bottomless evil' (Steinbrunner 1979: i). Emerging as a narrator character in 1931 when '[o]rganised crime was assuming alarming proportions that only a modern crusader could crush' (Gibson 1979: 1), the Shadow's own show assumed its form in 1936, though its commercial imperative was always questioned: 'It always seemed strange that the Shadow could find time to plug the sponsor's product in the midst of his titanic battles with the forces of evil' (Gibson 1979: 79). By 1940 *The Shadow* was a brand entity in multiple media – screened serials, the radio series, the magazine and comic strips. Yet, while massively influential, *The Shadow* has arguably never succeeded as well in other media as it did on radio. It should be unsurprising that in 1938, when young comic book writer Bob Kane was asked by the head of National Publications (later DC) to create a powerful and appealing superhero, he looked to the Shadow for inspiration – and came up with Batman, arguably a more enduring and multi-faceted character, but with many of the same qualities as the Shadow.

What connects the populist *Shadow* with the artistic *Columbia Workshop*? The presence of Orson Welles.

The Columbia Workshop and art vs. commodity (1935–40)

In *The Columbia Workshop,* the perennial divide of art versus commodity in radio drama is starkly illuminated. As Douglas suggested previously, upper income Americans listened the least to radio while those in the middle and lower incomes listened the most. As early as the mid-1930s, radio was accused of infantilizing its audience. Uneasiness about radio's unfulfilled intellectual potential as well as the 1935 FCC commission into CBS' monopolistic tendencies created the environment that produced *The Columbia Workshop,* which in turn led to NBC, for a time, hosting more cultural programmes as well. *The Columbia Workshop* is hailed by many accounts as the 'best' commercial US radio ever achieved in terms of art, and Verma is right to note that network competition between CBS and NBC helped to fuel productions such as *The Fall of the City,* Archibald MacLeish's 1937 verse-play presented on *The Columbia Workshop.* Verma suggests that 1936 was a particularly aggressive year of competition between the two networks – 7000 unsolicited scripts were received that year – 'enabling a small group of dramatists to develop conventions that would in time influence so much of American broadcasting' (2012: 23). This brief period of creative flowering seems evident in many areas, with trade publications beginning to run reviews of broadcasts in 1938. That was also the year high schools and colleges began to teach radio drama as a subject.

Howard Blue has examined the political motivations of writers in this period of creative competition, and his scholarship seems to link exposure to European radio with the artistic efforts of drama-makers like Norman Corwin and Irving Reis. In Heidelberg, Corwin came face-to-face with Nazism, and by 1935 he saw a spillover of fascism in his home state of Massachusetts. Corwin, venerated by generations of radio historians (see, for example, Russo 2012), developed his political writing early. He was fired in Cincinnati for questioning the policy of not reporting on strikes. Political writing became important for Corwin and others during this creative period. Many Americans feared not only foreign propaganda but also their own government, based on a bitter experience during the First World War. US listeners in the Second World War wanted reassurance from their entertainment/news medium. Writers like Corwin, Archibald MacLeish and Arch Oboler were 'leftists who came of age in the 1930s' and developed a pro-union, anti-fascist, internationalist-minded, racially tolerant stream of radio drama (Blue 2002: 8).

Nevertheless, this period of creative competition had more or less ended by the 1940s. Baker and Dessart trace this to when Sarnoff was forced to sell the NBC Blue network due to charges of monopoly in 1943. Baughman notes that after the tenure of FCC chairman James Lawrence Fly, free enterprise values supplanted New Deal politics and that neither Presidents Truman nor Eisenhower gave the FCC a high priority (1997: 20). The Blue Book, or the *Report on Public Service Responsibilities of Broadcast Licensees,* according to Norman Corwin, 'was based on a study of the abuses of commercial radio […] I don't fault the broadcasters for being apprehensive' (1994: 14). Nevertheless, network broadcasters had absolute disregard for the Blue Book reform policies.

The sale of NBC Blue resulted in the formation of the third major US network, the American Broadcasting Company (ABC), which had to, in Baker and Dessart's words, 'claw its way upward with an almost total reliance on mindless mass-market programming' (1998: 16). ABC was at first a 'feeder web', though it introduced some original series like *The Adventures of Ozzie and Harriet* (1949–54). Verma has linked the changes in networks, FCC enforcement, and web-link creation with the voices and styles within radio drama itself, calling programmes like *The March of Time* (1931–45) and *War of the Worlds* (1938) 'kaleidosonic', segueing 'from place to place', as if 'nobody is in charge of the broadcast – or of the world' (2012: 66, 71). Corwin suggested, too, that audiences needed to be taught the rules for listening and that writers and producers needed to learn what the audiences were capable of. In the early 1930s, 'radio was still new. It hadn't yet realized the extent to which it could exploit the public commercially' (Corwin 1994: 12). The audience's learning capacity mattered less than 'the naiveté of the writer who wasn't aware of what he could do. He was not yet trained to use the listener as a collaborator and to play on his imagination' (Corwin 1994: 22).

Upon its formation, ABC joined the existing networks, NBC, CBS and Mutual. Mutual Broadcasting System (MBS, also known as Mutual), the other important national/regional network, was founded in 1934 out of a quad-station alliance: WGN Chicago (a subsidiary of the *Chicago Tribune*), WLW Cincinnati, WXYZ Detroit and WOR Newark. WXYZ is the station that created *The Lone Ranger* in 1933 and would go on to create *The Green Hornet* (1936–52) and *Challenge of the Yukon* (1938–55). WLW billed itself as the 'Nation's Station', run by an eccentric executive who set it at an extremely high wattage (500,000 watt range at night).[6] Mutual differed from networks previously discussed because the network itself owned no affiliated stations; it *was* owned by the stations. Its commercial programmes were derived from productions at originating stations by sponsors purchasing time. Sustaining features were selected from among those aired by stations linked with the network. With only four stations initially, each contributed towards a quarter of the web's expenses and line charges. Later the financial situation became more complex, and stations were divided into three categories: member stations, participating members and affiliates, each with different levels of monetary investment (Cox 2009: 73).

WXYZ left Mutual for NBC Blue in 1935, though it could not take with it *The Lone Ranger* until 1942 because of contractual obligations. It was replaced in the quad by Ontario's CKLW. By attracting more independents and regional webs between 1935 and 1940, MBS grew from 0.07 per cent to 19.3 per cent of all US outlets. However, many of the additions simultaneously linked to either NBC or CBS. Much of eastern and Midwestern America could tune into Mutual, but the rest of the country remained virtually unaware of it. Between 1942 and 1960, Mutual overtook everyone else as a leader in the number of outlets. Mutual could boast the *Chicago Theater of the Air* (1940–55), *The Shadow, Tom Mix* (1933–51), *I Love a Mystery* (1939–52) and *Family Theater* (1947–62). In 1938, in one three-week period, Mutual offered 87 sustaining hours (Balk 2006: 124). Beginning in 1938, it included re-broadcasts from the BBC.

As the 1930s drew to a close, all four major networks were the subject of great scrutiny from the BBC. Maurice Gorham writing in 1949 gives a unique perspective as a BBC radio producer whose job involved linking with US network radio and sometimes re-packaging British output for these audiences. 'Our slogan was "British in content, American in appeal"', he wrote of the programme *Britain to America* (1942–43), narrated by Leslie Howard (1949: 132). Gorham noted that Fred Bate (NBC), Edward R. Murrow (CBS) and John Steele (MBS) covered the

Second World War in London before the United States joined the conflict. Gorham cites a scheme for the BBC to broadcast live shows in the early morning, beamed and broadcast in sponsored time, but this never went into practice. Clearly, the war itself memorably impacted US broadcasting and programming, which we explore in the next section.

Suspense

From the mid-1930s, programmes specializing in what Verma terms 'shockers' (and Cawelti could equally term 'Gothic') proliferated on US network radio. Such programmes were by no means niche – *Inner Sanctum Mysteries* (1941–52, NBC) was listed among the top twenty US radio programmes for fourteen years (Verma 2012: 101). Allison McCracken notes that by the end of the Second World War, there were 43 thriller programmes on US radio (2002: 183). The storytellers of OTR ranged from cackling, half-mad fiends as in *The Witch's Tale* (1931–34) and *The Hermit's Cave* (1935–44) to the sardonic Raymond of *Inner Sanctum Mystery* and the stern figures of *The Weird Circle* (1943–47) and *The Sealed Book* (1945). *Suspense* (1942–62) was a particularly popular permutation, usually fulfilling the role of crime thriller but occasionally straying into horror drama territory. It featured different stories every week by various playwrights and scriptwriters. It also boasted big name performers who seldom performed on the airwaves (such as Cary Grant). McCracken believes its success was due not only to the ability of stars to play against type but also through gender-transgressive characters (2002: 184).

Suspense endured in the public imagination, in part, because of the 1943 William Spier-produced 'Sorry, Wrong Number' episode, written by Lucille Fletcher and with an impressive performance by Agnes Moorehead. The flurry of publicity post-'Sorry, Wrong Number' proved that not only was there an audience for suspense-thriller programmes, it struck a chord with many Americans who felt constrained by social requirements (McCracken 2010: 735). These original (rather than adapted) scripts 'foregrounded issues of gender, sexuality, family, and consumption', particularly situating its often female audience in stories of 'thwarted career ambition, the life-threatening dangers of unhappy marriages, and the isolation and narrowness of suburban life' (McCracken 2002: 183). Verma also notes that marketing and the fact the productions were politician havens for creatives contributed to the genre's popularity (2012: 102). In a post-war setting, *Suspense* seductively portrayed the 'Other' (McCracken 2002: 184).

Genre and audience (1940–55)

By the time the 1940s arrived, radio could be called a ubiquitous entertainment in the United States. According to Blue, by 1941, 90% of Americans had at least one radio set at home, and the average American listened to about four hours daily (2002: 13). Rural audiences made up less than 6% of all listeners, but nearly 76% of radios among those rural households were located in the family room (Russo 2013). Yet we should not over-sentimentalize radio's role within daily life and imagine it to be Marshall McLuhan's famous electric hearth or the embodiment of President Roosevelt's Fireside Chats, nor should we credit it solely as a device to keep up morale during the Great Depression or the Second World War. Radio during wartime, in fact, had many functions, and US radio in this period cannot quite be compared to the 'panacea' of German radio during the Weimar Republic. As Douglas has pointed out, there was a high correlation between 'serious listening' to political shows and union membership, yet at the same time, the proportion of the population, 11%, that listened to opera was the same as that listened to soap operas like *Today's Children* (1933–46, NBC) ([1999] 2004: 142). David Sarnoff was a devotee of opera, not soaps, and Douglas has credited radio with opera's resurgence in popularity and the social acceptance for American men to legitimately enjoy music ([1999] 2004: 89).

Much BBC creativity was expended in propaganda to bring the United States into the Second World War. However, by this point, the tentative debates on policy-making of the early 1920s had all but been forgotten, and each country seemed deeply entrenched in its chosen system. Baker and Dessart report that in 1930, CBS executives Cesar Saerchinger and Henry Bellows met in London with the head of the BBC to work out the use of BBC facilities for a series of live transatlantic radio presentations by over 30 British writers and statesmen, similar to a scheme Gorham detailed above. J.C.W. Reith, director-general of the BBC, reportedly said, 'what I'd like to know is how you Americans can successfully worship God and Mammon at the same time' (cited in Baker and Dessart 1998: 4). Blue has shown how necessary the British propaganda-by-radio was: one survey of Americans from June 1941 reported that 79% favoured neutrality, and a second survey showed that even after the US entrance into the war, fully 50% surveyed 'had no clear understanding of what the war was about' (Blue 2002: 2). The bald-faced political dramas of the period have been well-studied (Verma reports that CBS devoted 38.7% of its airtime to shows about the war) (2012: 95)), but dramas of all kinds presented a political front during these years. Soap operas allegedly appealed to women on the home front, though in general new programmes dealing specifically with the problems of wartime America were not successful. It was a much more secure practice to adapt storylines of existing soaps to the war. Only one important soap character died in action. In early 1944, Ma Perkins' son, in the eponymous long-running serial, was killed in Europe. The network was criticized for reporting his death, saying it would depress morale, but the writer defended his actions by arguing for verisimilitude in broadcast. The secularism of pre-war serials vanished, and *The Light of the World* (1940–50, NBC) was popular, dramatizing Bible readings chapter by chapter.

However, if we pause a moment and apply a radically different mode of thinking – the BBC's 'Reithian trinity of Information, Education, and Entertainment' – to this juncture in radio history, we can examine the humble sitcom[7] and its relationship to wartime entertainment (Giddings and Selby 2001: 1). Situational comedy had, firstly, found a successful home on radio. *Fibber McGee and Molly* (1935–56, NBC) starred real-life married couple Jim and Marian Jordan and was one of the programmes that challenged the dominance of *Amos 'n' Andy* in 1935. *Fibber McGee* became US radio's most popular programme in 1943. The recurring gag was an overstuffed closet. According to George Burns, 'no picture could have been funnier than what the listeners were seeing' when the closet door was opened (cited in Cox 2009: 147). *Fibber McGee*'s sound gag both underlined the strengths and unique character of radio and created links to other popular comedies of the era, including *The Jack Benny Program* and Britain's *ITMA*. The famous scene in *Jack Benny* where the notoriously thrifty comic was asked '[y]our money or your life?' by a thief had Benny replying 'I'm thinking, I'm thinking', which 'produced one of the biggest laughs he ever got' (Douglas [1999] 2004: 117).

For Douglas, the unparalleled success of *Amos 'n' Andy* is a bridge to discussions of race within American society at the time. *Amos 'n' Andy*, among other comedies, showcased 'linguistic rebellion' (Douglas [1999] 2004: 103). She also maintains that comedy reflected crises in masculinity and reflected well on radio comic actresses like Gracie Allen. Furthermore, she asserts that Americans from all ethnic backgrounds could find a place for themselves in radio drama. For example, Gertrude Berg's *The Goldbergs* (1929–48), about a Jewish family, premiered, unsponsored, on NBC locally. Within two years, it was a sponsored weeknight network series. 'The thick Ashkenazic' accents 'provided much of *The Goldbergs*' humor' (Marc 2005: 17). Regional comedies also proliferated, such as *Lum and Abner* (1931–54, KTHS/NBC/CBS), which was an Arkansas variant from 1931.

Given the tendency of critics and historians to single out *The Columbia Workshop* as the only worthwhile artistic endeavour to come out of US commercial radio, analysing general drama on radio of this period can be challenging. Nevertheless, Verma's scrupulous studies have paved the way. Anthology shows like *Cavalcade of America* (1935–53, CBS/NBC) were popular and offer critical insight. 'Some of the US's most serious radio dramatists cut their teeth on' *Cavalcade of America* (Hilmes 2012: 122). After a slow start, from 1940 the programme lured Broadway and Hollywood stars into portrayals of 'what really happened' in US history. The emphasis was on biographies of famous Americans from all walks of life. The serial was also sponsored by the Du Pont company, who used their sponsorship to improve their PR image. Du Pont was known as the 'merchant of death' in the First World War for selling gunpowder, and by its sponsorship of this patriotic programme, it slowly regained its wholesome image (Cox 2009: 149).

Another important anthology show, *Grand Central Station*, ran from 1937 to 1954 on NBC. By using the aural imagery of a train pulling into the station, the programme set its characters off in hundreds of different directions, allowing it to explore many different genres of drama with the station as simply its starting-off point. *Lux Radio Theater* was by contrast the most glamorous drama programme on radio. Beginning in 1934 on NBC and transferring to CBS a year later, this programme began by taking popular Broadway plays and adapting them for radio. By 1936, this included popular film scripts, which were reduced to 48 minutes and brought to life using three or four of the original actors. It was important for small towns that lacked cinemas: Malcolm Usrey of the rural Texas Panhandle recalled, '[o]nly a serious emergency kept us from hearing *The Lux Radio Theater*' (cited in Barfield 1996: 150). Douglas notes that until programmes like this, America had idolized heroes of production; now they were obsessed with movie stars. *Lux Radio Theater* inspired many imitators (*Screen Guild Theater* [1939–52], *Hollywood Premiere* [1941], *Academy Award Theater* [1946] and others).

Dragnet

The detectives of US radio drama of the 1940s and 1950s, influenced by film noir, were all disillusioned, embittered men, like their audiences desensitized to the squalid urban wasteland. Instead of instilling listeners with conviction or thrilling them with glamour, they were left with a feeling of uncertainty, that

> the greatest cities of the country – New York, Los Angeles, Chicago, San Francisco – were criminal cesspools with only a cadre of depressed public and private investigators defending them from anarchy.
>
> (MacDonald 1979: 185)

The (anti)heroes enjoyed an antagonistic relationship with law enforcement and a disdain for the wealthy. The most famous exemplar of this genre, *Dragnet*, ran on NBC from 1949 to 1957 and made the successful transition to television. *Dragnet* was incredibly influential and the product of serious scripting and research before it was ever broadcast – as Dunning notes, 'the seeds of *Dragnet* were sown on a movie set' (1998: 209). Jack Webb, who played Sergeant Joe Friday, also scripted and directed *Dragnet,* demonstrating an auteur-ish relationship to the radio crime serial that stands as a unique achievement. Closely associated with the LAPD, who provided the stories and approved rough edits, action in *Dragnet* preceded point by point (Hilmes 2014: 225). 'Realism', Webb believed, 'should be the show's hallmark: the stories should be authentic to the last sound effect' (Dunning 1998: 209). Indeed, the series used as many as 300 effects in its 'world of sound' approach. Joe Friday was cold and disciplined but believable, refined from Webb's previously hard-edged characters *Johnny Madero: Pier 43* (1947, MBS) and *Pat Novak for Hire* (1946–47, ABC), a character 'so hard-boiled it became high camp' (Dunning 1998: 209). Furthermore,

> Jack Webb had an extraordinary ear for the '*throwaway line*' most often associated with the work of *Raymond Chandler*. But it was Webb's genius for drolly and cynically delivering those *Chandleresque* lines, that made every radio program he recorded during that era some of the most often revisited recordings among Golden Age Radio collectors.
>
> (Digital Deli Too n.d., original emphasis)

Furthermore, the sense of Friday's character came from his sleuthing actions and crime notebook narrating approach; his personal life was never delved into (Hilmes 2014: 225). Yet, the show broke many taboos in the interests of verisimilitude, including depicting sex crimes and violence against children. When listener mail was received protesting the episode 'A .22 Rifle for Christmas' (22 December 1949), the show's approach was defended by LAPD Chief Parker. 'The cops promised such groups as the National Rifle Association "ten more shows illustrating the folly of giving rifles to children"' (Dunning 1998: 211).

Post-war radio trends (1945–55)

There is a palpable sense in the literature that US radio drama peaked in 1938.[8] Certainly, Verma gives the impression that this has been his experience: 'Scholars have long considered the play [*The Fall of the City*] to be a cerebral anomaly amid hours of schlock' (2012: 18). While he suggests that by the 1940s, commercialism had precluded the possibility of radio art, it is also conceivable that an overwhelming post-war sense of nationalism stunted creative growth. Gorham, one of the few British radio producers to use less-than-damning language about US radio, nevertheless expressed bafflement and even unease after a visit to the United States. He was alarmed by 'self-confident and self-righteous' nationalism (1948: 231). This was dangerous, as he saw it, because it suggested that Americans 'really thought foreigners should adopt the American way of life as soon as they heard of it' (1948: 231). Similarly, Dr Jeanne Kenmore made trips to England in the 1950s and found that America's representation of itself, particularly through its government-funded international outlet The Voice of America, created hostility: 'Have you no problems in the USA?' she was asked.

> Why do Americans think that they have the best country – for EVERYTHING? [...] What is the point of The Voice of America? To beg people to move there? To brag? To look down on other places?
>
> (cited in Barfield 1996: 193)

Despite this, US radio drama's quality in the late 1940s did not suddenly decline. However, much of 1940s commercially sponsored radio drama, especially comedies, *sound* the same, sharing similar jokes across programmes. Nevertheless, there is a sense that such homogeneity was noticed and seen as less-than-desirable. Bill Paley, head of CBS, initiated what were known as Paley's Raids, in which he strove (and in many cases, succeeded) to lure NBC's top creative talents to CBS. Paley was passionate about radio, even after 1947 when he was forced to start considering the place of television in the coming media market. Baughman suggests that profits and ratings were not uppermost on Paley's mind; 'he also strove to alter his network's relationship with advertisers' and 'his engagements in scheduling and plot development could be significant' (1997: 122, 124). The raids, which took place in

1948, allowed CBS to lead primetime ratings for the first time in two decades. Columbia, unlike RCA, earned most of its revenue from radio.

Sylvester J. 'Pat' Weaver of NBC, whose contributions we will discuss in more detail in Chapter 6, also made a concerted effort in the late 1940s to 'reform' the soap operas, attempting to create fresher and more contemporary plots and styles. Post-war soaps, perhaps continuing the trend noted earlier of anti-secularism, had become melancholy and moralistic. Radio, Weaver believed, was degrading in quality 'by scheduling too many series, too many of which imitated one another' (Baughman 1997: 101). Furthermore, although it is dangerous to place changes in radio drama in the late 1940s under the lazy umbrella title of 'changing listening habits', it is asserted by both Douglas and Baughman that the percentage of women listening to soap operas declined during this period. We can also cautiously assert that former listeners were not listening together every evening as they had been in the 1930s and 1940s. As cheap radio sets became available, each person could have a personal set rather than listen as a group. Not only were these changing trends dictated by social mobility, in the late 1940s, 'advertiser demand for airtime rose, gradually reversing the ratio of sustaining to commercial programs in favour of the latter' (Baughman 2007: 24).

As Sarnoff, Paley, Weaver and others realized, tired reworkings of familiar radio drama themes, changing social habits and altered business and rules of radio contributed towards setting the US stage for television. However, radio's fate was by no means certain, as Baughman has noted that Americans in the 1950s 'proved even more homebound than in the 1930s' (2007: 25). Yet radio was beginning to follow Americans everywhere via broadcasts in public venues and on public transport. Russo has examined the case in the late 1940s of Transit Radio, Inc., which, 'after three years of legal back and forth', was seen to have engendered a 'resentment over the intrusion of commercialism into new areas of personal lives' such as buses and streetcars (Russo 2009: 2). Verma argues that post-war radio, obsessed with technology and the 'closed world' narratives of the Cold War, ironically featured the theme of running out of time (2012: 163–80).

Yours Truly, Johnny Dollar

Yours Truly, Johnny Dollar (1949–62, CBS) hailed back to the earlier tradition of the glamorous detective, though as Philip J. Lane suggests, Johnny Dollar was hardboiled, cynical and a bit of a ladies' man (2010: 291). Dollar was 'America's fabulous freelance insurance investigator'; the programme took the form of his expense summaries that detailed his exciting investigative life. Originally named 'Lloyd London', the eventual eponymous hero is a transparent emblem for his role working with money. This seems to mirror early TV sitcoms from the same period, such as *Life of Riley* (1941–51) and *Mama* (1949–56), which espoused a hedonistic, capitalist spending agenda (see Chapter 6). The charming Dollar was played over the course of the series by six actors and became less cynical a character as time went on. When the show returned to the air in a new format in 1955, its new incarnation prefigured the early twenty-first century audio storytelling obsession with the serialization technique. The format moved from a weekly 30-minute episode to five 15-minute episodes per week.

MacDonald has quoted Charles J. Rolo in saying that 'the detective story is modern man's Passion Play' (1979: 157), a sentiment that not only invokes a simplified and powerful moral message, but also suggests what Cawelti calls 'resistance to closure' (1984: 347). MacDonald has also stressed the individualism highlighted in detective stories, with the suggestion that even one person can make a difference within mass modern life (1979: 159). The 'resistance to closure' is similar to 'hyperdiegetic universes', a sense of breadth and depth in the text's setting, a sense that any one story being told is only the tip of the iceberg in a larger universe – and what Matt Hills calls in *Fan Cultures* 'an endlessly deferred narrative' (2002: 128). Johnny Dollar's narrative was seemingly endlessly deferred as one of the last OTR dramas on US network radio to cease broadcast.

Conclusion

To conclude, the US radio network system was very different than the British monopoly-in-public-trust of the BBC, although, as this chapter has shown, the differing format was never a foregone conclusion. After a period of chaos and creativity in the early 1920s, the 1927 Radio Act formalized a system that came to be deeply entwined with commercialism, a decision that did not come to pass without debate and unease. Nevertheless, by the 1930s, US network radio had developed its own distinctive body of drama broadcasting, largely (though not solely) characterized by serials. While the late 1930s were characterized by a creative flowering due in part to network competition, radio drama continued to flourish through the Second World War and into the 1950s. Comedy and mystery literature were just some among the many forms of drama that flourished on air. However, commercial homogenization in the late 1940s set the stage for radio's decline.

Notes

1 An exotic music programme sponsored by the Great Atlantic & Pacific Tea Company first on station WEAF, then NBC, running from 1923 to 1936.
2 Sponsored by the beauty product company, NBC 1934.
3 Atwater-Kent was a well-known radio manufacturer; this programme ran from 1925 to 1934, first on WEAF, then on NBC.
4 A CBS and then NBC programme in various forms from 1933 to 1954, sponsored by the cigarette company.

5   NCER is separate from the National Advisory Council on Radio in Education (NACRE), founded in 1926 by the Carnegie Corporation's American Association for the Education of Adults.
6   In 1941, of the twenty regional networks, only six targeted coverage beyond a single state. This is due to the different ranges of wattage. The highest category is clear channel (up to 50 kW). The next is classified as regional (5 kW by day and 1 kW by night). Finally there is local (250 watts by day and 100 by night). All stations unless otherwise mentioned were on the AM band.
7   As David Marc pointed out, the term 'situational comedy' was only in common usage from 1953.
8   Bernard Shaw (2000) even mistakenly blames *War of the Worlds* for the 'almost fatal decline in radio drama'!

Chapter 6

Why US Audio Drama Died and British Audio Drama Survived

> Even for the less fortunate members of society, television has long since come to be regarded as a necessity rather than a luxury.
> – Michael Kammen (2001: xi)

Radio policy in the United States was set relatively early, based on a desire for control over chaos, an understandable concept that was shared with many European countries, though their eventual reactions differed. Control became the key concept for advertisers in the United States, who, at the dawn of the 1950s, were examining with interest the new medium of television. They were led by strong personalities in the business world, men who could be described as both visionary and ruthlessly capitalist, such as David Sarnoff, Pat Weaver and Bill Paley. These men were aided and abetted by a post-war audience fatigue, reacting to a radio drama system inherently dictated by commercialism. Ironically, Weaver and Paley saw the new medium as a clean slate for new, more experimental drama. Then advertising fled radio for television, and radio drama in the United States more or less ceased to exist.

Although some US advertisers expected television to boom, this was by no means a widespread conclusion. Why, then, did the dramatic content on US radio fade away so rapidly, disappearing almost entirely by 1960, while dramatic content has become a core part of US TV? Succinctly, it was because advertising moved from radio to TV. The soaps and serials that could have sustained radio moved along with the advertising onto TV. However, more than a change of medium was in store for these forms of dramatic content when they shifted allegiance. There was a palpable sense of exhaustion about post-war radio drama in the United States. Broadcast network executives somewhat naively saw an opportunity to approach the new medium of television with artistic ambitions they believed had been frustrated by the over-commercialization of radio. Radio had become intrinsically linked in their minds, as well as the minds of their audiences, with nostalgia. Ironically, their efforts at throwing off these old shackles rebounded as the homogeneous atmosphere of US network TV and its strict self-imposed censorship began to emerge. Ironically, the networks, too, wanted to reverse the control advertisers had exerted over the medium of radio (Boddy 1990: 94).

Meanwhile, the BBC had a long tradition of observing US media policy and using these observations to help it make its own decisions. Had the BBC lost its TV monopoly before 1955, and had the same amount of capital been outlayed in Britain for TV as in the United States, would radio have withstood the TV challenge so well? Many employed by the BBC, especially those who sought to develop television in the early 1950s, felt that radio was holding television back. As discussed in Chapter 4, the 1950s were a strong decade for BBC Radio in terms of cultural prestige. The prowess of BBC radio-makers of that era made it difficult for television to crawl out from under its shadow. In this chapter, we will first look at the various contributing factors to the transfer of almost all dramatic content from radio to television in the United States in the 1950s, and then look at some of the reasons why Britain was able to continue its radio drama throughout these decades.

Commercial advertising and control in the United States

In the history of US broadcasting, there is a tendency to believe that the commercial model has always been accepted. 'The majority of American radio listeners have become accustomed to the inclusion of commercial credits in the programs they hear', Seymour and Martin wrote in 1938 (251). It is not generally known that a system similar to that of the BBC, or at least one between what became the US system and the BBC, could have come into play in the early to mid-1920s. The radio network system in the United States was by no means as stable as hindsight suggests. Not only was there dissent, there was ennui with what the commercial system had produced. The debate immediately before the Radio Act of 1927 proves this: such a debate would not have been necessary had there been universal agreement about a commercial network system. The radio reform movement of the 1930s was also a clear, if somewhat critically neglected, sign. Clearly, some people in the United States did not want advertisements within their listening space. As Douglas noted, ad listening remains an area of deep ambivalence – TV ads can be muted; the violation in radio is very personal ([1999] 2004: 35).

In the 1940s and 1950s, there was no great certainty that television in the United States was going to become as popular as radio, cinema, stage theatre or any of the other forms of entertainment that preceded it. As William Boddy has pointed out, even in 1946, only 6500 TV sets were sold in the United States, 'mostly for use in taverns and the homes of media professionals' (2004: 46). As noted previously, the 1920s had been characterized in US radio, at least officially, as an aural bedlam that needed to be controlled. Advertisers had eventually enforced that control and did not want to lose it, should television prove to be a successful entertainment medium. Post-war advertisers had learned from the 1930s and the radio experience and wanted to prevent what happened there – the costly and annoying dissension from groups like the National Committee on Education by Radio (NCER). In short, commercial advertisers wanted absolute control over TV – despite the networks wanting the exact opposite. Frederick Greenhalgh frames the shift of interest and funding from radio drama to television as 'a planned assassination of radio drama' (2007). Baughman describes the three networks (NBC, ABC, CBS) getting into television as 'slow suicide' (1997: 66). McChesney emphasizes the consumer lack of choice as the Federal Communications Committee (FCC) and US government adopted 'the commercial model without a shred of public debate over prospective alternatives' (2008: 447).

Michele Hilmes (2012) has persuasively explained how the Second World War brought out the best of broadcasting from both the United States and the United Kingdom and how the frequent collaborations also pushed the envelope in radio production. However, the relief that came when the war ended also seems to have opened Americans' eyes to the shortcomings of their heavily commercial-sponsored programming. Many Americans were tired of formulaic soap opera-style dramas with product plugging at regular intervals. The novelty of television would only go so far, but it had a fertile market ready for change.

US network executives shape policy

Sylvester J. 'Pat' Weaver and Bill Paley provide us with fascinating examples of how good intentions can change very much in the execution. We will see how these two men in positions of power were exhausted with radio content and came to approach the new medium of television with heightened artistic ambitions. Furthermore, we will see how such lofty ambitions ultimately yielded to homogeneity. James Baughman has noted that a movement led by NBC executives, some entertainers, writers and ad agents considered TV an opportunity 'to break the monotonous rush to formula that denoted the evolution of motion pictures and radio' (2007: 3). There was, however, no need to reinvent the way popular drama functioned – both NBC and CBS seemed convinced that daily or weekly serials could be continued successfully on TV.

For Baughman, Weaver's influence on early US television is almost mythic. Weaver was so convinced of the clarity of his vision that he approached all four television networks (NBC, CBS, ABC and DuMont) about heading their departments. NBC accepted his leadership in August 1949, and he spent much of 'his early tenure duelling with CBS for talent' (Baughman 2007: 86). Weaver put it bluntly: 'I told them, "Look, we ruined radio. Let's not let it happen to television. Let's stage our own programs and just sell advertising time to the agencies"' (cited in Boddy 1990: 103). David Sarnoff, convinced of television's qualities as early as 1936, was willing to be aggressive in his policies. Though Weaver's appointment at NBC was originally to 'keep the seat warm' for Sarnoff's son Robert (Barnouw 1975: 189), he quickly proved his worth. Weaver, left with diminished talent after Paley's Raids, had to work harder to create innovative must-see television rather than relying on well-known names to carry his programmes (Baughman 2007: 54). He also poached 'spectaculars'. These were what became known as 'event' television, originating in New York City on CBS. Costing far more than any one advertiser could (or would) invest, their multiplicity of sponsors helped fund them. NBC publicized the 'spectaculars' heavily, and nine of the top ten programmes of 1954, the network claimed, were spectaculars, culminating in *Peter Pan* in 1955 (one out of every two Americans watched this extravaganza) (Baughman 2007: 54). Indeed, many critics of the era felt that live spectacles represented opportunities for freedom and nonconformism, with Rod Serling noting, '[w]hatever memorable television moments exist were contributed by live shows. Whatever techniques were developed that were television's own are live techniques' (cited in Boddy 1990: 75).

Gilbert Seldes, who worked at CBS between 1937 and 1945 as its first director of television, had much in common philosophically with Weaver. Seldes' classic work that blurred the boundaries between 'lowbrow' and 'middlebrow' art, *The Seven Lively Arts* (1924), of course predated television (and mentioned radio only in its infancy). However, like Weaver, Seldes was scornful of the 'vast snobbery of the intellect which repays the deadly hours of boredom we spent in the pursuit of art' (Seldes 2001: 311). Weaver, similarly, 'refused to hold his viewers in contempt' (Baughman 2007: 105). Weaver's belief that the average American merely needed to be exposed to high culture to gain appreciation (inform while you entertain) seems almost Reithian in retrospect, a commitment to '*real* thought and *real* beauty; *real* sweetness and *real* light' (Arnold 1993: 79, original emphasis). 'Let us dare to think and let us think with daring', Weaver said (cited in Barnouw 1975: 190). Weaver is termed by Baughman a high cultural democrat; Seldes is termed a classic liberal by Michael Kammen, though in terms of background Seldes had much more in common with David Sarnoff (both were of Russian Jewish immigrant ancestry). In any case, all three men seemed to have had a burning desire to 'overturn a century-long imposition of class over culture' in America (Baughman 2007: 107). When NBC showed a telecast of Laurence Olivier's *Richard III* several hours before its theatrical release in 1956, up to 25 million Americans watched (Baughman 2007: 109). Indeed, Barnouw characterizes Weaver's departure from NBC in 1955 as signifying the end of an era: 'it was because the whole structure he represented showed signs of crumbling' (Barnouw 1975: 191).

Bill Paley was Weaver's counterpart on CBS, NBC's rival. Paley's real love was radio. However, he saw the potential of television after 1947, and was responsible for *Alfred Hitchcock Presents* (1955–65) and *Gunsmoke* (1954–57), the idea for which he originated himself. *Gunsmoke* lasted twenty seasons and worked well in both sound and vision. Paley's strategy was to create 'good drama in period dress' (Baughman 2007: 150). Anthologies like *Alfred Hitchcock Presents* served well on early network television. In the 1950s, anthology writers 'were white, nearly all male, and all in their late twenties and thirties' (Baughman 2007: 180). Most had served in the Second World War and brought their suspicions of authority (much like *The Goons* and other off-the-wall post-war British comedy). Such writers were playing out their psychological struggles in 'kitchen sink' dramas and plays like *Marty* (1953). Between 1955 and 1957, US television moved away from Weaver's theatrical roots and became more filmic. While commercial sponsors like Philco and Kraft gave writers considerable artistic freedom, for writers like Rod Serling it was not nearly enough (Feldman 2010: 56; Barnouw 1975: 163).

David Sarnoff

Paley's and Weaver's visions drove television content forward as they tried to correct the mistakes they believed had occurred in radio. Neither of them could have made their contributions if not for the single-minded aggression of David Sarnoff. A lack of capital for investment into new media can be crippling, or at least obstructive. As with radio some decades earlier, TV networks had to 'invest ahead of demand from consumers and advertisers' (Baughman 2007: 4). As Marc has noted, all 108 stations were either owned by or affiliated to the existing networks. Sarnoff may have felt a personal rivalry with business opponents like Paley who, although of Jewish immigrant ancestry like Sarnoff, was college-educated and middle class, which may have fuelled Sarnoff's relentless pursuit of RCA dominance. In the early days – Sarnoff poured money into television research after 1936 when he saw the first BBC telecasts – RCA 'obviously had a greater immediate interest: popular programming would promote the sales of TV sets' (Baughman 2007: 34). US technological advancement in television would probably not have been driven at its steady pace if not for Sarnoff. Sarnoff's vision looks remarkably prescient to us now. Baughman has discovered that 'an overproduction of radios immediately after the war' flooded the market and caused the price of radios to drop (2007: 33). 'Manufacturers could earn far more money on television sets, if the TV boom ever arrived' (2007: 33). For those who thought like Sarnoff, the TV boom was an anxiously anticipated event.

Sarnoff, Paley and Weaver are merely the most visible of the figures moving from what they saw as the tired world of radio to the novel world of TV. Mistakenly, the large film studios did not believe the radio networks that had taken control of TV had the resources to compete with Hollywood visually, so they did not pool their resources until it was too late. It was this assumption – that the cheapness of TV drama production values would not cut into cinema-going – that helps to explain some of the directions of the earliest US television programming. In the event, it was musical star Milton Berle who brought the New York urban audience to TV drama, hosting *The Texaco Star Theater* on NBC from 1948. Though the show, like most TV at that point, was produced in New York, it did well nationally with an 86.7 per cent audience rating. Next, *I Love Lucy* (1951–57, CBS) showed how canny television producers had become. Lucille Ball had starred in a vacuous radio sitcom called *My Favorite Husband* (1948–51, CBS), but took the initiative with her company DesiLu to film *I Love Lucy* in Los Angeles even though it took place in New York City. Until then, the film industry had managed to hamper television dramatic content by causing most of movie talent to live in and around LA. Other companies, such as Ziv and Four Star 'built programs around major radio personalities, selling them as a "package" […] both to single sponsors via their ad agencies or, increasingly, directly to the networks themselves' (Hilmes 2012: 218).

Censorship and TV

Sarnoff's aggressive drive for television stemmed from a belief in the entertainment business possibilities of the medium. Paley and Weaver were at least partially driven by genuine artistic vision. But how did their intentions translate under the realities of commercial advertisers? Radio had always been censored, sometimes elaborately so. In 1938, Seymour and Martin noted the high level of self-censorship in the radio industry during that time, which they claimed would always be more severe than that of the stage, the novel or film. This, they said, was because audiences would always be prepared in advance for the likelihood of offence in film or theatre and were making a choice. Radio, transmitted directly into the home, offered no such choice. They gave a list of five radio taboos, including sex, 'irreverent references to the Deity', racism, slander and 'dissemination of false information' (Seymour and Martin 1938: 292).

In the United States in the 1950s, TV networks and stations soon 'understood that ignoring the profanity clause ran a regulatory risk' (Baughman 2007: 15). More than merely regulating bad language, TV now also had to contend with giving visual offence. Baughman notes that behaviours like excessive drinking and suicide were not allowed in NBC comic routines or TV dramas, nor were TV audiences at all comfortable with displays of the female body (Baughman 2007: 26, 28). Networks, ad agencies and commercial sponsors would censor anything they thought likely to give offence. Such was the case with a 1948 episode of CBS' *Studio One* (1948–58), 'Thunder on Sycamore Street', in which the original protagonist was a black man. In order to avoid appalling southern viewers, the 'beleaguered protagonist' became, instead, an ex-convict (Barnouw 1975: 165). TV advertisers were even more fearful of offending their audiences than radio advertisers, because an offended audience could be a boycotting audience that could severely limit profits. In early 1954, only 20 per cent of Arkansas homes had a TV and only 8 per cent of homes in North Dakota had one. TV executives had to make sure, however, that these more conservative rural audiences as well as an urban New York one was catered for and could not be offended. Indeed, a 1951 article warned, '[o]ff color jokes, swish routines, city humor hits the small towns and suburbs with unpleasant impact, focusing reaction upon certain entertainers – and their sponsors' (cited in Boddy 1990: 101).

Advertising executives, in their tremendous drive towards commercially motivated censorship, were hoping no one would speak up against anything they saw on TV. TV's messages of prosperity were thought to have the power to hold off another Great Depression (Baughman 2007: 43). George Lipsitz goes as far as to suggest that commercial TV sponsors feared broadcast messages would combat 'awakened militancy among workers' and 'physical fragmentation of suburban growth' (2003: 106, 107). Furthermore, US intellectuals lost the chance – it proved 'a fatal nightmare' – to engage with and influence TV's content, retreating instead into 'television snobbism' (Marc 1996: 186). This contrasts clearly with the reform movement of the intelligentsia in the early 1930s regarding radio, in which broadcast reform received its 'nearly unconditional support' (McChesney 2008: 197). Instead of influencing policy-making (voting with their financial patronage the way minority letter-writers caused BBC controllers no end of agony), these Americans – among them ministers, rabbis and older, childless couples – paved the way for networks and national advertisers to appeal to 'middle-class crusaders' and the moral/cultural guardians (such as Catholic and Protestant leaders) (Marc 1996: 2, 11). This led to an extreme homogenization of content, which upon reflection seems exactly the same as the radio restrictions that people like Paley and Weaver had struggled to keep from TV's *tabula rasa*. Instead, TV became known by such epithets as 'goggle box', 'idiots' lantern' and 'chewing gum for the eyes'. 65 per cent of stations in 1948 were not network affiliates, but 'few high-powered stations were independent' (Marc 1996: 17).[1]

Nostalgia

Another cause for the death of dramatic content on US radio is a corollary to the artistic ennui noted above. Radio had linked itself intrinsically with nostalgia. Nostalgia is a powerful concept in both a negative and positive sense. Garrison Keillor (see Chapter 8) was relieved to have escaped his hometown. Yet, to many who listen to his stories of Lake Wobegon, this relief is not apparent and is instead replaced by a sense of nostalgia for a life – and a radio – long gone. Fake ads in *Prairie Home Companion* (1974–2016), as Susan Douglas perceived, 'ridiculed what many, in their nostalgia for radio's "golden age", had forgotten: its overabundance of schlocky commercials that sought to turn everything into a commodity' ([1999] 2004: 324). Indeed, the term 'old time radio' appears to originate in 1963 when networks began re-broadcasting *The Shadow* (1937–54) and *The New Adventures of Sherlock Holmes* (1939–50) (Patterson 2016: 7).

The 'good old days' on US television are often now recognized as somewhat deceptive. This nostalgic approach to TV drama in the 1950s often involved the transfer of earlier radio programmes, a hearkening back that has been described as a 'desiccated and eviscerated' version of working-class life in programmes like *Mama* (1949–56, CBS) and *The Goldbergs* (1949–56) (Lipsitz 2003: 119). George Lipsitz examined family, class and ethnicity in early network TV programmes like the above examples and how they misremembered and commoditized the recent past, linking nostalgia with consumer products. In the case of *Mama*, memories of the narrator's Norwegian-American working-class family were very appealing for TV viewers (Lipsitz 2003: 102). Lipsitz found that these shows lost their emphasis on kinship and ethnicity when they moved from radio to TV, embracing a new US consumer future. For example, in *The Goldbergs*' episode 'The In-Laws', matriarch Molly Goldberg's Depression-era ethic is reversed when she is convinced by her children that 'living above our means' is the 'American way' (Lipsitz 2003: 108). *Life of Riley's* (1949, 1953) main character's 'shortage of cash becomes a powerful failing caused by incompetent behaviour as a consumer'; Jack Benny's stinginess on radio caused a great deal of ritual mirth by contrast (Lipsitz 2003: 109). What is clear is that the rather old-fashioned nature of radio drama in the United States contributed to the demise of the form – only for television to borrow, and then subvert, those same old-fashioned values.

The BBC and US radio policy

The BBC with J.C.W. Reith at the helm had the advantage of observing the US approach to broadcasting. As Reith's biographer has noted, 'John Reith had a great love of the sea and a considerable fondness for nautical metaphor' (McIntyre 1993: 119). It was this metaphor that he used to describe the BBC's mission and progress, titling a chapter in his 1924 *Broadcast Over Britain* 'Uncharted seas', and writing in the 1928 *BBC Handbook* that broadcasting 'was a sea full of more or less unchartered rocks, and to be navigated at fairly high speed into the bargain'. Reith's influence on the BBC cannot be – and seldom is – underestimated. However, how he came to create and shape the policy he rigorously maintained is often obscured by an emphasis on his strict religious upbringing.² Underexplored is the period during and after the First World War that he spent in the United States.

Michele Hilmes has been particularly observant of the effect of aural bedlam that the British perceived in the United States in the years between 1918 and 1922, before the formation of the British Broadcasting Company. She appears to have been the only scholar to document the direct impact of the US broadcasting situation in the early 1920s upon Britain's Sykes Committee in 1922 (2012: 42–44). She quotes Cecil Lewis in 1924, expounding the attitude that, 'others [should] rush at the new inventions, and do the experimenting, spend the money, get the hard knocks, and buy their experience at a high price' (cited in Hilmes 2012: 37). Meanwhile, the British, Cecil Lewis implied, would learn from others' mistakes. To Reith, US broadcasting would always remain chaotic, and he, and his policies, would remain the British antidote to it. Thus, the formation of the British Broadcasting Company is directly influenced by aural bedlam in the United States; in turn, President Hoover's management of 'public interest' in the late 1920s was directly influenced by the British organization of their system, which further directly influenced the formation of the Crawford Committee and the incorporation of the British Broadcasting Corporation. This system of international cause and effect continued throughout the first half of the twentieth century.

The intellectual high ground

We know, too, that from 1922, British broadcasters had almost nothing good to say about the US system (or, as many of them perceived, the lack of one). Even radio dramatists who had visited the United States, such as Maurice Gorham, often had extremely dismissive reactions to the quality of US radio drama in particular.³ They may have admired some of the modes of US radio production, but they felt British radio drama was unparalleled. In the 1940s and 1950s, 'American initiative and "wide awakeness", all based on commercial competition', was contrasted in the US press with 'British complacency and sleepiness' (Hilmes 2012: 76).

Early TV, as Val Gielgud says in the British context, 'had been something of a joke' (1957: 139). Programme-makers at the BBC were slower to promote and explore the possibilities of television and certainly they were not going to adopt a US commercial model in their use of it. Perhaps one incident is the best indication of British feelings about US broadcasting in the early 1950s. *The Today Show,* launched on January 1952, was the first early morning television programme in the United States, broadcasting between 7 and 9 a.m. EST. No single advertiser would underwrite it, but ratings went up when they put a chimpanzee on the show. When

NBC's coverage on *The Today Show* of Queen Elizabeth's coronation in 1953 failed to show what the British audience considered due respect by interrupting the service with product commercials, the British were horrified (Crisell 2002: 80). It is, in a sense, not surprising that radio programme-makers at the BBC should treat their medium with pride and think little of the television usurper, if the US display as typified by NBC was anything to go by.

Maurice Gorham was among several ex-employees of the BBC who felt radio in the 1950s was holding TV back. His 1949 book on television was written well before the BBC's commercial rival ITV had been formed. Nevertheless, he was a supporter of television's interests, and the fact that he left the BBC shows a parting of the ways on television policy. Before the war, the BBC's skills in television production were hampered by a lack of technical finesse. Certainly the implication is that if British broadcasting had had the resources (financial and otherwise) of their US counterparts, British television would have been more technically proficient and therefore perhaps more worthy of BBC pride. Gorham was eager that television's potential in quality broadcasting be recognized. 'Many people bought their television sets so that they could watch the Derby or the Cup Final or the Trooping of the Colour', Gorham observed, even if they later found their investment had repaid itself by 'steady value from the studio plays' (1949: 45).

As happened a few years later with NBC, Shakespeare was the source of British television drama's elevation to higher culture in February 1949 with BBC TV's *Macbeth,* one of the most elaborate productions ever staged at Alexandra Palace. Events like these had convinced Gorham that television had a sophisticated future. To Gorham and his allies, 'radio represented the enemy' (Bridson 1971: 244). It is difficult to know in what direction the BBC would have gone with TV if it had had the budget and the resources. Gorham wrote witheringly, 'if television can kill organised entertainment, it will have accomplished one of the biggest social revolutions of modern times' (1949: 114). He thought television would be used for 'communal viewing' and that radio 'will have its use for slack periods when there is no real point in adding sight to sound' (1949: 110, 140). It must be remembered what kind of television was being produced in the United Kingdom roughly around the time Gorham was writing. Early TV had been aimed at an affluent and frivolous audience based in London and the Home Counties, fed on a diet initially of Noel Coward and Brandon Thomas plays. Other programmes included *Come Dancing* (1950), *What's My Line?* (1951), *The Grove Family* (1955), *The Quatermass Experiment* (1953) and *1984* (1954).

In the United Kingdom, the frustration of people like Gorham was at last appeased when the Independent Television Authority (ITA) allocated a number of regional franchises on fixed-term basis to various programming companies, responsible for selling airtime to the advertisers. There was an average of six minutes advertising in one hour. Norman Collins, it is said, originated the name Independent Television (ITV) (Crisell 2002: 85). There were split franchises on a weekday/weekend basis. The financial backing came from those within theatre, cinema, radio and TV rentals, and newspapers – a startling contrast to the financial backers of US TV.

Let's pretend: Was there any US radio drama 1948–58 that could have saved the genre?

We have now looked at the radio and TV of 1940s and 1950s for both the US and British arenas and examined reasons for the rise and fall of each. For enthusiasts of radio drama and those who yearn for an alternative to US commercial network radio, it is a tempting (and not completely self-indulgent) exercise to imagine what might have saved US radio from being eclipsed by TV as a lasting form of entertainment. If one could return to 1948, how would one go about giving US radio the boost it needed to compete with TV and ensure an existence for drama and other non-music programming beyond 1960? What kind of evasive action, programming-wise, would one engage in? It seems likely that offering technically explosive and aesthetically iconoclastic forms to the US public in 1948 would not have guaranteed success; it may instead have alienated the radio listening audience further. David Marc suggests the natural forms of television were basically inherited from radio, such as sitcoms, cop shows, game shows and soap operas (1996: xxvi).

As Neil Verma has reported in the opening to *Theater of the Mind* (2012), CBS executive Guy della Cioppa had begun receiving letters from listeners requesting new radio dramas in 1956. In the United Kingdom, writer Clemence Dane was disturbed that in 'a recent quiz [about] colour-television [where] somebody was asked: "Why are you for it?" The answer came pat: "I shan't have to use my imagination so much"', implying that television's appeal for many was the fact viewers did not have to use their imaginations (Dane 1961: 3). Verma suggests that the CBS backlash in 1956 was due to disappointed TV viewers reaching 'a point of saturation at which they started to yearn for something that would involve more of their own "imagination"' (Verma 2012: 1). Imagination, apparently, was in short supply on early US network TV, and in that moment radio drama seemed, once again, to offer audiences an alternative. Audiences were right back where they started with radio in the early post-war era. They were bored, going from one medium to another. It didn't seem to be the medium that mattered, it was the content, and the content lacked imagination.

The marvellous world of the ordinary ('genre paintings') characterized early TV offerings and 'most advertisers were selling magic' (Barnouw 1975: 163). Early US TV stations could choose from an inventory of older feature films from a few distributors, such as those owned by Alexander Korda and William Boyd (Hopalong Cassidy). The popularity of *Howdy Doody* (1947–60) underlined that TV programming had to appeal to the whole family. The point of such WABC TV programmes as *I Cover New York Times* and *A Couple of Joes* (both 1950) was interactive entertainment with a local angle (Allen 1997: 8). WPTZ-TV Philadelphia offered *The Handyman* in 1946, a combination of infomercial and handyman tips. With TV's programming so apparently unsophisticated and mundane,[4] surely radio drama in the United States should have stood more of a chance. Verma's point, however, was that few new radio dramas would attract the kind of advertising money needed to justify national distribution. The short answer therefore, is, no, there is unlikely to have been any drama programming on radio introduced between 1948 and 1958 that could have saved its continued existence.

Looking at Marc's list of 'natural' inheritance from radio, what genres of programming on radio did survive the transition (i.e. continued to broadcast after 1948 and through to 1958) and why? Westerns are one clear example. Specific programmes granted multiple manifestations in various media include *The Lone Ranger* (MBS/ABC radio 1933–54; ABC television 1947–54), *Gunsmoke* (CBS radio 1952–61; CBS television 1955–75) and *Have Gun, Will Travel* (CBS television 1957–63; CBS radio 1958–60). *The Lone Ranger*, previously discussed in the history of the MBS network, originated on radio on Detroit's celebrated WXYZ in 1933. Notably, it thrived on both TV and radio between 1949 and 1954. It seemed to appeal to all age groups with an ethical and moral simplicity. Yet the very fact that *The Lone Ranger* and *Gunsmoke* had recognizable brands from radio would have assisted with the outlay of capital and no doubt by the mid-1950s, with television access to Hollywood's location filming, more realistic recording could be achieved. Perhaps, as Frederick Faust said, a good horse is more important than a woman in the western, and all a TV western needed to make a convincing show were horses and men in costume. It is certainly possible that the television competition spurred radio westerns to new artistic heights, with some of the most complex and interesting series ever made debuting during this period, such as *Straight Arrow* (1948–51), *Frontier Gentleman* (1958, CBS), *The Six-Shooter* (1953–54, NBC), *Gunsmoke* and *Have Gun, Will Travel*.

Crime shows are another obvious choice. However, some of these transferred from radio to TV more successfully than others. *Gangbusters* finished in eighth place during its first full Nielsen season on television. It was cancelled after only eighteen months on air scheduled against and bested by *Dragnet*. Jack Webb had created *Dragnet* on radio in 1949, and Baughman offers some clue to why it outlasted the crime competition: Webb's auteur-esque authority, such that he was 'already synonymous with the show when he brought it to television' (Baughman 2007: 74). 'After years of the highly stylized theatrical artifice of *Martin Kane* and *Man Against Crime*', *Dragnet*'s television incarnation must have mirrored its radio reputation in seeming realistic (2007: 75).

Several sitcoms and soap operas transferred from US radio to TV, such as those already mentioned as well as *The Honeymooners* (1934–36, NBC), *Our Miss Brooks* (1948–57, CBS) and *Life with Luigi* (1948–53, CBS). However, early TV sitcoms seemed to most easily fall foul of McCarthyism, which had begun to brew. In 1947 in House testimony, J. Edgar Hoover had referred to communists who had 'infiltrated the airwaves' (Baughman 2007: 207). Then in February 1950, when Republican senator Joseph R. McCarthy 'accused the State Department of harbouring precisely 205 Communists, i.e. traitors', the new red scare, embodied in McCarthyism, went 'on and on for decades, and became a way of life' (Fried 1997: 1, 4). In June 1950, the effect had snowballed to the point that three ex-FBI agents published *Red Channels,* 'a book that cut a wide swath' across the entertainment industry; of the 151 entertainers and writers it smeared as communists, most never recovered their careers (Fried 1997: 119). Although its devastating effect was fictionalized by Philip Roth in *I Married a Communist* (1998), the reality was shattering when actor Philip Loeb was named in *Red Channels* for attending an antifascist rally. Loeb played Jake Goldberg in the TV version of *The Goldbergs* (1949–56). Gertrude Berg, the writer and showrunner, initially backed Loeb but eventually chose to cut him loose in order to regain commercial sponsorship of her TV show. Sponsors resumed their support after Loeb left the show in 1952. The actor received a $45,000 settlement but never worked again and committed suicide in 1956 (Lipsitz 2003: 101–34).

The essential conservatism of US society during this period is evident not only in McCarthyism's effect on media, as noted above, but also in its emphasis on physical appearance. It is worth mentioning that many of radio's best beloved personalities did not belong on TV and could not make it on the new medium. Lipsitz details a failed sitcom property that tried to transfer Bing Crosby in sitcom mould as a crooning repairman who has given up show business stardom for family life. *The Jack Benny Program* enjoyed a modest but abbreviated run on television (1950–65). On the other hand, no one would dream of watching *Baby Snooks* (1936–51) on television. Fanny Brice introduced 'the most notorious brat of the air' on NBC in 1937 (Cox 2009: 146). Brice was a former Ziegfeld Follies girl whose surprisingly charming portrayal of an incorrigible toddler and her long-suffering 'Daddy' made her popular on radio between 1944 and 1951. In the 1920s, her career on stage in both musical performance and comedy caused Gilbert Seldes to consider her a genius of her craft (she was also the inspiration behind the musical *Funny Girl* [1968]). Certainly, here was an example of a middle-aged woman playing (and often dressing up as, in publicity photographs) a toddler. Such could not be acceptable on television. *Snooks'* Depression-era ethic, as well, would have been out of place on television.

Baughman suggests that the networks' radio 'risk aversion' strategy was ultimately what doomed radio, as they did not make any real attempts at innovation on radio to save the medium (1997: 66).

Outside intervention?

If programming alone could not have saved radio drama's continued existence, perhaps some outside intervention could have? The FCC, US policy-maker for radio, had to oversee the technical aspects of television. Perhaps unsurprisingly in light of its record with radio, it 'proved an inconsistent policy-maker, as well as an incompetent and, on several occasions, corrupt licensor' (Baughman 2007: 57). Furthermore, support for the idea of an educational TV channel espoused at the very beginning of television development in the United States was doused fairly quickly. The radio network model was, in Lipsitz's view, guaranteed to triumph over arts, culture or educational TV (2003:106). This failed movement for educational TV initially enjoyed 'bipartisan congressional support' (Baughman 2007: 66). However, the movement faced conflict from none other than Gilbert Seldes as the head of CBS' television department. Seldes, quite characteristically, feared that setting up ETV would cause commercial broadcasting to eschew the content that 'mixed high and mass culture' (Baughman

2007: 67), the same argument against splitting the BBC's radio service into the Home Service, the Light Programme and the Third Programme in 1946. The creation of an American Public Broadcasting System would have to wait until 1970.

US commercial broadcasters have long held the view that a tripartite system such as Haley's cultural pyramid from 1946 is right and proper. As discussed in Chapter 5, in 1944 William Haley created the new tripartite system, the cultural pyramid. In the current context, the important thing to remember about this new approach was that 'some mixture of programming would be retained within each network, but more than this, listeners would be encouraged to work their way up through the network system' (Crisell 2002: 64). There were to be no surprises, no juxtaposition of Bach and Irving Berlin, but instead the pyramid system, 'leading' to 'high' culture, making this a voluntary choice, rather than Reith's philosophy of keeping the two side by side, making overlap unavoidable. In terms of the US system, a cultural pyramid approach lets the 'taxpayer pick up the obligations of commercial licensees', with entities such as the Public Broadcasting System serving as 'holding pens' for viewers who yearn for more than mainstream commercial television is providing (Marc 1996: 185).

Educational radio in the United States was even slower to materialize than ETV; as Douglas puts it, NPR was an afterthought of the Public Broadcasting Act of 1967 and was obliged to produce and distribute national programming, with less than 10 per cent of the total Public Broadcasting budget – the rest went, naturally, to TV. In extreme cases, opposition to commercial television is framed as 'opposition to the free market and, by easy extension, opposition to freedom itself' (Douglas [1999] 2004: 187), presumably why the US House of Representatives felt it could propose the elimination of the Corporation for Public Broadcasting in 2011 and 2017. Clearly, the tensions at work in the realms of culture, democracy, capitalism and media that were manifest from the beginnings of radio were just as intense in the first decades of the twenty-first century as they were in the late 1940s and 1950s.

In conclusion, this chapter has examined the ways radio policy, established quite early in the twentieth century in the United States and the United Kingdom, influenced TV policy. The decisions made in the late 1920s influenced not only the two countries, working off each other in a cause-and-effect relationship, but appeared in the long shadow of posterity when TV policy was made in the 1940s and 1950s. In the United States, it was the influence of commercial advertisers, as well as the genuinely ambitious artistic aims of men like Pat Weaver and Bill Paley, that ensured TV's ascendancy and radio's decline. The United Kingdom, watching the US broadcasting landscape since the nineteen-teens, made up its mind rapidly about what it didn't want: a US-type system, and this intellectual high-mindedness persisted to a point that it coloured the British approach to television broadcasting. British TV may have been retarded in its growth until commercial competition in 1955, but undeniably its radio drama has lived a lifetime longer than US radio's, partly as a result of the United Kingdom avoiding an all-or-nothing leap into early TV.

Notes

1 'Unlike New York, where much early television programming was produced by ad agencies directly for the sponsors, thereby cutting the stations out of the process, television sponsorship and program production at WPTZ was a collaborative effort' (Woal and Woal 1997: 52).
2 'We know that he was dominating and steeped in a rather rigid Presbyterian morality', as David Hendy puts it (2013: 21).
3 This attitude can partially be understood as 'Britain had more reasons than most to be concerned about being NOT American' (Hilmes 2013: 19).
4 It's impossible to know how WPTZ-TV Philadelphia's wartime soap *Last Year's Nest* would have held up against *Against the Storm;* seen by a handful of people with television sets in 1942, actor Leonard Valenta recalled, '[i]t was a wartime drama about the trials and tribulations of a German refugee and the family that took him in as a kind of second son. I played the young immigrant – my name was Blackie – and the story seemed to imply that I had left Germany to escape from the Nazis because I was Jewish. The episodes covered everything from Blackie's first love – tame compared with how we'd handle it today – to an episode with me being hunted by a Nazi' (cited in Woal and Woal 1997: 45).

Chapter 7

The Ascendance of the Background Medium: Drama on US and British Radio (1960–2010)

> It [radio drama] didn't die of natural causes, nor is it really dead.
> – Norman Corwin (cited in Nachman 2000: 500)

Radio drama did not uniformly disappear from US airwaves after 1960, nor did it disappear at all from the BBC, even after the end of the British broadcasting monopoly in 1955. Great changes took place in the radio drama landscape in both countries during the second half of the twentieth century. This chapter combines the histories of the United States and the United Kingdom over a period of 50 years. This period has been critically under-served in the radio annals of both countries, though as more radio studies scholars emerge, the drama offerings of the period will be understood in more depth. Furthermore, although changes in the media landscape in the United Kingdom dictated sometimes remarkably different radio drama content in the second half of the twentieth century than what preceded it, in the United States, the story is both simpler and more complex. This is due to the fact that radio drama, with a few notable exceptions, has been heard on terrestrial radio on public service broadcasting (PSB), which is not nearly as monolithic as the BBC. The varied and sometimes competing strands of US PSB make for a wide-ranging but complicated radio drama history.

Radio drama in Britain (1960–2010)

It may seem churlish if not downright misleading to condense radio drama in the United Kingdom during a period of 50 years into one half of a short chapter, especially as output continued to be prolific and diverse. The necessity for this is that very little has been written on radio drama of this period, and the research needed to write authoritatively on the subject has not been done, in part because of factors identified in Chapter 1, the sheer volume of work and its general inaccessibility. This section of the chapter deals with BBC restructure and policy post-1967 and its effects on drama, the legislation that made possible commercial radio broadcasting in the United Kingdom and commercial forays into radio drama, and briefly treats a number of important radio drama productions from the period, concluding with an extended examination of *The Archers* (1951–present).

Drama on the BBC and on commercial radio

In 1967, the BBC created the 'pop music' station Radio 1 in response to the pressure of pirate radio. This was part of a wider restructuring that, in very simplified terms, resulted in: Radio 1 (for contemporary, popular music), Radio 2 (for 'golden oldies'), Radio 3 (classical music, arts coverage, religious programming, some drama), Radio 4 (speech) and the World Service. Programming on BBC radio has changed a great deal from J.C.W. Reith's concept of what and when edifying programmes should be broadcast to the British nation as a whole. A variety of content is one of the BBC's hallmark features, and while Radio 4 has generally been the home to radio drama, it can in fact be heard on many strands. For example, Radio 2 had comedy slots until the 1990s (Hodgson 2014: 40). BBC Managing Director Frank Gillard cancelled *Children's Hour* in 1967, but children's radio programming, including drama, continued on Radio 4 for decades.

As Hendy has noted, BBC audience research suggested that 'the public's expectation of radio was higher' than of TV, and by extension, 'its abhorrence of something unexpected consequently all the more intense' (2007: 148), an observation borne out by recorded audience comments. These comments included complaints about 'musical jingles, sex, bad language, morbid themes, reception problems, scheduling, regional accents, and so on, though less often about what programmes said or signified' (Hendy 2007: 243). In the 1980s, the average age of the Radio 4 listener was around 53, which had not really changed since 1967. Revealingly, the audience remained, generally, middle aged, middle class and white. Hendy noted that this was due in part to younger listeners joining at roughly the rate that older ones were dying (2007: 267). Radio 4 was deemed to be for 'clever folk' but not intellectuals ('they had Radio 3'); an audience 'infused with the spirit of curiosity and modest self-improvement' (Hendy 2007: 268).

The long-term consequences of the re-structuring of the late 1960s unfolded in the 1970s, 1980s and 1990s. This ensured that Radio 3 retained the Third Programme's cerebral cachet, but more regionalism could be heard in drama, censorship slowly became more loosely controlled and unique features developed within the sphere of radio drama. Hendy has identified the strength of British regional theatres in the early 1970s that contributed to new forms of drama excellence, which was in turn rewarded by official awarding bodies. From Leeds, producer Alfred Bradley attracted talent like Stan Barstow, Barry Collins, Barry Hines, Alan Ayckbourn and Alan Plater. Andrew Davies, a Welsh writer, was first recognized on radio via the Birmingham studios, which produced his early plays including *Filthy Fryer and the Woman of Maturer Years* (1970). Newcastle native Lee Hall was the most lauded radio scriptwriter of the 1990s. Winner of the biennial Alfred Bradley Bursary (open to first-time radio dramatists living in the north of England), Hall created *Spoonface Steinberg* in 1997. Tim Crook has identified the essence of *Spoonface Steinberg*, a phenomenon that generated 'hundreds of letters and phone-calls', as the titular character's 'natural courage which we would all wish to find' (1999c).

Not everyone agreed that Radio 4 should be a natural home for speech radio. In the 1970s, there were plans within the BBC to break up Radio 4 and disperse its content to other BBC networks. However, among the arguments that ultimately saved Radio 4 was the contention that if BBC Radio Drama moved exclusively to Radio 4's sister channel, Radio 3, its audience would diminish into negligibility. Similarly, it was argued that eliminating radio comedy as heard on Radio 4 would destroy the creative environment for comics who often debuted on that station, to later transfer their talents to television. The point of it all was, in David Hendy's words, to allow 'talented individuals the creative time and space to practise their craft, try new techniques, take risks' (2013a: 56). Radio 4:

> set standards of technical and editorial quality that were a yardstick for the whole of British broadcasting; that popular programmes were as important as the demanding ones, since many heard the latter by accident if they had stayed tuned after hearing the former; that well written stories and plays provided a balance.
>
> (Hendy 2007: 273)

The 1970s were also characterized, according to Hendy, by 'a dangerously pent-up desire for greater artistic license had been created in Broadcasting House' (2007: 106). Historically, the main defence mechanism for allowing producers artistic freedom and not offending Radio 4's core audience has been scheduling. In the 1970s and 1980s, the easily offended knew to avoid the now-defunct *The Monday Night Play* slot. *After Liverpool* (1971) by Jamie Saunders and *Cries from Casement as His Bones are Brought to Dublin* (1974) by David Rudkin were the first dramas to feature potentially offensive language that their producers did not self-censor.[1] Elmes suggests such scheduling continues in 'raunchy books, spooky playlets […] and, these days, late-night risqué comedy [that] have populated the closing hours of Radio 4's schedule' (Elmes 2008: 289).

Radio legislation and alternatives to the BBC

In 1970, the BBC's radio broadcast monopoly was broken, and the Conservative Party inaugurated Independent Local Radio (ILR). While much of commercial radio had little interest in drama, there is evidence that regional responses to drama were successful. As early as 1972, there were rumours of a commercial radio challenge to *The Archers* on LBC or Capital Radio. ILR's soap, Capital Radio's *Bedsitter*, 'lasted only a few months' (Starkey 2004: 182) but incorporated phone-in interactivity (Crook 1999a: 24). Though this putative serial wasn't long-lasting, commercial stations Capital Radio and Radio Clyde boasted drama producers (Anthony Cornish and Hamish Wilson respectively). Wilson produced *The Slab Boys* for Radio Clyde in 1979 and went on to work in drama at the BBC. Wade notes that in 1978, Manchester's Piccadilly station's drama, *The Last Rose of Summer*, was a finalist in radio drama awards given by the Society of Authors (1981: 218). Radio City (Liverpool) also produced drama by Alan Bleasdale (Street 2006b: 121). Bleasdale presented *Scully,* an hour-long programme broadcast on Sunday mornings, produced by Robert Cooper. *A Nation in His Hand,* written by Mike Bartlett, was produced by David Lucas for Swansea Sound in 1981. It starred Philip Madoc and Sion Probert and was a retelling of Evan Roberts and the 1904–05 religious revival in Wales (Street 2006b: 129). Roger Harvey notes that there was also a short lived 'soap' at Metro Radio (serving Tyneside, Northumberland and Durham) in the late 1970s, and in 1978 he was commissioned to provide occasional drama for the ILR station. His productions included *The Only Child* (1980), *Prisoners* (1981), *Hassan* (1983) and *The Silver Spitfire* (1985). By the mid-1980s, 'all speech-based programmes except news and sport were dropped' from Metro Radio (Harvey n.d.).

Between 1987 and 2003, Independent Radio Drama Productions Ltd. (IRDP) produced drama that was heard via NPR in the United States as well as within Britain on LBC. Founded by Tim Crook, Richard Shannon and Marja Giejgo, IRDP ran festivals and competitions 'which resulted in the production and broadcast of many plays by new writers who would not otherwise have had the chance to hear their work aired on the radio' (IRDP 2003). IRDP had a subsidiary stage company and a mirror group in the United States, the Anglo-American Radio Drama Company, and pre-dated the BBC in terms of putting audio drama online (Crook 1999a: 28). IRDP 'demonstrated that there was a place for quality radio drama production outside the BBC' (Street 2005: 127).[2]

John Birt's tenure as director-general of the BBC in the 1990s initiated radical reforms. At least one writer has alleged 'Birtist management was responsible for eroding the BBC's creativity' (Born 2005: 6). A national shift in broadcasting policy, too, had wide-reaching consequences. The Broadcasting Act of 1990 disbanded the Independent Broadcasting Authority in favour of the Independent Television Commission and the Radio Authority. The Broadcasting Act of 1990 brought independent community radio to the United Kingdom for the first time. 'Public dissatisfaction with local radio was not restricted to *content:* in neither the BBC nor the independent stations had the dream of wider *access* been realised' (Crisell 2002: 215, original emphasis). According to Peggy Gray and Peter Lewis, both the BBC and ILR had 'claimed to serve the whole community', but their ability to serve smaller communities and tastes 'was severely limited' (Gray and Lewis 1992: 158). Homogenization in radio, too, was regarded as a consequence of the 1998 Competition Act (Starkey 2015: 131). Many frequencies for local radio appeared by the opening up of the FM band. Nevertheless, Starkey believes '[r]egional commercial radio did little that was positive for localness on local radio' (2015: 134).

Legislation and technology were both important influences upon radio audiences. For example, the transistor radio was introduced in Britain in 1960; by the end of the 1970s nearly 70 per cent of all radio sets in the United Kingdom were portable or mobile (Paulu 1981: 350). By contrast, the digital take up was slower. In 1995, the BBC began the world's first digital audio broadcasting (DAB) transmissions. Tony Stoller, one-time chief executive of the Radio Authority, characterized the move to digital radio in the United Kingdom from a thought process in the 1990s, moving towards the centre of radio thought in the early 2000s, to the concept of analogue switch-off in 2007 (Stoller 2012). The first portable 'kitchen' DAB radio for under £100 in the United Kingdom was not available until 2002. Five new digital radio networks were launched in 2002 (1Xtra, 5 Live Sports Extra, 6 Music, Radio 7 and the Asian Network).

Radio drama in the 1970s to the noughties

There has nowhere been suggested a 'canon' of important radio drama on the BBC between the 1950s Golden Age of Prix Italia-winning Third Programme dramas and contemporary drama, though individual historians have identified candidates (see the gamechangers section of Chapter 8). Long-time radio reviewers for popular British magazines and newspapers like Jane Anderson for the *Radio Times* and Gillian Reynolds for *The Daily Telegraph* and the extensive radio drama listings website Diversity (http://www.suttonelms.org.uk) can give a cumulative view of radio drama of the last 50 years but have yet to offer a critical commentary. For example, a number of top ten radio drama lists on Diversity display a general predilection towards thriller and detective adaptations, but no consensus has been adopted, with favourite dramas from writers as diverse as Henry Reed, Alan Bennett and Alick Rowe (cf. Bickerton n.d.; Cropper n.d.; Deacon 2007, 2008, n.d.; Hawley n.d.; Pike and Campbell n.d.; Whitby n.d.). The canon, therefore, is highly subjective. For example, Michael Mason's 26-part *The Long March of Everyman*, broadcast in 1971, scarcely fit the definition of drama, adhering more to a feature-like structure. A 'lovingly woven tapestry of music and location atmosphere', it had been inspired by Radio 3 programmes on the Bayeux Tapestry (Hendy 2007: 65). Between 500,000 and 1 million people listened to it. Mason didn't use actors for his production; instead, 'a baker's words from the fourteenth century would be spoken, albeit a little woodenly sometimes, by a baker from the late twentieth century' (Elmes 2008: 128). Martin Esslin, however, called it 'anti-radio and self-defeating' (cited in Elmes 2008: 129).

In 1981, Brian Sibley's adaptation of *The Lord of the Rings* attained 'near cult status' (Street 2006b: 123). Garrison Keillor's *Lake Wobegon Days* (see later in this chapter) was read on Radio 4's *Book at Bedtime* in 1986. *The Adventures of Superman*, produced by Dirk Maggs in 1994, brought further Americana to the BBC, using comic books and cinematic techniques in a radiogenic way. Len Deighton's novel, *Bomber,* set in 1943, was adapted in a novel way by Jonathan Ruffell in February 1995, adhering to a series of real-time episodes spread through a day and evening. It was repeated on Radio 4 Extra on Armistice Day 2011. Tim Crook has suggested that in form, *Bomber* most resembled a feature (1999a: 203). Comedy series also continued to be popular on BBC, such as *The Men From the Ministry* (1962–77), *The Burkiss Way* (1976–84)*, Wrinkles* (1980–81), *On the Hour* (1991–92), *Old Harry's Game* (1995–2012), *Chambers* (1996–99) and *Cabin Pressure* (2008–14).

The potential difficulties in establishing this canon returns us to our previous nexus of high/low art. Ed Hime's *The Incomplete Recorded Works of a Dead Body* won the Prix Italia in 2007, the first BBC original to do so in almost twenty years, and was considered an important, experimental new work of drama. *The Wheel of Fortune* (2001) and *The Dark House* (2003) demonstrate an occasional foray from BBC radio into interactive drama. *The Wheel of Fortune* by Nick Fisher 'comprised three simultaneous versions of the play in radio and online form'

(Hand and Traynor 2011: 72). *The Dark House,* written by Mike Walker and formulated by Izzy Mant and Nick Ryan, was another experiment in this vein. Instead of listeners being able to influence the plot by phoning, e-mailing or texting, by voting real-time, they were able to choose which POV to follow: Lucy (a radio reporter), Jim (an old man) or Kelly (a young girl). The shift occurred every three minutes. As suggested by Richard J. Hand, '[t]he play was really three simultaneous binaural productions of three parallel scripts, but on the day of broadcast was crafted by the audience into a single, experiential horror drama' (2014: 194–95). As a radio ghost story set on Halloween, its self-aware identity aligned it with previous 'haunted house exposés' like 'Ghost Hunt' (1949) from *Suspense* (1942–62). *Chain Gang* (2004, 2007, 2009, 2013) was a further effort in interactive storytelling, once again placing the emphasis on audience-generated storylines. Broadcast on BBC Radio 7 in six episodes, each series began with an episode scripted by the production team, which ended on a cliffhanger; further story ideas were contributed by listeners. Series 2 and 3 won Sony Radio Academy Awards (Shearman n.d.).

An institution that has stood the test of time in the last 50 years of BBC radio drama is the Radio Drama Company, also known as the 'Rep'. Once comprised of up to 30 actors, the BBC Radio Drama Company is one source from which BBC radio drama has always drawn its casts. By 1999, there were six actors in the Rep. Rep actors tend to be given lesser roles, with leads going to 'name' actors brought in. Today, the company numbers between ten and twelve and is based in London but can be used elsewhere if necessary and if the actors are available. In 1997, Beck reported that 14,000 actors per year were employed in radio drama in the United Kingdom, with a turnover in fees of £6 million (1997: 4). The core of the Rep is the five annual winners of the Carleton Hobbs Bursary Award and two winners of the Norman Seaton Fellowship. In the past, these winners have included Nerys Hughes, Richard Griffiths, Anthony Daniels and Julian Rhind-Tutt. The Carleton Hobbs Bursary Award (1953–present) and the Norman Seaton Fellowship (2003–present) are both now under the umbrella of (((soundstart))), which attempts to bring young British acting talent into radio drama. Hobbs was a well-known BBC radio drama actor, and Seaton was an accomplished Guyana-born broadcaster. Other awards that recognize radio drama excellence have included the Sony Radio Academy Awards (now the ARIAs – Audio and Radio Industry Awards). The BBC Audio Drama Awards, established in 2012, were created to reward audio drama, and have in the years since awarded British audio drama that has no connection with the BBC in the category of Best Online Only Drama. The categories of award include the Imison Award for Best Script by a New Writer, the Tinniswood Award for Best Radio Drama Broadcast, Best Use of Sound, Best Adaptation and Best Innovation.

The Archers and radio memory

While creating a BBC radio drama canon is the work of future historians and scholars, there is one programme that is emblematic of BBC radio drama of the last 50 years, whether people like it or not. During the week of 11–17 July 1998, the *Radio Times* assembled a panel of experts (see Appendix 3) to help readers vote on the best and most memorable radio drama they had heard. 'As there are so many memorable programmes and people to choose from, we asked a panel of experts to help you decide by nominating what they have enjoyed most' (Robinson 1998: 22). Although Tim Crook has highlighted the flaws in the selection criteria (1999a: 6), *The Archers,* rather unsurprisingly, won this battle of radio memory. This section of the chapter explores *The Archers* in relation to its emblematic status for BBC radio drama and also details some of the lesser-known serials with which it has competed for listeners.

As noted in Chapter 1, the BBC Radio 4 drama serial, *The Archers* garners large numbers of loyal listeners – according to RAJAR figures for the first quarter of 2014, 4.92 million weekly. There are 128 characters in *The Archers,* seventeen of which are silent roles. Fan involvement has been crucial and has carried blithely into the twenty-first century, as with Lucy Freeman's *Dum Tee Dum* podcast (2014–present) (Miller 2015: 36). Hand and Traynor suggest that the *Archers* website is a boon to the programme's continued success. 'Throughout the site, you can catch up with previous episodes, take part in the *Archers Quiz* […] an interactive map allows you to zoom in and out of the fictional village of Ambridge' (2011: 71). Furthermore, '[t]hese aspects of the website enhance the listening experience' by providing clues for new listeners who may become overwhelmed by 60 years of continuity (2011: 71). Metafictionally, *Archers* fans can follow a deceased character's ghost (Sid Perks) on Twitter, as well as the Ambridge Mice (Hodgson 2014: 123). *The Archers* produces 65 hours of weekly drama. The programme also seems to be a barometer of Radio 4's core audience's general mood (Hendy 2007: 88). Spatially, in radio terms there is little to compare with *The Archers.* The series'

> locations, constantly dichotomised between the traditional home, the field or the farm, relate to a society that is strongly attached to the countryside, but connected to the working class through the industrial revolution in Great Britain, a country where modernity always embraces customs and roots.
>
> (Rodero et al. 2014: 170)

Indeed, incredible attention to detail is demonstrated in the layouts of all the locations in Ambridge (Miller 2015: 21–22, 192–93; Country Channel TV 2010). Helen Walmsley-Johnson has suggested that Jennifer Archer's kitchen has an identity all its own (cited in Miller 2015: 154).

While spatially sophisticated, *The Archers* has never held completely supreme as the BBC radio soap. As Elmes discussed in the Radio 4 retrospective *Ambridge in the Decade of Love,* by the 1960s, *The Archers* was looking distinctively old-fashioned. *Waggoners Walk* was deemed one solution, a serial drama that debuted on BBC Radio 2 in April 1969, seeking to 'capture the tensions of student protest, sexual equality, contraception and a more socially mobile society', featuring 'three young women […] sharing a flat in Hampstead. One had an illegitimate child […] another's marriage broke up and the third lived in sin' (Crook 1999b). Crook alleges that its 1974 listening audience of 4 million was higher at that time than that of *The Archers,* but cites a 'money-saving plan' for its destruction in 1980 (Crook 1999b). By the 1980s, *The Archers* was being pilloried by critics as typifying the lack of (ethnic, class, regional) diversity they believed blighted the drama strands on Radio 4; indeed, Crook has questioned its ability to represent modern life in terms of Britain's ethnic makeup (1999a: 48). Part of Controller Michael Green's mid-1980s initiative was to create an alternative to *The Archers* that was less class-bound and designed for an audience a little younger than that of *Coronation Street* (1960–present) (Hendy 2007: 307). His solution was the serial *Citizens* (1987–91), produced by Marilyn Imrie and Anthony Quinn, which featured characters in their early twenties sharing a flat in SW21. The five young characters had met at Leicester University, 'symbolically dead in the centre of England', and then moved in together in East London (Elmes 2008: 113). The cast of *The Archers* met their 'urban soap-cousins' on air in an unusual case of radio drama crossover (Elmes 2008: 113). Elmes suggests that the reason *Citizens* failed was because it needed to be serialized every day, but could only logistically be scheduled twice a week. Hendy has speculated that the main reason audiences did not take to *Citizens* is that none of the characters were likeable; Street noted it was more of a 'soap box' than a soap drama (2006b: 123)

In summary, radio drama in Britain in the last 50 years has been found predominantly on the BBC, but also on commercial radio. It continues to navigate an identity between rarefied inheritor of the Third Programme and the populist drama that so enchants *Archers* listeners. Has a similar formula been at work in US radio drama of the same period? We will explore this in the second half of this chapter.

Radio drama in the United States (1960–2010)

Drama had a somewhat ghostly presence on US radio after 1960. People who had grown up listening to it and identified strongly with its imaginative qualities never forgot it, but drama on radio had been deemed unprofitable by an increasingly commercialized radio system. In response to its changed role in the wake of television, radio took on a new identity: as a DJ who brought music to young people; as home of shock jocks and talk radio; as home of serious current affairs programming on National Public Radio; as alternative fringe on low-power FM (LPFM). Within this system, there were pockets of revived radio drama, bound up within alternatives like audiobooks and, later, online audio drama.

KHFM, format radio and US radio legislation

The history of radio in the United States post-1960 hinges upon a succession of radio regulation, the birth of format radio, the introduction of maverick forms that rose and fell, the introduction of public service broadcasting and its multiple manifestations, then ultimately deregulation, the legalization of community/LPFM/activist radio and radio in the Internet age. The way drama has been threaded through this context is difficult to understand without historical basis. As an introduction, KHFM Albuquerque, 96.3 (a private, for-profit, regional classical music station not affiliated with any public radio network) serves as an example where some radio drama could and did exist in a local, commercial context that was ultimately homogenized through deregulation. 'The talk radio we love is always with us', Kevin D'Arcy noted (2007: 5), and thus I bring personal experience to bear in this chapter, with the example of my childhood radio station, KHFM. KHFM was unusual both in its approach to advertising and its position as a classical music station that proved very popular in the ratings game. During the 1990s through the early noughties, it also presented a unique business/audience model in which 'the business of education' was replaced by a business that occasionally provided 'educational value' (Allen 2001a). Part of this philosophy included space for radio drama such as a series of Canadian radio biopics for children, *Classical Kids* (1995) and when Director of Programming Kip Allen performed an uninterrupted reading of Charles Dickens' *A Christmas Carol* (1843) as part of a Christmas Day broadcast.

KHFM evolved as radio format in the United States evolved. The invention of the transistor radio in the 1960s changed radio's portability. Portable transistor sets allowed individuals to use personal radio receivers 'to stake out their social space' (Douglas [1999] 2004: 221). The 1960s also introduced underground radio, where the goal was to be as relevant and responsive to the community as possible (Keith 2002: 391). A late 1960s broadcasting ethos of contempt for Top 40 hit format radio then transformed in the 1970s into a focus on profit-making. While this was not inherently negative – a 2014 poll suggested that 80 per cent of Americans surveyed thought commercials were a fair price to pay for free AM/FM (Edison Research/Triton Digital 2014: 12) – it did give rise to an unfortunate and mostly ubiquitous homogeneity of content on US airwaves. David Barsamian blasts US format radio as 'vacuumed of content' and 'saturated' with 'recycled' propaganda from right-wing organizations such as the Cato Institute, the American Enterprise Institute and the Heritage Foundation (2002: 10).

Driven by the needs of the format, mainstream commercial radio in the United States has historically found no space for drama. Susan Douglas sees the rise of talk radio in the 1980s as a reaction against an otherwise colourless FM band, believing that both the publicly funded National Public Radio (NPR) and commercial talk radio arose at the same time due to a 'sense of loss of public life' ([1999] 2004: 285). She notes that over 80 per cent of political talk radio hosts, and a majority of the listeners, are male (2004: 485). US talk radio inspires passion and debate. Alfred Balk links the 'right wing shock jocks' of talk radio with the 'monopolization' of US airwaves by chains like Clear Channel Communications (2006: 12); Keillor links the 'blathering idiots' of talk radio with 'jackhammer' Top 40 music (2005 n.pag.). Yet talk radio's omnipresence in daily American life underlines its popularity. Contemporary US radio relies heavily on news, sports coverage and radio personalities who are frequently deceptively presented as local through use of such devices as 'voice tracking' (Perlstein 2002; Klinenberg 2007) and similar processes to video news releases (VNRs). Potentially ethically suspect, VNRs hypothetically 'deceive audience members into thinking they are watching news gathered by reporters, rather than a promotional pitch' (Broaddus et al. 2011: 283).

As for KHFM, in the early noughties, it was local, distinct – and commercial. It was the second-most listened-to station in Albuquerque in 2001 (it was the most listened-to station in Santa Fe between 2001 and 2003). In a station memo (December 2001) entitled 'Why KHFM sounds different from other stations', Kip Allen told staff that nuance in advertising and announcer 'links' was essential due to audience brand loyalty and demographic needs (2013d). KHFM cultivated listener loyalty. When perhaps less than 10 per cent of listeners tune into a single radio station in a given US city marketplace, loyal listeners are 'demographically desirable', and loyalty translates into economic buoyancy (Lochte 2004: 39).

In the 1970s to 1990s, 'in a dramatic transformation, the US media system came to be dominated by a handful of entertainment conglomerates', such as Time Warner, News Corporation, Viacom, Disney and General Electric (McChesney 2013: 120). As noted in Chapter 5, US radio is regulated by the FCC, and the FCC's members are 'appointed primarily for political reasons' (Ray 1990: xv), with its character 'based on the various personalities of the commissioners who serve and the political climate of the period' (Caristi and Sterling 2010: 283) and viewed by some as an industry lapdog (Smith 2014: 151). FCC interest in deregulation began with President Jimmy Carter, who viewed deregulation as 'a means to increase diversity in broadcasting' (Smith 2014: 154). Unfortunately, this aim has not been realized. In a 2011 study evaluating its long-term effects, the FCC discovered that of more than 18,000 stations in the United States, about 6 per cent 'are minority owned' (Smith 2014: 159).

The 1996 Telecommunications Act has been described as 'the largest policy shift in the history of US broadcasting' (Chambers 2012: 263), touching 'off an onslaught of massive consolidation within the broadcast industry' (Riismandel 2002: 424). Further deregulation took place after 19 April 2001 when the FCC voted to end the 'dual network' rule. What this period of deregulation meant in Albuquerque was that KHFM, which was occupying a particularly attractive frequency on Sandia Crest, became a desirable commercial target. KHFM majority owner Peter Beesher decided to sell the station to Citadel Communications, one of the large media conglomerates that was being formed (Ronish 2008a). Citadel leased KHFM to the American General Media Group. AGM brought a streamline format style to their new acquisition.[3]

The incorporation of stations like KHFM into national conglomerates may not have reduced KFHM's broader role culturally, as the station continued to play classical music. However, the adoption of streamlined formatting reduced the flexibility that could perhaps have guaranteed a space for radio drama on the station. Until 2017, the frequent station IDs trumpeted 'listener-supported KHFM', giving what Allen calls 'a pseudo-semblance of public radio' while the station remained private and commercial (2013a). KHFM at that stage was being forced into an increasingly curtailed existence to fit in with format radio norms. Format radio is highly typified across different music specialties. For example, in a breakfast show on commercial radio, broadcast from approximately 6 a.m. to 10 a.m., listeners are primarily interested in accessing the time, travel conditions, weather conditions and news (so that they feel they are connected to the rest of the world after eight hours of sleep). 'In the morning, ten times as many people listen to the radio than watch TV', so programmers showcase their best content, bookended by rapid changes of mode, commercial insertions and station IDs (Stewart 2006: 61). Daytime shows last between 10 a.m. and 4 p.m.

There is a sense from programmers' rhetoric that the function of radio is to be a companion in the banal yet challenging everyday nine-to-five. With a mostly music format by midday, music play is increased, says Stewart, during the day when most listeners are at work, to 'help listeners *get through the working day*' (2006: 64, emphasis added). Such programming is continued during 'drivetime' markets on commercial radio during the evening commute (4 p.m.–7 p.m.). One station might 'help you "survive the rush hour", presumably by stimulating enough nervous energy so that you can cope with it' as Truax speculates (2001: 170). Format radio has decreed that there are few radio listeners in the evening as most of the population is watching TV; the overnight shows (10 p.m.–6 a.m.) are, for Stewart, the one place where there is 'room for innovation' because 'little harm can be done to the listening figures or the style of the station' (2006: 67). Initially, the costs of commercial talk radio were high compared to music broadcasting, but it has become a profitable source of income for the makers of US commercial radio. One of the hallmarks of format radio is that each station's style is 'always readily identifiable' and is designed to target a specific group (Truax 2001: 162). It is indeed difficult to see where drama might fit into the highly codified schedule of commercial format radio, if not in the overnight show slot.

The logical implications of conglomerates like Clear Channel is that to make such arrangements profitable, they create a system that can be input across all the stations (Mitchell 2005: 174). In such instances, commercial stations owned by national chains are unable to afford to produce any but the cheapest programming. This creates the potential problem of radio stations failing 'to reflect their local communities very well' (Riismandel 2002: 424). In an interesting postscript, as of September 2017, Classical KHFM, now 95.5, re-formed as a community-supported, non-commercial radio, funded by a donation system, though still unaffiliated with a public-service broadcaster.

Public radio in the United States

As noted in the previous chapter, National Public Radio (NPR) was created by the Public Broadcasting Act of 1967 after President Lyndon Johnson had asked the Carnegie Foundation to make recommendations on a federally funded public/educational system. While radio may have been an afterthought to the Carnegie Commission, it was not to Johnson, a successful radio station owner himself (Flintoff and Sterling 2010: 504). With only $5 million in funding, the Corporation for Public Broadcasting (CPB) needed help, which it received from the Carnegie Commission, CBS, the Communications Workers of America and the Ford Foundation. A founding board member of NPR, Karl Schmidt wrote that NPR should be a place where:

- People talk to people
- People listen to people
- Unities as well as dissensions are explored
- Awareness of a shared humanity is emphasized
- Rhetoric is de-escalated
- Language is enriched
- Openness is risked
- The lives of people are our only concern (cited in Mitchell 2005: 413).

Some early NPR staff members wanted it to be everyone's second favourite station (Mitchell 2005: 415). This early idealism gave way to journalistic authority as time went on, and 'the familiar voices of hosts and reporters like Susan Stamberg, Nina Totenberg, and Linda Wertheimer gave audiences their first real taste of serious news from a female perspective' (Hilmes 2014: 332). NPR's news and current affairs remain paramount (its offices and studios are based in Washington DC), including *All Things Considered* (1971–present), *Morning Edition* (1979–present) and a number of programmes produced by individual stations and distributed by NPR, such as *On the Media* (1995–present, WNYC). Drama programming was never a priority to NPR, despite one of the original NPR tenets being to enrich language. Perhaps surprisingly, the only full-time drama programme on NPR was *Earplay* (1971–81), which crested a wave of nation-wide radio drama revival. This manifest in even commercial radio commissioning new anthologies in the style of OTR. *Earplay* contributed 'an experimental space on radio for young up-and-coming playwrights to practise crafting work writing for the ear' and represented collaboration with other countries' radio drama programming, such as Germany and the United Kingdom (Patterson 2016: 9–10).

Commercial OTR radio drama nostalgia

As early as 1964, radio drama was making a 'comeback' on US airwaves (Patterson 2016: 2). However, it wasn't until the 1970s that US radio networks decided to 'dust off' transcriptions of OTR drama and in some cases, create new programmes in the same mould for the 'post-network' era (Patterson 2016: 3). The result was, according to Jim Cox, 'authentic déjà vû' (2013: 148). The syndicators acquired distribution rights for *Lights Out!* (1934–47), *The Shadow* (1937–54), *The Lone Ranger* (1933–54) and other OTR programmes such as cult science-fiction anthology *Dimension X/X Minus One* (1950–51, 1955–58, NBC), re-broadcast to great acclaim in 1973. This inspired a new anthology series, *The Zero Hour* (1973–74), hosted by Rod Serling and produced by Himan Brown. Brown, an active drama-maker during the years of OTR, was responsible for the most influential series of the 1970s/1980s revival, *The CBS Radio Mystery Hour* (1974–82), a 'welcome treat to vintage radio buffs' (Cox 2013: 156). This comparatively late example of mystery literature on air won a Peabody Award. *The General Mills Radio Adventure Theater/The CBS Radio Adventure*

Theater was also produced by Brown, running between 1974 and 1978. *The Sears Radio Theater/The Mutual Radio Theater* (1979–80) tried to be all things to all listeners, giving listeners westerns on Mondays, comedies on Tuesdays, Vincent Price-introduced melodrama on Wednesdays, emotional dramas on Thursdays and adventure stories on Fridays.

On public radio, *NPR Playhouse* (1981–2002), produced by Andy Trudeau, commissioned an original series of new Sherlock Holmes dramatizations and seasons of the works of Samuel Beckett and German *hörspiel*. *NPR Playhouse* broadcast a thirteen-part dramatization of *Star Wars* (1977) in 1981, followed by *The Empire Strikes Back* (1982), and *Return of the Jedi* (1996), a project enthusiastically embraced by George Lucas. NPR's listening audience doubled during the 1981 broadcast. Using John Williams' score and Ben Burtt's original sound effects, including the nonverbal articulations of Chewbacca and R2-D2, the dramatization's length (six-and-a-half hours) de-compressed the film's story, 'meaning that the characters could be treated in more depth and the story told in more detail' (Kushner 2010: 718). Other *Playhouse* drama included serializations of *Doc Savage* in 1985 and the science-fiction/fantasy anthology show *2000^X* (2000, produced and directed by Yuri Rasovsky).

Financial difficulties within NPR as well as poor take-up from NPR affiliate stations resulted in *NPR Playhouse*'s demise in September 2002 (Crook 2010: 233). There were other short-lived radio drama offerings both on NPR and elsewhere: *Masterpiece Radio Theater* (1979–80) emulated PBS' TV *Masterpiece Theater* (1971–present) as well as the BBC's *Classic Serial*. *Alien Voices* (1996–2000), in which *Star Trek* aliens Spock and Q sparred against each other, developed a cult following (Wood 2008: 243). While not drama, *This American Life (TAL)* (1995–present), a weekly PRI-distributed programme, produced by former NPR reporter Ira Glass, has occasionally provided a forum for short drama. This has been primarily in *The Truth* (2009–present) slot by Jonathan Mitchell, whose experimental drama fits well within *TAL*, which has been said to stretch 'the boundaries of magazine-style entertainment radio with a poignant honesty' and a consummate artistic flair (Wallace 2010: 767).

NPR is the US' largest public radio producer and distributor (Flintoff and Sterling 2010: 503) but by no means the only one. This is due to the fact that in 1985, the CPB created the Radio Fund, permitting any radio organization to apply for money. NPR does not own or operate any of its member stations, with most stations licensed to universities or community groups (see KUNM in Chapter 9). Pre-dating NPR was the Pacifica Foundation, the first listener-supported, non-commercial radio network in the United States (Lasar 2010: 551). KPFA San Francisco, founded in 1954, broadcast 'poetry and music of the San Francisco Beat Generation' (Coyer 2007a: 26). KPFA was the founding station for the Pacifica network, which broadcasts from five stations[4] and 200 affiliates. KPFA 'provided an outlet for those with something important to say, even if few people were interested in hearing it' and was, as Mitchell alleges, more radical and more anti-establishment than its literary equivalent in the United Kingdom, the BBC's Third Programme (Mitchell 2002: 410) and consistently anti-war, an ethos stretching back to KPFA's founders who were conscientious objectors (Mitchell 2005: 181).

KPFA's drama broadcasts included programmes from the BBC, Canadian and Australian radio, 'but in addition KPFA produced original drama and literature programming with talents drawn from it's [sic] own community' (Bauersfeld n.d.). The Pacifica network emulated *Earplay* with *SoundPlay,* which ran between 1991 and 1992. Anthony J. Sloan's WBAI New York (a Pacifica affiliate) mid-1990s live drama productions were epic in length, 'philosophically challenging, politically controversial' with complex sound production techniques (Crook 2010: 233). Sloan was a self-taught broadcaster, specializing in dramas based on the works of black US writers (Sloan 2005). WBAI also hosted Joe Frank, who, in addition to producing and performing *Joe Frank: Work in Progress* weekly for KCRW Santa Monica between 1986 and 2002, produced radio drama between 1978 and 1984. These included *The Death of Trotsky* (1979) and *Across the River* (1984) (Frank 2015).

The San Francisco area has proven particularly receptive over the years to radio drama, with Bay Area Radio Drama (BARD) forming in 1987 (Bauersfeld n.d.). All BARD productions were first broadcast on KPFA, but those with outside funding remained the property of BARD and were re-broadcast on NPR, the BBC and WDR Köln (Germany) as well as Public Radio International (see below). BARD collaborated with Earwax Studios editing the sound production for KCRW's 29-part dramatization of Sinclair Lewis's *Babbitt* (1922). BARD's output has included a dramatization of *The Horla* (1992), a series of adapted horror stories, *Black Mass* (1963–70) and the *Hörspiel/USA* project (1981–92).

Another thread in US public radio drama is Public Radio Exchange (PRX), which began in 2003 'as a means of encouraging and enabling independent producers to place their material on public radio stations' (Mitchell and Sterling 2010: 62). Most public radio stations in the United States are members of NPR, PRI (formerly APR, see below) and PRX concurrently, and some belong to the Pacifica network. Individual stations have access to independently produced drama. 'Together, APM and PRI began the diversification process that revolutionized US public radio in the 90s, just as digital platforms began to emerge' (Hilmes 2013: 53).

With a final nod to KHFM, radio dramatist and actor Rick Huff's commercial spots on KHFM for local Albuquerque business Lieber's Luggage could be considered a form of (zany) short-form radio drama; Huff was part of Albuquerque's Southwestern Writers Workshop Radio Theatre, writing and performing dramas for radio distributed on tape cassette. No doubt many other US cities had similar initiatives. The potential zaniness and lack of discernible categorization also typifies the Firesign Theatre, described as a 'surrealist humour ensemble', a 'four-man comedy troupe of Phil Austin, Phil Proctor, Peter Bergman and David Ossman […] theater of the mind' who released LPs in the 1960s and 1970s and came to NPR in the noughties (NPR n.d.).

Activist radio and the LPFM movement

As has become evident, radio drama in the United States has often been produced by activist, community and/or non-commercial radio. LPFM stations are authorized for noncommercial broadcasting and cannot be operated by a company or an individual; their purpose is for community and education. They are so named because the service range of an LPFM station is roughly 3.5 miles radius. LPFM has been described as a direct result of 'pirate' stations (also called activist radio), such as WTRA, spearheaded by Mbanna Kantako in Springfield, Illinois. Operating without a licence from 1987, WTRA (later Human Rights Radio) was ignored by authorities 'until it broke a story about what became a high-profile police brutality case' (Coyer 2007a: 26). The National Association of Broadcasters (NAB) and NPR lobbied throughout the late 1990s and early noughties against LPFM because they said it would cause frequency interference for other communications media, a historically persistent fear (a concern that Riismandel finds difficult to take seriously, 2002: 442). LPFM became an 'explosively controversial topic' (Riismandel 2002: 423). In 2000, there were around 200 community radio stations in the United States, out of 12,000 nationwide. This is in contrast to the many radio stations in small Latin American countries that 'serve rural and urban communities with content that is appropriate to the local language, culture, and needs' (Hilliard and Keith 2005: 187).

When LPFM was launched in 2000, 590 stations went on air. However, users of LPFM would have to wait until 2011 before President Barack Obama passed the Local Community Radio Act that 'modified the technical restrictions' on licensing LPFM (Doyle 2012: 34). Part of the law opens up diversity of viewpoints by allowing for more LPFM, which Doyle calls 'an opportunity for the largest expansion of community radio in US history' (Doyle 2012: 34). Chambers (2012) sees evidence that LPFMs slow duplicating formats and may be seeking out new types of radio audiences, a potential for diversified radio content such as drama (see KZMU in Chapter 9). Public radio in the United States is clearly complex and does not uniformly include drama programming in its schedules. Therefore, other means have arisen to satisfy listeners' cravings.

Audiobooks

Audiobooks gave rise to new strands of US radio drama in the 1990s and noughties. In 2010, Trudi M. Rosenblum reported that movie tie-ins, the Internet and innovative promotions – such as free audio play giveaways in hotels – brought new fans to the genre. Stuffed Moose Audio, Spirited Yarns, Little Evil Things and Ziplow Productions were among the trailblazers, though Rosenblum reported that the first audio theatre title to be broadcast on the Internet was Patrick Seaman and Jim Cline's *A Small Percentage,* released on Broadcast.com in 2005 (Rosenblum 2010: 42). The high cost of casting – between $5,000 and $20,000 per show in 2010 – meant that a title that sold between 5000 and 10,000 copies was considered a success. Perhaps unsurprisingly, 'truck stops welcome audio theatre, particularly westerns and science fiction' (Rosenblum 2010: 42). Tim Crook suggested that in the early noughties, a niche interest in the radio western was created by Charles Potter and Random House (2010: 233).

The audio drama cassette market had its own fans and production companies, including Ziggurat, ZBS Foundation, Atlanta Radio Theatre, The Radio Repertory Company of

America, Shoestring Radio Theatre and Hollywood Theater of the Ear. The latter was executive produced and directed by Yuri Rasovsky between 1993 and his death in 2012. A prominent figure in US post-OTR radio and audio drama, Rasovsky had been artistic director of the National Radio Theater of Chicago between 1972 and 1986. He produced and directed hundreds of broadcast radio dramas, from re-stagings of OTR to classic stage plays like Aristophanes' *The Frogs* (405 BC) to staples of the BBC's Third Programme repertoire to pieces he authored himself. Many of his productions featured star-studded casts, such as *Craven Street: Ben Franklin in London* (1993), starring Nigel Hawthorne, David Warner and Martin Sheen (Rasovsky n.d.).

A Prairie Home Companion

Though not strictly radio drama, it is impossible to tell the story of US public radio and its potential as a venue for drama without Garrison Keillor's *A Prairie Home Companion* (1974–2016), despite recent allegations of improper behaviour that have clouded Keillor's profile (Ohlheiser 2017). Keillor's Lake Wobegon stories capitalize on a rich vein of nostalgic longing, wherein 'the memory of both the sound and its context has been idealized' (Truax 2001: 79). This is in many ways similar to Jean Shepherd's 1930s/1940s Indiana on late night WOR New York radio in the 1960s, dramatized in *In God We Trust, All Others Must Pay Cash* (1969) (and later, and very famously, in the film *A Christmas Story* [1983]). Kip Allen characterizes *Prairie Home Companion*'s 'nostalgic feeling' as the 'past you never had but wanted' (2013a). As explained by Michael Nelson, *Prairie Home Companion* began in the 1970s when Garrison Keillor hosted public radio programmes in Minnesota; it was here he developed the blend of 'live and recorded music, dramatic serials, comedy skits, mock commercials and greetings and announcements' that would prove successful enough to make *Prairie Home Companion* a national commodity by 1980. *A Prairie Home Companion* was produced by American Public Radio (APR), a Minnesota-based group of stations financed by the Radio Fund on a model based on PBS, scheduling and promoting national programmes produced by individual stations. *Prairie Home Companion*'s format had been rejected by NPR as 'elitist and patronising to middle-American values' (Flintoff and Sterling 2010: 507). After a respite between 1987 and 1989, the show returned and spawned an industry including novels such as *Lake Wobegon Days* (1985) and a film (2006). The programme's title, suggesting that 'radio is your companion as we head toward our ultimate prairie home', reflects Keillor's religious devotion (Nelson 2001). This is appropriate as Nelson has convincingly argued that the style, format and content of live *Prairie Home Companion* performances at the Fitzgerald Theatre in St. Paul, Minnesota are similar to a religious service.

However, the name of Keillor's fictional 'home town' speaks to a different reference point. The *Lake Wobegon* books include 'satirical gibes at small-town provincialism' that refer to Keillor's childhood among the Minnesota Plymouth Brethren (Nelson 2001: 10). Now a Lutheran, Keillor has successfully transformed the fundamentalist restrictions of his childhood – including the interdiction against listening to radio – into a source for entertainment and community (Keillor's background is Scottish, not Norwegian as commonly believed from the Norwegian-American characters that inhabit *Prairie Home Companion*). Furthermore, Keillor's storytelling religious background and deep-seated love of writing are transformed into tour-de-force when he performs his twenty-minute monologue about Lake Wobegon during *Prairie Home Companion.* Composed rather like BBC features of the 1930s, his monologues are written as 'a perfect blend of spontaneity and careful preparation' (Nelson 2001: 2). It is clear that Keillor values this kind of writing/performance; in 2005 he praised the other 'great artists of public radio' for their simulated spontaneity, including Terry Gross, Ira Glass and the *Car Talk* (1977–2012) Brothers (Keillor 2005 n.pag.). *Prairie Home Companion* remains highly visible and highly influential as a form of radio with dramatic elements.

Conclusion

The many strands of US PSB have fostered radio drama from time to time, as have commercial, community and activist radio, as well as audiobooks. In the United Kingdom, radio drama in the last 50 years has primarily found a home on the BBC but has likewise been found, infrequently, on commercial broadcasting. Far less well-researched than the rose-tinted past of OTR and early BBC radio drama history, this more recent period provides a fascinating mix of philosophically stimulating plays with roots in stage performance as well as more populist serials and comedies.

Notes

1. There is no official 'watershed' policy for radio in the United Kingdom as there is for TV.
2. IRDP's output is unfortunately no longer available, but its website is still online as a valuable archive.
3. David King Dunaway (2014) describes a similar process with KPCC FM Pasadena when it was bought in 2000 by APM.
4. KPFA Berkeley, KPFK Los Angeles, WBAI New York City, KPFT Houston, WPFW Washington.

Section III

Audio Drama Today

Chapter 8

Current British Audio Drama

> The idea of one radio station being all things to all men and women was formally abandoned in favour of four stations being four things to four sides of everyone.
>
> – Kevin D'Arcy (2007: 27)

Chris Patten, chairman of the BBC Trust from 2011 to 2014, declared, 'when people who work for the BBC talk to audiences or people from outside the United Kingdom, they're reminded what a fantastic national institution it is' (cited in Smith 2013: 29). The BBC's international reputation in, for example, the United States, is considerable. The apparent monolithic status of the BBC masks for many international admirers the fact that BBC Radio has for many decades walked a similar fine line to the one traced by NPR. Over the years, the BBC has been taken to task by some for being 'toffee-nosed' while others accuse it of dumbing-down or even of corrupting morals. These criticisms are specifically important to its radio drama reputation due to this book's focus on the accessibility of audio drama generally for wide audiences. The 1980s and 1990s represented unprecedented criticism of the BBC, but such criticism remains current, when the place of a licence fee in modern British society is fiercely debated (cf. Lévesque-Bartlett n.d.). As one extreme example, Boris Johnson, Conservative MP and then-editor of *The Spectator,* said in 1999,

> We men of moderate opinions are prepared to support the existence of this anomalous nationalised industry, this weird system of taxpayer-funded outdoor relief for 22,000 media folk, even if, in our hearts, we know that Norman Tebbit is right to say it is full of pinkos. For decades our wrath has been bated by the knowledge that it has produced some first-rate stuff. Dimly, inarticulately, we acknowledge that there is some kind of case for public service broadcasting.
>
> (cited in Born 2005: 4)

The BBC is 'blasted and buffeted on every side by powerful and ruthless enemies', Charlotte Higgins concluded (2015: 230).

Tim Crook, although often critical of BBC radio drama, notes that there is by no means 'a snowballing decline of BBC radio drama and the potential extinction of a great tradition' as is so often suggested (1999b). Radio 4 remains its primary home, with a mission to 'appeal to listeners seeking intelligent programmes in many genres which inform, educate and entertain' (Hodgson 2014: 9).[1] In 2004, Frances Gray noted that 8.87 million people would listen to Radio 4 in any given week, an audience share of 10.8 per cent of the total audience for radio in the

United Kingdom (2009: 253). In 2006, 9.3 million listened to Radio 4, which equates to 18.7 per cent of the then-British radio public. The average listener that year spent 13 hours a week with Radio 4. By 2007, that figure had risen to 9.5 million who tuned in at some point every week (Hendy 2007: 1). In 2017, a record-breaking 11.55 million tuned into Radio 4 each week (Terry 2017). Despite the repeated criticisms of the BBC generally – that it alternately dumbs down content or looks down upon ordinary people – the longevity and continued success of BBC Radio Drama is due to its engagement with serial continuity and a range of genres and forms to balance its output. It can achieve the latter only by ensuring the former.

Structure and strands

The BBC operates under a Royal Charter, and from 2007 to 2017 was governed by the BBC Trust. The BBC Trust was replaced by regulator Ofcom after criticism regarding transparency and a change in political government in the United Kingdom in 2010. Radio drama on the BBC is funded, as is all BBC programming, through the licence fee. The licence fee funds 54 BBC radio stations (including 10 national stations) (Ramsey 2017: 91). The director-general of the BBC is Lord Tony Hall. The director of BBC Radio at the time of writing is Helen Boaden. Under the director are the controller of production and deputy director; the head of group operations; and the finance and business manager. There are eight controllers, including controller of Radio 4 and Radio 4 Extra (at the time of writing, Gwyneth Williams). The head of drama (at the time of writing, Alison Hindell), reports to the controller of product. Her primary clients are the controllers of Radio 4 and the controller of Radio 3. According to the 2013 Radio 4 Service Licence, the service budget for 2013/14 was £94 million. 16 per cent of the television licence fee (£653 million) is spent on radio (Ramsey 2017: 90).

The contemporary production imperatives within BBC Radio Drama are not well documented in academic or popular literature on audio drama. Through interviews with Alison Hindell (2011, 2014), Caroline Raphael (2014) and Sharon Terry (2017), the workings of the BBC Radio Drama system were briefly explained to me. For example, the head of drama supervises editorial concerns United Kingdom-wide for in-house productions. Each geographical base has its own local manager, not a drama specialist but an administrative manager who manages staffing and budget issues. Under these managers, each core drama team is led by an editor. This person also produces his or her own programmes and is, in essence, the executive producer on all programmes produced by the teams he or she manages. The producers within each group also have production coordinators or production assistants to support them. Outside of this hierarchy are commissioners who operate within the networks and commission work both in-house and from independents for their relevant networks. Under the supervision of the head and their local editors, producers pitch ideas, which are sometimes brought to their attention through writers and are sometimes the ideas of the producers themselves. A successful project which is produced has gone through a lengthy and complex process by which it has been approved locally and then by the network commissioner. Generally, the producer who has pitched the work directs it once approved. If a producer is too over-committed to direct a project, he or she has a discussion with the head of drama and with the commissioner as to who should follow through with the project.

In response to many Radio 4 listeners objecting to 'the implied endorsement of the establishment and established religion' (Hodgson 2014: 201), in 2010, the Religious Broadcasting Department was renamed Religion and Ethics, reflecting a shift towards more inclusive religious programming. In addition to programmes like *Prayer for the Day* (1970–present), *Beyond Belief* (2005–present) and *Thought for the Day* (1970–present), Radio 4 maintains a specialty in dramas that reflect the Christian liturgical calendar, particularly at Easter, such as Nick Warburton's *Witness* (2009), and *Bach: The Great Passion* in 2017, a drama with significant use of music from Bach's Easter composition.

The continuing importance of regions within the BBC Radio Drama output is best illustrated with BBC Radio Wales and Radio Cymru and BBC Radio Scotland and Radio Nan Gaidheal. Wales represents the highest levels of radio listening in the United Kingdom (Johnson and Mitchell 2012: 7). Despite the fact that in some areas in Wales, 'broadcasts from London-based radio channels can be heard more easily than BBC Radio Wales or Radio Cymru', the latter is notable for creating original content, including drama, in the Welsh language (Johnson and Mitchell 2012: 8). BBC Radio Wales and Radio Cymru now have the highest reach of any in Wales, though the most listened-to stations in Wales are still BBC Radio 1 and Radio 2 (Johnson and Mitchell 2012: 12).

The BBC Asian Network initiated a radio serial, *Silver Street,* whose demise in 2010 was in fact debated in the House of Commons, firstly in 2009 and then again in 2010, where its supporters included Lynne Jones and Jeremy Corbyn. The motion welcomed 'the BBC's commitment to distinctive drama but expresses concern that the total yearly volume of drama on the Asian network will be reduced from 21 to six hours' (UK Parliament 2010). Created in 2004, *Silver Street* was script-edited and then produced by Naylah Ahmed and featured both Asian and non-Asian writers. It was available through DAB and Freeview and was Birmingham-based (Kennedy 2013).

Ken Garner has found that radio drama is particularly well-served in Scotland and that its audience is content with its radio choices. The current Scottish radio market is characterized by Britain-wide networks from London, Scottish national radio services from the BBC – Radio Scotland and Radio Nan Gaidheal, the Gaelic-language service – as in Wales, which dates essentially from the 1970s (Garner 2012: 43). In 1992, Garner found, BBC Radio Scotland was reaching nearly 1 million people, close to one-quarter of Scotland's population. BBC Radio Scotland produces a weekly half-hour comedy slot, and since 2006, a dozen new dramas per year. *Off the Ball*, a radio comedy about football, has been on BBC Radio Scotland since the 1990s. Comedy and drama 'are seen as touchstones of commitment to the national creative industries, both by listeners […] and by policy-makers' (Garner 2012: 52). Radio in Scotland 'has been experiencing a high-velocity onslaught of policy initiatives and proposals for legislative change since 2007' (Garner 2012: 40).

Currently, approximately 50 per cent of BBC radio's drama output originates in London and 20 per cent originates in the North region (Manchester as well as other suppliers based in northern England) (Terry 2017). The rest of the drama output is produced in Wales, Northern Ireland, Bristol and Scotland, with the latter contributing the most out of this final category. *The Archers* originates out of Birmingham, as does the 2014–18 series *Home Front*. Approximately 70 per cent of dramas, including *The Archers,* are made in-house and the rest produced by independent production companies.

As Ramsey (2017) has detailed, BBC Radio's output has been increasingly regulated through the lens of 'public value'. In the BBC's own policy document from 2004, public value was iterated as serving audiences

> not just as consumers, but as members of a wider society, with programmes and services which, while seeking to inform, educate and entertain audiences, also serve wider public purposes. Public value is a measure of the BBC's contribution to the quality of life in the UK.
>
> (BBC 2004: 7–8)

The policy-changing document of 2016, *A BBC for the Future,* noted that £88 million was currently spent on Radio 4 (2016: 39).

Radio drama on Radio 3 is usually confined to *Drama on 3* (2002–present), which continues the Third Programme's reputation for more cerebral, edgier drama. On Radio 4, the current drama slots are *15 Minute Drama* (formerly *Woman's Hour Drama* and still a broadcast serial after *Woman's Hour* [1946–present], five days a week), *The Archers* (at 7:00 p.m., repeated at 2:00 p.m., five days a week), *Afternoon Drama* (formerly *Afternoon Play,* a 45-minute slot five days a week), *Classic Serial* (one hour, broadcast Sundays) and *The Saturday Drama* (2008–present) (one hour). A week night 6:30 p.m. slot produces a half-hour of radio comedy, including sketch shows and sitcoms. There are also occasional comedy/drama series in the late morning (11:00 or 11:30 a.m.) and late night (11:00 p.m.) (which are not included in Table 1).

Table 1: Typical Radio 3 and Radio 4 schedule of drama (all appear on Radio 4 unless otherwise indicated).

	Sunday	Monday	Tuesday	Wednesday	Thursday	Friday[2]	Saturday
10:45–11:00		15 Minute Drama	15 Minute Drama	15 Minute Drama	15 Minute Drama	15 Minute Drama	
14:15–15:00		Afternoon Drama	Afternoon Drama	Afternoon Drama	Afternoon Drama	Afternoon Drama	
14:30–15:30							Saturday Drama
15:00–16:00	Classic Serial						
19:00–19:15		The Archers	The Archers	The Archers	The Archers	The Archers	
19:30–21:00	Drama on 3 (Radio 3)						

Woman's Hour, one of BBC Radio's longest-running programmes, launched in 1946, has featured a drama slot (a 15-minute serial) since its inception. Its remit and structure has remained virtually unchanged, other than a 1990 change from afternoon to morning (and it resisted a name change vetoed by public outcry). Mirroring the overall Radio 4 audience, its audience is found to be predominantly older, middle-class, educated and white (Minić 2013: 308). While *Woman's Hour* has seen much analysis from radio scholars, almost no attention has been paid to its drama output.

BBC radio drama, body of work: Statistics

As suggested in previous chapters, it is difficult to generalize about BBC radio drama given its volume. In his 2008 thesis, Roger Wood decided to take a quantitative approach to British radio drama for the year 2006. This was reasonable, given that 'no one could possibly listen to 677 hours of product, not counting *The Archers, Silver Street* or anything on BBC 7' (2008: 26). A qualitative and quantitative approach, nevertheless, seemed the most worthwhile option for building up an accurate picture of BBC radio drama, which I adopted for the year 2012.[3]

The methodological focus was on number of hours of new drama (defined by first transmission date), rather than including repeat material. (Please see Appendix 1 for a longer prose write-up of these statistics.) In 2012, the *Afternoon Drama* slot broadcast over 114 hours of new content, the equivalent of 25.4% of the entire Radio 4 and Radio 3 drama output.[4] The *15 Minute Drama,* formerly known as *Woman's Hour Drama,* was heard in excess of 59 hours. The *Classic Serial* was roughly equivalent to those figures in both hour-production and percentage. Over 37 hours were produced on Radio 3 for *Drama on 3.* In addition to these regular drama slots on Radio 4 and Radio 3, new series of either drama or comedy in varying lengths were a regular occurrence each week in 2012. New series hours totalled 83.25. Furthermore, *The Archers* produced an impressive 65 hours in 2012, along with 19.5 hours of *Ambridge Extra* (2011–13). BBC Radio 4 Extra, although primarily an archive of past productions, also produced 30 new hours of radio drama (Raphael 2014).[5] With nearly 450 hours produced in regular slots for Radio 3 and Radio 4, 84.5 hours of *The Archers/Ambridge Extra* and 30 hours produced by Radio 4 Extra, BBC radio drama production in 2012 in total was around 564 hours. Alison Hindell (2014) confirmed that the ballpark figure for drama production on Radio 4 and Radio 3 in a year is equivalent to 500 hours (including repeats but excluding Radio 4 Extra productions). This was in keeping with Radio 4's Service Licence, released in May 2013, which vowed to broadcast at least 600 hours of original drama and readings[6] each year, excluding repeats (2013: 5). The BBC's analysis of its performance against public commitments (2014–15) continued this statistical pledge, producing 617 hours of drama, 68 hours of comedy weekly, 66 hours of drama weekly, while ensuring that only 7% of Radio 4's programming was catch up (meaning that 93% was original) (2016: 10).

BBC radio drama: Range of work

Is there any validity to the notion that BBC radio drama is made up entirely of cosy contemporary stories, or all adaptations, or all historical works? In pursuing my quantitative approach, I also recorded statistics on BBC Radio Drama in 2012 as *range* of work in addition to *body* of work. These statistics look at genre, form and type, so far as can be determined. A *range* of output has been crucial to BBC drama ethos; even if serious plays were the only ones worthy of Val Gielgud's attention, for example, such attitudes have changed. Gielgud, it may be recalled, liked to present stage drama on BBC Radio and was happiest when commissioning adaptations of stage pieces. Later drama producers like Martin Esslin preferred contemporary European theatre, and later still, John Tydeman seemed to enjoy producing contemporary British satire, ranging from *Adrian Mole* (1982) to Rhys Adrian's cynical two-handers. Over the years, the 'typical' Radio 4 drama has come to represent any number of things, but the *whole* should include all the categories above and more.

In 2012, by a slight margin (53%), most dramas on Radio 4 and Radio 3 were set in the present day.[7] 35% of dramas were set in a clearly defined historical past. The third category, which I invented for the purposes of statistic-gathering, was 'other', used for plays that were parables, allegories, speculative fiction or spent a significant amount of their scope in settings both contemporary and historic; for example drama in which a significant amount of the action was in 'flashback'. Perhaps surprisingly, such drama accounted for just under 13%.[8] This data suggests that, in 2012 at least, a clear emphasis was placed on plays with a contemporary setting, though there was obvious variety in other categories.

The concept of adaptations into radio form has become increasingly sophisticated. During radio drama's earliest days, adaptation from stage was de rigeur, initially out of necessity, though later film-to-radio adaptations were popular. By 2012, adaptation continued to employ a range of source material. That year there were 50 adaptations from novels on Radio 4 and Radio 3. Interestingly, only twelve stage plays were adapted during the year on Radio 4 and Radio 3. Just over 10 per cent of hour-production adaptations in 'other' categories were produced in 2012 (see Appendix 1 for more details). Adaptations from languages other than English were comparatively scarce in 2012. In total, there were twelve works adapted from non-British English-speaking sources, the majority of them US novels of the twentieth century. The full-day adaptation of James Joyce's *Ulysses* (1922) represented the single adaptation from Irish literature, while two plays written by Louis Nowra and produced in Australia represented the Antipodes.

Range of work: Anecdotal evidence

These statistics give a general picture of the output on Radio 3 and Radio 4 in 2012. I have chosen now to take the qualitative approach and examine in more detail the works that were produced as detailed above. Based on these findings, BBC radio drama can fairly claim that its current repertoire is varied and wide-ranging. What is the function of adaptations on BBC radio within the scheduling continuity? BBC radio has been adapting classic novels since 1925 (*Westward Ho!* [1855]). How varied were they in 2012, in terms of theme, plot, genre and source categorization? A new production of *The Count of Monte Cristo* (1844) was the longest *Classic Serial* in 2012. In three parts, Thomas Mann's epic of nineteenth-century merchant life, *Buddenbrooks* (1901), was a cornerstone of *Classic Serials* translated from other European languages in 2012. At the beginning of the year, a new adaptation and translocation of *Martin Chuzzlewit* (1843–49), newly titled *The Mumbai Chuzzlewits* by Ayeesha Menon, transposed the action of the nineteenth-century novel to contemporary India in three parts, with fascinating results. Produced and directed by John Dryden, this vision of Dickens' novel was recorded on location in India. Adaptations from the novel form that were perhaps more modern in their flavour were John Wyndham's science-fiction novel *The Chrysalids* (1955), produced by Nadia Molinari; Robert M. Pirsil's *Zen and the Art of Motorcycle Maintenance* (1974), produced by Melanie Harris and Malorie Blackman's futuristic young adult series *Noughts and Crosses* (2001), produced by Marion Nancarrow. Not all of these productions were necessarily deemed successful by radio reviewers, but they did show that *Classic Serials* were not confined to nineteenth-century triple-deckers.

As noted above, fewer stage plays than perhaps might be expected were adapted for radio in 2012, though those that were adapted showed a considerable range. One was the Arnold Wesker socialist classic, *Chicken Soup with Barley* (1959), broadcast live, from stage performance, in the *Drama on 3* slot. *Tamburlaine* (1587) by Christopher Marlowe was a jump back of nearly four hundred years directed by Peter Kavanagh on *Drama on 3*. David Hare's popular 2011 Chichester Festival stage play, *South Downs,* especially commissioned to play opposite Terence Rattigan's drama *The Browning Version* (1948), was sensitively adapted for radio. One of the most interesting stage play adaptations of 2012 was Tamika Gupta's reworking of Ibsen's *A Doll's House* (1879) to a colonialist Indian setting in *Drama on 3*.[9] An adaptation of this kind follows in the footsteps of past BBC radio adaptation successes, particularly Ronald Mason's *Plain Tales from the Raj* (1974–75), which Elmes called a 'mesmerizing' attempt at capturing 'the often unedifying experiences of British colonial rule' (2008: 131). Considered against the entire Radio 3 and Radio 4 schedule, the number of adapted stage plays is rather small, especially compared to novels.

Perhaps one of the most surprising findings in this data collection was how much speculative fiction was broadcast on Radio 4 and Radio 3 in 2012. Despite BBC Radio Drama's reputation for cosy drama of 'everyday country folk', or its long history with the *Classic Serial* and adaptation, there is also a prestigious and overlooked sub-genre of BBC speculative stories. In the early years of BBC Radio, Lance Sieveking's broadcast works included at least two speculative fiction plays. Radio 4 Extra (and BBC Radio 7 before it) had an interesting function, which has addressed, up to a point, Wood's (2008) concern for the availability of archival programming, making available programmes as diverse as archival *Hancock's Half Hour* (1954–61) to *The Revenge* (1978). However, its brief was also to provide for more 'family-friendly' drama offerings and more niche interests, one of which could well be described as 'speculative fiction' (Raphael 2014). BBC Radio 4 Extra has a dedicated science-fiction slot in the early hours of the morning known as *The Seventh Dimension* (2003–present), and it is true that a good deal of archival material that can be heard on Radio 4 Extra to this day could be characterized as horror or science fiction.

Without such a dedicated slot, however, on Radio 4 and Radio 3, the two channels cover a very wide range of thought-provoking speculative fiction. 'Speculative fiction' includes within it science fiction, fantasy and certain types of satire that posits a different world to the one we know in order to make a point. Speculative fiction accounted for 66 hours and 14.6 per cent of the total drama output on Radio 4 and Radio 3. The majority of these dramas were heard in the *Afternoon Drama* slot with the others spread more or less evenly amongst other slots; however, there was an unusually high number of new speculative fiction comedy series broadcast during the summer of 2012, and an understandably higher number in October during the Gothic Imagination Season, in the *Classic Serial* slot. Roughly one-third of the speculative fiction dramas in total were comedies. A special 2012 Olympic Games-inspired half-hour drama broadcast on Radio 2 recorded in front of a live audience, *Welcome to Our Village, Please Invade Carefully* by Eddie Robson, was more a satire on British village life as personified in Cresdon Green, than an attempt at hard science fiction.[10] On the other end of the spectrum is a series loosely described as creative nonfiction, written by Jon Canter and produced by Clive Brill, based on the life of British actor Richard Wilson, *Believe It!* (2012–18)[11] As one reviewer wrote, 'like all the best tales, it's difficult to tell where the truth really ends' (Manning 2012: 127).

In its single dramas, too, BBC radio drama shows a good degree of range. The two poles of criticism levelled at the BBC, as mentioned at the beginning of this chapter, would suggest that BBC Radio Drama is either all over-intellectualized, edgy, foul-mouthed drama, or all cosy, too-safe, too-sweet serial adaptations. The truth is that both tendencies are present, but returning to the concept of BBC radio drama 'range', much is found in between. For example, *Erebus,* broadcast on Thursday 12 January 2012 in the *Afternoon Drama* slot, was written by poet Jo Shapcott, mixing poetic monologues with factual information about ice and excerpts from historical documents. The drama told the true story of a doomed nineteenth-century expedition to the Arctic, 'that is by turns bleak, elemental and poignant' (Anderson 2012a: 136). This contrasted with Kwame Kwei-Armah's *Father, Son, and Holy Ghost* (2012). A 'tough but brilliant listen', investigating the world of Afro-Caribbean church communities in London, the play 'examines the consequences of inter-generational conflict' and 'the vexed question of church finances' (Raw 2012).

The reason BBC Radio is able to offer a wide range in programming is due to continuity in scheduling and a marked stress on serials and series. It is obvious when reading the *Radio Times* that programming has a strong tendency towards the cyclical. Longer works are serialized in five or ten parts, spread over the week, in *15 Minute Drama*. With increasing frequency, the *Afternoon Drama* is part of a series of two to five related plays. Series continue in the same slot on a particular day each week for up to six weeks. *The Archers* remains a fixture at 7:00 p.m. (with repeats at 2 p.m.) on weekdays throughout the year and maintains its continuity as a single serial. The advantages of this heavy emphasis on serialization and series are two-fold: firstly, in terms of resources and as a 'selling point', a successful series is more economical. If listeners have enjoyed a series in its first run, there is less risk involved in giving them a second series of the same. Secondly, reinforcing the idea of 'wait until next week to find out more' creates a loyal audience that feels secure within its radio schedule. If 'a particular voice comes to contain a specific time of day' in speech radio, knowing what to expect in form if not content can be reassuring (Karpf 2013: 67).

With an emphasis on series and serials, how does BBC Radio Drama of today escape the trap of monotony engendered within US network radio in the late 1940s? There is an effective tension between form and content. In form, the short-term series may be quite circumscribed, though their length does vary between fifteen and 45 minutes per episode, as does their scheduling (between four and ten episodes). For example, *Clare in the Community*, which debuted in 2004, epitomized the contemporary BBC series. Written by Harry Venning and David Ramsden, it was considered 'an instant hit, catching the PC tone of our times' (Elmes 2008: 132). This kind of comic drama is well-suited to a format that stresses continuity. *Clare in the Community* began as a comic strip drawn for *The Guardian* by Venning, and the radio series sometimes breaks the fourth wall by referring to the strip. By 2014, the show was on its ninth series and still, apparently, as relevant as ever: its eighth series ended in 'incredible form, in an episode allying absurdism, pratfalls and a rearguard action against the mother-in-law' (Petty 2013).

The *15 Minute Drama*, long known somewhat pejoratively as the *Woman's Hour Serial*, also shows a good range of material, from a series of Hattie Naylor's popular adaptations of Samuel Pepys' diaries to Robert Forrest's tenth-century Japanese romantic thriller *The Pillow Book*. The range of the *15 Minute Drama* was tested by the politically charged *An Everyday Story of Afghan Folk* (2012), which was translated from Pashtun from a series of PACT-created radio soap operas broadcast to the border area between Pakistan and Afghanistan. The tongue-in-cheek English title acknowledged the complex ties between the drama produced for PACT and *The Archers*, exploring 'the conflict between religion and tribal law' (Crawford 2012: 130).

Beyond the forms that were already suitable for serialization, Radio 4 and Radio 3 have a tendency to create 'seasons' that organize themes around which to pin drama and create a sense of continuity. This is, of course, similar to Radio 3's thematic programming with certain classical music composers or types of music. In drama, these seasons can (and tend) to capture quite large and complex concepts. In 2012, for example, Mike Walker continued his contemporary dramatization of *Holinshed's Chronicles of England* with his series *Plantagenet*, this time on the reigns of Richard II, Henry IV and Richard III; produced by Jeremy Mortimer and directed by Sasha Yevtushenko, these plays used very traditional themes – the English monarchy – in Walker's characteristically adult style. The 2012 Olympics in London spawned a loose conglomeration of themed drama, but one particular aspect of British culture was celebrated in Radio 3's Shakespeare Season that year, including new stagings of *Twelfth Night, Romeo and Juliet* and *The Tempest,* which were recorded in front of a live audience. 'The Gothic Imagination' was a banner title for a series of interrelated dramas in October 2012, including new adaptations of *Frankenstein* (1818) and *Dracula* (1897), a radio version of Howard Brenton's *Bloody Poetry* (1984), and several new dramas on Radio 4 Extra. The Mystery Plays on *The Essay* celebrated Advent in the Christian calendar, as did *The People's Passion* for Easter. Five dramas, written by Nick Warburton and directed by Jonquil Panting, these were set in a fictional cathedral and echoed in a contemporary setting the themes attendant on the last days in the life of Christ.

Finally, it is difficult to find a genre more beloved on contemporary British radio than the crime drama. In forms both comic and deadly serious, one could find permutations in each of the weekly drama slots as well as in new series. Most of these were adaptations from novels, such as Ian Rankin's Edinburgh-based sleuth, Rebus, in *The Black Book* (Rankin 2008); Joyce Porter's darkly comic Inspector Dover and a reworking of three of Georges Simenon's standalone novels in the *Afternoon Drama* slot. Scottish writer David Ashton's police inspector, McLevy returned for another series in December. Amelia Bullmore's eponymous Manchester-based DI *Craven* produced by Justine Potter, dominated the schedule in 2012, putting in three separate appearances. The trend for Nordic noir was fulfilled by a five-part serialization of Maj Sjowall and Per Wahloo's *The Martin Beck Killings* (1965–75) in the *Saturday Drama* slot, produced by Sara Davies, over six hours of drama.

In conclusion, BBC Radio Drama succeeds with its philosophy in providing something for everyone at least some of the time by using its repetition and continuity to balance out its range of genres. It has, as David Hendy has pointed out, survived on a diet of 'continuity and change' (2013a: 3).

Audiences

The average listening audience for a Radio 4 *Afternoon Drama* is just under 1 million, according to Hindell (2014), with listenership peaking early in the week. Weekly listening figures in 2014 according to RAJAR were 2.66 million (Hodgson 2014: 17). No one programme can be held up as the most listened-to drama of all time on BBC Radio, as statistics are measured in three-month periods rather than on a programme-by-programme basis (Raphael 2014). Hindell noted that the average weekly listening audience for Radio 4 has been steadily rising over the past five years and remains at a steady 10.4 million. However, the amount of time each listener has spent listening has been decreasing, suggesting, as she has noted, that listening habits are changing to encapsulate shorter listening periods. Simon Elmes has attributed several factors to the changing habits of listeners in the United Kingdom. Over the past 40 years, he notes, more people have been living alone and working from home. People are, he says, 'less willing to defer to authority and more willing to make their own judgement on a growing number of issues' (2008: 37). Naturally, the abundance of podcasts and other listening options also plays a part. Chris Patten believes 'the BBC has to endlessly balance, to reach and also challenge the audience' (Smith 2013: 33). BBC Radio, and Radio 4 in particular, have very ardent supporters. 'Even if Britain does not have an intelligentsia, it does have Radio Four', Kevin D'Arcy wrote, elevating Radio 4's audience to a moral and political compass by the dint of the fact those who listen to it are among the most influential in the country (2007: 42). Such an elevation is not new – David Hendy wrote that Radio 4 was considered more influential than Parliament or the Church of England in a 1972 poll of men and women listed in *Who's Who* (2007: 117).

Who is the average Radio 4 listener? Hindell found it difficult to offer generalizations when I asked her to describe the average BBC radio drama listener, but did admit that the core audience tends to be more female than male,[12] middle class and aged 55 or older (strikingly similar in makeup to the core audience for NPR in the United States). Hendy believed that the core Radio 4 audience could be defined by some characteristics, such as its 'pragmatism, understatement, mild eccentricity, and willingness to laugh at' itself (2007: 1). Christian Brochand in his history of French radio wrote of the 'ossification' that took place on national radio channels in the 1960s, and it is well-known that 'for an older generation especially', Radio 4 is 'a legacy of the close rapport with a Home Service many grew up listening to during and after the War' (Hendy 2007: 7). When I asked Alison Hindell what sort of audiences she, as the head of drama, wished to attract, she replied, '[l]arge and varied. Young audiences are not the Holy Grail for R4' (2014). 'Most producers' on the BBC, as Hendy found,

> regard their tasks simply as ensuring that a richer range of human activity reaches the screen or loudspeaker than would be the case if it were left either to market forces or the fore of aggregated public demand – forces that intrinsically favour the familiar over the new.
>
> (2013: 79)

When I asked Hindell how she intended to attract the desired audiences, she said, '[k]eep spreading the editorial net as widely as possible' (2014). Technology has always played a part in the way people listen to radio, and this has been illustrated in part by the evolution of BBC iPlayer.

iPlayer

The combined development, implementation and use of BBC Radio 4 Extra and BBC iPlayer for radio have made a demonstrable difference to the way BBC radio drama can be consumed. The possibility of listening to the enormous back catalogue of BBC drama has enriched listening for radio drama enthusiasts in the United Kingdom. More widely, iPlayer radio fits in with the time-shifting properties of catch-up media and pushes the portability of traditional broadcast radio even further. The BBC website was the United Kingdom's third most popular site in 2007, and a variety of its incarnations won online awards at the Prix

Europa (Connor 2007). The first incarnation of iPlayer was BBC radioplayer, which, from 2002, allowed people to 'listen again' to broadcasts they had heard on terrestrial radio. Post-2006, the BBC needed to 'reinvent' its web presence, 'fill it with dynamic audio-visual content, personalise it, open it up to user-generated content' (Thorsen 2012: 18). iPlayer developed as 'trusted guide' within the 'potentially disruptive world of digital distribution' (Grainge 2017: 143). The BBC was one of the first European national broadcasters to lead the 'digital revolution' (European Parliament 2011). The BBC's history of Prix Europa wins in the category of online presence showed that its online audio and video experimentation, initiated in 1996, could provide a highly usable system. All web content for the BBC was produced in-house. By the end of 2012, iPlayer Radio reached around 6 million British browsers per week, an increase of 30 per cent from October 2011. In 2014, Grainge argues, BBC advertisements for iPlayer emphasized it as a travel companion, representing the BBC's 'burgeoning digital identity' and an unfolding meta-commentary on online TV in the 2010s (2017: 139, 140, 141). The profile of BBC iPlayer remains strongly under-55 in terms of age (Andersson 2016: 2). In January 2016, comedy programmes (and the *Test Match Special*) topped the radio iPlayer requests, as did *The Archers* (Andersson 2016: 15).

In 2012, Chris Kimber recorded in his official BBC blog that iPlayer Radio had brought together all of the BBC's English language radio stations 'into one coherent digital product across desktop, tablet and mobile' (Kimber 2012). By rising to the necessity of engaging audiences through interactivity, iPlayer can compete with 'the multimedia extravaganza to be found on a home computer or a smartphone' (Balick 2013: 16). Thorsen believes iPlayer's success is due to the 'simplicity of access (i.e. streaming), quality of content, clarity of message and platform neutrality' (2012: 26). Kimber acknowledged that there were user issues with iPlayer Radio, such as inability to find the programmes users want to listen to (2012). This correlates to Renata Salcecl's formulation of tyranny of choice: 'the consumer [has] to choose not to choose and often [has] to pay for advice on how to do this […] they may have wanted to limit their choices, but not too much, and they wanted someone else to do it for them' (2010: 5–6). Hendy suggests that only one-third of requests on iPlayer have been for radio rather than TV, but 'more than a million radio programmes are heard through iPlayer each day' (2013: 115). David Hepworth suggests '[w]hether it's punk rock, reggae, true crime, comedy or chat, the "listen again" function enables you to download a treasure trove of audio delights' (2015).

Anthony Rose, in a BBC blog entry, highlighted the importance of programming and scheduling as a sort of metadata for BBC iPlayer.

> When you turn on your TV in the evening peak viewing hours and idly flip through the available channels, the programmes that you see are carefully chosen by each channel's scheduler. […] But what if you no longer watched linear TV? Who becomes the tastemaker then? Right now this is a largely theoretical problem as very few people watch no live TV at all.
>
> (Rose 2010)

In the intervening years, however, this has certainly become the case for some segments of the population. In the 1960s and 1970s, the DJ became a cult figure for youth radio audiences in the United States for his (it was usually a man) ability to put together playlists. Without a guiding scheduler, will future audio listeners assemble their own drama playlists and how will metadata feature? In 2018, the BBC iPlayer radio app transformed into BBC Sounds (Priday 2018). This platform acknowledged the pull of mobile podcast content and has re-packaged the BBC iPlayer radio app to fit these conventions, though still with an element of curation (BBC 2018). Lord Tony Hall suggested that BBC Sounds gives listeners 'easier access to the great British content we make' (BBC 2018).

The gamechanger and *Life and Fate*

The role of a gamechanger is to widen the editorial net, which, as Hindell remarked, was the ongoing mission of radio drama production within the BBC in terms of gaining the audience it seeks. The gamechanger is the mirror image to the steady and sturdy *Archers,* the *Classic Serial* adaptations of Dickens, Trollope and Dumas, and the Radio 4 crime serials. It would be impossible to feel the impact of gamechangers, the programmes that really push the envelope, no matter their source or genre, without the background of good, dependable and varied everyday drama. Not every gamechanger is a Prix Italia-winning play, and not every Prix Italia-winning play would be universally acknowledged as a gamechanger. Different audiences accept different modes of nominating excellence. In the history of British radio drama, the standard for a prestigious play began with the flurry of Prix Italia-winning original radio drama in the 1950s. The Prix Italia differs from the Prix Europa, in that its selection is not limited to European countries, accepting entries from over 90 public and private broadcasting entities, including those from Canada, Australia, Japan and the United States. RAI (the Italian state broadcaster) presents the competition. International juries are made up of expert judges selected on a rotating basis from a variety of countries, and the competition includes public debate. Since the 1950s, BBC successes at the Prix Italia have been far less frequent.

The Prix Europa – which has a slightly more adventurous tone – was established in the mid-1980s with its first award ceremony in 1987. Originally awarding excellence in European TV, a radio drama category was added in 1997, and the first winners of this award included a Special Commendation for a BBC play, *Vox Humana* (1996). It was another six years until another British radio drama was honoured, and it was not until 2004 that a British radio drama production was honoured as Best European Radio Drama of the Year (*The Colony* [2005], made for the Radio 3 slot *The Wire*, was the winner). In more recent years, British radio drama has been recognized more consistently, with Special Commendations in 2012 and 2013 (see Appendix 2).

Since the 1950s, there has been less consensus among historians and critics on the next big gamechangers. A few of the suggestions for BBC Radio drama gamechangers are posited below.

Douglas Adams' *The Hitchhiker's Guide to the Galaxy (HHGTTG)* was broadcast without a studio audience at 10:30 p.m. on a Wednesday, 8 March 1978. Broadcast in a little-trumpeted late night slot, it was not considered to be a high-profile series. However, within the week, two national papers carried reviews of *HHGTTG*, highly unusual when reviews of radio in newspapers are scarce to non-existent. Science fiction, which the BBC had 'condemned' as 'very fifties' and lacking 'popular appeal' came into vogue (Hendy 2007: 191). The word of mouth publicity suggested *HHGTTG* was universally enjoyed, not just by science-fiction fans or comedy fans, but 'most people liked it because it was accessible, fast, and funny' (Gaiman 2003: 36). It soon had an audience of half a million per week. The typical listener was 31 years old, 'more upmarket' than even the typical Radio 3 listener (Hendy 2007: 193). By 1980, it had become a television show, novel, stage play and an LP. It changed public perceptions of Radio 4, bringing in a younger audience, 'attracting a generation uninspired by Radio Four's usual tone' (Hendy 2007: 194). It also created a vogue for hi-fi experimentation in radio sound. 'We were actually having to invent the process by which we worked', said Adams, 'because nobody was doing multi-track recording, electronic effects, and so on' (cited in Gaiman 2003: 33). Despite *HHGTTG*'s great popular success, it won no major awards.

The gamechanger of the 1980s was *Adrian Mole*. The play by Sue Townsend, *The Secret Diary of Adrian Mole Aged 13 ¾*, was broadcast on Radio 4 on New Year's Day 1982. The broadcast was overheard by publishers at Methuen, who immediately contracted Townsend to write a book. By the time the book version had been released, *Adrian Mole* had run again on Radio 4 as a *Morning Reading*. Head of Drama John Tydeman recognized Townsend's talent and continued to commission her in various *Adrian Mole*-related plays, not the least of which was transferring the radio play into a stage play that debuted in Leicester (with the diary extracts pre-recorded). Hendy speculated that the reason Townsend's writing captured the heart of the Radio 4 audience was because it was 'a comedy straight from the heartlands of Radio Four audiences: British suburbia' (2007: 374). While this is no doubt true, it cannot account for the continued success of the Mole saga in print; one suspects this was due to the fact it was accessible, fast and funny – the same descriptions Gaiman employed of *HHGTTG*.

Life and Fate (2011) differs from *HGTTG* and *Adrian Mole* in that it is dramatized from a novel, but the unique experiment in terms of the novel's complexity and the way it suffused the Radio 4 schedule, made it a gamechanger. Before the broadcast, few people in the United Kingdom had heard of *Life and Fate* (1960), a novel arrested by the KGB but smuggled to the West. The Radio 4 dramatization had a remarkable effect. Post-broadcast, Random House printed in excess of 13,000 copies just to keep up with demand. The book topped the charts on Amazon, and downloadable versions of the play topped iTunes. Mark Damazer, one-time controller of Radio 4, had commissioned Hindell to produce a radio version of *Life and Fate* after having been impressed by the book in 2008. The challenge faced by the *Life and Fate* team was that the book was said to be 'undramatizable'. With more than a thousand named characters in Grossman's work, the production team were in the end able to reduce it to 159, played by 67 actors. Two structures consistent with the BBC presentation of adaptations were immediately obvious: the *Classic Serial*, the *Afternoon Drama* or a special series. Ultimately, no single drama slot per week, or even per day, was given over to *Life and Fate*. Instead, every drama slot during one week of broadcast, from Sunday, 18 September to Sunday, 25 September 2011, was linked to *Life and Fate*. Many listeners praised the structure as adventurous and imaginative. One listener expressed a desire to have drama like *Life and Fate* on television as he or she could find nothing of similar calibre to watch on TV. Jane Thynne, radio reviewer for *The Independent*, suggested that the gamble of filling every slot on the network 'paid off fabulously' (2011: 16).

The unprecedented amount of publicity for *Life and* Fate, including TV trails that are unusual for radio programmes, was foremost 'to raise consciousness' of Grossman and the novel, noted Hindell. Critics noted that the trails were 'endless' and ubiquitous. The use of iPlayer and downloading the plays was extremely important in how *Life and Fate* was disseminated. Clare Heal felt this kind of radio event would be 'impossible without the iPlayer on the internet' (2011: 63). Gillian Reynolds, for example, confessed she could not listen to a whole week of *Life and Fate,* having listened to three plays, then downloading a fourth via iPlayer. In 2012, *Life and Fate*'s schedule-spanning prerogative was echoed by a full-day adaptation of *Ulysses,* heavily abridged and nearly eight hours long.

Concerns about language, propriety and scheduling were registered by listeners writing in, phoning in and e-mailing Radio 4 regarding the conceptually adult *Life and Fate*. Of these complaints, some were in the category that objected to the Radio 4 schedule being swamped with the series, from which some listeners felt there was no escape. Some listeners felt the content was too mature for the time of day it was broadcast, objecting to bad language, murder and torture.[13] Such complaints have a long history; Gielgud refers to a feature called *Narvik* from 1940 that reconstructed the Battle of Narvik in Norway. A widow of the campaign wrote after its broadcast, 'to impersonate the voices of the living and the dead is unpardonable' (Gielgud 1957: 168).

'Listeners to Radio 4 in 1967 were expected to look in *Radio Times* to decide what they wanted to hear and then make a date', Elmes has reflected (2008: 16). Although the notion of 'appointment listening' has changed dramatically in the twenty-first century, a vein of necessity seems to run through the critical reaction to *Life and Fate*. Hendy noted 'publicity for radio in a television age has been a scarce commodity', while the judgements of the radio critics (an ever-dwindling group) 'feed the wider nexus of critical "opinion" by which the BBC's reputation as a whole has been judged' (2003: 70). *Life and Fate* received unprecedented attention in the press, not just in Britain but worldwide. In contrast to listener concerns about scheduling and propriety, there were also critics who decried the BBC for eliminating 'every trace of genius' from Grossman's novel. The BBC could have chosen to broadcast *Life and Fate* exclusively in the *Drama on 3* slot, the inheritor of the Third Programme, which as we have seen was for 'intellectuals'. The scheduling of *Life and Fate* in the broad range of slots suggested the BBC was seeking to find a wider audience for the novel, even at the risk of alienating listeners (like the complainant above). Despite the general success of *Life and Fate*, as with other BBC gamechangers, it garnered no European radio awards.

The future of radio drama at the BBC

Despite the statistical and anecdotal evidence offered in this chapter to the contrary, many people persistently believe that British radio drama is in its twilight. This criticism does not come from one side but many. The tension between elitism and popular appeal is well-defined, both in terms of radio drama in general and BBC radio drama in particular. Writers like Lance Sieveking and producers like Donald McWhinnie have always formed a group that devotes its energy to 'clearing a space' for material they believe in, 'no matter how small its audience was likely to be' (Wardle 1968: 14). In the United Kingdom generally, both sides of the political spectrum have their criticisms. The criticisms from the right opened this chapter and scarcely need re-stating; those critics on the left 'feel it [the BBC] does not engage with the right people' (Smith 2013: 29). For example, although admitting this was based on anecdote, Anne Karpf wrote that her young students at London Metropolitan University, many from ethnic minorities, felt completely disengaged from speech radio, 'the rich, baritone middle-aged, bourgeois male voice of a BBC Radio 4 presenter connotes not safety and resilience but an oppressive authoritarianism' (Karpf 2013: 67). Just as television is perceived as always on the verge of being sophisticated, radio drama is always on the verge of being inclusive. 'The absence of young writers is the result of something more complicated than an absence of young listeners', Allen (1988: n.pag.) went on to say, though perhaps, as Hindell has suggested, ensnaring a young audience is not the highest priority.

Alternatives to the BBC

Not being able to appeal to a youth audience, and indeed, not training enough young audio drama-makers, is one criticism that Tim Crook of Goldsmiths College has levelled against BBC radio drama (1999a: 43). As a radio drama scholar and member of the IRDP, Crook's critiques of BBC radio drama in the 1990s were many, including an elitist attitude to radio drama (1999a: 152) as well as believing that most broadcast radio drama was not very good (1999a: 155, 157); cultural manipulation of the Holocaust and grief through *Spoonface Steinberg* (1997) (Crook 1999a: 148); as well as the fact that IRDP were not approved as one of the BBC's independent producers (meaning their drama was not broadcast on the BBC) without, Crook felt, sufficient explanation (1999a: 29).

For those desiring a wide palette of audio drama in the United Kingdom, the trailblazing efforts of IRDP have led to many options for creating and distributing drama independently of the BBC, and listeners likewise have many sources and options. *Sophia Square* (2012–13) is one example of a United Kingdom commercial station producing and broadcasting new drama, which was freely available over the Internet. Based out of Radio Cardiff, show-run by Alison Plant, Jeremy Rhys and Rhys Phillips, and satisfying the station's public service remit, *Sophia Square* was very much an example of a radio serial written by and for the particular community it served. Another up-and-coming source of non-BBC original plays is universities, such as University Radio York, which produced *The Prince of Humberside* in

2011 or the University of Lincoln, which produced *Rose* in 2012. *Above and Below* (2012), written and produced by Daniel MacNaughton for Aboveandbelowseries.co.uk, won the 2013 BBC Audio Drama Award for Best Online Only Drama. There are other community outlets such as the Yorkshire-based Holmfirth Writers' Group.

Between 1998 and 2011, Crazy Dog Audio Theatre, headed by Roger Gregg, produced audio drama that was heard on the BBC and NPR affiliates. Gregg, Dublin-based and RTÉ-trained, 'pioneered his own audio sound, a wacky blend of Captain Beefheart sonic assault and an intimate, fine theatre sensibility', according to Greenhalgh (2017). Subtitled 'Modern Drama for a Modern World', the Wireless Theatre Company suggests it caters for 'existing radio lovers and for the "Facebook Generation"' (The Wireless Theatre Company 2014). Founded by Mariele Runacre-Temple, Wireless has a strong connection to both stage theatre (through founding members Robert Valentine and Jack Bowman) and BBC-style radio drama (through producers who have included Cherry Cookson). Wireless can also be heard through British hospital radio. Founded in 2007 and based in central London with access to studio space, Wireless' productions are generally quite polished. While they began by accepting open script submissions, due to their growing popularity, Wireless have had to restrict their solicitation process. Wireless originally made use of a rather unique business model – most plays were free to download but prestigious bonus dramas were subscription-based – which was supplemented by offering the recording of voice reels for aspiring actors. In early 2014, Wireless turned to a paid subscription service with different prices for different packages (as of 2017, each play costs £1.49 to download or £25 for an annual subscription). Wireless also sponsors competitions and live performances/recordings. As of June 2017, Wireless have also teamed up with Audible to produce a large-scale dramatization, though its distribution mechanism is so far unclear.

The genre output of Wireless is also more diverse than many contemporary Internet-only audio drama producers. They range from comedy musicals to horror to the puzzlingly named 'audio drama plays'. Laurence Raw[14] reviewed *Grimm at Christmas* in 2011, a Wireless drama that highlighted 'the essential brutality of the world, and how individuals have to acquire inner strength in order to negotiate it' (Raw 2011b). *The Strange Case of Springheel'd Jack* (2011–13)*,* a multi-part epic by Gareth Parker and Roger Valentine, is a historical detective story with touches of the macabre. The first series won the 2011 Silver Ogle Award for Best Fantasy Audio Production of the Year and the second won the 2013 Gold Ogle Award. *Springheel'd Jack* remained one of Wireless' most popular downloads in July 2017 along with Sherlock Holmes stories, an H.G. Wells spin-off, and two comedies, *Ladies* (2016, recorded live in front of a pub audience) and the spoof *Radio Hoohah* (2016).

The scale of the Wireless Theatre Company cannot be matched by many other British independents; nevertheless, a multitude exists, usually making productions freely available on the Web. *The Tin Can Podcast* (2010–present) gives as its mission statement 'to supply the public with high quality diverse and entertaining podcasts on a regular basis' (Brown n.d.). As a tongue-in-cheek parody of Hammer Horror and productions like Wireless' *The Strange Case of Springheel'd Jack,* Newgate Productions' *The Monster Hunters* has been bringing its brand of politically incorrect, time-warped-in-the-1970s horror comedy since 2013. Some other commercialized independent production companies exist, such as Spiteful Puppet. Spiteful Puppet shot to a widespread acclaim in 2014 with its Robin Hood series *Hood,* which won the BBC Online Only Audio Drama in 2014 and 2015. *Wooden Overcoats,* a freely available comic podcast created by David K. Barnes, is set in the Channel Islands and since 2015 has won great acclaim. Resonance FM also exists as an important platform for new audio/radio art, where the boundaries between drama and other aural art forms are pushed to extremes. The aural artwork found on Resonance is that which 'has no other place on the radio dial' (Coyer 2007b: 117). Another platform for experiencing such works but in a very different context is In the Dark, based in London and Bristol, which presents collective listening events 'in the dark'. Primarily, In the Dark focuses on the feature/documentary tradition, especially as epitomized by international podcasting developments, with previous events including a chance to hear the Third Ear's *Kvinden på Isen (The Woman on the Ice)* (2015), and a night of stories with the Kitchen Sisters (2014). Among these events have been collaborations with the British Library utilizing their BBC archive collections of both radio features and drama, including a 2014 dramatization of Virginia Woolf's *To the Lighthouse* and a selection of Giles Cooper plays.

Finally, Big Finish Productions, based in Maidenhead, has been commercially producing studio-based audio drama on CD since 1999. Big Finish's fan audio dramas have consistently placed in the BBC Audio Drama Awards for Best Online Only Drama,[15] such as *Absent Friends* (2017) and *Dark Eyes* (2012). The company began with an exclusive *Doctor Who* range, having successfully negotiated the licence from the BBC (when *Doctor Who* was off television). It has since expanded to other fan audio. With an audience loyal to infinite spin-offs of the *Doctor Who* universe, Big Finish has had some difficulty introducing non-fan ranges, though it is now experimenting with titles by Shakespeare and Victorian writers. Big Finish attracts a good level of guest stars, including Anthony Stewart Head, Benedict Cumberbatch, David Tennant, the late John Hurt and Keeley Hawes. Also, Big Finish's quantitative output is phenomenal with approximately eight new releases every month across dozens of product ranges.

Liveness is another important component of some contemporary non-BBC British audio drama. The group Fitzrovia Radio Hour are recreating radio-as-performance in a series of retro performances complete with costumes and sound effects as they would have been made in OTR productions. Jon Edgley Bond, Letty Butler, Samara Maclaren, Tom Mallaburn and Phil Mulryne's earliest works were straight adaptations ('American to English') of thrillers from the Golden Age of Radio, such as *Escape's* (1947–54, CBS) *Leinigen and the Ants* (2008), which they performed live and recorded in front of a cabaret audience. Their newest material is completely original, combining short sketches with advertisements in what is either a homage to Radio Luxembourg or a creation of a radio drama past that never existed. This idea of performance practice as 'consciously arcane' and tapping into a sense of 'homely nostalgia' appears to be popular, as the performance radio programme at the University of South Wales has trumpeted this trend (Challis et al. 2014: 252, 254). The idea of 'American to English' is also an important part of the appeal, with Challis et al. highlighting '[t]he post-war setting', the 'extremely sardonic humour' as well as the workaday approach (demonstrably different to the Gielgud-esque theatre approach that would have existed on the BBC in the late 1940s).

It is worth noting, however, that many British radio researchers feel the medium is still not taken seriously by academics, politicians and many media professionals (Tacchi 1997: 3). 'Critical coverage of radio output', Kevin D'Arcy admitted, 'is generally nearly invisible' (2007: 56). A body of specialists is growing, assisted in part by online networks such as the Radio Studies Network, but there is a problem of coordination and communication. Richard Rudin (2011: 61) and Roger Wood both agree that the United Kingdom is curiously diffident about preserving and making available its broadcasts, especially in contrast to the United States.

> The only practical way of accessing previously broadcast British radio plays is through the National Sound Archive at the British Library, which acts as a portal to the BBC Archive. The microfiche archive of play scripts at the BBC Written Archives Centre is equally invaluable but again incomplete and impossible to access remotely.
>
> (Wood 2008: 23)

'In the British Library of 2012, this self-ethnographer feels', Peter Lewis wrote, 'like Marty in *Back to the Future,* a stranger' (2012: 54). Despite this, time has proven that the British Library's collections, among others, are invaluable and rewarding for the patient scholar. Shaun Ley, a BBC presenter, also described Radio 4 Extra as 'a standing rebuke to those in the past who neglected our broadcast heritage' (cited in Hodgson 2014: 72). However, more recently, websites in particular have made radio drama archival research easier. BBC Genome, a searchable database of the *Radio Times* 1923–2009, has brought some BBC-based sources to researchers' fingertips. A growing number of university programmes are offering theoretical and production-based modules on radio drama, such as the above-mentioned University of South Wales, as well as the University of Sunderland and the University of Salford.

Conclusion

If a rounded audience is the one that BBC radio drama-makers want, then it seems this is the audience it will get, if the output, as surveyed in this chapter, is representative of the direction in which the network is headed. BBC radio drama succeeds with its philosophy in providing something for everyone at least some of the time, as we have justified through close examination of its statistical output. By using repetition and continuity to balance out its range of genres, BBC radio drama may continue, as Hindell hopes, to keep casting its editorial net widely. Elmes does not overstate the situation by much to call the BBC radio drama output 'a genuine and, in these days of media profusion and strained resources, a truly astonishing and little-trumpeted achievement' (2008: 181). British audio drama is also enriched by a varied and vibrant community of independent audio-makers, succeeding in the footsteps of the IRDP, from Big Finish's fan audios to the live OTR performance exploits of the Fitzrovia Radio Hour to Wireless Theatre's unique business model. To borrow the title of Humphrey Carpenter's book on Radio 3, British audio drama may be reasonably called the envy of the world.

Notes

1. Though in the same book, Radio 4's output is also referred to as 'undemanding' (28), an evident case of radio drama once again straddling the continuum of highbrow and lowbrow.
2. In 2010, *The Friday Play* was cut from the schedule, to the disappointment of listeners who believed it was a last bastion of cutting-edge drama (Hodgson 2014: 105).
3. I describe my statistical methodology in detail in Appendix 1, but the two main sources for my quantitative approach are the *Radio Times* listings for 2012 and interviews with the BBC's United Kingdom Head of Audio Drama Alison Hindell.
4. Unless otherwise indicated, the total number of drama programmes for Radio 4 and Radio 3, and the total number of collective hours, necessarily exclude Radio 4 Extra for reasons explained in the Methodology, and exclude *The Archers* and *Ambridge Extra,* to avoid skewing the data towards the highly prolific serials.
5. From 2015, Radio 4 Extra ceased to produce new drama.
6. It should be noted that, despite the fact that, for the purposes of the statistical analysis, I did not include dramatic readings, they constitute an important part of the dramatic speech strands on BBC Radio.
7. Discounting *The Archers/Ambridge Extra,* which would give a distorted picture, as indicated above.
8. These figures are for the percentage of number of dramas in these categories divided by the whole.
9. Gupta's adaptation won Best Adaptation in the 2012 BBC Audio Drama Awards.
10. The programme was so popular it went into two series as a comedy with a live audience.
11. *Believe It!* won Best Scripted Comedy in the BBC Audio Drama Awards 2013.
12. Though, interestingly, in Tacchi's 2001 study of radio listeners in Bristol, the men she interviewed were more likely to be the loyal Radio 4 listeners than the women.
13. A listener complaint on 23 September 2011 felt *Krymov in Moscow* being transmitted at 2:15 p.m. was 'appalling', citing the fact that in the broadcast a woman was raped, murdered and tortured. While the story dealt with Nikolai Krymov being tortured for not towing the Party line, the alleged rape and murder did not occur, suggesting that sometimes listeners' outrage can literally deafen them to the finer points of a radio broadcast.
14. Laurence Raw's Radio Drama Reviews website, from 2007 onwards, was an extremely valuable resource for critical reflection on contemporary audio drama in English. His reviews later moved to his Academia.edu page (https://baskent.academia.edu/LaurenceRaw/Radio-Drama). When Raw passed away in 2018, his Academia.edu collection of radio reviews numbered over 100.
15. Though this raises some ethical issues such as the fact these *Doctor Who* dramas are based on a BBC series, and why they are listed in an online-only category when Big Finish dramas are available through paid subscription or CD/download sales.

Chapter 9

Current US Audio Drama

Today's modern [US] radio drama scene can be characterised as an orphaned medium with a lot of guts but not a lot of polish. There is [a] hard-core niche audience that keeps [the] producer faithful of [*sic*] a resurgence, and dropping costs of equipment and the interconnectivity of the Internet certainly has allowed for more communication and community-building of this niche than ever before.

– Frederick Greenhalgh (2007)

Podcasting is drawing on so many skills that it can be hard to get right, and, not very celebrated, even if it does get it right.

– Dana Gerber-Margie (cited in Hilmes and Lindgren 2016: 6)

It is the age of the audience.

– Germán Arango-Forero, Sergio Roncallo-Dow and Enrique Uribe-Jongbloed (2016: 25)

'Radio in the digital age is arguably becoming more prolific, more fragmented, more manipulable, more mobile, more global, more personal', argued Lacey (2013: 9). Digitalization, Dubber notes, 'has taken place at a far broader societal level' (2013: 180). The digital and the analogue, in fact, most frequently sit side by side (Starkey 2004: 32; Dubber 2013: 35). While sound scholars are getting to grips with the changing nature of radio (Hilmes 2013: 49; Gordon 2018), listeners themselves (especially younger listeners) are unclear. 'I suppose podcasts are sort of radio?' one of Tacchi's 2012 informants suggested (235). Younger listeners are frequently unaware that radio-like media (such as the podcast) still perform the same roles as radio. This mirrors a general lack of understanding about audio drama by large parts of the population, who usually associate it with the past (OTR or crusty old BBC dramas that don't have relevance for certain parts of the audience). Yet radio in the digital age links up with so much, from the traditional to the more technologically innovative, and this variety should be better understood.

Since 2005, podcasts have exploded into the ears, iPods and mobile phones of listeners everywhere, but particularly in the United States. Podcasting's 'first age' for fiction meant either re-worked 'techniques and tropes of OTR drama' such as *Tales from Beyond the Pale* (2010–present) and *We're Alive* (2009–present), or adopted frameworks from analogue radio programming, such as *Welcome to Night Vale* (2012–present) (Hancock and McMurtry 2017). What Bonini (2015) terms as the 'second age' of podcasting (in the spirit of Web 2.0),

Siobhán McHugh has defined as being influenced by the ethos and production techniques of US public service broadcasting (PSB) with innovative/combinatory funding sources (2016: 3), necessarily influenced by liberatory advances in technology. Bottomley takes the properties of the podcast too far, however, by suggesting that without podcasts, 'there would likely be no contemporary radio drama being made' (2015: 183), an assertion disproven in this chapter!

In 2014, 30% of those surveyed in the US study 'The Infinite Dial' reported having ever listened to a podcast, around 39 million people (Edison Research and Triton Digital 2014: 41). By 2017, that percentage had increased by 10% (to 40%), an estimated 112 million people (Edison Research and Triton Digital 2017: 40). According to Sterne et al., 'approximately 6 million of the 22 million US adults who own a portable audio player have downloaded a podcast' (2008). McClung and Johnson noted that the 'time-shift' feature of podcasts allows users to choose 'from a variety of other podcast content including technology and education-related programming' (2010). McHugh associates podcasting with Anderson's 'long tail' (2016: 66) (for more on the 'long tail', see page 201).

Podcasting appeared in 2004 and exploded onto the scene in 2005 as iTunes 4.9 began podcast hosting. According to a 2010 US survey, only 23% of those surveyed had ever listened to a podcast. By 2014, that number had risen to 30%, and that year, approximately 39 million said they had listened to a podcast in the last month (Arbitron Inc./Radio Research Consortium 2011: 41–42). There was also a 17% increase in those who listened to podcasts on smartphones (2011: 44). Podcasts' popularity is evident from an outfit called Personal Audio (labelled by Mike Masnick of TechDirt as a 'patent troll') that has sued various podcasting creators with allegations in 2013 that it patented podcasting (Masnick 2013). Greenhalgh has called podcasting 'almost a revolution', and these patenting allegations prove how important the form has become (2007). How much do we actually know about those who make and listen to podcasts? Private, commercial audience research companies, unsurprisingly, keep data on podcasting audiences to themselves, so that little has been available for academic study. Bonini surveying the field in 2015 found only fourteen available scholarly articles on podcasting (cited in McHugh 2016: 2), though as the academic community has caught up with *Serial* (2014–present) and the podcasting explosion, much more has been written. Audience data on podcast-makers and listeners therefore appears, on the surface, to be somewhat contradictory.

In Markman and Sawyer's study, both podcast-makers and -listeners were characterized as 'technologically savvy, educated, older, professional males' (2014: 30). Andréa Baker found slightly different results. She studied the music-listening habits among college students. Her data showed a corollary with Markman and Sawyer's: the main music podcast-makers were 18–24 years old, urban-based, white, male and from the middle and upper classes. She did suggest that 'young women participate in net-radio *consumption* in roughly equal numbers to young men' (2012: 86, emphasis added). In 2017, those surveyed in 'The Infinite Dial' were most likely to listen to between two and five podcasts weekly (Edison Research and Triton Digital 2017: 45). Crucially, what needs to be understood about these statistics so far is that they do not exclusively represent audio drama podcasts. This kind of data is not yet easily accessible. Critics in 2014 already suggested that podcasts were played out (Zurawik 2014a). In 2018, are we in danger of being subsumed by podcast production? If everyone can and does make podcasts, who is still around to listen? It seems podcasts currently present us with a tyranny of choice.

A tyranny of choice

The concept of the tyranny of choice questions whether having more and more choices in daily life has helped or hurt humans psychologically. Siva Vaidhyanathan characterized modern people's habits as a desire to trust, inertia and impatience (2011: 15), which has implications for how much or how little choice people want. David Hendy has questioned whether actual choice exists in a deregulated media environment (2013: 98). Kate Lacey similarly queried, 'the proliferation of forms and formats for individual expression is assumed to be coterminous with a plurality of voices, which in turn is taken to be the marker of a properly functioning communications democracy' (Lacey 2013: 16).

In the current US podcasting scene, we are reminded of the opposite poles of human behaviour that seem to want infinite choice but then often succumb to being overwhelmed by so much choice. This tendency was, indeed, interpreted by Matthew Arnold in the 1860s as a reason for promoting culture as not only innate but something that needed to be cultivated amongst others. This, of course, was taken keenly to heart by J.C.W. Reith as part of the operating ethos for the BBC. As Ien Ang has determined, television, based on what it learned from radio, introduced parameters that give some choice as far as consumers are concerned. These parameters can be summarized simply: the choice to watch or not to watch, how little or how much to watch. Ang characterizes this as a method of television appearing to grant complete freedom while desperately holding onto control, as it cannot afford to lose its audience.

While I have attempted to situate podcasting within a potential tyranny of choice, podcasting is not necessarily emblematic of all audio drama production today in the United States. As in the United Kingdom, there are many strands, and in fact it is clear that the US audio drama scene is even more fragmented than its counterpart in Britain. If it provides both an embarrassment of riches and a potential tyranny of choice, it must be understood within the framework of US radio regulation and PSB. The contemporary US radio scene is familiar because the commercial format it originated has been exported worldwide. Thus the structure of this chapter looks at what PSB means in the United States within the current radio legislation landscape and ponders distinct areas where audio drama can be found. These areas include local radio (NPR-affiliated or otherwise); audiobooks and in particular Audible; performatory OTR recreations; satellite audio drama freely available including gamechangers like *Welcome to Night Vale;* and audio drama podcasts based on the *Serial* model.

Serial

Torey Malatia, WBEZ's general manager between 1996 and 2013, reports that in 2007, the production staff behind WBEZ Chicago, a public radio success story and NPR-affiliate, decided to engage in a radio makeover. Like KERA Dallas and WABE-FM in Atlanta, WBEZ was 'in the unusual position of being the primary public radio service in a major market, without a full power public service non-commercial competitor' (Malatia 2007: 6). WBEZ also served parts of northwest Indiana, 'a densely populated, highly diverse area that is economically, socially, and environmentally tied to the Chicago metropolitan region' (Malatia 2007: 4). WBEZ's identification with its Chicago and Indiana listeners, however, took on a national (even international) dimension in 2014 when it began broadcasting *Serial*, a spin-off of Ira Glass' extremely popular *This American Life* (*TAL*) (1995–present) radio programme. *Serial* was also a podcast, and it was through this platform that its success was most revelatory. A trending pop culture event (McMurtry 2016: 306) mainly fuelled by word of mouth (McCracken 2015: 8), *Serial* used the techniques of audio drama to tell a nonfictional story, in keeping with *TAL*'s and US public service radio's talking point, high-quality nonfiction stories and investigative journalism (McMurtry 2016: 307).

Serial was, at the conclusion of its first season, deemed manipulative, disappointing and potentially unethical (McMurtry 2016: 318). However, it was also considered compelling, addictive and *The Wire* (2002–08) of podcasting (McMurtry 2016: 312). While seriality was an undeniable component of its triumph, much of *Serial*'s appeal was due to its host, Sarah Koenig. Undoubtedly influenced by Glass' 'movies for sound' approach to audio documentary-making – characterized by McHugh as part of continuity in audio documentary/feature-making where the producer is placed at the heart of the programme to personalize the narrative (2016: 5) – Koenig projected a typically *TAL*-esque persona of equal parts self-deprecating intimacy and quirk. Koenig and her team were maintaining a high standard of control over the way *Serial* unfolded to its listeners, a trait no doubt learned from Glass' tutelage (Glass 2010: 459). In 2000, Dunaway worried that the manipulable qualities of digital radio would create '[a]n entirely new – or false, depending on your perspective – ambience [that] can be superimposed on actuality, raising potential ethical dilemmas' (2000: 37), a description that seems apt for *Serial*.

Serial was not drama, though many non-radio drama specialists chose to lump it in with OTR. Nevertheless, in reviving what some considered the 'moribund' medium of podcasting (Zurawik 2014a), *Serial* paradoxically demonstrated some of the most effective weapons in audio drama's arsenal, as highlighted in Chapter 2: its use of narratives (Berry 2015: 171), its centripetal power, its intimacy, its macro-micro scale. The use of the podcast form (its accessibility and the eventual ability to 'binge' consume it) were also clearly a factor. *Serial* established conventions within its structure whose repetition seemed deeply resonant for its audience (Hancock and McMurtry 2018). Furthermore, *Serial* hearkened back to BBC 'appointment listening', in that listeners had to exert their full attention on content; it would not submit to being a background medium. As David Letzler pointed out, *Serial*'s listeners must listen to eight states of mind in a single setting (Letzler 2017: 146). Accordingly, '[t]he podcast is no-longer a side project of radio, but a self-regulating and generating media form in its own right' (Hancock and McMurtry 2018: 100). *Serial*'s importance to podcasting and radio is undeniable.

What does public service broadcasting mean in the United States?

Serial unquestionably emerged from the public service broadcasting context. The US PSB environment is complex and often embattled. The US House of Representatives proposed eliminating the Corporation for Public Broadcasting, one of the most important sources of funding[1] for public radio and television, in 2011 (Kinnally and Brinkerhoff 2013: 2) and again in 2017 (Johnson 2017).[2] While NPR may be the most well-known of PSBs in the United States, all organizations connected with public service broadcasting are affected by such threats. To what extent do these many entities currently make use of drama programming? As noted in Chapter 7, besides NPR, there is the Pacifica network, Public Radio Exchange (PRX) and Public Radio International (PRI). Because PRX provides public radio programmes of nearly all genres, there is a higher ratio of non-fiction/documentary content to fictional/drama content, which is unsurprising, given US public radio's predilection towards factual speech content.

Hugh Richard Slotten remarked that NPR 'uses public funds to support advertising-free programming meant to entertain, inform, and enlighten' (2009: 3). This phrasing is surprisingly similar to J.C.W. Reith's founding principles for the BBC and highlights a significant link between the two nations' public broadcasting endeavours. One difference is in how NPR is funded, not by a licence fee, but from a variety of other sources. US public service broadcasting, McChesney argues, was 'never lavishly funded or supported' and 'struggles to survive in a fairly small niche of the media market' (2008: 445). As NPR is funded overwhelmingly by private donations, its fight to keep its audience is fierce, and its main competitor for public money is PRI. Businesses, foundations, colleges and universities, state and federal governments all fund public radio and TV, but individuals are exhorted constantly for their support. If the United States adopted the BBC's licence fee, for example, McChesney estimated in 2008 that PSB would have a budget of $20 billion annually (2008: 446). The US public service broadcasting landscape may be usefully compared to the one in New Zealand, which initially followed a BBC-like system before being released to deregulation in the 1990s. 'The effect of conglomeration – a seemingly inevitable outcome of deregulation on this scale', Dubber argues, 'was to significantly reduce the number of media interests and therefore also diversity and dissenting voices' (2007: 25). While it is clear that NPR is not the only example of PSB in the United States, this section explores how NPR is funded and structured as well as identifying its audiences and online presence, to provide a clearer picture of its organization and structure.

NPR and PBS in the United States walk a similar tightrope to the one described regarding the BBC in the previous chapter – and are much maligned by both sides of the political spectrum. Certainly NPR would seem, by default, to offer an alternative and a critique to a trend of 'dumbing-down', what Crook describes as a social anxiety of cultural decline (2012: 154). When Douglas wrote that she was tempted to suggest, despite inadequate evidence, that radio listening 'made people smarter while TV viewing dumbed them down', she seems to be acknowledging that listeners to US public radio do so as a remedy for 'dumbing themselves down' ([1999] 2004: 355). Indeed, Kristine Johnson's findings from the NPR website users indicate that, among 514 NPR.org users, the majority were white, highly educated, female (more than two-thirds) and between the ages of 25 and 44 (Johnson 2012). This is similar in makeup to the audience of BBC Radio 4, with the key component here being the education levels of the audience.

Listeners to NPR, in addition to being educated, are also seen to be invested in technology, evidenced by the fact that National Public Radio formally changed its name to NPR in 2010. This was, it said, to reflect the fact that it was no longer 'just' radio. As Paul Fahri of *The Washington Post* reported, its programming is heard 'over a variety of digital devices that aren't radios' (2010). NPR's podcast programmes are often listed among the top downloads on iTunes, and the NPR.org website offers streaming audio, mobile phone apps and links to local stations. A February 2010 poll of 1753 people aged 12 and older corroborated just how important the online listenership of any given US radio market is (Arbitron/Edison Research 2010). By 2014, 47% of Americans surveyed had listened to online radio in the last month, compared with 45% in 2013 (Arbitron Inc./Radio Research Consortium 2011: 5). 75% of those surveyed between the ages of 12 and 24 listened to online radio in the last month, with a surprising percentage of those 55 and older (21%) who had done so (2011: 5). The estimated weekly reach was 94 million people (Arbitron/Edison Research 2010: 6).

As Hendy notes, the audience for most NPR programmes 'dwarfs the number of subscribers to, say, the *New York Times*' (2013: 128). However, despite the size of its audience, NPR does not satisfy all listeners who seek speech radio and alternative programming in the United States. Douglas in 2004 more or less pleaded for something of this type. 'But I, and millions like me, don't have a radio station to listen to anymore […] And we miss that' ([1999] 2004: 356). Some have found NPR's general ethos to be smug, self-satisfied and discouraging to '"ordinary" Americans' (Tracey 1998: 159). Others have felt that NPR has betrayed its 'raw, cutting-edge quality' by becoming 'predictable and ever so polite' (Barsamian 2002: 11). Jack Mitchell summarizes the many variations of criticism from the left as regards public broadcasting in the United States and insists that 'public radio was never any further from the political mainstream than other academic and journalistic institutions' (2005: 179), in contrast, perhaps, to the politically-charged Pacifica. As detailed in Chapter 7, there have been a number of scattered slots for contemporary radio drama on US airwaves, some of them long-serving, others local and short-lived. The brief examples below build on Chapter 7's survey to provide contemporary ways to listen to drama on US radio. They give an idea of the range as well as the way US public radio stations can take advantage of the several threads of public service broadcasting available. As in Chapter 7, we begin with the author's personal experience, which is rooted in Albuquerque, New Mexico.

Local radio and drama

KUNM (Albuquerque)
KUNM Albuquerque, frequency 89.9 FM, broadcasts drama with limited resources, as a member station of NPR, PRX and PRI. KUNM's studio is physically based on the University of New Mexico's campus, and the station is affiliated with the university, beginning broadcasting in 1960 as KNMD. KUNM's programmes with a drama content, both in-house and external, include *Children's Hour, Other Voices, Other Sounds* and *Radio Theater*. *Radio Theater* is in-house and hosted by Linda López-McAlister and David Hughes. López-McAlister, who is also the founder of Camino Real Productions LLC that produces stage and radio theatre in New Mexico and Mexico, detailed the range of outlets from which KUNM's *Radio Theater* draws its output, including the LA Theater Works ('actors and plays you've heard of') and *Playing on Air* (2013).

As co-producer of KUNM *Radio Theater,* López-McAlister accesses PRX in order to obtain quality drama programming from public and independent production companies across the United States. PRX, she explains, offers public radio station subscribers a point-based system. She is given permission by KUNM's managing staff to purchase on the point-based system one LA Theater Works' show every other month. With a theatre background in LA, New York, and a 30-year career as a professor of philosophy and women's studies at universities in New York, California and Florida, López-McAlister appreciates the freedom provided by independent radio productions – producers, she says, don't feel compelled to keep to a 58-minute slot (unlike, as she acknowledges, in Britain, where BBC drama slots are more codified). However, she also has to take the time and initiative to trim or elongate productions bought on PRX from other companies – such as Chatterbox Theater's three-act production of *Oedipus the King* (2013). She also notes that British independents like the Wireless Theatre Company are welcome on KUNM's airwaves. Some years ago, she attempted and failed to get the rights to broadcast BBC radio drama. Now that this is possible, it is not, for KUNM, financially feasible.

KZMU (Moab)
KZMU, 87.9/106.1 FM, is staffed by volunteers in remote Moab, Utah. Initiated in 1992, the station became solar powered in 2008 with the assistance of a grant from Rocky Mountain Power and its listener base. Its programming is entirely locally produced, and this includes, from 2016, the live drama production of *Downtown Abbey,* a 'satirical spoof' of Edward Abbey set in a 'parallel universe' Moab (Durlin 2016). *Downtown Abbey* was written, produced and directed by Station Manager Marty Durlin during evenings and weekends (Richards

2016), seemingly influenced by the live radio drama/foley aesthetic of OTR and *Welcome to Night Vale* in its satire on a western US community. KZMU differs from KUNM, in that it is not affiliated with a university. It seems significant that original drama in community public service environments in the United States is originating from western, predominantly rural states, despite the long association of radio drama with metropolitan areas, like California's Bay Area, the East Coast and cities like Chicago and New York.

As Tim Crook indicates, what all new forms of audio drama have in common is the desire to tell stories 'artfully' (2012: 121). Audio drama in the United States as represented online differs in provenance, form, production values and manner of dissemination.

Audiobooks

Already discussed in detail in Chapter 7, the extent to which audiobooks can be considered audio drama is debatable[3] and, in practice, their adherence to 'drama' as opposed to 'reading' is based on the level of performances given by the readers as well as the addition of other features (such as music or special effects). By 2011, 'the 18–34 year-old crowd, bringing with it a new generation of tech-savvy and voracious listeners' were enjoying audiobooks in mainly digital formats (Publishing Trends 2011). Audiobooks provide acting opportunities broadly similar in technique to those in audio drama (Kaufman 2013). Indeed, voice-over artists are warned that radio actors are more at the mercy of directors: 'The director makes all the decisions and the actors, usually, do what they are told' (Shaw 2000: 172). Audiobooks also have their own awards, the Audies (http://www.audiofilemagazine.com/audies/). Audible, a New Jersey-based audiobook company, was founded in 1995 and acquired by Amazon in 2008. Audible's pervasive marketing strategy focuses on introducing new listeners to audiobooks and retaining brand loyalty. The company has expanded into audio dramas in addition to traditional narrated audiobooks with titles such as *Alien: River of Pain,* an *Alien* (1979) universe fill-in starring Anna Friel, Philip Glenister, Colin Salmon and Alexander Siddig and produced by Dirk Maggs. In the second half of 2017, their *X-Files* fill-in, *Cold Cases,* also produced by Maggs, starred David Duchovny and Gillian Anderson.

Performatory OTR recreations

LA Theater Works, mentioned previously, have been producing audio drama since 1988. Theirs is a relatively traditional approach, recording live stage drama and re-packaging it for audio listeners, a tradition that hearkens back to OTR and *The Lux Hollywood Radio Theater* (1934–55, NBC/CBS) that sourced film scripts and realized them for radio, using many of the same cast members. LA Theater Works similarly boasts accomplished, household-name actors, and the non-profit media arts organization claims to have the world's largest recorded play archive. *Playing on Air* represents an East Coast alternative to LA Theater Works, using the readily available talents of Broadway in its traditional studio recordings of mostly stage theatre work.

Chatterbox Audio Theater, mentioned previously by López-McAlister, until 2018 represented another independent audio drama production outlet preferring the traditional methods of studio recording. Also key to their process was liveness – in part due to executive director Robert Arnold's experience listening to old cassette tape recordings of *The Shadow*, in part due to a reaction against the tedium and isolation engendered by post-production techniques (Dunn 2010).[4] Their material was drawn both from existing sources that they adapted ('Luckily, we all paid attention in English class, so we know that there are a ton of great stories out there just waiting to be reborn') and original stories (Chatterbox Audio Theater 2017). According to Arnold, 'Chatterbox is a community theater, and we rely heavily on our community' (cited in Hand and Traynor 2011: 80).

More recently, referencing an aesthetic more reminiscent of the performatory nature of *A Prairie Home Companion* (1974–2016), anthology podcast dramas have been playing live shows. Perhaps most notably, the *NoSleep* horror podcast, which originated in 2010 from a subReddit forum, and has been hosted since that time by David Cummings (Cummings 2017). The 2017 Sleepless tour performed live in major cities in the United States in traditional theatre venues as well as in cafes. *NoSleep*'s interactive quality was a well-established part of its aesthetic, given its Reddit forum origin, a nature highlighted in its fifth anniversary podcast show, celebrating 250 hours' worth of horror storytelling and 750 stories adapted (Cummings 2016).

Satellite audio drama

Despite this profusion of outlets for audio drama in every imaginable genre, it is the vastness and lack of connection that can be daunting for a first-time listener. Small-scale productions, often funded out of their originators' own capital, can offer first-rate drama but rely on word of mouth, good Internet street cred or, increasingly, social media and iTunes top downloads to advertise and to attract new audiences. As Julie Hoverson, creator of *19 Nocturne Boulevard* (2008–present), suggested in her 'making-of' audio drama podcast, the difficulties involved for the small-scale, independent audio drama producer mean that many operations do not succeed beyond producing a single play (2010a).

19 Nocturne Boulevard, however, has proven its staying power with a barrage of productions. *19 Nocturne Boulevard* also highlights the heavy genre-fication of the current independent audio drama scene in the United States. A dedicated listener can find the genres/modes one hears on radio and audio all over the world: comedy, fantasy, science fiction, adaptations of classic texts, adaptations (or live recordings) of stage plays, the perennially popular thriller or detective story and satire. *19 Nocturne Boulevard* has carved itself a niche in the genre of horror audio drama, with a plethora of counterparts from Icebox Audio Theater to KC Wayland's *We're Alive*, a zombie saga. Hand and Traynor summarized Icebox as 'an education and charitable and literary group dedicated to the study, practice, and production of radio theater and the related arts to include, but not be limited to script writing, production, acting, sound effects, music composition and directing' (2011: 80). *We're Alive,* also examined in detail by Hand and Traynor, 'is set in an apocalyptic Los Angeles where a disparate group of survivors struggle to keep alive in the face of a multitude of zombies as well as other living rivals fighting for the remnants and fragments of a crumbling civilization' (2011: 88). Horror audio drama is particularly well-served, with *Campfire Radio Theater* (2011–present) showrunner John Ballentine crediting 1980s Canadian horror radio drama anthology *Nightfall* (1980–83) with inspiration for his long-running horror series (Ballentine 2011).

One of the original prolific online independent audio producers is Misfits Audio, the project of CEO 'Capt.' John Tadrzak that embraces a variety of genres and stories under its umbrella production title. One genre in particular seems to acknowledge this nostalgic quality while not necessarily building upon it. When Garrison Keillor wrote in 2005, 'I am old enough to be nostalgic about radio […] but I don't feel a hankering to hear any of it ever again', he represented a majority in the first sentiment and a minority in the second (Keillor 2005 n.pag.). Simply put, those who remember radio drama of the 1940s, 1950s and 1960s (and perhaps their nostalgic and enthusiastic revivals in the 1970s and 1980s) are often drawn to recreating these types of stories. Nearly every active audio anthology production succumbs to this nostalgia; radio scripts of the Golden Age are often recorded anew with little or no innovation from the original. Some of these genre pieces are pastiche, but many are po-faced tributes. *Stage Door* (n.d., Gypsy Audio Productions), is one of these straight remakes, though an undeniably well-made piece of audio drama (it was originally written by Edna Ferber and adapted for *Lux Radio Theater* in 1937). While Challis et al. argue that reproducing OTR-era scripts for live performance does not 'merely reproduce antique radio but re-animates the vibrancy of the form' (2014: 255), I would disagree and suggest this approach binds audio drama practice in a certain era and a certain nostalgic mode of production. Some productions combine studio-based recording with features of satellite audio drama, such as Audioblivious Productions based out of a basement in Cincinnati, Ohio. Others form an industry: *Our Fair City,* a multi-season Chicago-based award-winning drama of 'post-apocalyptic sci-fi', began in 2011. They further expanded to include comic book anthologies and short fiction, all freely available online.

From what sources does contemporary audio drama draw its actors? In 1946, as Duerr discovered, 50 per cent of the radio acting in New York City was done by 20 per cent of the members of the American Federation of Radio Actors (1950: 6). In the context of the BBC, Piers Plowright was quoted by Simon Elmes regarding recurring radio talent: 'you'd expect to hear the same voices, that was half the pleasure of it' (Elmes 2008: 190). To an extent, this also occurs with satellite audio drama; freelance voice artists can interact without national borders preventing them. As a consequence, a number of in-demand voices proliferate, such as North Yorkshire-based David Ault, having appeared in pieces by Darker Projects, 1138 Productions, the Voice Realm, the *NoSleep* podcast, Pendant Productions, Unseen Shadows, Campfire Radio Theater, Misfits Audio, BrokenSea, the Mercenary Artist, the Wicked Library, Colonial Radio Theatre, Cooperantem Audio and Voices in the Wind, among others (!).

Fan audio

Fan audio-makers take their cue from (text) fan fiction, traditionally the 'literature of the subordinate' (Derecho 2006: 73). M. Mackey and J.K. McKay summarize fan fiction as 'one relatively democratic version of that impetus to rework, to open up a previously finished story' (2008: 133). While text fan fiction usually involves only one writer, fan audio uses the source texts of media, literature and culture and 'democratically reworks it', using actors, composers, writers, directors, producers, sound recordists and mixers in a joint effort. One of the appeals of what some might call derivative creation is in the 'endlessly deferred narrative', which is, after all, one of the selling points of serial fiction (Hills 2002: 128).

One of the most famous examples of fan audio production was Pendant Audio Productions, which, since 2004, had been offering fan audio serials based on a number of copyrighted franchises, such as *Star Trek, Indiana Jones* and *Batman*. The threat of legal action from the copyright holders in 2012 forced the production company to remove all fan audio content from its website, even though all of Pendant's productions were free to download; it is suggested unofficially that because the franchise sold items such as t-shirts and mugs through the website, the concept of 'fair use' was challenged. The law is still open to interpretation. Pendant continues to operate, but with original and copyright-lapsed material. Fan audio in general ranges from *Doctor Who* to adaptations of the manga *Fruits Basket* (2011); another of the most ambitious forays into fan audio was Misfits Audio Productions' *Snape's Diaries* (2008), based on J.K. Rowling's *Harry Potter* novels (1997–2007) and the Warner Brothers' films (2001–11). More recent fan productions include the award-winning *Improvised Star Trek* (2011–present) and *The Katniss Chronicles* (*c*. 2011), based on *The Hunger Games* (2008–10) series of books.

Welcome to Night Vale

In July 2013, the relatively unknown podcast *Welcome to Night Vale* (*WTNV*) leapt to the top of the iTunes podcast charts. It had debuted one year previously, releasing twice-monthly episodes. *WTNV*'s popularity on Tumblr helped it reach 2.5 million downloads by July 2013. *WTNV* largely emulated (and inspired) anachronistic, nostalgic community radio formats and cultures (Hancock and McMurtry 2018). It is emblematic of current audio drama, especially that which is based out of the United States, because of its continuity with OTR, oral horror storytelling and its DIY aesthetic. Created by Joseph Fink and Jeffrey Cranor, the short drama is notable for its form and its production. Originally mixed on Freeware Audacity and (usually) featuring one voice, that of Cecil Palmer (Cecil Baldwin), it is distributed through podcast distributor Libsyn with music provided almost exclusively by a single composer/performer. *WTNV*'s production simplicity belies its many layers of engagement with audiences, with narrator Palmer epitomizing local radio's scripted/spontaneous speech; 'he *sounds* like a serene, reassuring local radio host' (Bottomley 2015: 185, original emphasis) despite the bizarre science-fiction events he narrates as public service bulletins on the fictional Night Vale Community Radio station. Palmer narrates a world with more than 50 characters, describing as commonplace disturbing events and uncanny characters in a fictional desert southwest community. Hancock would argue that *WTNV* is less a horror or comedy podcast and more a vision of inclusive community. 'Night Vale', she suggests, 'is a town where anybody can find community' and has engendered a truly worldwide following (2018: 2–5; Włodarczyk and Tyminska 2014). *WTNV* has spawned a veritable empire, with its live shows typified by cosplaying and directed roleplaying (Hancock 2018: 13).

Audio drama curators

Many contemporary audio dramas rely heavily on online forums and social media such as Facebook and Twitter to support and develop their respective communities. To navigate this impressive but disjointed treasure trove hanging somewhere in cyberspace, a number of self-appointed connoisseurs of the field have established podcast reviews in order to publicize and encourage the audio drama community. It should be here noted that many contemporary audio drama efforts cannot be easily categorized within the national context as 'American'; perhaps more accurately, a 'North American' aesthetic can be said to be in place. Indeed, the most influential of the audio drama curators are the *Sonic Society* and *Radio Drama Revival* (2007–present). Jack J. Ward of Halifax, Nova Scotia, created the *Sonic Society,* a weekly podcast and radio broadcast (CKDU 88.1 FM), in 2005. The anthology/discussion show grew out of *The Shadowlands,* an OTR showcase (The Sonic Society n.d.). Now co-hosted by the ubiquitous David Ault, the *Sonic Society* is also a blog and has a social media presence with excellent up-to-the-minute news about all aspects of audio drama worldwide. Similarly, *Radio Drama Revival* was founded in 2007 by Frederick Greenhalgh, whose production entity is FinalRune, based out of Portland, Maine. Now hosted by David Rheinstrom, its archive boasts over 450 hours of original audio fiction. Both anthologies grew out of a love for OTR transformed into a dedication to sharing new audio drama online. In addition to these shows, the Audio Drama Directory (also curated by Jack J. Ward) organizes available drama by genre and presents it with 'Audio Drama Ratings'. Ward writes, '[a]s an educator and a father, I know I would love to be able to point more families, teachers and students to a number of different audio play productions', thus the ratings system (Ward n.d.b).

There are a number of audio drama awards that have rewarded audio drama excellence in the last decade (see Appendix 4). The Audio Verse Awards arose in 2013 after frustration over a lack of dedicated awards purely for *free online audio drama*. Run by a team of volunteers, the Verse Awards define audio drama as 'dramatization, not prose, with multiple characters and using sound effects or/and music to present the piece' (Beall et al. 2017). Winners receive 'fortune and glory' and a special Web graphic. The longer-established Mark Time and Ogle Awards have existed since 1996 for the specific genres of science-fiction/fantasy/horror/mystery/detective audio drama. The Parsec Awards cover similar territory, speculative fiction, though their definition of 'fiction podcasting' is less rigid than the Audio Verse Awards. The Sarah Awards for Audio Fiction are by comparison brand-new (2017), originating from Sarah Lawrence College, and feature a fee to enter. The National Audio Theater Festival (NATF) bestows a reward annually, the Norman Corwin Excellence in Audio Theatre Award. The annual festival is a practical and hands-on training ground for aspiring audio-makers.

Audio drama podcasts

The audio drama audience in the United States in the second decade of the twenty-first century faces an embarrassment of riches. Technological advances such as the podcast have made the creation of audio drama easier, less expensive and potentially more accessible and democratic. Technological change has dictated that some audiences adapt to listening to audio drama in the car or on MP3 players, but many more still listen on traditional equipment in more traditional settings if provided with the opportunity. While there are many models for audio drama beyond the freely available gift economy recognized by the Audio Verse Awards, a number of for-profit companies (see previous section on Audible) have emerged, chief among them Gimlet Media. Gimlet, run by Alex Blumberg and Matthew Lieber, was financed initially by $1.5 million, which was then supplemented through crowdfunding. Gimlet mainly produced nonfiction podcasts but created a single drama strand in 2016, a high-profile production starring Catherine Keener and David Schwimmer, *Homecoming*, whose TV rights were almost immediately snatched up (Andreeva 2017). Verdier of *The Guardian* notes that it's 'impossible not to become immersed in the opening episode of the psychological thriller' (2016), though Conor Donovan of HeadStuff remarked, 'the plot seems a little flat. Characters are hastily shaded in, and any tension is cranked up just as quickly' (2016). It seems likely Gimlet will create more series in this vein.

Markman and Sawyer have suggested that most podcast-makers podcast not to make a profit, but because 'they can express themselves and their expertise and potentially become famous doing so' (2014: 32). Speaking more generally about net-only radio, Baker commented that it was 'a space that provides participants with opportunities for innovation and empowerment, not only as users but also as producers and managers' (2012: 213). Malatia goes on to suggest that the human desire to be heard is of high importance:

The ambition to be heard by all, to have one's voice or creative work beamed to everyone at the same time remains the hidden highest goal of all, including Internet users. This is not motivated only by ego, but also impact. The desire to make a mark.

(2007: 15)

As a very informal survey conducted by Cochrane et al. in April 2014 noted, of a sample of 1180 podcasters, 15.52 per cent had been engaged in podcasting for nine years. Understanding why listeners choose to seek out podcasts will give us valuable insight into the kinds of potential audiences they represent.

We know more about the way people consume podcasts. 'The Infinite Dial' survey results on US media consumption in 2017 suggests that most people (80% of those surveyed, who had ever listened to a podcast) listened to it at home while 47% listened in the car, 28% on foot and 19% while on public transportation (Edison Research and Triton Digital 2017: 47). (Curiously, 29% reported to listening to a podcast while at work!) So although Ira Glass defined *Serial* at its debut as '[l]ike *House of Cards* or *Game of Thrones* but you can enjoy it while you're driving' (Glass 2014), 82% of those who listen to audio in the car still use AM/FM radio (Edison Research and Triton Digital 2017: 54). 'At home' was still the location *most* listened to (52 per cent) (Edison Research and Triton Digital 2017: 48). While Michael Bull has suggested that the drivetime audience is often a solitary one (2003: 364), *Serial* and other podcasts in its mould seem to be consumed more frequently at home than anywhere else. This may reflect the concentrated listening supposedly needed for podcast listening as opposed to radio as the 'background medium', although audiobooks still reflect this breakdown, with the majority (almost 19%) listened to at home and 15% in the car (Kozlowski 2016). This listening does not seem to be particularly gendered, with 27% of men surveyed in 2017 and 21% of women saying they had listened to a podcast in the last month (Edison Research and Triton Digital 2017: 43).

The post-*Serial*

This chapter will conclude with a short discussion of a particular sub-genre of audio drama podcasting that has grown both from the rich tradition of radio/audio drama horror/thrillers (touched upon briefly in this chapter), OTR thrillers and oral folktales that have inspired *Welcome to Night Vale,* and, indeed, the non-fiction podcasting sensation *Serial.* This sub-genre, which Danielle Hancock and I have dubbed the 'post-*Serial*', is emblematic of the cutting edge of US audio drama podcasts, due to their engagement with their multiple modes, their production aesthetic and undeniable popularity. In 1999, Crook argued that 'radio has not lost its importance as a huge and significant source for news and entertainment and the opportunity to hoodwink the audience is as strong as it's ever been' (1999a: 105). Indeed, nearly twenty years after his pronouncement, the enjoyment to be had in exploiting framing errors is still present, though with less emphasis on 'hoodwinking' and more on 'playing the game'. As suggested previously, *WTNV* harnessed an existing satellite audio drama horror aesthetic shared and pioneered by programmes such as *Pseudopod*[5] (2006–present), *The Drabblecast* (2007–present), *Tales from Beyond the Pale*, *Tales to Terrify* (2012–present), *Earbud Theater* (2012–present) and the previously mentioned *19 Nocturne Boulevard*, *We're Alive*, the *NoSleep Podcast* and *Campfire Radio Theater*. As Hancock and I have argued, podcast horror has existed longer than the concept of the podcast itself.

The list of post-*Serial* podcasts includes (but is not limited to) *Lime Town* (2015–present), *The Black Tapes* (*TBT*) (2015–present), *TANIS* (2015–present), *The Bright Sessions* (2015–present), *The Message* (2015–present), *Archive 81* (2016–present), *The Deep Vault* (2016–present), *Within the Wires* (2016–present), *The Box* (2016), *Akiha Den Den* (2016) and *Rabbits* (2017). Notably, all of these fictional podcasts were made after the first season of *TAL's Serial*. While some podcast listeners/makers have expressed annoyance with the nonfiction *TAL*-soundalikes, such as Gimlet Media's *StartUp* (2015–present) and Radiotopia's *Criminal* (2014–present) (McHugh 2016: 8), it seems the *TAL/Serial* aesthetics have crossed over to the fictional. If, before *Serial*, fiction podcasts often depended upon radio's frameworks, conventions and even aesthetics, Hancock and I have argued elsewhere that Sarah Koenig and team 'established a narrative style which was informed by, and exploratory of, podcast media identity, and its noted properties of mobility, fragmentation, and individualistic listening culture' (Hancock and McMurtry 2018: 83). Despite *TAL's* 'highly conversational' and 'audio vérité feel', Ira Glass and his producers 'spend a great deal of time editing pieces and copy to create the "relaxed" style of the program' (Wallace 2010: 767–68). Fictional podcasts like *Lime Town, TBT* and *TANIS* have adopted such an aesthetic. These podcasts were notable for their enthusiastic connection to the audio-visual nature of the Web, not just the 'inner world' created by the podcast/headphone-based playback (Bull 2007, 2010). Indisputably, these drama podcasts utilize the techniques previously discussed in Chapter 2, centripetal intimacy along with the engaging pull of seriality. However, they also make use of website imagery, logos, show episode 'posters' and other paratexts, which have been used in pre-podcast audio drama to an extent, but have come to full fruition with post-*Serial* podcasts. This sub-genre also tends to engage with technostalgia, part of a wider fascination with radio nostalgia as evinced in *WTNV* and live performatory audio drama as discussed earlier in this chapter, and something that seems to be part of a wider Zeitgeist (Winters 2016: 46).

The Black Tapes, TANIS, Lime Town, The Message and *Archive 81* are all programmes that, like *Serial*, investigators/journalists who relay the progress of their mystery-solving to audiences through bi-weekly installments of the podcast medium (Hancock and McMurtry 2017). In particular, *TBT* and its sister-show *TANIS* inhabit a fictional NPR-like network, Pacific North West Stories, where the respective hosts, Alex Reagan and Nic Silver, 'work' as reporters, lending a credibility to the Gothic frame story holding together Reagan and Silver's supernatural, fictional exploits. PNWS doesn't exist as such, but by making the implicit reference to NPR, these series demonstrate a certain self-awareness in the genre.

What are the artistic reasons for adopting the post-*Serial* approach? On a superficial level, these fictional podcasts 'sound' like *Serial* and perhaps garner some listeners that way. Through emulating *Serial*'s recognizable form, podcast fiction becomes intelligible to an unfamiliar audience (Hancock and McMurtry 2018). More relevantly, these podcasts tap into the inherent Gothic nature of *Serial*'s investigations, deriving adventure and suspense from investigating notions of 'what is truth?' *Serial* tried to tap into an ultimately unsustainable hybrid between reality and storytelling, because the cases examined were real-life investigations, without the neat conclusions of fiction, despite the adept sleight-of-hand aesthetic of Ira Glass. The post-*Serial* fictions had no such problems. While the conception of *Lime Town* in particular predates *Serial*, it seems that Berry is correct to assert that *Serial*'s success is due to a combination of factors, that its success was, if not inevitable, partly the result of many elements coming together with a similar Zeitgeist in mind (2015: 171). It is possible that post-*Serial* podcast fiction has (or will) reach a saturation point, but for the moment, it is not only very popular – *TBT* and *TANIS* gained over 12 million listeners in their first year – but very artistically satisfying, even garnering a post-*Serial* influenced serial drama on BBC Radio 4, *That Was Then* (2018).

Conclusion

To conclude, individuals in the United States are listening to audio drama and have a wide access to a range of productions, whether on terrestrial community radio such as KZMU Moab, or through podcasts and satellite audio drama. It is not commercial radio itself that precludes the possibility of drama in the United States finding a home, but rather it is symptomatic of the stifling environs of format radio. US PSB providers, such as NPR, have not had a consistent relationship with drama. This is a historic and chronic problem; it is predicated on the role of public radio in US consciousness as well as a lack of awareness of where public radio funding originates. Individuals who want to listen to audio drama are more likely to find it online (or on their smartphones or iPods). The rise of podcasting has helped with audio drama access: the descending price of equipment along with the widespread use of Web 2.0 has also contributed. Audio drama can now be found on the fringes of audiobooks, online, in podcasts, or even in performatory live shows. However, because it is difficult to engage in a full framework, the multitude of choice is a double-edged sword, or as Renata Salcecl put it, 'a tyranny of choice'.

Notes

1 More than 700 radio stations receive programming grants from CPB (Lochte 2004: 47).
2 See Tsakalidou (2013).

3   Yuri Rasovsky evidently thought the two were separate. 'Narrating is not acting', he wrote (n.d.b).
4   Anthony J. Sloan (2005: 136), the arts director of WBAI, the New York Pacifica station, gave much the same reasoning for his live action epics (Crook 2010: 233).
5   It is debatable whether some of these titles strictly constitute full audio drama as some are mainly readings.

Section IV

The Future of Audio Drama

Chapter 10

Listening Now

> But radio is also comprised of comedy podcasts, archived discussion programs, time-shifted voice tracking, public radio news magazines, short and long-form audio documentaries, curatorial sites, interactive audio drama, sound installations, audio tours of urban spaces, audiobooks with or without musical soundtracks, historic sound events posted on YouTube, spoken word collections, nostalgic broadcasts of old-time radio, audio collectors' online offerings, and hundreds of audio apps available for iPhones and tablets.
>
> – Michele Hilmes (2013: 44)

This book has attempted to provide an extended valediction of audio drama through its history and aesthetics, by looking at its particular properties, in an attempt to prove its continued relevance and in order to suggest ways to make it more inclusive and more vital. As previously argued, the concept of 'radio' in the twenty-first century is still fluid. To follow that to its logical conclusion, definitions of how radio or audio drama might be defined in the twenty-first century are likewise fluid. As Dubber seems to suggest, the methods and means may have changed a great deal, but presumably the essence of what makes an audio drama has not: 'Radio producers use tape, or they use digital editors; technicians may have broadcast engineering or software development roles; presenters may sit in air conditioned studios or in their bedroom at home' (2013: 22). One of the most important points broached in the previous chapters is that radio policy does not exist in a vacuum, and we can now take that to mean mass media culture in general. As Shingler and Wieringa (1998) point out, radio has the advantages of being flexible, affordable, accessible and immediate – all of the reasons given in the Introduction for the continued existence of audio drama. How can we 'treat' audio drama of today, and how do we chart where it is going? Traditional broadcast radio looks warily at its continued existence, and podcasts struggle towards sustainability and recognition in a flooded market. How can audio drama continue to be heard, upon which platforms, and how to entice new audiences while retaining existing ones?

In 2014, I completed the Ph.D. thesis that inspired this book. At the time, I suggested that a future recipe for successful, popular, well-made and engaging audio drama within a US national distribution context might be:

Seriality + high production values + star casting = success?

Subsequently, and to my surprise, the emergence of *Serial* (2014–present) from *This American Life (TAL)* (1995–present)/WBEZ Chicago and its consequent overwhelming and gamechanging popularity fulfilled, in part, this recipe. The salient difference was, of course, that *Serial* was not fictional drama. Nevertheless, as I explained in a 2016 article in *The Journal of Popular Culture, Serial* (and the post-*Serial* fiction described in Chapter 8), freely exploited strategies taken from fictional drama in ways that helped it achieve incredible listener loyalty. Thus, while I asked in my 2014 Ph.D. thesis conclusion what could be done to convince the US audience that it wants and needs audio drama, the current question is how to turn the almost obsessive desire of some audiences for *Serial*-like content into a wider and more productive desire for audio drama content, as well as answering ongoing questions of distribution. As I noted in the 2016 article, *Serial* to some extent solved the most pressing problem for widespread US audio drama production and proliferation – namely issues of financial support for production and distribution – through the eventual monetization of the podcast. Nevertheless, making audio drama financially viable in a wholly commercial environment is still a challenging and problematic proposition. As discussed in the previous chapter, podcasts are by no means the end-all and be-all of audio drama now, and, I would argue, in the future. Nevertheless, as some writers have introduced a dichotomy between 'old' aural media like radio and 'new' like podcasts (Cridland 2018), it is worth exploring podcast production and audiences in order to understand listening now.

In order to consider how people are listening now and *may* listen in the future, it's instructive to examine various issues in *Serial*'s production and reception, as no success is 'unqualified'. Since its emergence, podcasting has approached funding in many different ways and has flirted to varying degrees with audio/online utopianism. In that regard, satellite audio drama and other formats have been closer to a 'free Internet' ideal, with a potential gift economy in place. Hilmes (2013: 55) argued that part of *TAL*'s success was its ubiquity of access, and as I will argue further in this chapter with the example of *Welcome to Night Vale* (2012–present), free, easy and fast-to-access, on-demand, multi-platform, digitally distributed audio proliferation can lead to remarkable fan engagement and online buzz. In this chapter, we will explore the ways *Serial* has pre-empted some of the questions about how podcast/audio drama is listened to now and what this might mean for the way podcast/audio drama is listened to in the future, including issues of monetization and advertising; what audiences *Serial* reached and didn't reach and the implications for those listening to podcasts and online audio content.

Shrimp sale at the Crab Crib: Advertising in podcasting paradise?

'A single, short line – "There's a shrimp sale at The Crab Crib" – uttered in the *Serial* podcast' by producer Dana Chivvis in Episode 5 of the first season (Andrews 2015) not only struck a chord with listeners, who thereafter wanted 'Shrimp Sale at the Crab Crib' merchandise like t-shirts, but they also descended *en masse* to the Woodlawn, Maryland-area business. This was an instance of a throwaway line (unintentionally?) turned into free advertising, but in recent years, podcasting and advertising have had a varied and sometimes uneasy relationship. As a recent *New York Times* article noted,

> A podcast hosting gig has become a new status symbol for top journalists, entertainers and talking-head politicos. Hosts can discuss whatever they want, usually for a rapt audience of in-car drivers and on-train commuters. Most podcasts are available free on iTunes, and advertising is often necessary to cover productions costs. So A-list talent is now singing for its soup, routinely peddling products like audiobooks, bedsheets and delivery meal services.
>
> (Geiger Smith 2017)

This section examines the different ways that podcasts/audio drama have been funded and in particular how *Serial* was funded (and how that changed between the beginning of Season 1 and the conclusion of Season 2). There will also be a short exploration of why audio advertising works and the implications of Audible investing in new audio drama writing.

There is accumulated evidence for the efficacy of advertising on radio in general. 'Radio remains a very cost-effective way of creating durable images in listeners' minds' (Starkey 2004: 180). An influential and no doubt effective example was given by Stan Freberg in 1965 in the promotional record *Who Listens to Radio?* Freberg's character convinces a sceptical advertiser that radio advertising can be incredibly rich:

> I want the 700-foot mountain of whipped cream to roll down into Lake Michigan which has been drained and filled with hot chocolate. Then the Royal Canadian Air Force will fly overhead towing the ten-ton maraschino cherry which will be dropped into the whipped cream.
>
> (Freberg et al. 1965)

Freberg sought to convince advertisers in rich, imaginative language; researchers have subsequently demonstrated the psychological basis for such arguments. For example, according to Paul Bolls, 'an entertaining story that is relevant to the targeted audience is the foundation of excellent high-imagery radio ads' (2006: 209). Bolls' findings are unsurprising, given that Stephen Kosslyn (1983) has determined that we use images to remember facts about objects or events, such as when we are recalling something we saw in passing (such as how many windows are in our kitchen); a description has been stored that would allow us to deduce the information, but it is too cumbersome spatially to use it. Kip Allen, former programme director of KHFM Albuquerque, the classical music radio station, was proud of his system of attuning the commercial advertisements, heard on air during breaks in music, to the specific audience. Allen characterized this audience as 'affluent, educated, loyal' as well as 'opinionated, judgemental, and anxious for facts in order to form an opinion' (Allen

2013e). Years of listening to Allen's KHFM in my youth has given me a wealth of anecdotal evidence of the kind of radio advertising that disturbs listeners least, and this kind of advertising chimes with Bolls' (2006) findings: cognitive/visually clever ads, of relevance to the audience, composed of like-sounding music and tone to the content and narrative-driven. Radio advertising obviously works in a similar fashion, though the less visually creative methods currently employed in some drama podcasts (discussed below) take a much more literal approach.

Advertisers, therefore, use imaginative radio to sell a product or a service, but, as we know, not all radio is funded by advertising. The public service broadcasting (PSB) ethos has found other ways to generate funding. Yet these methods have problems of their own, chiefly how to cause donors to consistently give money to support PSB stations or networks. In Andréa Baker's case studies of net-radio users in the United States and Australia, one of her respondents, a university student/music radio fan who rejected traditional terrestrial commercial format radio, was also unable to cope with NPR because of its emphasis on fundraising from its listeners. As he put it,

> Every morning I wake up with NPR, and for the past 5 days they have been begging people to send them money, and it's 5 minutes of news, 10 minutes of 'Hey send us some money', and it's 5 minutes of news, 10 minutes of 'Hey send us some money, we need your support' and it's very annoying.
>
> (Baker 2012: 197)

'Programming that is relatively expensive, relatively uncompetitive, and of relatively low value to listeners is not only tough to sustain financially', Walrus Research & AudiGraphics Inc. found in 2006; 'it is hard to justify using any public service rationale' (Walrus Research 2006d: 15). Kinnally and Brinkerhoff found that a third of NPR's budget comes from individual donations. Therefore, NPR 'must make donors feel good about giving' (2013). A range of motives, they found, that drive people to pledge to PSB include the need for public recognition; the incentive of tax deductions; a sense of connection; and emotional needs such as guilt. 'Should listeners give directly to NPR, with all those famous names and velvety voices, or give to the local station which provides the infrastructure to deliver that signal?' (Dunaway 2014: 178).

Podcasts operate in yet a different way. Those that have a commercial funding element cannot utilize advertising the way traditional radio has, due to their discreet form, though some take a more traditional radio approach than others: related technology Spotify, for example, sandwiches its ads in between music selections, though the kinds of ads and their frequency depends on platform (tablet or mobile) as much as subscription level. Despite the ads, Spotify has 10 million paying subscribers, a 25 per cent conversion rate (Slattery 2014). McClung and Johnson advised that 'advertisers [should] continue use of the sponsorship approach by placing ads only during the beginning and end of the podcast program', sound advice for not alienating and irritating listeners (2010). Markman and Sawyer found that, in addition to time-shifting, podcast listeners enjoyed the fact podcasts offered little to no advertising and that they could seek a more personalized approach (2014: 20). PSB-originating podcasts like *Serial* have been noted for their ability to remove the PSB exhortation to keep funding. But do they all make such a distinction? Early episodes of *The Black Tapes* (2015–present), *TANIS* (2015–present), and others thanked listeners for their (presumably at least partial financial) support. This is known as underwriting, where donors are named and described if not actually endorsed. The podcast production company Maximum Fun, for example, is also listener-supported like NPR. However, Kyle Wrather has shown that Maximum Fun has 'dabbled in branded content and native advertising', for example with an episode of *My Brother, My Brother and Me* (2011–present) called 'The McElroy Family Fun Hour Brought to You by Totino's', sponsored by the microwave pizza company (2016: 47–48).

Underwriting on the post-*Serial* podcasts (*TANIS*, for example) has become closer to actual product endorsement. Indeed, this has even given way to reflexive, 'meta parody' (Wrather 2016: 48). This seems like the aural equivalent of product placement. Robin Nelson suggests that 'product placement and direct sponsorship have become increasingly important' to sustaining TV (2007: 67) and Geiger Smith (2017) notes that '[t]he practice of podcast hosts reciting advertisements is reminiscent of the early days of radio and television', an aspect frequently parodied in modern audio drama (such as in *Prairie Home Companion* [1974–2016], BBC Radio 4's 2011 production *The Big Broadcast,* and the Fitzrovia Radio Hour). It is particularly disconcerting to listen to podcasts like *TANIS* severed midway by exhortations by host Nic Silver to put on some Bombas Socks, though perhaps in a drama podcast like *TANIS*, such disconnect is intentionally drawing focus back to the partially invented, partially real persona of hosts like Silver. Matteo Cacchia would have ruined the verisimilitude of *Amnèsia* (2008–09) if he had started talking about his Gucchi shoes, but in audio drama's recent climate, perhaps the unsettlingly real nature of *Amnèsia* is no longer possible. The celebrity endorsements, particularly, seem to jar, perhaps because many of these A-listers 'would not be likely to flop down on a mattress in a television commercial' (Geiger Smith 2017).

In this section, we have noted that many podcasts have employed underwriting as an advertising strategy, celebrity endorsements and/or PSB exhortations to donate. As noted earlier, by 1938 Seymour and Martin stated that US audiences were inured to advertising on radio, despite the vigorous efforts of radio reform groups in the 1930s, but how do twenty-first century audio drama listeners feel about advertising in podcasts? McHugh cites opinions of British listeners who, familiar with commercial-free BBC, may not tolerate ads in their podcasts (2016: 12). Unlike NPR, naturally, BBC radio does not interrupt broadcasts to chide their listeners for not paying their licence fees; this radical difference has grown out of the dissimilar approaches of the PSB national contexts, as discussed in detail in Chapters 7, 8 and 9. Sterling argues that podcasts allow 'for an instant world-wide appeal to very targeted or specialized audiences' similarly to blogging, 'thus raising the potential for commercial applications' (2010: 565). If so, then podcasting would seem to represent the natural progression of 'the long tail' as described by Chris Anderson in his book *The Long Tail: Why the Future of Business is Selling Less of More*. Anderson suggested that while 'hits, in short, *rule*', they are less important now as a concept and less money-spinning than in the 1970s and 1980s (2006: 1, original emphasis). Instead, he suggests, that the cost of reaching niches has fallen, and niche products can now find consumers (2006: 6). He cites the Internet as the main factor for this transformation, the 'unlimited and unfiltered access to culture and content of all sorts' (2006: 3). 'The great thing about broadcast', he notes,

> is that it can bring one show to millions of people with unmatchable efficiency. But it can't do the opposite – bring a million shows to one person each. Yet that is exactly what the Internet does so well.
>
> (2006: 5)

Siva Vaidhyanathan has also noticed the increasing potency of niches; Facebook, Google and Amazon 'want us to relax and be ourselves. They have an interest in exploiting niche markets that our consumer choices have generated' (2011: 112).

Dana Gerber-Margie seems to see an inevitability to podcasting monetization, not only in terms of commercial sponsorship but also that '[m]ore ads will also mean a side industry forming to support podcasts; there are already countless apps out there claiming to be the app that will finally solve all of podcasts' problems with sharing and going viral' (cited in Hilmes and Lindgren 2016: 7). She also suggests that experimentation can be done with other models such as subscription services (such as those employed by Audible, Gimlet, Big Finish and Wireless Theatre). When there is still so much equivalent drama freely available on the Web it is interesting to speculate as to how subscription-only services will continue to thrive.

Other funding options have been cited. Crowdfunding (with companies such as Kickstarter and Indiegogo) is a contemporary and often very effective funding venture. *Our Fair City* (2011–present), for example, started with a Kickstarter. 'On the web', Steffen suggests, 'the start-up and scale-up costs are low' and social media catalyses popularity, 'meaning that once good work reaches a critical mass of public awareness, it can spread like wildfire' (Steffen 2011: 90). As Kyle MacLellan reported in the *Huffington Post*, banks have been curtailing their lending 'due to tougher capital rules and greater regulatory scrutiny', whereas crowdfunding 'has expanded rapidly as an alternative source of finance' (2013). According to a study for the first quarter of 2014, for every hour in the month of March, more than $60,000 dollars were raised via worldwide crowdfunding (Clifford 2014). Patreon has also proven popular with audio drama and podcast-makers. Patreon's method is for patrons to pay monthly towards their creators, who are funded not only to 'work for themselves' but also must provide 'rewards' to their patrons. Currently, more than twenty audio drama groups are pursuing this method, from Icebox Radio Theater to Ars Paradoxica, either as a sole means to fundraising or (more commonly) in conjunction with other methods. Icebox, for example, has 34 patrons and raises $140 per month (at the time of writing) through Patreon. Their patrons get immediate access to exclusive content, so Patreon functions much like a subscription model while being 'ad-free'.

WBEZ Chicago's Vocalo funded itself through a combination of foundation grants, Chicago Public Radio venture funds, and underwriting messages, although 'the web is the primary source of funding for the service, largely through advertising, e-commerce, layered subscriptions for institutional restricted use, and donations' (Malatia 2007: 20). Its descendent, *Serial,* also used a variety of funding models. It was funded initially by *This American Life* and advertiser MailChimp, with Squarespace and Audible providing support mid-season (Griffin 2014; Baysinger 2015). These advertisers eagerly renewed their sponsorship for Season 2. Other audio drama series have followed a mixed model; Chatterbox Theater, for example, appealed to potential donors by publishing a 'Wish List' on their website that ranges from equipment to the rent for their radio studio. Contributors received recognition on the website in return for their beneficence.

'But I'm an American, and therefore I'm a little cynical: I've watched money ruin a lot of art', noted Devon Taylor (cited in Hilmes and Lindgren 2016: 7). There is, then, clearly some opposition to commercial models in audio drama and podcasting. Interestingly, *Welcome to Night Vale* is committed to providing its podcasts for free, supporting itself through crowdfunding, merchandizing and live performances, as well as making premium paid content available (all methods discussed above). This is sustainable/practical for their production methods; theirs is a small cast and was originally edited on Freeware like Audacity.

It is admittedly possible to produce audio drama that can be accessed for free (though with the potential for donations) on a long-term basis (Chatterbox may be the best example), but it assumes that writers, producers, actors, web designers and others will not use the production as a basis for making a living. In the increasingly monetized podcast world, this could be difficult to sustain, as audio drama producers see themselves going from amateurs to professionals, with attendant increasing costs (for equipment, self-remuneration, distribution and publicity). Currently, listeners to audio drama are doing what they have always done – accessing audio drama wherever and however they can find it, some investing in subscription services, some investing in crowdfunding, some not paying anything. This core group of listeners will probably continue in their practices, but new audiences accessing podcast drama in the near-future may see things differently. When Audible-produced original plays are released, their commercial model may have an impact on the way audio drama is consumed, due in part to Audible's pervasive abilities in advertising and distribution (due to its being ultimately owned by Google).

In this next section, we will pause for a moment in the discussion of the monetization of podcasts and focus on the audiences that traditional radio and podcasts have failed and what can be done about it.

Serial's sophomore slump

It has seemingly been the case in the annals of radio and audio drama that one-hit wonders are the norm rather than the exception. While *TAL* has banked on a long run of successes, uncharacteristic for the medium but perhaps not for US public radio and the

PRI/NPR modes, some listeners (and fellow podcast-makers) were perhaps struck with *schadenfreude* when *Serial*'s second season (2015–16) was less popular than the first, though generally still critically acclaimed. Many critics wrote that *Serial* Season 2 was extremely accomplished, yet fans determined that it didn't have the 'must-listen' factor. 'Sure, it's not as exciting as the breakout first season', Nick Quah admitted (cited in Hilmes and Lindgren 2016: 6). '[T]he story is bigger, the scale is more complex, and the stakes are so much more abstract […] this is still a three-dimensional chess game that no one's even tried to play' (Hilmes and Lindgren 2016: 6). Nevertheless, a post on a Reddit forum summed up the fan response: 'I, like pretty much everyone else, loved S1. But I got an episode or two into S2 as they were coming out and I just didn't like it as much' (MorboReddits in Reddit 2017).

Baron (2016) blamed Season 2's weekly-to-biweekly release as a reason for disenchantment. In general, though, listeners found the series somewhat boring, with the central mystery upstaged by 'more tenuous' ethical conversations, 'riveting for some and dull as dry toast for others' (Locker 2016). *Serial* Season 2 followed the very public saga of Bowe Bergdahl, a US soldier captured by the Taliban and released five years later under a cloud of allegations as to why he had gone AWOL. *Serial* Season 2 still had Sarah Koenig and the same production team; the theme music was still produced by Nick Thorburn, though it was not identical to the first season's. Season 2 had a more ruminating visual aesthetic on its website, but it was still a production by WBEZ Chicago and *TAL,* heard both online/in downloadable podcast form, and through terrestrial radio. In Season 2, relatively obscure murder mystery was exchanged for very high-profile case (Locker 2016). The cachet of exclusivity, perhaps even in closed community, had gone. 'Where's the excitement in waiting for the next instalment when you can just look up the guy's story on Wikipedia or in any US newspaper?' (Shakamalaka in Reddit 2017). Despite the continuing presence of Koenig, she did not interview Bergdahl directly; filmmaker Mark Woal mediated for her, which destroyed arguably the most important aspect from *Serial* Season 1, Koenig as narrator, as stand-in for ourselves. I argued in my 2016 article that, despite being real people, the speakers in *Serial* Season 1 became characters as soon as they were transformed by the *TAL* aesthetic – and the characters in Season 2 weren't as good. Reddit forum user TulipSamurai (Reddit 2017) wrote, 'Sarah Koenig made some really good points about Bo's [*sic*] mental state and the military's questionable recruitment at the time, but I find Bo [*sic*] really unsympathetic, inarticulate, and not horribly intelligent'.

The proprietary attitude of the Reddit poster above towards constructed portrayals of real people is not atypical; some listeners even objected to Koenig's 'paternalistic attitude toward the people and narratives she covers. She trusts only her team to get Bergdahl's story right' (Waldman 2015). Conversely, the things that annoyed many listeners about Season 1 (the lack of a concrete resolution, which, though true to real-life, was not a satisfying conclusion to a dramatized narrative) were part of the backbone of Season 2, potentially creating the sense of 'disappointment' felt by some. As Baron (2016) suggests, there was also less scope for listeners to weigh in and help 'solve' the case. Ironically, Season 2 is also more like its progenitor *TAL,* a mode that Waldman (2015) calls 'novelistic'.

Critics have suggested that even if *Serial* Season 2 was a 'cultural disappointment' (Baron 2016), it achieved wider journalistic/artistic attainments, demonstrating for the greater truth that despite the 'strong beliefs of some of Bergdahl's fellow soldiers and superiors, his poor decision cost no one their lives' (Locker 2016). 'The podcast', Waldman suggested, was 'growing up', as reflected by Season 2 (2016). Nevertheless, it is fruitless to argue that the *Serial/TAL* team did not take on board the criticisms of *Serial* Season 2 when devising their next spin-off project, *S Town/Shit Town* (2017). It's clear from the outset that *S Town* emulates *Serial* Season 1 with its central investigation of corruption in the United States justice system and in particular, allegations of murder that have gone under the radar (Bibb County, Alabama is little-represented online). These potential miscarriages of justice were, crucially, not discovered by host Brian Reed, but the idea for the podcast was actually *launched* by a listener, John B. McLemore, the native of 'Shittown, Alabama'. For many of the Nancy Drew-esque armchair detectives of *Serial* season 1, this must appear a dream come true (McMurtry 2016: 317). However, journalist Reed is still the mediator for listeners, not McLemore. McLemore is – mirroring Adnan Syed and rejecting the model of the inarticulate Bowe Bergdahl – incredibly articulate. He makes a good character. He is engaging and yet culpable, a depressive who may be a conspiracy theorist, a geek and/or genius, and a potential George Bailey who has stayed in his hometown despite aspirations to do something important and far-reaching with his life. Perhaps his ultimate fate – and the true subject of *S Town* – makes this even more poignant. It can be argued that Season 2 of *Serial* appealed to the more high art side of audio storytelling, as discussed in Chapter 1.

Mirroring *Serial* season 1's aesthetic, *S Town* includes the requisite phone interviews and keeps the regional accents. Indeed, the American South begins in *S Town* as Other, eerily reminiscent of *Lime Town* (2015–present) where the Eastern urban interloper was fictional investigator Lia Haddock rather than real-life journalist Brian Reed. Goudeau (2017) felt the characters wafted a sense of Southern Gothic, and Callahan (2017) accuses Reed of being a 'cosmopolitan reporter congratulating his backwoods subject[s] for having a moral compass'. Reed is represented as eagerly trolling people's Facebook pages, triggering the same questions of journalistic ethics and privacy as were raised with *Serial* Season 1 (McMurtry 2016: 318). Indeed, as shock developments in *S Town* make clear, the ethical stakes are perhaps even higher (Goudeau 2017); *S Town* is 'morally indefensible' (Alcorn 2017). While at first glance, the show's title *S Town* seems to reflect the self-censorship of radio and US advertising (Young 2017), listening to the podcast reveals an aesthetic that emulates HBO television's promise of 'quality' and 'exclusivity' served up with adult content, including nudity, sexual content and profanity. 'For all the world cloned from a movie studio of the classical Hollywood era', HBO can construct itself in the very image of the *Lux Hollywood Theater* (1934–55) (Miller 2008: x), and indeed, the *TAL* podcast can 'grow up' by not bleeping out frequent profanity – though necessarily excluding listeners to *TAL* and *Serial* who could access those shows on terrestrial radio, as *S Town* has been released solely in podcast form.

Reed is, perhaps, no Koenig, an ironic reversal of decades-discarded received wisdom about the perceived lack of authority in a woman's broadcasting voice (Barnard 1989: 149), and *S Town* occasionally borders on being overwritten, straying too blatantly into *TAL*'s wholesome quirk (Hirschom 2007). Alcorn (2017) suggests that Reed does not adhere closely enough to *TAL*'s reputation of 'garnered trust', that he is too slick, too heartless. While *Serial* Season 1 was criticized for wavering between genres, Season 2 was condemned for not including enough mystery (Bissrok in Reddit 2017), whereas *S Town* has once again re-aligned to the central mystery of Season 1 regarding a character's inherent truthfulness. *S Town*'s producers have certainly paid attention to listeners' gripes about *Serial* Season 1 and 2 release schedules and therefore released all 7 episodes of *S Town* at once. 'I've always been better at binging [*sic*] than keeping up', Reddit user MorboReddits (Reddit 2017) confessed. Now, that listener need not worry.

Close reading of the whole *TAL/Serial/S Town* cycle suggests that a documentary feature serial in this mould must adhere to a familiar structure and focus on a central mystery to achieve widespread popularity and critical acclaim or risk 'whatever hold it had on the Zeitgeist' dissipating (Baron 2016). Deviating from the conventions – even for a slow TV-esque 'thinkpiece read aloud over the course of three months' (Locker 2016) – risks alienating the audience (and the Zeitgeist). By virtue of the form, the audio drama podcasts that top iTunes favour serialized stories in the mould of 'soaps' (i.e. Continuing Drama) (*Homecoming* [2016–present], *The Black Tapes* podcast, *TANIS*, *Alice Isn't Dead* [2016–18], *Rabbits* [2017]), though one-off anthology dramas also feature (*NoSleep* [2011–present]). It is impossible to extrapolate a one-to-one parallel of the *TAL/Serial/S Town* cycle onto audio drama, but it does seem evident that serialization plays a key role in current listening, both for nonfiction podcasts and audio drama (online and podcast).

Claybourne

The evidence suggests that, as *Serial* did not emerge out of a vacuum, there is an 'almost inevitability to the structure and format' of *Serial* and the post-*Serial* (Hancock and McMurtry 2018: 85). I would argue that this 'almost inevitability' is manifest in pre-digital radio dramas like *Claybourne*, indeed down to this very notion of the prominence of seriality. I highlight *Claybourne* here because of its notions of accessibility and seeking out listeners who might not usually be reached by radio drama. *Claybourne* ran for 96 episodes on New Zealand radio station Newstalk ZB in 1998. Written by and starring Jim McLarty and William Davis and produced by Andrew Dubber and Belinda Todd, *Claybourne* was genre-crossing, a sci-fi/thriller soap opera broadcast four days a week in extremely short chunks (around five minutes), a highly addictive format. Set in New Zealand and with many Māori characters and a clear focus on Māori culture, it was, in Dubber's words 'deliberately and proudly New Zealand in its language, humour and accent. It was consciously cinematic in production and sound design' (2006). Furthermore, the serial drama was scheduled just after the 3:00 p.m. news:

> we imagined an audience member that would turn the radio on in the car as they waited outside for the school pickup, hear the next instalment, then switch off again (or at least turn the radio down) as the kids got in the car.
>
> (Dubber 2017)

Newstalk ZB was also characterized as having an audience skewed towards 'white, conservative, middle class, male' listeners (Dubber 2017).

The listener's 'way in' was Thompson, an American employed by Koestlers, a mysterious corporation. On holiday in New Zealand, Thompson is called to investigate a crisis in Claybourne, a town in the remote part of the north island. Thompson quickly becomes embroiled in the local community, interacting with Māori *kaumātua* (elected tribal leader) Mata. With a televisual emphasis on 'storyarcs within story arcs' (Dubber 2006), *Claybourne* was almost literally too large for its palette, ending after one season when two had been planned. It was resurrected in 2006 as a podcast by the Podcast Network, became one of the most popular spoken word programmes in the history of mp3.com (Hopkinson 2007) and subsequently became available on Bandcamp and Archive.org.

Claybourne had many of the elements that made *Serial* irresistible:

- The strong pull of seriality and episodes available in digestible chunks
- A seemingly infinite series of cliffhangers
- Centripetal storytelling
- Genre slipperiness
- Bookending litany
- Compelling characters
- Accessibility.

Although set in what some listeners might consider an alien culture, it was presented in an accessible way (i.e. Thompson was initiated into Māori traditions and exposed to pervasive elements of Kiwi culture like Vegemite). Dubber describes this as:

> The relationship between Mata and Thompson meant that audiences were generally situated somewhere in between. The idea was that any pakeha [white person] who lives in New Zealand is less ignorant of Māori culture than Thompson. As a kaumātua, very few Māori know as much about the culture as Mata.
>
> (Dubber 2017)

The major difference between *Serial* and *Claybourne* was in the *way* the story was told. *Claybourne* used an omniscient voice. *Serial* had the noughties idea of the probing, self-reflexive reporter, a sort of true crime/Gothic protagonist. Another important difference was the way in which *Claybourne* was distributed: by traditional means, on terrestrial radio. In subsequent years, then, it has taken on an afterlife probably not envisaged by its creators, and it's a testament to the series' quality that a drama produced by and for a New Zealand audience could be globally engrossing. One thing that *Claybourne* had that *Serial* didn't was that it (potentially) reached people who aren't in the white, middle class, affluent, educated demographic. This has ramifications for audio drama reaching audiences whom it has traditionally failed to reach; as we have seen, the audiences for BBC Radio 4 have tended to be white, educated and middle class, which is a similar demographic to those who listen to public radio in the United States.

Serial's audience: Those who don't listen

Who did *Serial* reach?

As far as we are able to determine, *Serial* reached, generally, public radio's core audience – young-ish to middle-aged, technologically savvy, generally white, middle-class people. It is difficult to build up a demographic understanding of *Serial*'s audience beyond inference and anecdote. iTunes charts can only reveal so much: for the most part *numbers* of listeners, not who they are. Collecting 'accurate demographic information from' websites can often be 'almost impossible', as Pinch and Athanasiades found in a study of online music-makers (2012: 486). In Richard Berry's (2015) informal, 100-participant survey about *Serial* conducted on Twitter, 54 per cent of respondents came to *Serial* who already listened to *TAL*, and 72 per cent were already public radio listeners. The demographics of US public radio listeners have already been discussed, but broadly this group adheres to the white, middle class, affluent, educated part of the population, though it tends to be more female than male (in common with BBC Radio 4 listeners).

Who didn't it reach?

In repeatedly discussing the core audiences for speech-based radio like BBC Radio 4, NPR and public service broadcasting-launched podcasts like *Serial*, it is important to explicitly state what audiences are not being reached. These audiences are as follows: the elderly (who do not feel technologically comfortable with accessing podcasts); working-class listeners and those with lower standards of education; the very young (teens) and people of colour. As regards elderly listeners, *TAL* producers are actively seeking them. They urged older listeners to follow in the late Mary Ahearn's footsteps and 'change their worlds' by listening to podcasts, as opposed to traditional broadcast radio (This American Life 2014b).

With this in mind, how do we reconcile the audience of *Serial* in their twenties, thirties, forties with the existing audience of older people who still remember original OTR or later 1970s/1980s permutations? Is there a way to unite the two audiences under the auspice of a single audio drama? Decades of commercially released OTR cassette tapes and CDs have demonstrated that the ageing group of consumers who were young in the 1940s, 1950s and 1960s and remember listening to radio drama is prepared to spend money listening to OTR favourites. Brian Ott's findings on nostalgia television (2011) suggest that although currently an undeniable market exists for straight replays of OTR drama, whether on terrestrial radio, or on CD, MP3 player or in the car, this audience could well be interested in new drama in *the style* of OTR. Verma writes, 'if what we long for about the theater of the mind is less *The Shadow* and more the mode of "pictorial listening" that *The Shadow* invents' (2012: 10), then this audience may be interested in accessing the classics of its youth repackaged in a more grown-up style with the same ethos with which they grew up.

The 'nostalgia' radio audience and the US PSB audience are not necessarily mutual. Hilmes notes that non-music radio audiences in the United States grew slowly in the 1970s, only reaching about 3 per cent of the population (2013: 47). She also suggests that the reasons speech radio was difficult to create on US radio post-1970 were:

> Once missed, a program could not be heard again; titles and credits were announced once or twice and then lost to memory; complex and tightly constructed soundworks passed rapidly before the ears and vanished, never to be heard again. Under these conditions, a coherent and sustainable sound culture simply could not develop.
>
> (Hilmes 2013: 48)

Perhaps a coherent sound culture could have been maintained if modes of address that 'make listeners feel engaged and welcome' (Chignell 2009: 63) had been developed. As noted by Charli Valdez (2017), ultimately *Serial* did not adequately deal with the dimension of race.

Is this a public radio problem?

In 2007, WBEZ Chicago, *Serial*'s parent station, was concerned that it was not reaching parts of its core potential audience and reinvented itself as Vocalo. Before the makeover, the Chicago Public Radio audience was 91% white, 5% black and 4% Latino. This was deemed a serious problem as it did not represent neighbourhood demographics. The NPR and PBS brands, including Chicago Public Radio, were perceived very negatively within the minority groups in the potential listenership (Malatia 2007: 14).

Remarkably, those programs we see as our most entertaining and most appealing to new listeners, like our own *This American Life, Wait, Wait…Don't Tell Me!* along with Minnesota Public Radio's *A Prairie Home Companion*, and even WBUR's *Car Talk*, were perceived to be just as clubby as NPR's weekly debrief with Cokie Roberts.

(Malatia 2007)

This consultancy project underlined an undeniable 'lack of variability in voice, accent, and dialect' on US radio, what Riismandel calls 'a symptom of the overwhelming homogeneity and lack of diversity' (Riismandel 2002: 427).

If racial/ethnic diversity of representation is a problem for public radio in the United States, it is certainly not one that has been ignored (Flintoff and Sterling 2010: 507). On the other hand, some public radio stations choose not to go the way that WBEZ did, perhaps in fear of what befell Dr Wally Smith at KUSC Los Angeles, as described by Mitchell (2005: 188): Dr Smith drove KUSC to the top of the classical music market in his listening area, then decided that the station wasn't adequately serving its (multiracial) community. Mitchell argues that trying to make the station appeal to Latino, East Asian and young audiences failed, in the process alienating its core (white, middle class, affluent, educated) audience. As suggested above, *Serial* was criticized for elevating white privilege in journalism. As argued by Valdez, 'the failings of *Serial* that are so glaringly obvious to critics of color exist precisely because Koenig and her team worked from a white majoritarian privilege' (2017: 335). *S Town* has also been criticized for erasing black America from the South that was so much part of the show's narrative (Mengiste 2017). However, this may be an access problem that extends beyond US public radio and is an area of concern in the British public service broadcasting environment as well. The BBC's Diversity Strategy 2011–15 is described by Hendy as 'fair-minded', inclusive and 'a marker of genuine progress' (2013: 49). Nevertheless, Aujla-Sidhu's examination of the BBC Asian Network argues the BBC's diversity objectives for 2020 'are not as ambitious as those of other broadcasters, for instance Sky, who want 20 per cent of significant on-screen roles to be filled by black, Asian and minority ethnic (BAME) actors' (2017: 107).

The crux of my concerns are represented in questions of why, for example, WBEZ Chicago pre-2007 was listened to an audience that was 91 per cent white, and why 'Pakistani, Indian and Bangladeshi audiences consume less radio than the general British population' (Aujla-Sidhu 2017: 110). This has implications for audio drama, because PSBs in both the United States and United Kingdom celebrate a speech culture that includes and in some cases celebrates aural drama; if the listeners are not racially and ethnically diverse as representative of the multiracial makeup of these countries, can we expect listeners who have felt traditionally excluded by public service speech radio to discover and embrace audio drama? It has been difficult to discover any statistically relevant data on the demographics (including race) behind audio drama and podcast-makers and listeners, but anecdotally I believe that, generally, online audio drama and podcast drama to be more diverse than terrestrial radio drama. The situation is, I believe, improving. Despite a commitment to reflect greater diversity at IRDP, only 7 per cent of IRDP's new writers were non-white (Crook 1999a: 42), though production photographs from Crook's text imply a high level of ethnic diversity. Also, Aujla-Sidhu characterizes the BBC Asian Network as 'a revolutionary attempt on the part of the public service broadcaster (PSB) to reflect contemporary British society' (2017: 107).

The examples of *Silver Street* (2004–10), *Atching Tan* (2008), *Sophia Square* (2012–13), *Claybourne,* and the work on WBAI New York (which celebrated the literature of the black diaspora) suggest to me that if a community feels underrepresented, then it will create something based on its own background with a DIY ethic. In all of these cases, the presence of an existing broadcasting framework within which to address community concerns in the form of drama (the BBC, commercial stations like Radio Cardiff and NewsTalk ZB and a Pacifica affiliate, respectively) was an essential element. On the other end of the spectrum, audio drama conceived and edited on a smaller, less financially intensive scale like *Welcome to Night Vale* can also metaphorically open up diverse representation. Hancock (2017) suggests that people who traditionally find themselves excluded from society (people of colour, LGBT, disabled people) find community in *WTNV*. There is also the example of Mutual Broadcasting System's Mutual Black Network, narrowcasting to a specific community in 1973, including its own radio soap, *Sounds of the City* (*c.* 1973–74), targeted to black housewives (Patterson 2016: 12). Although NPR is 'more inclusive than most media', Mitchell argues that '[i]f public radio divides the nation, it is by education level, not by race, gender, handicap, or sexual preference' (2005: 187). This begs the same question: are audio drama and podcasting reaching a wider audience in terms of class, or is this only possible through the democratizing, low-cost ubiquity of terrestrial community radio broadcasting?

Conclusion

In late May 2017, the audio drama world was rocked by the news that Audible had created a $5 million fund for emerging playwrights (Hoffelder 2017; Barone 2017). This signalled a shift from an audio fill-in culture (*Alien, The X-Files*) to a more contemporary approach to original audio drama writing, akin to Gimlet's *Homecoming*. With the advisory board created to award the funding reportedly headed by Annette Bening, Lynn Nottage, Tom Stoppard, David Henry Hwang, Trip Cullman, Leigh Silverman, Oskar Eustis and Mimi O'Donnell, a clear connection was made to stage writing (in particular, Off Broadway dramatic writing), with no reference to specifically audio drama-makers or anything approaching an OTR style. The announcement was generally received with excitement, though some commentators were more sceptical (Hon 2017).

Some have seen Audible's announcement as a significant shift, but in what way this announcement will impact future audio drama is unknown. If we treat the previous chapters of the study as ways people *have been* listening, we now have to look to the future and predict ways in which they might listen. The chapter analyses the way the

Serial phenomenon adhered to my 2014 hypothetical model of nationally distributed, accessible US audio drama content. Seriality clearly struck a chord with nonfiction and fiction podcasting. The much-explored tension between high and low art seems to be present in the differences between 'boring' but intellectually stimulating 'thinkpiece' *Serial* Season 2 and ethically challenged *S Town* that zeroed in on compelling characters, voyeurism and the central question of a character's trustworthiness and a journalist's reaction to that. The chapter also discussed the many different methods of funding that have arisen for online and podcast drama, speculating that a core of audio drama listeners will continue to seek out productions that are free as well as those that are crowdfunded and monetized, though the balance could be shifted if commercially sponsored mega-productions like Audible's become the norm. The chapter also discussed ways that *Serial* potentially let diverse audiences down, ways to overcome this and whether this is a wider PSB representation problem.

Chapter 11

The Post-*Serial* World and Listeners of the Future

> Radio as a mythic force – the same mythic force that shaped both my imagination as a child and to a large extent the person I have become as an adult – is back. It's already back.
>
> – Andrew Dubber (2013: 179)

Accessible audio drama of all kinds, and the seriality that often accompanies such drama, have been a major focus of this book. Just as BBC Radio Drama has survived on a diet of continuity and change, so, I believe, has audio drama in general, and so it will continue to be. We are not yet in a position to suggest that interactive hybrids between gaming/VR and audio drama as we know it will represent the future of the form, nor can we discount the pervasive influence of the audiobook format. Hybrid forms have arisen that seem to combine more traditional narrative audio drama, audiobooks and podcasts, such as those created by Gimlet Media, and the seductive pull of licensed fan audio (Audible's experiments with *Alien* [2016–present] and *The X-Files* [2017–present] and Big Finish). It should be no surprise that such diverse efforts have in common narrative formats relevant to the postmodern listenership (fan fiction/metafictional approaches and true crime narrative made famous/palatable by *Serial* [2014–present]) as well as big star names – it is perhaps unsurprising that Val Gielgud wrote in a BBC context in 1957, 'the public needs "stars" […] to which it may hitch the wagons of the Drama' (1957: 40).

Nevertheless, recent serialized audio dramas that have proved genuinely popular, in terms of downloads, and on the iTunes charts (*NoSleep* [2011–present], *The Black Tapes* podcast [*TBT*] [2015–present]), have, for the most part, reflected the gift economy of satellite audio drama, which Dana Gerber-Margie likens to the democratic qualities of fanzines and blogs for ease of access/production (cited in Hilmes and Lindgren 2016: 7). They also reflect Vincent Meserko's contention that '[m]ainstream media […] is incapable of the nuance and intimacy that the podcast provides' (2015: 797). That *NoSleep* and *Welcome to Night Vale* (*WTNV*) (2012–present) also co-exist successfully as live shows should remain unsurprising if we treat the online audio drama and/or podcast as an extension of radio itself and the broadcaster–solo relationship. Clearly, what gives the 'fillip' (in Gorham's words) to fans of *NoSleep*, *WTNV*, *TBT* and the like is still the feeling that the audience is one of being addressed directly, despite the obvious cognitive reality that the listener is literally, in the case of the live shows, amongst hundreds. Such a relationship was also clearly important to listeners of *Serial* as they contacted *This American Life* (*TAL*) (1995–present) to contribute their investigative leads on the Adnan Syed case, to the point of harassing real-life people caught up in the juggernaut. However, the real question of the future of audio drama concerns monetization of the form and whether audio drama will remain freely available on the Internet or through traditional (public service) broadcasters or become a subscription paid industry.

Throw us your pennies and we'll make you a kingdom

In 2007, Frederick Greenhalgh of FinalRune Productions, veteran producer of audio drama and long-time listener and theorist, offered this business model:

> I think an 'all you can eat' subscription based radio drama/audio theater store is apt to be more successful than anything else. Say a dozen or so of us producers opt-in, upload all of our work to a centralized server that distributes the work to all subscribers (or have the ability to offer it to bronze, silver, or gold level memberships). As a subscriber, you can sign up for a variety of levels, which offer tiered levels of programming; say the $10/month subscriber gets 4 of your 30 minute episodes while the $30/month subscriber gets access to your 5-hour epic mini-series. […] The money gets split up on a democratic, server-controlled manner based on the number of downloads of each respective work.
>
> (2007, original emphasis)

Seven years later, Greenhalgh persisted that the future of audio drama remained with his 'All-You-Can-Eat' subscription store. Naturally, the time he was writing preceded the impact of *Serial,* the post-*Serial* drama podcasts, Audible's involvement with *Alien* and *The X-Files* and Gimlet Media, but Greenhalgh did not seem that interested in these kinds of drama permutations in any case. Echoing Tim Crook's rhetoric of audio drama representing a vast wasteland of sub-par productions, Greenhalgh suggested that audio drama must abandon podcasting. His solution was an app for audio drama, insisting that a discovery platform was the most efficient means for ensuring not only audio drama's survival, but its ascendance. That Audible represented a 'long tail' space for audio drama, he feared, was part of the problem: 'Some people enjoy panning the great wide 'net in a desperate hope for gold, but most people have 100,000 other things to get to and wading through crummy RSS feeds is not on their to-do list' (2014). In the intervening years, it seems unlikely that Audible – or anyone else – has adequately addressed this critique.

Netflix, not Pandora

Netflix, launched in 1997, has participated in one of the great changes in the consumption of media in the twentieth century. Keyed in to technological convergence, its ease of access appealed to busy media consumers, as did its gathering of content (McDonald and Smith-Rowsey 2016: 2). Following rapidly in its wake is Audible. Audible, despite the gesture of confidence shown by the 2017 announcement, remains deeply invested in the traditional audiobook and has not suddenly rolled over to exclusive audio drama production overnight. 'Listening is the new reading', Audible claimed in 2017. Yuri Rasovsky optimistically anticipated a day when original audio drama was in demand, as Greenhalgh seems to, 'when many first rate creators regard audiobooks as their primary medium, when books, TV specials and movies are based on audiobooks, not the other way around' (2001b). So far we've not yet seen any television or film adaptations of *Serial* or the post-*Serial*,[1] though the BBC has frequently adapted extremely popular one-off radio dramas (such as *Spoonface Steinberg* [1997] or *Stan* [2004]) for television, usually less successfully.[2]

The great joy of online audio drama and much of podcast drama has been the gift economy ethos inherent in the form (though Greenhalgh would suggest this has led to its mediocrity). Whereas many makers of US radio drama (Rasovsky, for example) had to turn to commercially produced, and, they felt, inferior audiobooks in order to pay the bills so they could produce more enjoyable drama, the access enabled by technology (through Web 2.0, the development of the MP3, the proliferation of Freeware DAWs, etc.) has allowed today's generation of audio drama-makers to circumvent such a process should they choose. This means that many pursue the hobby in their spare time for the sheer fun of it, but it also means many young podcast drama-makers want and feel they deserve to make their living out of quality audio drama production, as noted in the previous chapter. It seems that companies like Audible may agree with them. So is the only solution a commercial one? If, and how, can these conditions be reconciled?

It is worth noting that Wireless Theatre's subscription model is in some ways the practical embodiment of Greenhalgh's 'All-You-Can-Eat' subscription. Differing from more niche, genre-driven audio drama production formats (for example, Big Finish), Wireless' strength seems to be in offering general drama and comedy, which have proved popular with audiences. Nevertheless, to adopt Wireless on a wider scale and within the US nationalized environment would take an extra 'little sumthin' sumthin", to paraphrase Greenhalgh. Greenhalgh, indeed, made the connection with HBO (Greenhalgh 2007), suggesting that his co-op shop idea appeals to those who watch HBO; he admires their ethic for keeping their audiences in rapt suspense every week. HBO absorbs its audience's cultural values in its mode of production, 'even to the detriment of its supposed economic bottom line' (Santo 2008: 20). If the survival of the medium is the whole reason for the medium, as Marshall McLuhan famously alleged, then HBO both acts contrary to this dictum and for its overall adherence as it sticks so doggedly to its brand. Robin Nelson suggests that channels like HBO 'appeal to busy professionals who have little time' to watch TV and that 'a more sophisticated product is required to attract them' (2007: 18). Further to this, 'HBO's programming choices have, in part, been influenced by a public service model of television' (Santo 2008: 25).

More recently, however, Greenhalgh has suggested that what audio drama needs is not HBO, nor Pandora, but Netflix. Rewinding for a moment, it is perhaps surprising that there does not currently exist a Pandora-like service to match listeners up with audio dramas they like (the Audio Drama Directory being the closest thing, interactive to the point that it offers a search function). Pandora Radio began in the early 2000s as part of the Music Genome Project; by 2008 it had 1 million average daily users in the United States (Whoriskey 2008).

In 2017, 40 per cent of Americans surveyed used Pandora, and it topped audience brand awareness (Edison Research and Triton Digital 2017: 29, 21). Pandora 'allows customers to create stations tailored to their own tastes' (Whoriskey 2008). After overcoming financial problems, in 2011 Pandora accrued 11 per cent of US listening (Blodget and Gobry 2011). In 2014, Pandora One's base subscription cost was $5 annually (Burns 2014). Pandora Radio operates similarly to Yahoo!'s music recommendation service, which Anderson described in detail. 'Unlike a traditional radio station, Yahoo! knows quite a bit about those listeners who liked the song […] gender, age, zip code, and a lot about their musical taste from having tracked their listening behaviour and ratings' (Anderson 2006: 101). There are podcasts, websites and review databases to direct listeners to what audio drama exists, as we have noted, but nothing that utilizes the algorithmic software like Pandora. This has frustrated podcasters and audio drama listeners, who have to rely on word of mouth or the recommendation services listed above – or trawl through RSS feeds, of which Greenhalgh clearly despairs.

However, as stated previously, Greenhalgh is not advocating a Pandora for audio drama. The BBC's great (and well-nigh un-replicable) strength is the Reithian ideal of surprising listeners with things they didn't know they wanted to listen to. Paolo Massa warns against the concept of the 'echo chamber' or 'daily me', now so dangerously prevalent in our post-Web 2.0 era: everyone has 'the ability to listen to and watch just what they want to hear and see', suggesting a closing-down of thought processes instead of an opening of horizons, never being 'confronted with people with different ideas and opinions' (2011: 158). This is exactly the kind of environment that Matthew Arnold, in the 1860s, thought was the anathema to culture, and whose ideas so influenced J.C.W. Reith and his idea of mixed programming.

We are not necessarily in danger of a subsuming of culture within Massa's 'echo chamber'; as highlighted by the 'Infinite Dial' 2017, 68% of those surveyed said they discovered new music on the advice of friends and family, though YouTube had slightly surpassed AM/FM radio (64% and 63% respectively). This is perhaps something we need to remember as we interact with the future of audio drama. This has been less achievable on the chronically underfunded NPR; '[i]n a sense, public radio's audience, an unrepresentative slice of America if ever there was one, enslaved it' (Mitchell 2002: 416). Mitchell goes on to suggest that public service broadcasting (PSB) could squeeze contributions from all its listeners if it became a subscription-only service (2002: 417), citing the example of Minnesota Public Radio benefiting financially from *Prairie Home Companion* (1974–2016). A Netflix approach to audio drama might circumvent some of the evils of the 'echo chamber', but its strength would have to lie within its diversity.

Fan audio

Are we right to dismiss fan fiction audio drama wholesale as Greenhalgh does? 'I'm fairly confident that the concept of "the podcast" is going to die off', Nick Quah predicted rather pessimistically in 2016. Like Greenhalgh, he had little confidence in the podcast form, but for different reasons. He suggested podcast content would either become a live form or revert to on-demand (cited in Hilmes and Lindgren 2016: 7). If that is true, the genre spin-off or fill-in could have a rosier future than Greenhalgh predicts. Audible itself has somewhat overtaken events by offering this with its *Alien* and *X-Files* dramas. If the listening audience to NPR doubled for *Star Wars* in 1981, what prevents the *Stars Wars* universe producing audio drama fill-ins based on that vast and radiogenic fictional world? In 2012, Disney bought Lucasfilm for $4 billion; Disney-owned Marvel released new *Star Wars* comic tie-ins in January 2015, which grossed 25 times more than the last Dark Horse title released seven months previously (McLaughlin 2015). Key to the success of the NPR *Star Wars* radio adaptations was George Lucas' full cooperation that guaranteed access to crucial world-building *Star Wars* special effects and music. In 1978, *The Hitchhiker's Guide to the Galaxy* brought new listeners to radio drama on the BBC. Similarly, in 1981, *Star Wars* on NPR brought new listeners to the public service broadcaster and to radio drama. Given that Audible itself has so far created genre spin-offs in audio drama, could this be part of a wider strategy for bringing in new audiences? If so, could Audible's drama writing proposal pave the way for more democratic, original audio drama availability, belying Quah's cynical suggestion? Marvel/Disney, indeed, already seem to be making tentative forays in this direction, with Marvel teaming up with podcast subscription service Stitcher in 2018 to produce high-budget 'scripted podcast' (i.e. audio drama) *Wolverine: The Long Night*.

As suggested above, entities like Netflix have benefited greatly from technological convergence. This undeniable factor suggests a collaborative element to future audio drama. D.G. Bridson used actuality while making the radio feature *Ballarat* from a film that was recording at the same time, calling it 'the most evocative sound that I ever cut' (1971: 147). To give a more recent example, Danish playwright Trine Damgaard's production company Keep Talking has enacted an improvisatory attitude towards dialogue, which sees actors abandon scripts completely as they physically interact with each other, much as they would on the stage. The well-known Danish film *Festen* (*The Celebration*) (1998) was adapted for radio by Keep Talking. Instead of a straightforward, traditional adaptation, film-to-radio, the existing text was so well-known to the Danish audience that the adapters created 42 different scenarios based on the premise of the film and allowed the actors to improvise their way to a conclusion (Boss and Holm 2014). This has intriguing implications for the world of meta-fictional audio drama.

Zubernis and Larsen in their study of fan interaction with the TV programme *Supernatural* (2005–present) suggested that 'in order for a media text to be a successful cultural attractor, there must also be a way in for fans, with meaningful ways to participate' (2012: 3). Audio drama fill-ins could offer this. Pottermore, a website launched in 2011, was J.K. Rowling's 'give-back' to *Harry Potter's* fans (Flood 2011). Free to access and collaborative, Pottermore was redesigned in 2015, giving visitors the opportunity to be sorted into Hogwarts houses and to read news items and features. Pottermore does not feature any audio drama fill-ins – yet. In theory, Pottermore might not be a perfect fit – the *Harry Potter* phenomenon, now two decades old, celebrated the visual (and sometimes tactile) act of reading. However, its great success in audiobook form and the diversification into stage (*Harry Potter and the Cursed Child,* 2016) suggest a possible fruitful collaboration. This could represent an extremely potent way in to audio drama (via the fill-in) for younger people and a more diverse audience, two groups who have traditionally lacked access to radio drama.

Interactivity

Hilmes (2013: 44) drew attention to radio as a screen medium, a factor magnified by greater and greater dependence on smartphone usage. Indeed, greater interactivity between audio drama and other media may slowly overtake more traditional conceptions of audio drama. Tuomi has suggested that '[a]udiences are now combining different mediums and content in order to gather a coherent media experience', (2016: 250) and increasingly interconnected space within that media experience may be the future of audio drama. One of the undoubted advantages of the MP3 player was in what Chris Anderson called 'massive, unbounded selection' of music tracks, more than any one traditional shop could contain (2006: 34). Simultaneity – 'second screens' – is also a major feature of this:

> The time spent on consuming media services based on converged technologies such as mobile phone calls and Internet surfing, text messages, traditional and web radio listening as well as TV has rapidly increased and most of these consumption activities take place simultaneously.
>
> (Lugmayr and Dal Zotto 2016: 7)

While Henry Jenkins (2008) dismissed the idea of a Black Box device, a single device that would do everything, we are also far removed from Stan Freberg's 1965 sketch in which a US household consisted of eleven discreet radio sets, including the one in the car (Freberg et al. 1965). Second screening and online radio are both demonstrably important methods of radio consumption today. Smartphone usage is nearly ubiquitous among 12–24 year olds in the United States, at 95%, and has risen to 60% of those aged 55+ (Edison Research and Triton Digital 2017: 6). 61% of Americans in 'The Infinite Dial' listened to online radio in 2017, and though this trend represents only a small increase over previous years, adults who do listen to online radio are spending an average of fourteen hours per day with online radio (Edison Research and Triton Digital 2017: 14, 18).

These different methods of radio consumption suggest possibilities for further interactivity, pushing the boundaries of our definitions of audio drama. While Subramaniam S. Sundaram at the University of Edinburgh has been working on audio cues and sound effects for the blind and visually impaired (Sundaram 2015), the similarities in performance between the gaming industry and radio and audio drama have scarcely been discussed. Interactivity has already seen some success in Germany and seems to be becoming increasingly popular. In 2013, Nele Heise recorded the trends towards MixCloud, Podlove and Showno.tes, and the case of the narrow-caster who hacked a Wii controller to produce his own podcasts (2013a). What is sought is a successful example of a game is an aural landscape matched to the visual one either to 'provide further information about the environment or to confirm the information already provided by one sense' (Grimshaw 2012: 347). A first-person shooter (FPS) game without sight would seem antithesis to the medium, but it is certainly possible an FPS might be developed in which the aural sense is more important than the visual one in providing tactical information. For example, apps like Soul Trapper have already been singled out by Hand and Traynor as extensions of the mode of audio drama (2011: 73). Adrian Hon's company, Six to Start, was financed by Audible to produce *The Way of All Flesh* (2017), an audio drama based on his app Zombies, Run! (Hon 2017).

Along a different but related track, in 2014, Vito Pinto highlighted the work of *hörspielmacher* Paul Plamper, including two highly interactive pieces, the installation piece *Ruhe 1* (*Silence 1*) (2008/2012), and *Das akustische Kleistdenkmal* (*DAK*) (*The Acoustic Kleist-Monument*) (2011), an audio guide/drama. The latter in particular presents great possibilities for the future of audio drama. Presented as an audio guide to the area Kleiner-Wannsee near Berlin and to the life and death of poet Heinrich von Kleist, *DAK* has its own cast of characters masquerading as tour guide and participants who at one point leave the auditor behind. In Denmark, the artistic collective VONTRAPP have pushed this concept even further with site-specific installation *Beva mig vel* (*Keeping Well*) (2014), which uses binaural sound to subsume audio guide with audio drama while visually a kaleidoscope of theatre, dance and lighting underlines the 'ghostliness' of the set-up. Visitors wear earphones, guided around the Bellajøg estate, the fictive world increasingly interrupted by the reminiscences of an imaginary old woman. Interactive audio guides and 'treasure hunts' using geolocation apps on smartphones are among the audio drama-related activities pursued by John Barber's class in digital storytelling at Washington State University Vancouver (2014). The BBC's Research and Development Department have also been pushing the boundaries of audio drama. In 2017, they experimented with semi-interactive audio drama on the Smartspeaker (Google Home, Alexa) platform, science-fiction drama *The Inspection Chamber* (Gartenberg 2017). *The Turning Forest* (2016) was marketed as VR but could also serve as audio drama due to its meticulously recorded sound (BBC n.d.). These experiments are exciting but characterized by disconnect and a lack of formal, sustained research funding.

A rewrite of US communications legislation

At the crux of all this discussion is something that has been evident from the very beginning of our story, from the 1920s onwards: the tension between radio as public service broadcaster and commercial entity. Quah's prediction from above highlights an undeniable difficulty present both within BBC and US PSB: how to reconcile online and podcast audio drama within a capitalist economy. In Chapter 7 we noted how advertisers abandoned radio for television and therefore contributed irrevocably to the loss of radio drama from US airwaves in the 1960s (for better or worse; as we have seen, creative leaders of the 1950s felt radio was saturated with homogeneity and advertising and wanted to have a crack at the whip of the new medium of television). While it is by no means certain that radio drama would not have been offered on commercial stations had, for example, the BBC broken up its radio monopoly in 1955 as it broke up its television one, it seems likely that the continuity of British radio drama would have suffered for a time at least. Public service broadcasting in the Reithian mode seems unsustainable without a monopoly, yet the BBC has managed to provide this for more than 50 years.

Anecdotal evidence suggests to me that radio and audio drama are poorly understood by most of the population of both the United States and the United Kingdom, and for audio drama to survive, this needs to change. Jack J. Ward is in agreement: 'I fear the ugly truth is, if we did a better job telling people about the glories of the modern audio drama movement', there would be less misinformation (Ward 2017c). There is nothing more irritating to a scholar or enthusiast of audio drama than the constant assertion from mainstream media that Audible invented the twenty-first century audio drama ('Audio fiction seems to be having a moment'; Barone 2017), or, worse, that *Serial* did (Ward 2017b, 2017d). What is necessary for the future of audio drama to go anywhere is a widespread recognition of audio drama for its own sake, with its own literary canon, that it didn't just spontaneously emerge out of a *Welcome to Night Vale* vacuum, that continuity has been in place from OTR to *Serial*. This idea is borne out by the revelation that Gimlet's *Homecoming* (2016–present) was inspired in part by the 1940s network radio thriller *Suspense*'s most famous episode, 'Sorry, Wrong Number' (1943), something that is not widely advertised, as if Gimlet were ashamed of the influence rather than letting it add rich context to their creation.

Currently, there is a fractured audio drama landscape in part because PSB in the United States has been unable to sustainably offer radio drama. Until political priorities in the US government change to the extent that nationwide audio drama programming becomes a concern at the executive level, 'public radio is not and will not ever really have the money or incentive to produce original plays', as Greenhalgh put it (2007). Before the 1995 elections, convinced that Republicans would eliminate federal funding for public radio, heads of public radio stations worked hard to attract more listeners and more private income (Mitchell 2005: 174). Instead, President Clinton passed the Communications Act of 1996. It removed 'any pretext that commercial radio existed for any reason other than to make as much money as possible' (Mitchell 2005: 174). Some listeners, then, desire the Reithan system, but no one is willing to pay the price. Furthermore, McChesney suggests that '[m]ost Americans have no idea that debates on policy could even exist or what the deliberations actually are, due to an effective news blackout on the topics, except on occasion in the business press' (2013: 217).

Where do we go from here?

It has already been a long journey from the beginning of this book, in 1919, to this moment. In 2017 on the *Audio Drama Production Podcast* Facebook group, Steve Schneider alleged, not that most of the audio drama available was of poor quality, but that it was 'boring'.

Just really, really boring, to the point where I can't even keep listening and have to turn it off. I know I introduced myself as Steve the 'avid listener of many audio dramas', but it's truer to say 'avid listener to the BEGINNING of many audio dramas, but more than half of them I give up on inside of three minutes because they are so damned booooring'. […] What's that? Oh yeah, of course – blame me… yeah, it's MY fault. Blah, blah, blah… that I have ADD, that I'm listening while distracted, that I have poor taste in storytelling, that I don't love the medium enough, that I don't understand 'Great Art' when I hear it, and all the rest of your nonsense.

(Schneider 2017)

This echoes something noted by John Taranto, that the off switch for audio drama and podcasts is much easier than an actual radio set broadcasting either analogue or digital radio (cited in McHugh 2016: 7). Audio drama in the twenty-first century must, therefore, work harder than previous generations, due in part to the tyranny of choice inevitable in today's media landscape. I cannot agree with Greenhalgh or Crook regarding the general mediocrity (or worse) of the vast majority of audio drama available either on public service broadcasters or online, nor can I agree with Schneider that most of the audio drama available is 'boring', as long as (potential) listeners have hours to fill on, for example, a commute ('despite all of the other distractions out there, you still aren't allowed to watch TV while driving a car' [Greenhalgh 2014]). The world of radio and audio drama has picked up speed between 2010 and 2014 when I was writing the Ph.D. thesis this book is based on, and exponentially so between 2014 and 2018. While these rapid developments are encouraging, it makes speculation on the future of audio drama extremely difficult and perhaps a bit unrewarding. This section provides a final collection of advice, a 'wish list' if you will, which I believe will enable us to make stronger and more useful predictions about the future of audio drama and enable us to make it as rich and enjoyable for listeners and makers as possible. The following areas are just some of the ways we can improve our collective understanding of audio drama both as scholars and theorists and as listeners and practitioners.

- Gathering, collating and interpreting data on audio drama podcast-makers and podcast listeners. Who are they? What motivates them? What is their demographic makeup? Do they consume audio drama podcasts solely or is it just one genre within a larger constellation of podcast listening? Do they also listen to terrestrial radio? Where do they listen to podcast drama (is it part of their daily commute, for example, or do they listen to drama while at work)?
- More efforts towards a radio and/or audio drama canon, both British and American (and other Anglophone countries, for that matter). Thousands of dramas are offering themselves up to researchers in many disciplines; they just need to be rediscovered (particularly now that Genome and Archive.org are making this easier).
- Qualitative social scientific experiments on the aural imagination. The early efforts have been described on page 41 but much more can be done. As evidenced by Charlotte

Russell's, and Rodero's and Bolls' research into Alzheimer's, there is broad application for these findings.
- Researching venues and audio drama consumption. Are there differences between the way listeners respond to audio drama in groups and/or in the dark as opposed to functioning as background aural/mental stimulation during housework, exercising, commuting? Is there an aural equivalent to the 'cinematic gaze' as opposed to the 'televisual glance' and what are the implications?
- A Pandora-like service, would, I think, be useful, especially for newer listeners to audio drama. It would function at its best if it worked alongside BBC Radio 4 Extra. This is unlikely, given the BBC's current rights entanglements that limit the amount of radio drama heard outside the United Kingdom, but possible, given a large enough demand. The BBC/Dirk Maggs adaptation of Neil Gaiman's *Neverwhere* (2013) was perhaps another gamechanger of the noughties; Greenhalgh certainly interpreted it thus:

> Oh, of course there's Dirk Maggs, with Neverwhere, starring Benedict Cumberbatch and Sir Christopher Freakin' Lee and promoted by Neil Gaiman himself. And what happens? The BBC runs it for a week and then buries it forever in obscurity. As of this writing, there is nowhere legal to purchase the drama (not quite true, apparently it's available on Audible – thanks EC Bond). And you wonder why the medium is obscure.
>
> (Greenhalgh 2014)

- The BBC, indeed, require an overhaul of how they make their radio drama commercially available. I have taken advantage of the almost unique opportunity of having access to British audio drama like that offered by the BBC in the United Kingdom and enjoying audio drama recommendations from across the world. I may have a bit more patience than Greenhalgh in trawling through the Internet to find new listening material (McMurtry 2016b), but, like him, I lack time. The explosion of drama podcasts has made keeping up impossible.
- Increased interaction between makers/fans/theorists. Social media has made interacting in the audio drama community easy and accessible, but as with the above, the sheer volume can be daunting. Practitioners of all stripes are active online, but there remains a gap between drama-makers/fans and theorists writing from a scholarly perspective. As has been argued ad nauseum, Web 2.0 is supposed to have broken down the distances between us, but many more bridges need to be built amongst people who have a genuine love and interest for audio drama in order to harness the collective passion for the form.

Audio drama in the political landscape

This book is not ostensibly a political text. However, in arguing genuinely and passionately for the survival and proliferation of audio drama, it almost inevitably becomes one. Jack

Mitchell has said of donations to NPR in the late 1970s, '[i]n my opinion, listeners responded because they genuinely valued public radio and did not want to see it hurt but also because they wanted to protest against the Reagan philosophy' (2005: 166). Arguing from a public service broadcasting perspective, as radio drama has historically been so closely entwined with this tradition, it is difficult not to be suspicious of commercial interests interacting with audio drama, and we can perhaps appreciate better than others the difficulties inherent in PSB.

> The case against the BBC is led by a wide coalition of politicians, other broadcasters, the right-wing press and free-market think-tanks, who ensure that the case against the BBC is anything but evidence based, and is instead marked by arguments redolent of moral panic, such as the one that the BBC stifles markets and that the imposition of the licence fee removes choice and is thus illiberal.
>
> (Ramsey 2017: 102)

This does not mean that we cannot be critical of audio drama within a PSB context, and the concluding chapters have not let PSB off the hook for failing to be sufficiently diverse in the realms of audio drama.

Notes

1 There has been a documentary TV show *Adnan Syed: Innocent or Guilty* from June 2016, but it does not replicate *Serial's* format. *The Bright Sessions* (2015–present) is being developed for TV, and Gimlet's *Homecoming* (2016) was developed by Amazon Prime in 2018.
2 Disregarded in this pattern are the numerous BBC radio comedies that have graduated into TV adaptations with great acclaim.

Conclusion: We're Listening

Using research methods to describe and interrogate the historic past of radio drama, this work has attempted to survey, primarily, the field of audio drama of the United Kingdom and the United States, as extensively as possible as it exists at this moment. Working our way from contemporary trends and collective behaviours, the work has attempted to extrapolate from this some predictions for the future.

In the opening section, audio drama's aesthetics and crafts were examined, in Dubber's phrase, the *techné* of audio drama. Cognitively, audio drama uses imagination and mental imagery. These are skills that everyone has (though to what degree is unclear). The ear and the brain together compensate in a way that the eye and the brain do not – the ear is more forgiving, it constructs a galloping horse out of coconut shells. Therefore, audio drama is less expensive to employ than many other media in a way that doesn't impinge on the results. Audio drama is peripatetic, both in terms of the way it can be produced and the way it can be consumed. As the transistor radio transformed the aural landscape of the 1960s, so radio is still being used as the medium par excellence in developing countries. Production of audio drama has traditionally shown greater adaptability and lesser costs, even when studio-bound, than many other media, and this is now truer than ever. With audio drama being produced on-location and via satellite audio means, the form becomes even more fluid. Obviously, of course, audio drama is ideal for portraying settings that can be limiting in another media. An audio drama is set on Mars or in ancient Rome if you say it is, with the SFX and heightened language to accentuate it, of course.

Audio drama possesses a unique blend of macro and micro scale. It can reach many at the same time it personally engages an audience of one. Evan Eisenberg referred to the kingdom of music within us when we put on headphones; several times, I have lifted this metaphor to suggest audio drama's personal resonance. Dermot Rattigan noted that sound waves are *felt* through the body, not just *heard* in the ears and interpreted in the brain. Audio drama also excels at techniques of collage and serving as a palimpsest. Kenneth Burke called the process of convention/invention 'proverbs writ large', while John Cawelti and Raymond Williams noticed the value of this technique in 'lowbrow' and 'middlebrow' genres such as radio drama. This leads into another inevitable factor of audio drama: the association with nostalgia, which carries both a positive and a negative connotation.

These are the factors retained in what Andréa Baker has called radio's 'elasticity'. These have remained a constant despite, first, radio's constant reinvention, and the continual flux that exists today because of audio and radio drama. Therefore, the following are the aspects that will carry it through and make it a new medium. *Serial* (2014–present), post-*Serial* audio drama, satellite audio drama and podcasts, in general, suggest future audio drama will retain all of the above plus a continued stress on serialization. The strong continuity shown on the case study year of 2012 on BBC Radio suggests that continuity in general – grouping of dramas around themes – is highly prized by audio drama audiences.

Serialization and continuity, however, cannot exist without their opposites: the gamechangers. Space must be, at the same time, retained for experiment. Innovation plus a framework of bedrock, bread-and-butter 'everyday' drama seemed to be a workable mix for the BBC in 2012, and *The Archers* (1951–present) shares place with, in theory, the eccentric writing of Lance Sieveking and Giles Cooper. The high-flying writerly ambitions of *The Columbia Workshop* (1936–47) and the experimental air that arose on US radio in the mid- to-late 1930s could not, by definition, be sustained. The staid diet of radio drama throughout the 1940s, however, made room for another period of innovation and excellence in the last decade of US radio's Golden Age.

In the 1920s, the United Kingdom reacted to a widespread fear of the lurkers of radio, and the corporation system became a force for protection and moral uplift. Into this political and geographical context appeared drama, eventually. It began its existence within the confines of each system. Styles and approaches varied according to the different environments. Into this dynamic arose the tyranny of choice. If, as Matthew Arnold argued, people desire the power of choice but don't know how to use it appropriately, this was the BBC's concern in the 1930s. When British listeners had the choice of silence or the BBC, then there could arise within the audience an appropriate debate over quality. In the United States, the choices were (usually) between the networks, NBC, CBS and MBS. When the choice was between tuning into what all your neighbours were tuning into – the collective consciousness engendered by *Amos'n' Andy* (1926–55) – and gentle social ostracism, the idea of choice within a drama context took on a social dimension. There became some exchange and overlap – Archibald MacLeish cited the BBC's *March of the '45* (1936) as an influence on *The Fall of the City* (1937), his gamechanging play for CBS. But in the main, Britain reserved scorn for the US radio system, and that included its drama, too.

The present-day leaves us with a fractured commercial radio scene in the United States. This is, in turn, a product of a media landscape dominated by television for decades. This is, also, the legacy of the early legislation for radio policy in the United States, decided in 1927 after lively debate, and never intrinsic or inevitable. Without the benefit of codified study (like close reading for literature), we have picked up a motley inventory of devices to explain what audio drama 'does', what work it performs. These are not mere tricks – mostly through trial and error and a blending of techniques from other media, we grope for a language to describe what audio drama does. We ignore the historical context at our peril. While few broadcast or media professionals will ignore the history of radio completely, the lack of work placing radio/audio drama into the literary canon has stunted our self-reflexivity. Gielgud said that television took the glass slipper and married the prince. Many have tried to drag 'the Cinderella medium' back into the lights of the ball, but we've not yet achieved as great an impact upon society at large as we would like.

It's important, therefore, that we continue *producing* drama if we want to keep an audience. This may seem facile, but the importance of this concept cannot be underplayed. The audiences of *The Archers* may not be the same ones who seek out *TANIS* (2015–present), *Wooden Overcoats* (2015–present) or *Our Fair City* (2011–present). BBC Radio has navigated the high and low art spectrum, at least post-war, when its production teams were forced to address the popular audience craving for serialized drama, despite its apparent distaste for populist soaps. From this emerged the effective formula, the diet of continuity and change, which, though it leaves BBC radio drama open to accusations of homogeneity or 'dumbing down', at least provides a secure platform for radio drama (with the opportunity for the occasional gamechanger). To ensure this platform continues to be available, the BBC needs to widen its horizons, especially at the BBC Audio Drama Awards, which, despite the name, gives very little opportunity for independent drama producers to be recognized. Even if Radio 4 is not putting new, younger listeners as its first priority, drama-makers in general have to look at the full range of audiences. This includes not only younger audiences, particularly teens, but also more ethnically diverse audiences, less educated audiences and audiences outside the middle class. Bringing the sounds of podcast drama to the elderly, many of whom still yearn for OTR, would be a fantastic breakthrough. Similarly, if the teens and young adults who are currently obsessed with subscription video on demand dramas like *Black Mirror* (2011–present) could find their equivalents on audio, real change might be enacted. To that end, we must listen widely. The broader the listener casts his or her net for audio drama, the more informed he or she will be. This, in turn, will engender more ideas and will lead to an improved understanding of audio drama's past, present and future.

Appendices

Appendix 1 – Methodology: Statistics on BBC Radio Drama 2012

Original drama

For the purposes of this data-gathering exercise, original drama was taken to mean either drama or comedy that had not been previously broadcast. (Repeated material is indicated in *Radio Times* with an '(R)' in daily listings.) As the first issue began on Saturday, 31 December 2011, the records begin from Sunday, 1 January 2012. A series that was new in 2011 and was concluding its episodes in 2012 was not counted.

Information gathered on each drama

- Date of transmission
- Day of transmission (Saturday, Sunday, etc.)
- Programme/slot (if applicable; if not applicable, recorded as new series with start time and duration)
- Title and number of parts, if applicable
- Language of original and language of adaptation, if other than English
- Writer(s) and adapter(s), if applicable
- Director(s) and producer(s)
- Cast – where possible, every listed actor was recorded
- Page number in *Radio Times* where described
- Summary
- Special mention (if drama highlighted in *Today's Choice, Pick of the Week*, or *Five of the Best* and any relevant comments, as well as the writer who made them).

Radio 4 Extra

The *Radio Times* listings did not accurately record whether programming for Radio 4 Extra was on first transmission; therefore, Radio 4 Extra data was not recorded. A general picture was solicited from Alison Hindell, head of drama at Radio 4, and, later Caroline Raphael, head of Radio 4 Extra.

Single, serial and series

The decision was made to record data with broadcast drama hours as units rather than individual plays. This decision was made because of the prolific inclusion of serials and series in BBC Radio scheduling. A *Classic Serial* was recorded as a single story in serial and as three hours of radio drama. I define 'serial' as one story that is a single story broken up into more than one broadcast. Examples include, but are not restricted to, the *Classic Serial* and *15 Minute Drama*.

Series signifies either a group of stories connected by a grouping in the listings, or a series using the same cast but with a new story in each episode. Metadata that helped evaluate in such circumstances were episodes that were given individual titles rather than merely the series title each time a part of the whole was listed.

Where the category was not implicit, I made my best judgement based on the information available.

New nomenclature

In the week of 14–20 January, *Radio Times* changed its listings in the following way:

Afternoon Play → *Afternoon Drama*
Woman's Hour Drama → *15 Minute Drama*
Saturday Play → *Saturday Drama*
Friday Play → *Friday Drama*

Adaptations

Adaptation was used to signify any work that was adapted from another source, including but not limited to, novels or stage plays. Some critics make a distinction between adaptation, which is looser, and dramatization, in which a prose work is altered for radio drama broadcast. I have not made such a distinction, but have taken the degree to which the original work has been altered into consideration. A third category was created, 'blend', to signify that source material was being used in a novel way. The source material could be used more verbatim than in the case of adaptation, but the difference in genre or form between original material and radio drama version had to be significant. Examples in blend include radio dramas based on historical diaries, case histories or other non-fiction documents. I did not consider a spoof, satire or drama that used characters from an established work to be adaptation or blend (using theories of fair use as my guide). Naturally, I chose these categories at my own discretion.

Moment in time

Dramas were considered to take place in the past if an effort was made to locate them in a particular year, decade or historical period before 2011. All other dramas were considered to take place in the present, if the mode of the drama was consistent with what is known of the present-day. The only dramas included in the 'other' category were those set in no particular moment in time, those that were parables or allegory or those that were speculative fiction and might be set in the future or any other time.

Genre

Of course, many works of art (and therefore, many radio dramas) belong to several genre categories. Genre is a difficult thing to define as a set of rules that can be used for all time by all people, and I admit my categories are subjective. I used my best judgement to choose the genre that best described the drama, based on the information I was given. When possible, I used the metadata written in the programme listings themselves, though once again choices had to be made when descriptions like 'romantic comedy thriller' were given. In general, preference was given to the broadest category descriptor: comedy or drama. The exceptions to this rule were usually when the summary of the work suggested supernatural elements, a future or 'anytime' setting; or a satire or farce – these dramas I took to use imaginative elements not necessarily delineated by the normal genre categories 'comedy' or 'drama'.

The genre categories included:

- Family saga
- Comedy (with sub-categories of dark comedy, romantic comedy, musical comedy and spoof)
- Drama (with sub-categories of legal drama and political drama)
- Poetry
- Thriller
- Creative non-fiction
- Faction
- Speculative fiction
- Historical fiction
- Biography
- Mystery and crime drama

Creative non-fiction I meant to signify memoir or any reflective piece of writing identified by the writer as having been based on their life story. *Faction* was the category that strongly resembled documentary, and in some cases the only fictional element in this otherwise non-fiction were recreations of speeches by actors standing in for the real people who said them.

Of these 32 works, 7.75 hours were based on historical diaries; 4.75 hours were based on historical documents; 6.25 hours were based directly on news stories; 5 hours were based on short stories; 5 hours were based on legal or medical casebooks; 1.25 hours were based on poetry; 3.25 hours were Biblical parables[1]; 3 hours were from memoirs; 1.5 hours were from dramas that used characters from existing works of literature in original stories; 1.25 hours were an adapted and translated radio soap opera from Afghanistan; 2 hours were retellings of fairy tales; 1 hour was a radio drama based on a film.

The majority of these were German works, a total of five works in adaptation but 9 hours' worth of listening (mostly novels).[2] Furthermore, on the BBC in 2012 there were four works in French, representing 8.5 hours (due to a four-part adaptation of Alexandre Dumas *The Count of Monte Cristo* in December 2012). There were 2.5 hours in Italian and 1.5 in Danish; a special adaptation of Swedish crime fiction produced 6.25 hours. Perhaps surprisingly, given Britain's colonialist legacy, only one adaptation each came from the Pashtun and Bengali languages.

The sub-categories I included to make up speculative fiction were fantasy/fairy tale (9); supernatural (6); satire (4); political speculation (2); science fiction[3] (4); psychological speculation (6); horror (3); alternate history (2) and parable (2). Anecdotally, some of the fiction captured in this category ranges from ongoing fantasy drama series *Pilgrim* (2008–16) by Sebastian Baczkiewicz[4] to the *15 Minute Drama* series 'The Resistance of Mrs Brown', written by Ed Harris and directed by Jonquil Panting, set in 'an alternative past in which the Nazis have invaded London' (Preston 2012e: 125). I also included satire from the realm of the fantastic, such as a new adaptation of *Gulliver's Travels* (1726), and fairy tales such as the *Saturday Drama* adaptation of *Pinocchio* (1883).

Notes

1 '*Songs and Lamentations*' was a two-part *Classic Serial* by Michael Symmons Roberts based on the story of the destruction of Jerusalem in 587 BC from the Hebrew Bible, broadcast the last two weeks of June 2012. During Advent, *The Essay* on Radio 3 presented a five-part series of new mystery plays by contemporary playwrights setting New Testament parables in modern settings. These were produced by Jessica Dromgoole.
2 This is somewhat ironic, given the fact that Germany's Deutschlandfunk/Deutschlandradio Kultur/DRadio Wissen's 'Krimmis' (midnight thriller series) in spring 2014 were heavily weighted towards translations from English-language originals.
3 I defined science fiction as distinct from supernatural, psychological speculation and political speculation by identifying recognized science-fiction devices (e.g. robots).
4 The episode 'Sookey Hill' won a Special Commendation in the Prix Europa Awards of 2012.

Appendix 2 – British winners of the Prix Italia and Prix Europa in Radio Drama since 1949

Prix Italia

2013

Adapted Drama
1984

2007

Original Radio Drama
The Incomplete Recorded Works of a Dead Body
written by Ed Hime, directed and produced by Jessica Dromgoole, actors included Khalid Abdalla, Ameet Chana, Elaine Lordan, Saikat Ahamed, John Dougall, Mark Straker, Anthony Glennon, Jasmine Callan
BBC

Adapted Drama
Metropolis
written by Peter Straughan, directed and produced by Toby Swift, adapted from a work by Thea von Harbou, sound by Pete Ringrose, actors included Edward Hogg, Tracey Wiles, Damian Lynch, Peter Marinker, Kim Wall, Elizabeth Bell, Anthony Glennon, Liz Sutherland, Jaqueline Cloake, Thomas Wheatley
BBC

2005

Adapted Drama
My Arm
written by Tim Crouch, directed and produced by Toby Swift, music and sound by Chris Dorley-Brown, actors included Tim Crouch, Owen Crouch
BBC

2004

Adapted Drama
'M'
written by Peter Straughan, directed by Toby Swift
BBC

1997

Special Prize for Fiction
The Voluptuous Tango
written by David Zane Mairowitz, produced by Ned Chaillet, music by Dominic Muldowney, sound by Ian Dearden
BBC

1988

Prix Italia for Fiction
Hang Up
written by Anthony Minghella, directed by Robert Cooper
BBC

1985

Prix Italia for Drama
Scenes from an Execution
written by Howard Barker, directed and produced by Richard Wortley
BBC

1982

Prix Italia for Drama
Florent and the Tuxedo Millions
written by Peter Redgrove, directed by Brian Miller
BBC

1974

Prix Italia for Programmes in which the Text Plays the Dominant Part
The Mystery
written and directed by Bill Naughton, produced by Guy Vaesen
BBC

1973

Prix Italia for Programmes in which the Text Plays the Dominant Part
The Pump
written by James Cameron, directed by R.D. Smith
BBC

1970

RAI Prize for Literary or Dramatic Programmes
Evelyn
written by Rhys Adrian, produced by John Tydeman
BBC

1968

Prix Italia for Literary or Dramatic Programmes with or Without Music
Albert's Bridge
written by Tom Stoppard, directed by Charles Lefeaux
BBC

1965

RAI Prize for Literary or Dramatic Programmes with or Without Music
The Anger of Achilles
written by Robert Graves, directed by Raymond Raikes, music by Roberto Gerhard
BBC

Prix Italia for Stereophonic Musical and Dramatic Programmes
The Founding
written by Peter Gurney, produced by Raymond Raikes, music by Humphrey Searle

1962

Prix Italia for Literary or Dramatic Programmes with or Without Music
The Ballad of Peckham Rye
written by Muriel Spark, music by Tristram Cary
BBC

1959

RAI Prize for Literary or Dramatic Programmes
Embers
written by Samuel Beckett, directed by Donald McWhinnie
BBC

1957

RAI Prize for Literary or Dramatic Programmes
The Dock Brief
written by John Mortimer, directed by Nesta Pain, music by Anthony Hopkins
BBC

1954

Prix Italia for Literary or Dramatic Programmes
Under Milk Wood
written by Dylan Thomas, produced by Douglas Cleverdon, music by Daniel Jones
BBC

RAI Prize for Literary or Dramatic Programmes
Prisoner's Progress
by Louis MacNeice
BBC

1953

RAI Prize for Literary or Dramatic Programmes
The Streets of Pompeii
written by Henry Reed, produced by Douglas Cleverdon, music by Anthony Smith-Masters
BBC

1951

1st Prize (*ex aqueo*)
The Face of Violence
written by Jacob Bronowsky, produced by Douglas Cleverdon, music by Anthony Hopkins
BBC

1949

2nd Prize
The Old and Truthful Story of Rumplestiltskin
written and directed by Francis Collins, music by Francis Collinson
BBC

Prix Europa

2014

Everything, Nothing, Harvey Keitel
written, directed and sound by Pejk Malinovski

Falling Tree Productions/BBC

2015

Boswell's Lives: Boswell's Life of Freud
written by Jon Canter, directed by Sally Avens, sound by Anne Bunting
BBC

2013

Special Commendation
Good News
written by Melissa Murray, directed by Marc Beeby, sound by Colin Guthrie and Jenni Burnett
BBC

2012

Special Commendations
Use It or Lose It
written by Peter Blegvad, directed by Iain Chambers, produced by Alan Hall, sound by Peregrine Andrews
Falling Tree Productions

Pilgrim: Sookey Hill
written by Sebastian Baczkiewicz, directed by Marc Beeby, co-produced by Jessica Dromgoole, sound by Colin Guthrie
BBC

2008

Best European Radio Drama of the Year
The Picture Man
written by David Eldridge, directed and produced by Sally Avens, sound by Keith Graham, Ross Burman and Ali Craig
BBC

Special Commendation
Q&A – 1,000,000 RUPEES
written by Ayesha Menon, directed and produced by John Dryden, sound by Nick Russel-Pavier
BBC

2004

Best European Radio Drama of the Year

The Wire: The Colony
written by Dennis Kelly, directed by Pam Marshall and Peter Ringrose, sound by Ros Mason
BBC

2003

Special Commendation
The Monotonous Life of Little Miss P
written by Enda Walsh, produced by Gemma McMullan, directed by Enda Walsh, sound by John Simpson
BBC

Prix Europa Exploration: Fiction – Special Commendation
Ghosts
http://www.bbc.co.uk/ghosts
realization and presentation by Martin Trickey

1997

Special Commendation
Vox Humana
written by Nick Fisher, directed and produced by Peter Kavanagh
BBC

Appendix 3 – Panel of experts for *Radio Times* survey

Experts:
Edward Barnes – Former head of BBC Children's programmes
Biddy Baxter – First editor of *Blue Peter*
Lord Asa Briggs – Historian and authority on broadcasting
Ted Childs – Producer/executive producer of series
Bill Cotton – Former managing director of BBCTV. Currently manager of Meridian Broadcasting
Paul Donovan – *Sunday Times* radio columnist
Chris Dunkley – *Financial Times* radio critic
Nick Elliott – ITV controller of network drama
Lord Grade – Film and TV producer
Roy Hudd – Actor and broadcaster
Jonathan James-Moore – Head of BBC light entertainment radio production
Robert Kee – News journalist
Verity Lambert – Drama producer, now head of Cinema Verity
Mark Lewisohn – *Radio Times* TV expert
Edward Mizoeff – Executive producers, BBC Documentaries
Jim Moir – Controller of Radio 2
Sir David Nicholas – Former chairman and editor of ITN
Geoffrey Perkins – Head of comedy and entertainment, BBC Production
John Pilger – Journalist and filmmaker
Alan Plater – TV writer and playwright
Jonathan Powell – Director of drama and co-producer, Carlton
Libby Purves – Broadcaster and *Times* journalist
Gillian Reynolds – *The Daily Telegraph*'s radio critic
Angela Rippon – Broadcaster
Sue Robinson – Editor, *Radio Times*
Rt Hon Chris Smith – Secretary of State for Culture, Media & Sport
Alan Whicker – Broadcaster
Barbara Windsor – Actress

Appendix 4 – Audio drama awards

	Awards	Most Recent Winners
Audio Verse Awards	• Best Music for a Self-contained, Comedic Production	'Simple Life' by Matt Berger for *The Fall of the House of Sunshine*
	• Best Music for a Self-contained, Dramatic Production	'Blood Heart' by Michael Aquino and Ernio Hernandez for *The Last Call*
	• Best Music for a New, Ongoing, Comedic Production	'HellMart' by Thoreau Smiley for *Attention HellMart Shoppers!*
	• Best Music for a New, Ongoing, Dramatic Production	'Misadventure by Death Theme' by Rosemary Derocher for *Misadventure by Death*
	• Best Music for an Ongoing, Comedic Production	'But How Do We Tell the Children We Are Allergic to Their Smiles' by Alan Rodi for *Wolf 359*
	• Best Audio Engineering for a Self-contained, Comedic Production	Michael Aquino for *Something Inside That Head of Yours*
	• Best Audio Engineering for a Self-contained, Dramatic Production	Alexander Danner for *What's the Frequency?*
	• Best Audio Engineering for a New, Ongoing, Comedic Production	Laura Bramblette for *OtherVerse*
	• Best Audio Engineering for a New, Ongoing, Dramatic Production	Mischa Stanton for *The Far Meridian*
	• Best Audio Engineering for an Ongoing, Comedic Production	Laura Bramblette for *OtherVerse*
	• Best Audio Engineering for an Ongoing, Dramatic Production	Mischa Stanton for *Ars Paradoxica*
	• Best Writing for a Self-contained, Comedic Production	Alison Crane for *Uncanny County: The Ballad of Bobby Blue*
	• Best Writing for a Self-contained, Dramatic Production	Gabriel Urbina for *Beyond the Door*
	• Best Writing for a New, Ongoing, Comedic Production	Shannon Sawyer for *Otherverse*
	• Best Writing for a New, Ongoing, Dramatic Production	Jessica Best for *The Strange Case of Starship Iris*
	• Best Writing for an Ongoing, Comedic Production	David K. Barnes for *Wooden Overcoats*
	• Best Writing for an Ongoing, Dramatic Production	Lauren Shippen for *The Bright Sessions*

- Best Production for a Self-contained, Comedic Production	*Generic Hospital*
- Best Production for a Self-contained, Dramatic Production	*The Strange Case of Starship Iris*
- Best Production for a New, Ongoing, Dramatic Production	*The Far Meridian*
- Best Production for an Ongoing Comedic Production	*The Strange Case of Starship Iris*
- Best Production for an Ongoing Dramatic Production	*Wolf 359*
- Best Actress in a Role for a Self-contained, Comedic Production	Devin McCall as Lydia Hanlon in *Uncanny County: Home is Where the Spice Is*
- Best Actress in a Role for a Self-contained, Dramatic Production	Tanja Milojevic as Whitney in *What's the Frequency?*
- Best Actress in an Ensemble Role for a New, Ongoing Production	Stacey Taylor as The Librarian in *Ray Gunn and Starburst*
- Best Actress in an Ensemble Role for an Ongoing Comedic Production	Michaela Swee as Hera in *Wolf 359*
- Best Actress in a Supporting Role for a New, Ongoing Comedic Podcast	Elise D'Amico as The Wicked Witch of the West in *The Chronicles of Oz*
- Best Actress in a Supporting Role for a New, Ongoing Dramatic Production	Sarah Golding as Camellia in *Oakpodcast*
- Best Actress in a Supporting Role for an Ongoing Comedic Production	Leticia Leon as Debbie in *King Falls FM*
- Best Actress in a Supporting Role for an Ongoing, Dramatic Production	Kate Jones as Rita in *The Penumbra Podcast*
- Best Actress in a Leading Role for a New, Ongoing Comedic Production	Laura Bramblette as The Broadcaster in *Otherverse*
- Best Actress in a Leading Role for a New, Ongoing Dramatic Production	Eli Barrazza as Hesperia in *The Far Meridian*
- Best Actress in a Leading Role for an Ongoing, Comedic Production	Julia Morizawa in *The Bright Sessions*
- Best Actor in a Role for a Self-contained, Comedic Production	Simon Kane as Sir Maxwell House in *The Monster Hunters*
- Best Actor in a Role for a Self-contained, Dramatic Production	Karim Kronfli as Walter 'Troubles' Mix in *What's the Frequency?*
- Best Actor in an Ensemble Role for a New, Ongoing Dramatic Production	Fox as Fox in *Point Mystic*
- Best Actor in an Ensemble Role for an Ongoing Comedic Production	Frank Sjodin as Andrew Snidge in *Our Fair City*
- Best Actor in an Ensemble Role for an Ongoing, Dramatic Production	Zach Valenti as Doug Eiffel in *Wolf 359*
- Best Actor in a Supporting Role for a New, Ongoing Comedic Production	Kevin Townley as Allen Dentist in *The Fall of the House of Sunshine*

	• Best Actor in a Supporting Role for a New, Ongoing Dramatic Production	Neimah Djourabchi as Matt Salem in *Steal the Stars*
	• Best Actor in a Supporting Role for an Ongoing, Comedic Production	Kyle Brown as Sammy Stevens in *King Falls AM*
	• Best Actor in a Supporting Role for an Ongoing, Dramatic Production	Noah Simes as Lord Arum in *The Penumbra Podcast*
	• Best Actor in a Leading Role for a New, Ongoing Comedic Production	Taylor Hunter as Kevin Weathers in *Kevin's Cryptids*
	• Best Actor in a Leading Role for a New, Ongoing, Dramatic Production	Jonathan Groff as Jase Connelly in *36 Questions*
	• Best Actor in a Leading Role for an Ongoing Comedic Production	Noah James as Ben Arnold in *King Falls FM*
	• Best Actor in a Leading Role for an Ongoing, Dramatic Production	Joshua Ilon as Juno Steel in *The Penumbra Podcast*
Mark Time/Ogle Awards	• Gold Mark Time (Best in Science Fiction Audio Theater)	*Brad Lansky and the Result War* Producer, Dieter Zimmerman, Protophonic (Cape Town, South Africa)
	• Silver Mark Time	*Cerebrus Rex* Producer, Jason Hardcastle, Heorot Media LLC, (Wilmington, DE)
	• Bronze Mark Time	*Marsfall* Producer, Erik Saras, Amity Bros. (Jersey City, NJ)
	• Gold Ogle for Horror	*The Floodgates of Willowhill* Producer, William Dufris, Dagaz Media (S. Portland, ME)
	• Silver Ogle for Horror	*The White Vault* (Season 1) Writer and creator, Kaitlin Statz, Fool and Scholar Productions (Sarasota, FL)
	• Bronze Ogle for Horror	'The Boy Who Cried Martian' and 'Coulrophobia', from the series *Uncanny County* Producer, Todd Faulkner (New York, NY)
	• Gold Ogle for Fantasy	*The Fairy Tree*, The Owl Field Producer, Michel Lafrance (London, UK)
	• Silver Ogle for Fantasy	*The Muse Unbidden* Producer, Roger Gregg (Dublin, Ireland)

	- Bronze Ogle for Fantasy	*Nairobi Jack Rackham and the Lost Gold* (Episode 8) Producer, David Benedict, Atlanta Radio Theater Company (Atlanta, GA)
	- Gold Nick Danger Prize (Best in Mystery and Detective Audio Theater)	*Sight Unseen* William Dufris, Pocket Universe Productions (S. Portland, ME)
	- Bronze Nick Danger Prize	*Rex Rivetter: Private Eye* Producer, Greg McAfee, Downstairs Entertainment (San Diego, CA) *Houdini's Secret Life* Producer, James Wortman, Every Now and Then Theatre (Ventura, CA)
	- Gold Squeaky Pickle Award (Best in Comedy Audio Theater)	*Right Between the Ears: Over and Out Show* Producer, Darrell Brogdon, Right Between the Ears (Parkville, MO)
	- Silver Squeaky Pickle Award	*The Fall of the House of Sunshine* Producer, Jonathan A. Goldberg, Roi Gold Productions (Westwood, NJ) Julia Whalen as Amanda Houston in *Sight Unseen* Producer, William Dufris, Pocket Universe (S. Portland, ME)
	- BettyJo Award for Performance	William Stout Matthew Barton
	- Bradshaw Award for Service to Audio Theater - Grand Masters in the Field of Science Fiction Audio Theater	Dieter Zimmerman Darrell Brogdon
Parsec Awards	- Best Speculative Fiction Comedy/Parody Podcast	*Star Wars Best in Galaxy Season 3* by Mark Restuccia and Patch Hyde
	- Best Speculative Fiction Audio Drama (Long Form)	*Uncanny County* by Todd Faulkner, Alison Crane and Nicole Greevy
	- Best Speculative Fiction Story: Large Cast (Long Form)	*Return Home* – 'Genie' by Maia Brown-Jackson
	- Best Speculative Fiction Story: Small Cast (Long Form)	*The Raven and the Writing Desk* – 'Things Unseen' by Chris Lester
	- Best Speculative Fiction Story: Small Cast (Short Form)	*The Wicked Library* – 'Shadows' by K.B. Goddard
	- Best Speculative Fiction Audio Drama (Short Form)	*Campfire Radio Theater* – 'Woods Ferry' by John Ballentine

Sarah Awards (Audio Fiction)	No categories	*Almanak* by Wederik De Backer
		Celestial Blood by Gisele Regatao
		Jayne Lake by Matthew Graham, Steve Bond, Kate Rowland and Russell Finch
		Krleža, Stand in Line! by Vesna Mačković
		Romeo & Juliet by Mira Burt-Wintonick and Cristal Duhaime
		Voices of the Revolution by Vincent Calianno, Anne Coburn, Eli Susser and Luke Taylor

References

Adorno, Theodor (2013), 'On the fetish character of music and the regression of listening', in M. Bull (ed.), *Ecologies of Hearing and Listening*, Sound Studies: Critical Concepts in Media and Cultural Studies, vol. 2, Abingdon: Routledge, pp. 3–27.

Adorno, Theodor and Horkheimer, Max (2007), 'The culture industry: Enlightenment as mass deception', in S. During (ed.), *The Cultural Studies Reader*, London: Routledge, pp. 405–15.

The Agency, Ltd (2018), 'Joe White', http://theagency.co.uk/the-clients/joe-white/. Accessed 20 July 2018.

Ahıska, Meltem S. (2000), 'An occidentalist fantasy: Turkish radio and national identity', Ph.D. thesis, London: Goldsmith's College.

Alcorn, Gay (2017), '*S-Town* never justifies its voyeurism, and that makes it morally indefensible', *The Guardian*, 22 April, https://www.theguardian.com/commentisfree/2017/apr/22/s-town-never-justifies-its-voyeurism-and-that-makes-it-morally-indefensible. Accessed 20 July 2018.

Aldana Reyes, Xavier (2015), 'Reel evil: A critical reassessment of found footage horror', *Gothic Studies*, 17:2, pp. 122–36.

Allen, Craig (1997), 'Tackling the TV titans in their own backyard: WABC-TV, New York City', in M.D. Murray and D.G. Godfrey (eds), *Television in America: Local Station History from Across the Nation,* Ames: Iowa State University Press, pp. 3–18.

Allen, Kip (2000), Unpublished correspondence.

—— (2001a), 'Classical KHFM: Station philosophy', internal company memo.

—— (2001b), 'Why jingles don't work on KHFM', internal company memo, 17 May.

—— (2001c), 'Mission statement for KHFM', internal company memo, December.

—— (2013a), e-mails to Leslie McMurtry, 1 January–1 February.

—— (2013b), letter to Leslie McMurtry, 11 January.

—— (2013c), interviewed by Leslie McMurtry, Albuquerque, 29 April.

—— (n.d.a), 'Between the earphones', multiple newsletter columns.

—— (n.d.b), 'Why KHFM sounds different from other stations', internal company memo.

—— (n.d.c), 'Your message on KHFM', press pack.

Ambridge in the Decade of Love (2003), BBC Radio 4, UK, 9 and 10 May.

Anderson, Chris (2006), *The Long Tail: Why the Future of Business is Selling Less of More,* New York: Hyperion.

Anderson, Jane (2012a), 'Today's choice', *Radio Times*, 7–13 January, p. 136.

—— (2012b), 'Pick of the week', *Radio Times,* 28 April–5 May, p. 123.

Anderson, John (2012), 'Human Rights Radio turns 25', DIYMedia.net, 25 November, http://diymedia.net/human-rights-radio-turns-25/601. Accessed 20 July 2018.

Andersson, Mimmi (2016), 'BBC iPlayer monthly performance pack', BBC, https://downloads.bbc.co.uk/aboutthebbc/insidethebbc/mediacentre/iplayer/performancepackaprmayjun2016.pdf. Accessed 1 July 2018.

Andreeva, Nellie (2017), 'Julia Roberts in talks to star in Sam Esmail TV series *Homecoming* based on podcast', Deadline Hollywood, 5 June, https://deadline.com/2017/06/julia-roberts-homecoming-tv-series-sam-esmail-podcast-1202106692/. Accessed 20 July 2018.

Andrews, David (2015), '*Serial* fans find there's still a shrimp sale at the Crab Crib', *The Baltimore Sun,* 9 February, http://www.baltimoresun.com/features/baltimore-insider-blog/bal-serial-shrimp-sale-crab-crib-20150209-story.html. Accessed 5 August 2017.

Ang, Ien (1985), *Watching Dallas: Soap Opera and the Melodramatic Imagination* (trans. Della Couling), London: Methuen.

—— (1991), *Desperately Seeking the Audience,* London: Routledge.

Anon. (1935), 'Judy's hour-at the Midland Regional', *Radio Pictorial*, 67, 22 November, p. 17.

—— (1939a), 'Newsmongers radio gossip from the studios', *Radio Pictorial*, 80, 26 July, p. 8.

—— (ed.) (1939b), *Radio Times*, 1 September.

—— (ed.) (1939c), 'Revised programmes for Sept. 4–10, broadcasting carries on', special issue, *Radio Times,* 4 September.

—— (ed.) (1939d), *Radio Times*, 8 September.

—— (ed.) (1975a), *Radio Times,* 5–11 April.

—— (ed.) (1975b), *Radio Times,* 12–18 April.

—— (ed.) (1975c), *Radio Times,* 19–25 April.

—— (2011), 'BBC launches *Archers* spin-off show *Ambridge Extra*', *The Daily Telegraph,* 17 March, http://www.telegraph.co.uk/culture/tvandradio/8386596/BBC-launches-Archers-spin-off-show-Ambridge-Extra.html. Accessed 20 July 2018.

—— (2017), '2017 winners & finalists', The Parsec Awards, http://www.parsecawards.com/2018-parsec-awards-2/2017-finalists/. Accessed 6 October 2018.

—— (2018), '2018 Sarah Awards winners!', The Sarah Awards, 8 April, http://thesarahawards.com/article/2018/4/8/2018-sarah-awards-winners. Accessed 6 October 2018.

Arango-Forero, Germán, Roncallo-Dow, Sergio and Uribe-Jongbloed, Enrique (2016), 'Rethinking convergence: A new word to describe an old idea', in A. Lugmayr and C. Dal Zotto (eds), *Media Convergence Handbook – Vol. 1, Journalism, Broadcasting, and Social Media Aspects of Convergence,* Berlin: Springer-Verlag, pp. 17–28.

Arbitron and Edison Research (2010), 'The Infinite Dial 2010: Digital platforms and the future of radio', http://www.edisonresearch.com/wp-content/uploads/2015/08/infinite_dial_presentation_2010_final.pdf. Accessed 20 July 2018.

Arbitron Inc. and Radio Research Consortium (2011), 'Public radio subscribers – Fall 2010 quarter (September 16–December 8) Arbitron PPM markets only Monday–Sunday, 6 AM to midnight: Ranked by Metro 6+ AQH persons', 25 January, http://www.rrconline.org/reports/pdf/Fa10%20PPM%20eRanks.pdf. Accessed 20 July 2018.

Arnheim, Rudolf (1971), *Radio: An Art of Sound* (trans. Margaret Ludwig), London: Faber and Faber.

Arnold, Matthew (1993), 'Culture and anarchy: An essay in political and social criticism', in S. Collini (ed.), *Culture and Anarchy and Other Writings,* Cambridge: Cambridge University Press, pp. 53–188.
Attali, Jacques (2013), 'Listening', in M. Bull (ed.), *Sound Studies: Meanings and Scope*, Sound Studies: Critical Concepts in Media and Cultural Studies, vol. 1, Abingdon: Routledge, pp. 25–42.
Aujla-Sidhu, Gurinder (2017), 'How to serve British Asian communities? The dilemmas facing the BBC', *The Radio Journal: International Studies in Broadcast & Audio Media*, 15:1, pp. 107–24.
Ault, David (n.d.), 'David Ault, voice actor, narrator, and science communicator', http://www.davidault.co.uk/acting.html. Accessed 20 July 2018.
Avery, Todd (2006), *Radio Modernism: Literature, Ethics, and the BBC, 1922–1938,* Aldershot: Ashgate Publishing Ltd.
Babin, Laurie A. and Burns, Alvin C. (1998), 'A modified scale for the measurement of communication-evoked mental imagery', *Psychology and Marketing,* 15:3, pp. 261–78.
Baker, Andréa Jean (2012), *Virtual Radio Ga-Ga, Youths, and Net Radio: Exploring Subcultural Models of Audiences,* New York: Hampton Press.
Baker, William F. and Dessart, George (1998), *Down the Tube: An Inside Account of the Failure of American Television,* New York: Basic Books.
Balick, Aaron (2013), 'The radio as good object: An object relational perspective on the curative and protective factors of a BBC public service broadcast for young people', *The Radio Journal: International Studies in Broadcast & Audio Media,* 11:1, pp. 13–28.
Balk, Alfred (2006), *The Rise of Radio: From Marconi Through the Golden Age,* Jefferson: McFarland & Co.
Ballentine, John (2011), 'Origins of *Campfire Radio Theater*', Campfire Radio Theater, 22 July, https://campfireradiotheater.podbean.com. Accessed 20 July 2018.
Barber, John (2014), 'Future audio drama: Imagine the possibilities', *Audio Drama – Histories, Aesthetics, Practices*, University of Copenhagen and the Radiodrama Network, Copenhagen, 19 August.
Barfield, Ray (1996), *Listening to Radio, 1920–1950,* London: Praeger.
—— (2010), 'The Shadow', in C.H. Sterling, C. O'Dell and M.C. Keith (eds), *The Concise Encyclopedia of American Radio*, New York: Routledge, pp. 688–91.
Barnard, Stephen (1989), *On the Radio: Music Radio in Britain,* London: Open University Press.
—— (2001), 'Mother's little helper: Programmes, personalities, and the working day', in C. Mitchell (ed.), *Women and Radio,* London: Routledge, pp. 126–36.
Barnouw, Erik (1975), *Tube of Plenty: The Evolution of American Television,* New York: Oxford University Press.
Baron, Zach (2016), '*Serial* Season 2 wasn't a phenomenon – But it was still pretty phenomenal', *GQ,* 2 April, http://www.gq.com/story/serial-season-2. Accessed 20 July 2018.
Barone, Joshua (2017), 'Audible creates $5 million fund for emerging playwrights', *New York Times,* 30 May, https://www.nytimes.com/2017/05/30/theater/audible-creates-5-million-dollar-fund-for-emerging-playwrights.html. Accessed 20 July 2018.
Barsamian, David (2002), *The Decline and Fall of Public Broadcasting,* 2nd ed., Cambridge, MA: South End Press.

Barthes, Roland (1979), *Elements of Semiology* (trans. Annette Lavers and Colin Smith), New York: Hill & Wang.

Bauersfeld, Erik (n.d.), 'Bay Area radio drama', BARD, http://www.bardradio.com/. Accessed 20 July 2018.

Baughman, James L. (1997), *The Republic of Mass Culture: Journalism, Filmmaking, and Broadcasting in America since 1941*, Baltimore: The John Hopkins University Press.

―――― (2007), *Same Time, Same Station: Creating American Television, 1948–1961*, Baltimore: The Johns Hopkins University Press.

Baysinger, Tim (2015), 'Heading into Season 2, has *Serial* sold advertisers on podcasting?', *Adweek*, 29 November, http://www.adweek.com/digital/heading-season-2-has-serial-sold-advertisers-podcasting-168280/. Accessed 20 July 2018.

BBC (2004), *Building Public Value: Renewing the BBC for a Digital World*, London: BBC.

―――― (2011), 'The BBC's diversity strategy 2011–2015: Everyone has a story', May, https://downloads.bbc.co.uk/diversity/pdf/Diversity_strategy_110523.pdf. Accessed 20 July 2018.

―――― (2014a), 'WRITERSROOM BLOG', 29 July, http://www.bbc.co.uk/blogs/blogwritersroom. Accessed 24 August 2014.

―――― (2014b), 'BBC structure', Inside the BBC, http://www.bbc.co.uk/aboutthebbc/insidethebbc/managementstructure/bbcstructure/. Accessed 20 July 2018.

―――― (2016), 'Performance against public commitments', http://downloads.bbc.co.uk/annualreport/pdf/2014-15/bbc-papc-2015.pdf. Accessed 20 July 2018.

―――― (2017a), 'Genome', http://genome.ch.bbc.co.uk/. Accessed 20 July 2018.

―――― (2017b), 'The BBC Carleton Hobbs Bursary Award', (((soundstart))), http://www.bbc.co.uk/programmes/articles/3PvhNflP5QSWWj8jQFmGKv1/the-bbc-carleton-hobbs-bursary-award. Accessed 28 July 2017.

―――― (2017c), 'Previous Carleton Hobbs Bursary Award winners', (((soundstart))) http://www.bbc.co.uk/programmes/articles/47fxKVYdTN1wFVbSPsn5kqn/previous-carleton-hobbs-bursary-award-winners. Accessed 28 July 2017.

―――― (2018), 'Why has BBC iPlayer Radio changed to BBC Sounds?', BBC Sounds, https://www.bbc.co.uk/sounds/help/introducing-sounds. Accessed 16 November 2018.

―――― (n.d.) '*The Turning Forest, An Interactive Fairy-Tale*', Virtual Reality, http://www.bbc.co.uk/guides/z6nttv4. Accessed 16 November 2018.

BBC Marketing & Audiences (2011), 'BBC radio log and daily overview', 18 September–2 October.

BBC Trust (2013), *Radio 4 Service Licence*, http://www.bbc.co.uk/bbctrust/our_work/services/radio/service_licences/bbc_radio_4.html. Accessed 20 July 2018.

Beall L., Kelly, C., Podteen and Whitelaw, D. (2017), 'Eligibility and FAQ', Audio Verse Awards, http://www.audioverseawards.net/site/faq/. Accessed 20 July 2018.

'The Beauty of Bulldog' (2007), *Street Stories*, Australian Broadcasting Corporation (ABC), 8 July, https://www.thirdcoastfestival.org/explore/feature/disappearing-show. Accessed 24 August 2017.

Beck, Alan (1997), *Radio Acting*, London: A & C Black.

Benedictus, Leo (2010), 'Don't touch that dial: The threat to radio drama', *The Guardian*, 20 June, https://www.theguardian.com/tv-and-radio/2010/jun/20/radio-drama. Accessed 20 July 2018.

Berkeley, Reginald (1925), *The White Château*, London: Williams and Norgate Ltd.

—— (1927), *Machines: A Symphony of Modern Life,* London: Robert Holden & Co., Ltd.

Berland, Jody (1994), 'Toward a creative anachronism: Radio, the state, and sound government', in D. Augaitis and D. Lander (eds), *Radio Rethink: Art, Sound, and Transmission,* Banff, AB: Walter Phillips Gallery, pp. 33–46.

Berrigan, Frances (1977), *Access: Some Western Models of Community Media,* Paris: UNESCO.

Berry, Richard (2004), 'Speech radio in the digital age', in A. Crisell (ed.), *More than a Music Box: Radio Cultures and Communities in a Multi-Media World,* New York: Berghahn Books, pp. 283–96.

—— (2013), 'Radio with pictures: Radio visualization in BBC National Radio', *The Radio Journal: International Studies in Broadcast & Audio Media,* 11:2, pp. 169–84.

—— (2015), 'A golden age of podcasting? Evaluating *Serial* in the context of podcast histories', *Journal of Radio & Audio Media,* 22:2, pp. 170–78.

Bickerton, Roger (n.d.), '10 favourite plays', Diversity Radio Plays, http://www.suttonelms.org.uk/articles10.html. Accessed 28 September 2018.

Blesser, Barry and Salter, Linda-Ruth (2012), 'Ancient acoustic spaces', in J. Sterne (ed.), *Sound Studies Reader*, New York: Routledge, pp. 186–96.

Blodget, Henry and Gobry, Pascal-Emmanuel (2011), 'Pandora still growing like gangbusters – Now 4% of total US radio listening', *Business Insider,* 23 November, http://www.businessinsider.com/pandora-q3-earnings-2011-11#ixzz3994JS0Lm. Accessed 20 July 2018.

Blue, Howard (2002), *Words at War: World War II Era Radio Drama and the Postwar Broadcasting Industry Blacklist,* Oxford: Scarecrow Press.

Boddy, William (1990), *Fifties Television: The Industry and Its Critics,* Urbana: University of Illinois Press.

—— (2004), *New Media and Popular Imagination: Launching Radio, Television, and Digital Media in the United States,* Oxford: Oxford University Press.

Boer, John James de (1938), 'The emotional responses of children to radio drama', Ph.D. thesis, Chicago: University of Chicago.

Bolls, Paul D. (2002), 'I can hear you, but can I see you? The use of visual cognition during exposure to high-imagery radio advertisements', *Communication Research: An International Quarterly*, 29:5, pp. 537–63.

—— (2006), 'It's just your imagination: The effect of imagery on recognition of product- versus non-product-related information in radio advertisements', *Journal of Radio Studies,* 13:2, pp. 201–13.

Bolls, P.D. and Potter, R.F. (1998), 'I saw it on the radio: The effect of imagery evoking radio commercials on listeners' allocation of attention and attitude toward the ad', *Proceedings of the Conference of the American Academy of Advertising,* Lexington, KY, 27–30 March, pp. 123–30.

Bond, Martyn A. (1970), 'A comparative study of postwar radio drama in Great Britain and West Germany', Ph.D. thesis, Brighton: University of Sussex.

Bonini, Tiziano (2011), 'Blurring fiction and reality: The strange case of *Amnèsia,* an Italian "mockumentary"', in A. Gazi, G. Starkey and S. Jedrzejewski (eds), *Radio Content in the Digital Age: The Evolution of a Sound Medium,* Bristol: Intellect, pp. 83–104.

—— (2015), 'The "Second Age" of podcasting: Reframing podcasting as a new digital mass medium', *Quaderns del CAC,* 41, pp. 21–30.

Born, Georgina (2005), *Uncertain Vision: Birt, Dyke and the Reinvention of the BBC,* London: Secker & Warburg.

Boss, Sandra and Holm, Astrid Hansen (2014), 'Augmented listening – The sound media and the listening act as a spatial and time-defining factor in site-specific audio drama', *Audio Drama – Histories, Aesthetics, Practices,* University of Copenhagen and the Radiodrama Network, Copenhagen, 19 August.

Bottomley, Andrew (2015), 'Podcasting, *Welcome to Night Vale*, and the revival of radio drama', *Journal of Radio & Audio Media*, 22:2, pp. 179–89.

'The Boy Who Never Returned' (2007), *Maritime Magazine,* Canadian Broadcasting Corporation (CBC), https://www.thirdcoastfestival.org/explore/feature/disappearing-show. Accessed 24 August 2017.

Boyle, Darren (2014), 'BBC "apology" blames actors for mumbling in television drama *Jamaica Inn* after viewers said they could not hear as complaints surge and viewing figures slide', *The Daily Mail Online,* 24 April, http://www.dailymail.co.uk/news/article-2611942/BBC-apology-blames-actors-mumbling-television-drama-Jamaica-Inn-viewers-said-not-hear-complaints-surge-viewing-figures-slide.html. Accessed 20 July 2018.

Brett, Nicholas (ed.) (1992a), *Radio Times,* 10–16 October.

—— (1992b), *Radio Times,* 24–30 October.

—— (1992c), *Radio Times,* 31 October–6 November.

—— (1992d), *Radio Times,* 7–13 November.

Bridges, Jeffrey (2014), 'How can I submit an audition to Pendant Productions?' Pendant Audio Productions, http://www.pendantaudio.com/faq.php#audition. Accessed 20 July 2018.

Bridson, D.G. (1950), *The Christmas Child,* London: The Falcon Press.

—— (1971), *Prospero and Ariel: The Rise and Fall of Radio,* London: Victor Gollancz Ltd.

Briggs, Asa (1985), *The BBC: The First Fifty Years,* Oxford: Oxford University Press.

—— (1995a), *The History of Broadcasting in the United Kingdom, vol. III: The War of Words,* Oxford: Oxford University Press.

—— (1995b), *The History of Broadcasting in the United Kingdom, vol. IV: Sound and Vision,* Oxford: Oxford University Press.

—— (1995c), *The History of Broadcasting in the United Kingdom, vol. V: Competition,* Oxford: Oxford University Press.

Briggs, Nicholas (2013), interviewed by Matthew Kresal, *The Terrible Zodin,* 16, pp. 31–33, https://www.dropbox.com/s/c3wupqz5vw6luu4/TTZ16_final.pdf?dl=0. Accessed 20 July 2018.

Broaddus, Matthew, Harmon, Mark D. and Farley-Mounts, Kristin (2011), 'VNRs: Is the news audience deceived?', *Journal of Mass Media Ethics,* 26:4, pp. 283–96.

Brochand, Christian (1974), *Histoire générale de la radio,* vols 1 and 2, Paris: Documentation Française.

Brown, Mark A. (n.d.), 'Who we are', http://www.markacbrown.com/tin-can-podcast.html. Accessed 20 July 2018.

Brown, Michael Barratt (2013), 'Introduction to 2013 edition', in *Culture and Society 1780–1950,* Nottingham: Spokesman, pp. i–ii.

Bull, Michael (2000), *Sounding Out the City: Personal Stereos and the Management of Everyday Life,* Oxford: Berg.
—— (2003), 'Soundscapes of the car', in M. Bull and L. Black (eds), *The Auditory Culture Reader,* Oxford: Berg, pp. 357–80.
—— (2007), *Sound Moves: iPod Culture and Urban Experience,* London: Routledge.
—— (2012), 'iPod culture: The toxic pleasures of audiotopia', in T. Pinch and K. Bijsterveld (eds), *The Oxford Handbook of Sound Studies,* Oxford: Oxford University Press, pp. 526–43.
—— (2013a), 'Bergson's iPod? The cognitive management of everyday life', in M. Bull (ed.), *Sound Spaces, Places, Cultures and Technologies,* Sound Studies: Critical Concepts in Media and Cultural Studies, vol. 3, Abingdon: Routledge, pp. 57–70.
—— (2013b), 'iPod use: An urban aesthetics of sonic ubiquity', *Continuum,* 27:4, pp. 495–504.
Burke, Kenneth (1941), 'Literature as equipment for living', in *The Philosophy of Literary Form,* Louisiana: Louisiana State University Press, pp. 293–304.
Burns, Matt (2014), 'The Pandora One subscription service to cost $5 a month', TechCrunch.com, 18 March, http://techcrunch.com/2014/03/18/the-pandora-one-subscription-service-to-cost-5-a-month/. Accessed 20 July 2018.
Callahan, Maureen (2017), '*S Town* is just an excuse for urban liberals to rubberneck', *The New York Post,* 29 April, http://nypost.com/2017/04/29/s-town-is-just-an-excuse-for-urban-liberals-to-rubberneck/. Accessed 20 July 2018.
Camino Real Productions (2017), 'About Camino Real Productions', http://www.caminorealabq.com/about.htm. Accessed 20 July 2018.
Cantril, Hadley (1940), *The Invasion from Mars: A Study in the Psychology of Panic*, Princeton: Princeton University Press.
Cantril, Hadley and Allport, G.W. (1935), *The Psychology of Radio*, New York: Harper & Brothers Publishers.
Caristi, Dom and Sterling, Christopher H. (2010), 'Federal Communications Commission', in C.H. Sterling, C. O'Dell and M.C. Keith (eds), *The Concise Encyclopedia of American Radio,* New York: Routledge, pp. 282–86.
Carpenter, Humphrey (1996), *The Envy of the World: Fifty Years of the BBC Third Programme & Radio 3,* London: Weidenfeld & Nicolson.
Carter, Angela (1985), *Come Unto These Yellow Sands* (*Come Unto These Yellow Sands, The Company of Wolves, Vampirella, Puss in Boots),* Newcastle: Bloodaxe Books.
Cartwright, Andy (2014), 'Rediscovering the imagination: A practical exploration into the teaching of audio drama', *Audio Drama – Histories, Aesthetics, Practices,* University of Copenhagen and the Radiodrama Network, Copenhagen, 19 August.
Caulfield, Annie (2009), *Writing for Radio: A Practical Guide,* Ramsbury: Crowood.
Cawelti, John G. (1984), *The Six-Gun Mystique Sequel,* Bowling Green: Bowling Green University Popular Press.
—— (1995), 'The concept of formula in the study of popular literature', in C.L. Harrington and D.D. Bielby (eds), *Popular Culture: Production and Consumption,* Philadelphia: Temple University Press, pp. 203–09.
—— (2004), *Mystery, Violence, and Popular Culture,* Madison: University of Wisconsin Popular Press.

Challis, Ben, D'Arcy, Geraint, Dean, Robert, Hand, Richard, Smith, Rob and Traynor, Mary (2014), 'Wireless zombies! A re-creation of golden age radio drama for a contemporary audience', *Studies in Theatre and Performance*, 34:3, pp. 1–8.

Chambers, Todd (2012), 'Local ownership and radio market structure', *Journal of Radio & Audio Media*, 19:1, pp. 263–80.

Chatterbox Audio Theater (2017), 'The process', http://chatterboxtheater.org/node/29. Accessed 20 July 2018.

Chignell, Hugh (2009), *Key Concepts in Radio Studies*, London: London Sage Publications Ltd.

—— (2015), 'Out of the dark: Samuel Beckett and BBC Radio', *Peripeti Audiodrama*, 22, pp. 11–21.

—— (2016), 'Giles Cooper: Four radio dramas', *Giles Cooper: Four Radio Dramas*, CD booklet, Centre for Media History, Bournemouth University.

Chion, Michel (1994), *Audio-Vision: Sound on Screen* (trans. Claudia Gorbman), New York: Columbia University Press.

—— (1999), *The Voice in the Cinema* (trans. Claudia Gorbman), New York: Columbia University Press.

—— (2003), *Film: A Sound Art* (trans. Claudia Gorbman), New York: Columbia University Press.

Classical Public Radio 95.5 KHFM (2018), http://www.khfm.org/. Accessed 1 October 2018.

Clifford, Catherine (2014), 'Crowdfunding generates more than $60,000 an hour (infographic)', *Entrepreneur*, 19 May, http://www.entrepreneur.com/article/234051. Accessed 20 July 2018.

Cochrane, Todd (2014), 'Podcast RSS feed survey results', Podcaster News, 10 April, http://podcasternews.com/2014/04/10/podcast-rss-feed-survey-results/. Accessed 20 July 2018.

Connor, Alan (2007), 'Revolution not evolution', BBC Internet Blog, 4 December, http://www.bbc.co.uk/blogs/bbcinternet/2007/12/revolution_not_evolution.html. Accessed 20 July 2018.

Corwin, Norman (1994), interviewed by Douglas Bell, *Years of the Electric Ear*, Metuchen, NJ: The Directors Guild of America and Scarecrow Press, pp. 1–297.

Couldry, Nick (2000), *Culture: Reimagining the Method of Culture Studies*, London: SAGE.

Coulter, John and Lewis, Ivor (1937), *Radio Drama Is Not Theatre*, Toronto: Macmillan Company of Canada, Library and Archives of Canada, Records of the Canadian Broadcasting Corporation.

Country Channel TV (2010), '*The Archers*: Behind the scenes', YouTube, https://www.youtube.com/watch?v=FbHWq8Jdhr4. Accessed 20 July 2018.

Coward, Mat (2003), *Classical Radio Comedy*, Harpenden: Pocket Essentials.

Cox, Jim (2009), *American Radio Networks: A History*, Jefferson: McFarland & Co.

—— (2013), *Radio After the Golden Age: The Evolution of American Broadcasting Since 1960*, Jefferson: McFarland & Co.

Coyer, Kate (2007a), 'Mysteries of the black box unbound: An alternative history of radio', in K. Coyer, T. Dowmunt and A. Fountain (eds), *The Alternative Media Handbook*, Abingdon, Abingdon: Routledge, pp. 14–28.

—— (2007b), 'Access to broadcasting: Radio', in K. Coyer, T. Dowmunt and A. Fountain (eds), *The Alternative Media Handbook*, London: Routledge, pp. 112–22.

Crawford, David (2012), 'Today's choice, 17 June', *Radio Times,* 16–22 June, p. 130.
Creeber, Glen (2003), 'The origins of public service broadcasting', in M. Hilmes (ed.), *The Television History Book*, London: BFI Publishing, pp. 22–25.
Cridland, James (2018), 'What is radio?', comment, Radio Studies Network JISC Mail Group, 6 March.
Crisell, Andrew (1994), *Understanding Radio,* Abingdon: Routledge.
—— (2002), *An Introductory History of British Broadcasting,* London: Routledge.
—— (2004), 'Look with thine ears: BBC Radio 4 and its significance in a multi-media age', in A. Crisell (ed.), *More than a Music Box: Radio Cultures and Communities in a Multi-Media World,* New York: Berghahn Books, pp. 3–20.
—— (2006), *A Study of Modern Television: Thinking Inside the Box,* Basingstoke: Palgrave Macmillan.
—— (2009), 'Better than Magritte: How drama on the radio became radio drama', in A. Crisell (ed.), *Radio: Critical Concepts in Media and Cultural Studies,* Abingdon: Routledge, pp. 297–305.
—— (2012), *Liveness and Recording in the Media,* Basingstoke: Palgrave Macmillan.
Crook, Tim (1999a), *Radio Drama: Theory and Practice,* Abingdon: Routledge.
—— (1999b), 'British radio drama – A cultural case history', Independent Radio Drama Productions, http://www.irdp.co.uk/britrad.htm. Accessed 20 July 2018.
—— (1999c), 'The psychological power of radio', Independent Radio Drama Productions, http://www.irdp.co.uk/hoax.htm. Accessed 20 July 2018.
—— (2010), 'Drama', in C.H. Sterling, C. O'Dell and M.C. Keith (eds), *The Concise Encyclopedia of American Radio,* New York: Routledge, pp. 227–34.
—— (2012), *The Sound Handbook,* Abingdon: Routledge.
Cropper, Nigel (n.d.), 'My top 10 radio plays', Diversity Radio Plays, http://www.suttonelms.org.uk/articles8.html. Accessed 28 September 2018.
Cummings, David (2016), 'S7E10', The NoSleep Podcast, https://www.thenosleeppodcast.com/episodes/s7/7x10. Accessed 20 July 2018.
—— (2017), 'About – The history of the *NoSleep* podcast', The No Sleep Podcast, https://www.thenosleeppodcast.com/about. Accessed 20 July 2018.
Damgaard, Trine (2014), 'The vibrant radio drama – On improvisation in radio drama acting', *Audio Drama – Histories, Aesthetics, Practices*, University of Copenhagen and the Radiodrama Network, Copenhagen, 19 August.
Dane, Clemence (1961), 'Approaches to drama', The English Association presidential address, The English Association, London, July.
D'Arcy, Kevin (2007), *The Voice of the Brain of Britain: A Portrait of Radio Four,* London: Rajah Books.
Davies, John (1994), *Broadcasting and the BBC in Wales,* Cardiff: University of Wales Press.
Davis, Peter and Woodcock, Matthew (2013), The Monster Hunters, http://www.themonsterhunters.com/. Accessed 20 July 2018.
Deacon, Nigel (2007), 'Top 10 favourite plays: Your choice', Diversity Radio Plays, http://www.suttonelms.org.uk/articles38.html. Accessed 28 September 2018.
—— (2008), 'Ten more favourite radio plays', Diversity Radio Plays, http://www.suttonelms.org.uk/articles40.html. Accessed 28 September 2018.

—— (n.d.), '10 favourite plays – Nigel Deacon's choice', Diversity Radio Plays, http://www.suttonelms.org.uk/articles4.html. Accessed 28 September 2018.

Derecho, Abigail (2006), 'Archontic literature: A definition, a history, and several theories of fan fiction', in K. Hellekson and K. Busse (eds), *Fan Fiction and Fan Communities in the Age of the Internet*, Jefferson: McFarland & Co., pp. 61–78.

Digital Deli Too (n.d.), 'Dragnet', http://www.digitaldeliftp.com/DigitalDeliToo/dd2jb-Dragnet.html. Accessed 20 July 2018.

Dolan, Josephine (2003), 'Aunties and uncles: The BBC's *Children's Hour* and liminal concerns in the 1920s', *Historical Journal of Film, Radio & Television*, 23:4, pp. 329–40.

Douglas, Susan (1987), *Inventing American Broadcasting, 1899–1922*, Baltimore: John Hopkins University Press.

Douglas, Susan J. ([1999] 2004), *Listening In: Radio and the American Imagination*, Minneapolis: University of Minnesota Press.

Doyle, Brandy (2012), 'Low power community radio in the US: The beginnings, the first ten years, and future prospects', in J. Gordon (ed.), *Community Radio in the Twenty-first Century*, Bern: Peter Lang, pp. 33–54.

Driscoll, Catherine (2006), 'One true pairing: The romance of pornography and the pornography of romance', in K. Hellekson and K. Busse (eds), *Fan Fiction and Fan Communities in the Age of the Internet*, Jefferson: McFarland & Co., pp. 79–96.

Dubber, Andrew (2006), 'The end of *Claybourne*', 31 May, http://andrewdubber.com/2006/05/the-end-of-claybourne/. Accessed 20 July 2018.

—— (2007), 'Tutira Mai Nga Iwi (line up together, people): Constructing New Zealand identity through commercial radio', *The Radio Journal: International Studies in Broadcast & Audio Media*, 5:1, pp. 19–34.

—— (2013), *Radio in the Digital Age,* Cambridge, MA: Polity Press.

—— (2017), e-mail to Leslie McMurtry, August 10.

Dueker, Chris (2008), 'Aural sex?', Radio Drama Revival, 13 June, http://www.radiodramarevival.com/aural-sex/. Accessed 14 March 2018.

Duerr, Edwin (1950), *Radio and Television Acting: Criticism, Theory, Practice,* Westport: Greenwood Press.

Dunaway, David King (2000), 'Digital radio: Towards an aesthetic', *New Media and Society,* 2:1, pp. 29–50.

—— (2014), 'The conglomeration of public radio: A tale of three cities', *Journal of Radio & Audio Media,* 21:1, pp. 177–82.

Dunn, Larry (2010), 'Chatterbox on WKNO-TV's *Southern Routes*', YouTube, https://www.youtube.com/watch?v=RiJNNRBw26E. Accessed 20 July 2018.

Dunning, John (1998), *On the Air: The Encyclopedia of Old-Time Radio,* New York: Oxford University Press.

Durlin, Marty (2016), '*Downtown Abbey*: Season 1 a satirical spoof of modern Moab', KZMU, 1 February, http://www.kzmu.org/downtown-abbey/downtown-abbey-a-kzmu-radio-drama/. Accessed 5 August 2017.

Dylan Thomas Centre and City and County of Swansea (1991), 'Dylan Thomas: The broadcasts', in R. Maud (ed.), *Dylan Thomas – The Broadcasts*, http://www.dylanthomas.com/dylan/dylans-work/dylan-thomas-broadcasts/. Accessed 20 July 2018.

Eck, Hélène (2006), 'La radiodiffusion dans l'entre-deux-guerres: L'invention d'une culture médiathèques singulière', in J.-V. Mollier, J.-F. Sirinelli and F. Valloton (eds), *Culture de Masse et Culture Médiathèque en Europe et dans les Amériques 1860–1940,* Paris: Presses Universitaires de France, pp. 231–44.

Edison Research and Triton Digital (2014), 'The Infinite Dial 2014: Online radio, music discovery, social networking, podcasting, smartphones, in-car media', http://www.edisonresearch.com/the-infinite-dial-2014/. Accessed 20 July 2018.

—— (2017), 'The Infinite Dial 2017', http://www.edisonresearch.com/infinite-dial-2017/. Accessed 20 July 2018.

Eisenberg, Evan (1987), *The Recording Angel: Explorations in Phonography,* New York: McGraw-Hill Book Company.

Ellen, P.S. and Bone, P.F. (1992), 'The generation and consequences of communication-evoked imagery', *Journal of Consumer Research,* 19:1, pp. 93–104.

Elmes, Simon (2008), *And Now on Radio 4: A Celebration of the World's Best Radio Station,* London: Arrow Books.

Enns, Anthony (2013), 'Psychic radio: Sound technologies, ether bodies, and spiritual vibrations', in M. Bull (ed.), *Media Sounds,* Sound Studies: Critical Concepts in Media and Cultural Studies, vol. 4, Abingdon: Routledge, pp. 345–59.

European Parliament (2011), 'Digital Radio Conference 2011', http://digitalradi-oconference.ebu.ch/index.php. Accessed 4 June 2014.

Fahri, Paul (2010), 'National Public Radio is changing its name to NPR', *The Washington Post,* 8 July, http://www.washingtonpost.com/wp-dyn/content/article/2010/07/07/AR2010070704578.html. Accessed 26 April 2014.

Feldman, Leslie Dale (2010), *Spaceships and Politics: The Political Theory of Rod Serling,* Lanham: Lexington Books.

Ferguson, Douglas A. and Greer, Clark F. (2011), 'Local radio and microblogging: How radio stations in the U.S. are using Twitter', *Journal of Radio & Audio Media,* 18:1, pp. 33–46.

Fernández-Quijada, David (2017), 'Distinctiveness of public radio in the age of digitization', *Journal of Radio & Audio Media,* 24:1, pp. 77–89.

Ferrara, Alessandro (1998), *Reflective Authenticity*, London: Routledge.

Flintoff, Corey and Sterling, Christopher H. (2010), 'National Public Radio', in C.H. Sterling, C. O'Dell and M.C. Keith (eds), *The Concise Encyclopedia of American Radio,* New York: Routledge, pp. 503–09.

Flood, Alison (2011), 'Pottermore website launched by JK Rowling as "give back" to fans', *The Guardian,* 23 June, https://www.theguardian.com/books/2011/jun/23/pottermore-website-jk-rowling-harry-potter. Accessed 20 July 2018.

Forsslund, T. (2014), 'Young radio listeners' creative mental interaction and co-production', *The Radio Journal*: International Studies in Broadcast & Audio Media, 12:1&2, pp. 125–39.

Frank, Joe (2015), '*NPR Playhouse* and WBAI', JoeFrank.com, https://www.joefrank.com/shows/wbai-and-npr/. Accessed 20 July 2018.

Freberg, Stan, Vaughn, Sarah and Jones, Quincy (1965), 'Who listens to radio?', YouTube, https://www.youtube.com/watch?v=0C4e59yZExk. Accessed 20 July 2018.

Fried, Albert (1997), *McCarthyism: The Great American Red Scare: A Documentary History,* New York: Oxford University Press.

Frow, John (2006), *Genre*, London: Routledge.
Frye, Bob J. (1999), 'Garrison Keillor's serious humor: Satire in Lake Wobegon days', *The Midwest Quarterly*, 40:2, pp. 121–34.
Gaiman, Neil (2003), *Don't Panic: Douglas Adams and the* Hitchhiker's Guide to the Galaxy, London: Titan Books.
Garner, Ken (2012), 'We don't talk any more: The strange case of Scottish broadcasting devolution policy and radio silence', in R.J. Hand and M. Traynor (eds), *Radio in Small Nations: Production, Programmes, Audiences*, Cardiff: University of Wales Press, pp. 40–60.
Gartenberg, Chaim (2017), 'BBC is making interactive radio plays for Alexa and Google Home', The Verge, 16 September, https://www.theverge.com/2017/9/6/16261348/bbc-radio-plays-interactive-stories-audio-drama-google-home-amazon-alexa-echo. Accessed 16 November 2018.
Gaver, William W. (1993), 'How do we hear in the world?: Explorations in ecological acoustics', *Ecological Psychology*, 5:4, pp. 285–313.
Gearing, Brian (ed.) (1987a), *Radio Times*, 10–16 October.
—— (ed.) (1987b), *Radio Times*, 24–30 October.
—— (ed.) (1987c), *Radio Times*, 31 October–6 November.
—— (ed.) (1992a), *Radio Times*, 2–8 October.
—— (ed.) (1992b), *Radio Times*, 30 October–5 November.
Geiger Smith, Erin (2017), 'Welcome to the podcast: First a word from our celebrity', *New York Times*, 24 March, https://www.nytimes.com/2017/03/24/style/podcasts-advertisements-katie-couric-alex-baldwin.html?_r=0&referer. Accessed 20 July 2018.
Geraghty, Christine and Weissmann, Elke (2016), 'Women, soap opera and new generations of feminists', *Critical Studies in Television*, 11:3, pp. 365–68.
Gibbs, Nicholas (2006), 'Radio drama acting', BBC, 7 February, http://www.bbc.co.uk/cambridgeshire/content/articles/2006/02/07/raw_acting_guide_feature.shtml. Accessed 20 July 2018.
Gibson, Walter B. (1979), *The Shadow Scrapbook*, New York: Harcourt Brace Jovanovich.
Giddings, Robert and Selby, Keith (2001), *The* Classic Serial *on Television and Radio*, Basingstoke: Palgrave.
Gielgud, Val (1957), *British Radio Drama 1922–1956: A Survey*, London: George C. Harrap & Co.
Gilfillan, Daniel (2009), *Pieces of Sound: German Experimental Radio*, Minneapolis: University of Minnesota.
Glancy, Mark (2005), 'The war of independence in feature films: *The Patriot* (2000) and the "Special Relationship" between Hollywood and Britain', *Historical Journal of Film, Radio and Television*, 25:4, pp. 523–45.
Glass, Ira (2010), interviewed by Bill Moggridge, *Designing Media*, Cambridge, MA: MIT Press, pp. 445–60.
Goldin, David J. (2014), '*Against the Storm*', radioGOLDINdex database, 17 January, http://www.radiogoldindex.com/frame1.html. Accessed 20 July 2018.
Golding, Sarah and Thraille, Fiona (2017), 'The voice acting guide: Act 1 Episode 112', Audio Drama Production Podcast, http://audiodramaproduction.com/2017/06/acting-act-1-episode-112/. Accessed 20 July 2018.

Goodale, Greg (2011), *Sonic Persuasion: Reading Sound in the Recorded Age,* Urbana: University of Illinois Press.
Gordon, Janey (2012), 'The role of university radio in the development of community radio stations: A history', in J. Gordon (ed.), *Community Radio in the Twenty-first Century,* Bern: Peter Lang, pp. 367–84.
—— (2018), 'What is radio?', comment, Radio Studies Network JISC Mail Group, 6 March.
Gorham, Maurice (1948), *Sound and Fury: Twenty-One Years at the BBC,* London: Marshall.
—— (1949), *Television: Medium of the Future,* London: Percival Marshall.
Gosling, John (2009), *Waging the War of the Worlds: A History of the 1938 Radio Broadcast and Resulting Panic, Including the Original Script,* Jefferson: McFarland & Co.
Goudeau, Jessica (2017), 'Was the art of *S Town* worth the pain?', *The Atlantic,* 9 April, https://www.theatlantic.com/entertainment/archive/2017/04/was-the-art-of-s-town-worth-the-pain/522366/. Accessed 20 July 2018.
Graham, Adam (n.d.), 'Candy Matson', The Great Detectives of Old Time Radio with Host Adam Graham, http://www.greatdetectives.net/detectives/big-list-shows/candy/. Accessed 20 July 2018.
Grainge, Paul (2017), 'Moments and opportunities: Interstitials and the promotional imagination of BBC iPlayer', *Critical Studies in Television*, 12:2, pp. 139–55.
Gray, Frances (2004), 'Fireside issues: Audience, listener, soundscape', in A. Crisell (ed.), *More than a Music Box: Radio Cultures and Communities in a Multi-Media World*, New York: Berghahn Books, pp. 247–64.
—— (2009), 'The nature of radio drama', in A. Crisell (ed.), *Radio: Critical Concepts in Media and Cultural Studies*, Abingdon: Routledge, pp. 265–94.
Gray, Peggy and Lewis, Peter (1992), 'Britain: Community broadcasting revisited', in N. Jankowski, O. Prehn and J. Stappers (eds), *The People's Voice: Local Radio and Television in Europe*, London: John Libbey, pp. 156–68.
Greenhalgh, Frederick (2007), 'Original drama in the 21st century', Final Rune Productions, http://www.finalrune.com/original-radio-drama/. Accessed 20 July 2018.
—— (2008), 'Producing in the field – Doing it, and doing it on the cheap', Final Rune Productions, http://www.finalrune.com/producing-in-the-field/. Accessed 20 July 2018.
—— (2014), 'Audio drama needs a 21st century business model', Final Rune Productions, http://www.finalrune.com/audio-drama-needs-21st-century-business-model/. Accessed 20 July 2018.
—— (2017), 'RDR from the vault', Radio Drama Revival, http://www.radiodramarevival.com/rdr-vault-heart-morphine-roger-gregg/. Accessed 20 July 2018.
Griffin, Andrew (2014), '*Serial* podcast needs cash for second season, despite being one of the most popular shows ever', *The Independent,* 20 November, http://www.independent.co.uk/life-style/gadgets-and-tech/news/serial-podcast-needs-cash-for-second-season-despite-being-one-of-most-popular-shows-ever-9873086.html. Accessed 20 July 2018.
Grimshaw, Mark (2012), 'Sound and player immersion in digital games', in T. Pinch and K. Bijsterveld (eds), *The Oxford Handbook of Sound Studies*, Oxford: Oxford University Press, pp. 347–66.
Gruenberg, Axel (1998), interviewed by Irene Kahn Atkins, in I. Skutch (ed.), *Five Directors: The Golden Years of Radio: A Directors Guild of America Oral History,* Lanham: Scarecrow Press, pp. 45–75.

Guthrie, Tyrone (1931), *Squirrel's Cage and Two Other Microphone Plays,* London: The Camelot Press.
Hall, Alan (2010), 'Cigarettes and dance steps', in J. Biewen and A. Dilworth (eds), *Reality Radio: Telling True Stories in Sound*, Chapel Hill, NC: University of North Carolina, pp. 96–107.
Hall, Lee (2002), *Plays: 1 (Cooking with Elvis, Bollocks, Spoonface Steinberg, I Luv You Jimmy Spud, Wittgenstein on Tyne, Genie, Two's Company, Children of the Rain, Child of the Snow),* London: Methuen Publishing Limited.
Hancock, Danielle (2018), 'Our friendly desert town: Alternative podcast culture in *Welcome to Night Vale*', in J. Weinstock (ed.), *Critical Approaches to* Welcome to Night Vale: *Podcasting between Weather and the Void,* Basingstoke: Palgrave Pivot, pp. 35–49.
Hancock, Danielle and McMurtry, Leslie (2017), '"Cycles Upon Cycles, Stories Upon Stories": Contemporary audio media and podcast horror's new frights', *Palgrave Communications*, 3:17075, pp. 1–8.
—— (2018), '"I know what a podcast is": Post-*Serial* fiction and podcast media identity', in D. Llinares, N. Fox and R. Berry (eds), *Podcasting: New Aural Cultures and Digital Media,* London: Palgrave Macmillan, pp. 81–106.
Hand, Richard J. (2006), *Terror on the Air! Horror Radio in America, 1931–1952*, Jefferson: McFarland & Co.
—— (2014), *Listen in Terror: British Horror Radio from the Advent of Broadcasting to the Digital Age,* Manchester: Manchester University Press.
Hand, Richard J. and Traynor, Mary (2011), *The Radio Drama Handbook: Audio Drama in Context and Practice,* London: Continuum.
Hanrahan, Brian (2014), 'Reproducing traces of war: Listening to gas shell bombardment, 1918', Sounding Out! The Sound Studies Blog, 7 July, https://soundstudiesblog.com/2014/07/07/listening-to-traces-of-war-gas-shell-bombardment-1918/. Accessed 20 July 2018.
Harvey, Roger (n.d.), 'It's drama, but with adverts', Diversity Website, http://www.suttonelms.org.uk/articles39.html. Accessed 20 July 2018.
Hawley, David (n.d.), 'Radio plays – my top ten – David Hawley, VRPCC', Diversity Radio Plays, http://www.suttonelms.org.uk/articles11.html. Accessed 28 September 2018.
Haworth, Don (1976), '*On a Day in Summer in a Garden*', in J. Redmond and H. Tennyson (eds), *Contemporary One-Act Plays,* London: Heinemann Educational Books, pp. 103–36.
Heal, Clare (2011), 'Sprawling Soviet epic a treat', *Sunday Express*, 25 September, p. 63.
Heise, Nele (2013a), '"Radio activity": Theoretical perspectives on the interplay of radio, participatory practices and technology', *Radio Conference: A Transnational Forum*, University of Bedfordshire, Luton, 11 July.
—— (2013b), e-mail to Leslie McMurtry, 18 October.
Hendy, David (2000), *Radio in the Global Age,* Cambridge, MA: Polity Press.
—— (2003a), 'Speaking to Middle England: Radio Four and its listeners', in J. Aitchison and D.M. Lewis (eds), *New Media Language,* London: Routledge, pp. 65–74.
—— (2003b), 'Television's prehistory: Radio', in M. Hilmes and J. Jacobs (eds), *The Television History Book,* London: BFI Publishing, pp. 4–8.
—— (2004), '"Reality Radio": The documentary', in A. Crisell (ed.), *More than a Music Box: Radio Cultures and Communities in a Multi-Media World,* New York: Berghahn Books, pp. 169–88.

—— (2007), *Life on Air: A History of Radio Four,* Oxford: Oxford University Press.
—— (2013a), *Noise: A Human History of Sound and Listening,* London: Profile Books.
—— (2013b), *Public Service Broadcasting,* Basingstoke: Palgrave Macmillan.
—— (2013c), 'War, the emotions, and the origins of the BBC', *Radio Conference: A Transnational Forum*, University of Bedfordshire, Luton, Bedfordshire, 10 July.
—— (2013d), *Noise: A Human History,* BBC Radio 4, UK.
Heptonstall, Geoffrey (2009), 'Radio drama: A British art', *Contemporary Review,* 291:1693, pp. 204–16.
Hepworth, David (2015), 'Why the BBC's updated iPlayer app will change your life', *The Guardian,* 25 July, https://www.theguardian.com/tv-and-radio/2015/jul/25/iplayer-radio-app-david-hepworth. Accessed 20 July 2018.
Hewett, Richard (2015), 'The changing determinants of UK television acting', *Critical Studies in Television,* 10:1, pp. 73–90.
Higgins, Charlotte (2015), *This New Noise: The Extraordinary Birth and the Troubled Life of the BBC,* London: Guardian Books.
Hilliard, Robert L. and Keith, Michael C. (2005), *The Quieted Voice: The Rise and Demise of Localism in American Radio,* Carbondale: South Illinois University Press.
Hills, Matt (2002), *Fan Cultures,* London: Routledge.
Hilmes, Michele (1997), *Radio Voices: American Broadcasting, 1922–1952*, Minneapolis: University of Minnesota Press.
—— (2003), 'The origins of commercial broadcasting in the US', in M. Hilmes and J. Jacobs (eds), *The Television History Book,* London: BFI Publishing, pp. 26–29.
—— (2010), 'Hollywood and radio', in C.H. Sterling, C. O'Dell and M.C. Keith (eds), *The Concise Encyclopedia of American Radio,* New York: Routledge, pp. 363–67.
—— (2012), *Network Nations: A Transnational History of British and American Broadcasting,* London: Routledge.
—— (2013), 'The new materiality of radio', in J. Loviglio and M. Hilmes (eds), *Radio's New Wave: Global Sound in the Digital Era*, New York: Routledge, pp. 43–61.
—— (2014), *Only Connect: A Cultural History of Broadcasting in the United States*, 4th ed., Boston: Wadsworth.
Hilmes, Michele and Lindgren, Mia (2016), 'Podcast review and criticism', *The Radio Journal: International Studies in Broadcast & Audio Media,* 14:1, pp. 83–89.
Hindell, Alison (2011), interviewed by Leslie McMurtry, Cardiff, 4 November.
—— (2014), e-mail to Leslie McMurtry, 2 February.
Hinman, Tim (2014), 'Sound that makes drama is so much more than just the words – So what are radio dramas missing out on?', *Audio Drama – Histories, Aesthetics, Practices*, University of Copenhagen and the Radiodrama Network, Copenhagen, 19 August.
—— (2016), 'Blockbuster sound', *2016 Third Coast Conference*, Chicago, 11–13 November, https://www.thirdcoastfestival.org/explore/feature/blockbuster-sound. Accessed 20 July 2018.
Hirschom, Michael (2007), 'The unbearable lightness of Wes Anderson, Ira Glass, and other paragons of Indie sensibility', *The Atlantic Monthly*, 300:2, pp. 142–47.
Hobson, Dorothy (2002), *Soap Opera,* Oxford: Polity Press.

Hodgson, Caroline (2014), *For the Love of Radio 4: An Unofficial Companion,* Chichester: Summerdale.
Hoffelder, Nate (2017), 'Audible launches $5 million fund to pay emerging playwrights to write audio dramas', The Digital Reader, 30 May, https://the-digital-reader.com/2017/05/30/audible-launches-5-million-fund-pay-emerging-playwrights-write-audio-dramas/. Accessed 20 July 2018.
Hollingshead, Iain (2011), 'The Archers: The untold storyline', *The Daily Telegraph*, 3 April, http://www.telegraph.co.uk/culture/tvandradio/8423583/The-Archers-the-untold-storyline.html. Acccessed 20 July 2018.
Hon, Adrian (2017), 'The problem with podcast dramas: Is there anyone listening out there?', You Have a Lucky Face, 9 July, https://youhavealuckyface.com/the-problem-with-podcast-dramas-5e8833fc32c0. Accessed 20 July 2018.
Hopkinson, Doug (2007), *'Claybourne:* Single episodes', Archive.org, https://archive.org/details/OTRR_Claybourne_Singles. Accessed 20 July 2018.
Horspool, Maurice (1939), *Julius and the Bront: A Hyperbolical Anachronism in One Act,* London: Thomas Nelson & Sons, Ltd.
Horstmann, Rosemary (1991), *Writing for Radio,* 2nd ed., London: A&C Black.
Hoverson, Julie (2010a), 'Auditions/New producers', 19 Nocturne Boulevard, 12 January, http://hwcdn.libsyn.com/p/1/3/a/13a24a1559d75d5c/39_auditions_new_producers.mp3?c_id=2145097&cs_id=2145097&expiration=1530473012&hwt=f3d0d6e30bef1e3d552954231d79e8ae. Accessed 1 July 2018.
—— (2010b), 'Group', 19 Nocturne Boulevard, http://hwcdn.libsyn.com/p/3/7/c/37cecb04629010db/1_groups.mp3?c_id=2145746&cs_id=2145746&expiration=1530474007&hwt=000f0d2418c1c72c12ec239121d14fbc . Accessed 4 July 2014.
Hudson, Gill (ed.) (2002a), *Radio Times,* 31 August–6 September.
—— (ed.) (2002b), *Radio Times,* 7–13 September.
—— (ed.) (2002c), *Radio Times,* 21–27 September.
—— (ed.) (2002d), *Radio Times,* 28 September–4 October.
—— (ed.) (2002e), *Radio Times,* 19–25 October.
—— (ed.) (2007a), *Radio Times,* 1–7 September.
—— (ed.) (2007b), *Radio Times,* 8–14 September.
—— (ed.) (2007c), *Radio Times,* 6–12 October.
—— (ed.) (2007d), *Radio Times,* 27 October–2 November.
Huff, Rick (2013), interviewed by Leslie McMurtry, Albuquerque,10 May.
Hurdle, R. (n.d.), *'Alien Voices',* OTR Plot Spot, http://www.otrplotspot.com/alienVoices.html. Accessed 28 September 2018.
Huwiler, Elke (2005), 'Storytelling by sound: A theoretical frame for radio drama analysis', *The Radio Journal: International Studies in Broadcast & Audio Media,* 3:1, pp. 45–59.
IRDP (2003), 'About IRDP', http://www.irdp.co.uk/page1.htm. Accessed 20 July 2018.
Iser, Wolfgang (1980), 'Interaction between text and reader', in S.R. Suleiman and I. Crosman (eds), *The Reader in the Text: Essays on Audience Interpretation,* Princeton: Princeton University Press, pp. 106–19.
iTunes Charts (2017), 'Top 40 US arts podcasts', http://www.itunescharts.net/us/charts/podcasts/arts/. Accessed 5 August 2017.

J.A. (2011), 'BBC radio celebrates billionth download', About the BBC, 12 December (updated 18 March 2014), http://www.bbc.co.uk/mediacentre/latestnews/121211download.html. Accessed 20 July 2018.

James, Mary Louise (1994), 'British radio drama: A critical analysis of its development as a distinctive aesthetic form', Ph.D. thesis, Hatfield: University of Hertfordshire.

Jenkins, Henry (2008), *Convergence Culture: Where Old and New Media Collide,* New York: New York University Press.

Johnson, Kristine (2012), 'Audience use of new media technologies on NPR.org', *Journal of Radio & Audio Media,* 19:1, pp. 17–32.

Johnson, Steve and Mitchell, Philip (2012), 'In search of access, localness and sustainability: Radio in post-devolutionary Wales', in R.J. Hand and M. Traynor (eds), *Radio in Small Nations: Production, Programmes, Audiences,* Cardiff: University of Wales Press, pp. 7–26.

Johnson, Ted (2017), 'Trump budget proposes eventual elimination of public broadcasting funding', *Variety,* 22 May, http://variety.com/2017/tv/news/trump-budget-eliminates-public-broadcasting-1202440901/. Accessed 20 July 2018.

Johnstone, Jack (1999), 'Johnny Dollar', The Thrilling Detective Web Site, http://www.thrillingdetective.com/dollar_johnny.html. Accessed 20 July 2018.

Jones, Lyndon and Traynor, Mary (2013), 'Stand by studio! Reviving the golden age of live radio drama', *Radio Conference: A Transnational Forum*, University of Bedfordshire, Luton, 11 July.

Kammen, Michael (2001), 'Introduction', *The Seven Lively Arts: The Classic Appraisal of the Popular Arts*, Gilbert Seldes, Mineola: Dover Publications, Inc., pp. xi–xxxvi.

Karpf, Anne (2013), 'The sound of home? Some thoughts on how the radio voice anchors, contains and sometimes pierces', *The Radio Journal: International Studies in Broadcast & Audio Media,* 11:1, pp. 59–73.

The Katniss Chronicles (n.d.), 'About', http://www.thekatnisschronicles.com/index.php/about. Accessed 20 July 2018.

Katz, Elihu, Blumer, Jay G. and Gurevitch, Michael (1974), 'Utilization of mass communication by the individual', in J.G. Blumler and E. Katz (eds), *The Uses of Mass Communications: Current Perspectives on Gratifications Research*, London: SAGE, pp. 19–34.

Katz Marketing Solutions (2010), *Radio Usage Trends*, http://www.raisingthevolume.com/wp-content/uploads/2012/01/Radio-Usage-Trends.pdf. Accessed 20 July 2018.

Katz Radio Group (2008), 'RadioWaves #13', newsletter, http://katz-media.com/uploadedfiles/publications/radiowaves/RadioWavesOctober08.pdf. Accessed 4 July 2014.

Kaufman, Leslie (2013), 'Actors today don't just read for the part: Reading IS the part', *New York Times,* 29 June, http://www.nytimes.com/2013/06/30/business/media/actors-today-dont-just-read-for-the-part-reading-is-the-part.html. Accessed 20 July 2018.

Keillor, Garrison (2005), 'Confessions of a listener: Why I still love radio', *Utne Reader,* September–October, http://www.utne.com/arts/confessions-of-a-listener-garrison-keillor-radio-nostalgia.aspx. Accessed 20 July 2018.

Keith, Michael C. (1995), *Signals in the Air: Native American Broadcasting in America,* Westport: Praeger.

—— (2002), 'Turn on… tune in: The rise and demise of commercial underground radio', in M. Hilmes and J. Loviglio (eds), *Radio Reader: Essays in the Cultural History of Radio,* New York: Routledge, pp. 389–404.

Kelner, Simon (2012), 'Kelner's view: Liking *The Archers* is a simple question of heredity', *The Independent,* 28 March, http://www.independent.co.uk/voices/commentators/simon-kelner-liking-the-archers-is-a-simple-question-of-heredity-7594085.html. Accessed 20 July 2018.

Kendall, Bridget, Myerson, Jonathan, Walker, Mike and Hindell, Alison (2011), '*Life and Fate*: The radio dramatization', *BBC Radio 4 Presents* Life and Fate *by Vasily Grossman*, St Peter's College, Oxford, 9 September.

Kennedy, Ian (2013), 'Joining BBC Asian Network drama serial *Silver Street* as scriptwriter', IQK – Productions and Writing by Ian Kennedy, 6 April, http://iqkennedy.co.uk/writing/scriptwriting/joining-bbc-asian-network-drama-serial-silver-street/. Accessed 20 July 2018.

Khlebnikov, Velemir (1921), 'The radio of the future', Museum of Imaginary Musical Instruments, http://imaginaryinstruments.org/the-radio-of-the-future/. Accessed 20 July 2018.

Kimber, Chris (2012), 'BBC iPlayer radio: Two months on', BBC Internet Blog, 13 December, http://www.bbc.co.uk/blogs/internet/posts/iplayer_radio_traffic. Accessed 20 July 2018.

Kinnally, William and Brinkerhoff, Bobbie (2013), 'Improving the drive: A case study for modeling public radio member donations using the theory of planned behavior', *Journal of Radio & Audio Media,* 20:1, pp. 2–16.

Klinenberg, Eric (2007), *Fighting for Air: The Fight to Control American Media,* New York: Holt Paperbacks.

Konrath, Sara (2013), 'The empathy paradox: Increasing disconnection in the age of increasing connection', in R. Luppicini (ed.), *Handbook of Research on Technoself: Identity in a Technological Society,* Hershey: IGI Global, pp. 204–28.

—— (2015), 'Can text messages make people kinder?', in C. Miller, W. Fleeson and M. Furr (eds), *New Perspectives on Character*, Oxford: Oxford University Press, n.pag.

Konrath, Sara, Chopik, William J., Hsing, Courtney K. and O'Brien, Ed. (2014), 'Changes in adult attachment styles in American college students over time: A meta-analysis', *Personality and Social Psychology Review,* 18:4, pp. 326–48.

Konrath, Sara, O'Brien, E.H. and Hsing, C. (2010), 'Changes in dispositional empathy in American college students over time: A meta-analysis', *Personality and Social Psychology Review,* 15:2, pp. 180–98.

Kosslyn, Stephen Michael (1983), *Ghosts in the Mind's Machine: Creating and Using Images in the Brain,* New York: W.W. Norton & Company.

Kozlowski, Michael (2016), 'Global audiobook trends and statistics for 2017', Good EReader, 18 December, https://goodereader.com/blog/digital-publishing/audiobook-trends-and-statistics-for-2017. Accessed 20 July 2018.

Krapp, Peter (2011), *Noise Channels: Glitch and Error in Digital Culture,* Minneapolis: University of Minnesota Press.

Kuersteiner, Kurt (n.d.), Radio Horror Hosts.com, http://www.radiohorrorhosts.com/horrorhosts.html. Accessed 28 September 2018.

Kuffert, Leonard (2013a), '"Only radio could provide it": Drama on early Canadian radio', *Radio Conference: A Transnational Forum*, University of Bedfordshire, Luton, 11 July.

—— (2013b), e-mail to Leslie McMurtry, 13 July.

Kumar, Krishan (2003), *The Making of English National Identity,* Cambridge: Cambridge University Press.

Kushner, Frederica P. (2010), '*Star Wars*', in C.H. Sterling, C. O'Dell and M.C. Keith (eds), *The Concise Encyclopedia of American Radio,* New York: Routledge, pp. 718–21.

Lacey, Kate (1996), *Feminine Frequencies: Gender, German Radio, and the Public Sphere, 1923–1945,* Ann Arbor: University of Michigan Press.

—— (2013), 'Listening in the digital age', in J. Loviglio and M. Hilmes (eds), *Radio's New Wave: Global Sound in the Digital Era*, New York: Routledge, pp. 9–23.

Lander, Dan (1994), 'Radiocasting: Musings on radio and art', in D. Augaitis and D. Lander (eds), *Radio Rethink: Art, Sound, and Transmission*, Banff, AB: Walter Phillips Gallery, pp. 11–32.

Lane, Philip J. (2010), '*Yours Truly, Johnny Dollar*', in C.H. Sterling, C. O'Dell and M.C. Keith (eds), *The Concise Encyclopedia of American Radio,* New York: Routledge, pp. 891–92.

Lasar, Matthew (2010), 'Pacifica Foundation', in C.H. Sterling, C. O'Dell and M.C. Keith (eds), *The Concise Encyclopedia of American Radio,* New York: Routledge, pp. 551–54.

Letzler, David (2017), 'Narrative levels, theory of mind, and sociopathy in true-crime narrative: Or how is *Serial* different from your average *Dateline* episode?', in E. McCracken (ed.), *The Serial Podcast and Storytelling in the Digital Age,* London: Routledge, pp. 123–69.

Lévesque-Bartlett, Caroline (n.d.), 'To the House of Commons: End the BBC licence fee', 38 Degrees, https://you.38degrees.org.uk/petitions/end-the-bbc-licence-fee. Accessed 20 July 2018.

Lewis, Peter (2012), '"It's only community radio": The British campaign for community radio', in J. Gordon (ed.), *Community Radio in the Twenty-first Century,* Bern: Peter Lang, pp. 7–32.

—— (2013), 'Remembering radio', *The Radio Journal: International Studies in Broadcast & Audio Media,* 11:1, pp. 47–57.

Lindgren, Mia and Hilmes, Michele (2016), 'Editors' introduction to RJ 14:1 podcast 2016', *The Radio Journal: International Studies in Broadcast & Audio Media,* 14:1, pp. 3–5.

Lipsitz, George (2003), 'The meaning of memory: Family, class, and ethnicity in early network television programs', in M. Hilmes (ed.), *Connections: A Broadcast History Reader*, London: Thomson and Wadsworth, pp. 101–34.

Lochte, Bob (2004), 'U.S. public radio: What is it? – and for whom?', in A. Crisell (ed.), *More than a Music Box: Radio Cultures and Communities in a Multi-Media World,* New York: Berghahn Books, pp. 39–56.

Locker, Melissa (2016), '*Serial* Season Two: Why did the "must listen" show suffer a sophomore slump?', *The Guardian*, 5 April, https://www.theguardian.com/tv-and-radio/2016/apr/05/serial-season-two-bowe-bergdahl-podcast. Accessed 20 July 2018.

Lombardo, M. (2008), 'Is the podcast a public sphere institution?' in D.E. Wittkower (ed.), *iPod and Philosophy: iCon of an ePoch*, Chicago: Carus Publishing, pp. 215–28.

López-McAlister, Linda (2013), interviewed by Leslie McMurtry, Albuquerque, 10 May.

López-McAlister, Linda and Hughes, David (2013), 'Radio Theater', KUNM, http://www.kunm.org/programs/radio-theater. Accessed 20 July 2018.

Lugmayr, Artur and Dal Zotto, Cinzia (2016), *The Media Convergence Handbook, vol. 1: Journalism, Broadcasting and Social Media Aspects of Convergence,* Berlin: Springer.

MacArthur, Marit J. and Lee, Miller M. (2016), 'Vocal deformance and performative speech, or in different voices!', Sounding Out! The Sound Studies Blog, https://soundstudiesblog.com/2016/10/24/in-different-voices-vocal-deformance-and-performative-speech/. Accessed 20 July 2018.

MacDonald, Fred J. (1979), *Don't Touch That Dial!: Radio Programming in American Life,* Chicago: Nelson Hall.

Mackey, M. and McKay, J.K. (2008), 'Pirates and poachers: Fan fiction and the conventions of reading and writing', *English in Education,* 12:2, pp. 131–47.

MacLeish, Archibald (1937), *The Fall of the City,* London: Boriswood.

MacLellan, Kyle (2013), 'Global crowdfunding volumes rise 81% in 2012', *The Huffington Post,* 4 August, http://www.huffingtonpost.com/2013/04/08/global-crowdfunding-rises-81-percent_n_3036368.html. Accessed 20 July 2018.

Mahoney, Elisabeth (2011), '*Life and Fate*: Vivid, heartbreaking, illuminating and utterly brilliant', *The Guardian,* 23 September, http://www.guardian.co.uk/tv-and-radio/tvandradioblog/2011/sep/23/life-and-fate-radio-4. Accessed 20 July 2018.

Malatia, Torey (2007), 'Potential difference: Redesigning public radio for a changing society', Current.org, http://www.current.org/wp-content/themes/current/archive-site/radio/radio0708vocalo-extended.pdf. Accessed 14 June 2014.

Malpas, Simon (2005), *The Postmodern,* London: Routledge.

Mann, Sonya (2017), 'Patreon launches new ways for creators to make money (without stooping to ads)', Inc.com, 24 June, https://www.inc.com/sonya-mann/patreon-business-tools.html. Accessed 20 July 2018.

Manning, Stuart (2012), 'Today's choice', *Radio Times,* 5–11 May, p. 127.

Marc, David (1996), *Demographic Vistas: Television in American Culture,* rev. ed., Philadelphia: University of Pennsylvania Press.

—— (2005), 'Origins of the genre: In search of the radio sitcom', in M.M. Dalt and L.R. Linder (eds), *The Sitcom Reader: America Viewed and Skewed,* Albany: State University of New York Press, pp. 15–24.

Marcus, Daniel (2003), 'Public television and public access in the US', in M. Hilmes (ed.), *The Television History Book,* London: BFI Publishing, pp. 55–58.

Marinetti, F.T. and Masnata, Pino (1933), 'La Radia', http://kunstradio.at/THEORIE/theorymain.html. Accessed 20 July 2018.

Mark, Jason (2009), 'Sex sells: A tiny nonprofit uses mass media to encourage family planning', *Earth Island Journal,* Summer, http://www.earthisland.org/journal/index.php/eij/article/sex_sells/. Accessed 20 July 2018.

Markman, Kris M. and Sawyer, Caroline E. (2014), 'Why pod? Further explorations of the motivations for independent podcasting', *Journal of Radio & Audio Media,* 21:1, pp. 20–35.

Masnick, Mike (2013), 'Patent troll says it owns podcasting; Sues Adam Carolla, HowStuffWorks', TechDirt, 7 February, http://www.techdirt.com/articles/20130206/07215421891/patent-troll-says-it-owns-podcasting-sues-adam-carolla-howstuffworks.shtml. Accessed 20 July 2018.

Massa, Paolo (2011), 'Trust it forward: Tyranny of the majority or echo chambers?', in H. Masum and M. Tovey (eds), *The Reputation Society: How Online Opinions Are Reshaping the Offline World,* Cambridge, MA: MIT Press, pp. 151–61.

McCauley, Michael P. (2005), *NPR: The Trials and Triumphs of National Public Radio,* New York: Columbia University Press.

McChesney, Robert W. (2003), 'Crusade against Mammon: Father Harvey, WLWL, and the debate over radio in the 1930s', in M. Hilmes (ed.), *Connections: A Broadcast History Reader,* London: Thomson and Wadsworth, pp. 40–62.

—— (2008), *The Political Economy of Media: Enduring Issues, Emerging Dilemmas,* New York: Monthly Review.

—— (2013), *Digital Disconnect,* New York: New Press.

McClung, Steven and Johnson, Kristine (2010), 'Examining the motives of podcast users', *Journal of Radio & Audio Media,* 17:1, pp. 82–95.

McCracken, Allison (2002), 'Scary women and scarred men: *Suspense,* gender trouble, and postwar change, 1942–1950', in M. Hilmes and J. Loviglio (eds), *Radio Reader: Essays in the Cultural History of Radio*, New York: Routledge, pp. 183–208.

—— (2010), '*Suspense*', in C.H. Sterling, C. O'Dell and M.C. Keith (eds), *The Concise Encyclopedia of American Radio,* New York: Routledge, pp. 734–36.

McCracken, Ellen (2017), 'The *Serial* commodity: Rhetoric, recombination, and indeterminacy in the digital age', in E. McCracken (ed.), *The* Serial *Podcast and Storytelling in the Digital Age*, New York and London: Routledge, pp. 170–220.

McDonald, Kevin and Smith-Rowsey, Daniel (eds) (2016), *The Netflix Effect: Technology and Entertainment in the 21st Century*, London: Bloomsbury.

McDonnell, James (1991), *Public Service Broadcasting: A Reader,* London: Routledge.

McHugh, Siobhán (2016), 'How podcasting is changing the audio storytelling genre', *The Radio Journal: International Studies in Broadcast & Audio Media*, 14:1, pp. 65–82.

McIntyre, Ian (1993), *The Expense of Glory: A Life of John Reith,* London: HarperCollins Publishers.

McLaughlin, Jim (2015), '*Star Wars*' $4 billion price tag was the deal of the century', Wired.com, 14 December, https://www.wired.com/2015/12/disney-star-wars-return-on-investment/. Accessed 20 July 2018.

McLuhan, Marshall (1964), *Understanding Media,* London: Routledge and Kegan Paul Ltd.

McMahon, Daithi (2014), 'Docudrama: Bringing radio documentary to life through drama', *Audio Drama – Histories, Aesthetics, Practices*, University of Copenhagen and the Radiodrama Network, Copenhagen, 19 August.

McMurtry, Leslie (2012a), 'The neutral ground: Adapting Fenimore Cooper's *The Spy* for BBC radio', *Crossing Borders/Pushing Boundaries Postgraduate Conference*, Swansea University, Swansea, 12 September.

—— (2012b), 'Anatomy of a gamechanger: BBC Radio 4's *Life and Fate*', *Radio-Leituras*, 3:2, http://radioleituras.wordpress.com/2013/11/06/sumario-4/. Accessed 20 July 2018.

—— (2015a), 'The future of satellite audio drama', *Peripeti Audiodrama*, 22, pp. 45–54.

—— (2015b), 'Aurally bloodcurdling: Representing Dracula and his brethren in BBC radio drama', in I. Ermida (ed.), *Dracula and the Gothic in Literature, Pop Culture and the Arts*, Amsterdam: Rodopi and Brill, n.pag.

—— (2015c), 'Framing errors: Reality and fiction in audio drama', *Journal of American Studies in Turkey,* 41:1, pp. 5–16.

—— (2016a), '"I'm not a real detective, I only play one on radio": *Serial* as the future of audio drama', *Journal of Popular Culture,* 49, pp. 306–24.

—— (2016b), 'The magical post-horn: A trip to the BBC Archive Centre in Perivale', Sounding Out! The Sound Studies Blog, 26 September, https://soundstudiesblog.com/2016/09/26/the-magical-post-horn-a-trip-to-the-bbc-archive-centre-in-perivale/. Accessed 20 July 2018.

—— (2017), 'Imagination and narrative: Young people's experiences', *Journal of Radio and Audio Media,* 24:1, pp. 1–18.

McMurtry, Leslie and Plant, Alison (2013), 'Race, radio, and the soap opera', *Radio Conference: A Transnational Forum,* University of Bedfordshire, Luton, 11 July.

McNicholas, Anthony (n.d.), 'Soaps on the BBC: From the front line to the Queen Vic', History of the BBC, http://www.bbc.co.uk/historyofthebbc/research/programming/soaps. Accessed 20 July 2018.

McRobert, Neil (2015), 'Mimesis of media: Found footage cinema and the horror of the real', *Gothic Studies,* 17:2, pp. 137–50.

McWhinnie, Donald (1959), *The Art of Radio,* London: Faber and Faber.

Méadel, Cécile (1994), *Histoire de la radio des années trentes: du sans-filistes à l'auditeur,* Paris: Economica.

Meltzer, Tom (2011), 'Radio review: *Life and Fate: Journey', The Guardian,* 20 September, p. 24.

Mengiste, Maaza (2017), 'How *S Town* fails black listeners', *Rolling Stone,* 13 April, http://www.rollingstone.com/culture/how-s-town-fails-black-listeners-w476524. Accessed 20 July 2018.

Meserko, Vincent M. (2015), 'The pursuit of authenticity on Marc Maron's *WTF* podcast', *Continuum,* 29:6, pp. 796–810.

Messere, Fritz and O'Dell, Cary (2010), 'Regulation', in C.H. Sterling, C. O'Dell and M.C. Keith (eds), *The Concise Encyclopedia of American Radio,* New York: Routledge, pp. 667–74.

Miller, Beth (2015), *The Archers: An Unofficial Companion,* Chichester: Summersdale.

Miller, Toby (2008), 'Foreword', in M. Leverette, B.L. Ott and C.L. Buckley (eds), *It's Not TV: Watching HBO in the Post-Television Era,* London: Routledge pp. ix–xii.

Minić, Danica (2013), 'What makes an issue a *Woman's Hour* issue?: The politics of recognition and media coverage of women's issues and perspectives', *Feminist Media Studies,* 8:3, pp. 301–15.

Mitchell, Caroline (2001), *Women and Radio,* London: Routledge.

Mitchell, Jack (2002), 'Lead us not into temptation: American Public Radio in a world of infinite possibilities', in M. Hilmes and J. Loviglio (eds), *Radio Reader: Essays in the Cultural History of Radio,* New York: Routledge, pp. 405–22.

—— (2005), *Listener Supported: The Culture and History of Public Radio,* Westport: Praeger.

Mitchell, Jack and Sterling, Christopher H. (2010), 'Public radio since 1967', in C.H. Sterling, C. O'Dell and M.C. Keith (eds), *The Concise Encyclopedia of American Radio,* New York: Routledge, pp. 615–22.

Moore, Wil (2014), e-mail to Leslie McMurtry, 13 July.

Moores, Shaun (2000), *Media and Everyday Life in Modern Society,* Edinburgh: Edinburgh University Press.

—— (2001), 'From "unruly guest" to "good companion": Gendered meanings of early radio in the home', in C. Mitchell, *Women and Radio*, London: Routledge, pp. 116–25.

Mott, Robert L. (2014), *Sound Effects: Radio, Television, and Film*, Jefferson: McFarland & Co.

Moulton, Samuel T. and Kosslyn, Stephen M. (2009), 'Imaging predictions: Mental imagery as mental emulation', *Philosophical Transactions of the Royal Society, Series B: Biology*, 364, pp. 1273–80.

Nachman, Gerald (2000), *Raised on Radio: In Quest of the Lone Ranger, Jack Benny*, Amos'n'Andy, The Shadow, *Mary Noble…*, Berkeley: University of California Press.

Naughton, Pete (2014), '*Life and Fate*, Radio 4, review', *The Telegraph*, 19 September, http://www.telegraph.co.uk/culture/tvandradio/8774814/Life-and-Fate-Radio-4-review.html. Accessed 20 July 2018.

Nelson, Davia and Silva, Nikki (2010), 'Talking to strangers', in J. Biewen and A. Dilworth (eds), *Reality Radio: Telling True Stories in Sound*, Durham: University of North Carolina Press, pp. 36–43.

Nelson, Michael (2001), 'Church on Saturday night: Garrison Keillor's *A Prairie Home Companion*', *The Virginia Quarterly Review*, 77:1, pp 1–18.

Nelson, Robin (2007), *State of Play: Contemporary 'High End' TV Drama*, Manchester: Manchester University Press.

Nichols, Richard (1983), *Radio Luxembourg: The Station of the Stars: An Affectionate History of 50 Years of Broadcasting*, London: WH Allen.

Nicholson, Rebecca (2017), '*S Town* review: It's hard to recall a more touching, devastating podcast', *The Guardian*, 3 April, https://www.theguardian.com/tv-and-radio/2017/apr/03/s-town-review-its-hard-to-recall-a-more-touching-devastating-podcast-serial-john-b-mclemore-brian-reed. Accessed 20 July 2018.

Nielsen, Janne (2012a), 'Educating the public: A historical analysis of Danish broadcasting media as school', *Transformations in Broadcasting*, University of Leeds, Leeds, 13 July.

—— (2012b), e-mail to Leslie McMurtry, 20 August.

NPR (n.d.), 'Firesign Theatre, now playing on NPR', http://www.npr.org/news/specials/firesign/. Accessed 20 July 2018.

Nunes, Mark (2011), 'A million little blogs: Community, narrative, and the James Frey controversy', *Journal of Popular Culture*, 44:2, pp. 347–66.

Nwaerondu, N.G. and Thompson, Gordon (1987), 'The use of educational radio in developing countries: Lessons from the past', World Bank Global Distance EducatioNet, http://web.worldbank.org/archive/website00236B/WEB/RAD_01.HTM. Accessed 20 July 2018.

Ó Baoill, Andrew (2014), 'Copyright, community radio, and change: How the US community radio sector is negotiating changing copyright rules and the rollout of digital distribution', *Journal of Radio & Audio Media*, 21:1, pp. 163–76.

O'Donoghue, David (2016), 'Why podcasts are the hottest new medium for scary stories', Cultured Vultures, 6 April, http://culturedvultures.com/podcasts-scary-stories/. Accessed 20 July 2018.

O'Neill, Connor Towne (2017), 'Residents of so-called "Shit Town" are conflicted over *S Town*', Vulture, 25 April, http://www.vulture.com/2017/04/s-town-podcast-visiting-woodstock-alabama.html. Accessed 20 July 2018.

O'Sullivan, Tim (2003), 'Post-war television in Britain: BBC and ITV', in M. Hilmes (ed.), *The Television History Book,* London: BFI Publishing, pp. 30–34.

Ofcom (2013), *Communications Market Report 2013,* http://stakeholders.ofcom.org.uk/market-data-research/market-data/communications-market-reports/cmr13/. Accessed 26 April 2014.

Ohlheiser, Abby (2017), 'Here's why the Garrison Keillor allegations stand out', *The Washington Post,* 1 December, https://www.washingtonpost.com/news/arts-and-entertainment/wp/2017/12/01/heres-why-the-garrison-keillor-allegations-stand-out/?utm_term=.8513772b1975. Accessed 14 March 2018.

The Old Time Radio Researchers (n.d.), OTTRPedia, http://www.otrrpedia.net/. Accessed 28 September 2018.

Ott, Brian L. (2011), *The Small Screen: How Television Equips Us to Live in the Information Age,* Oxford: Blackwell.

The Owl Field (n.d.), https://www.owlfield.com/. Accessed 20 July 2018.

Palermo, Tony (2013a), 'Producing radio drama live, onstage', Ruya Sonic, http://www.ruyasonic.com/prd_stage.htm. Accessed 20 July 2018.

——— (2013b), 'Toward a radio drama 101', Ruya Sonic, http://www.ruyasonic.com/rdr_101.htm. Accessed 20 July 2018.

Parkin, Lin (2013), 'How smartphones are helping audio dramas reach new audiences', Audio Daily: The Audio Production Blog, 18 July, http://blogs.voices.com/audiodaily/2013/07/smartphones_help_audio_dramas.html. Accessed 16 May 2014.

Paterson, Robyn (2008), 'Comment: Trading tips: Audio mixing techniques', Audio Drama Talk Forum, 14 January, http://www.audiodramatalk.com/showthread.php?p=973&highlight=satellite#post973. Accessed 13 April 2014.

Patreon (2017), 'Radio Icebox', https://www.patreon.com/radioicebox. Accessed 27 August 2017.

Patterson, Eleanor (2016), 'Reconfiguring radio drama after television: The historical significance of *Theater 5, Earplay* and *CBS Radio Mystery Theater* as post-network radio drama', *Historical Journal of Film, Radio and Television,* 36:4, pp. 649–67.

Paulu, Burton (1974), *Radio and Television Broadcasting in Eastern Europe,* Minneapolis: University of Minnesota Press.

——— (1981), *Television and Radio in the United Kingdom,* London: Macmillan.

Pegg, Mark (1983), *Broadcasting and Society 1918–39*, London: Croom Helm.

Peover, Matt (dir.) (2012), *Cycle of Violence/Ava Carter: Girl Pilot!/The Day Dorking Stood Silent,* Martin Pengelly, The Fitzrovia Radio Hour, Udderbelly Festival, Southbank, London, September.

Perlstein, Jeff (2002), 'Clear Channel: The media mammoth that stole the airwaves', CorpWATCH, http://www.corpwatch.org/article.php?id=4808. Accessed 28 July 2018.

Peters, John Durham (2013), 'Phantasms of the living, dialogues with the dead', in M. Bull (ed.), *Sound Studies: Meanings and Scope,* Sound Studies: Critical Concepts in Media and Cultural Studies, vol. 1, Abingdon: Routledge, pp. 361–94.

Petty, Moira (2013), 'Radio review: *The Liberty of Norton Folgate; The Wind in the Willows; Mrs Updike*', *The Stage,* 18 February, http://www.thestage.co.uk/people/tv-radio/2013/02/

radio-review-the-liberty-of-norton-folgate-the-wind-in-the-willows-mrs-updike/. Accessed 20 July 2018.

Picker, John M. (2013), 'The recorded voice from Victorian aura to modernist echo', in M. Bull (ed.), *Media Sounds,* Sound Studies: Critical Concepts in Media and Cultural Studies, vol. 4, Abingdon: Routledge, pp. 10–54.

Pike, Barry and Campbell, Donald (n.d.), 'Ten Favourite Tapes', Diversity Radio Plays, http://www.suttonelms.org.uk/ARTICLES.HTML. Accessed 28 September 2018.

Pilkington, John (2012), e-mail to Leslie McMurtry, 23 November.

Pinch, Trevor and Athanasiades, Katherine (2012), 'Online music sites as sociotechnical communities: Identity, reputation, and technology at ACIDPlanet.com', in T. Pinch and K. Bijsterveld (eds), *The Oxford Handbook of Sound Studies,* Oxford: Oxford University Press, pp. 480–504.

Pinto, Vito (2014), 'Listen and participate – The work of the >Hörspielmacher< Paul Plamper', *Audio Drama – Histories, Aesthetics, Practices*, University of Copenhagen and the Radiodrama Network, Copenhagen, 19 August.

Plant, Alison (2012), 'Between the ears: Imaginative listening as personal construct', *Crossing Borders/Pushing Boundaries Postgraduate Conference*, Swansea University, Swansea, 12 September.

Potter, R.F. and Choi, J. (2006), 'The effects of auditory structural complexity on attitudes, attention, arousal, and memory', *Media Psychology,* 8:4, pp. 395–419.

Potter, R.F., Lang, A. and Bolls, P.D. (1997), 'Orienting responses to structural features in media', *Psychophysiology*, 34: 1, p. S72.

Preston, Ben (ed.) (2011), *Radio Times,* 17–23 September.

—— (ed.) (2012a), *Radio Times,* 7–13 January.

—— (ed.) (2012b), *Radio Times,* 24–30 March.

—— (ed.) (2012c), *Radio Times,* 28 April–4 May.

—— (ed.) (2012d), *Radio Times,* 1–7 September.

—— (ed.) (2012e), *Radio Times,* 8–14 September.

—— (ed.) (2012f), *Radio Times,* 15–21 September.

—— (ed.) (2012g), *Radio Times,* 29 September–5 October.

—— (ed.) (2012h), *Radio Times,* 6–12 October.

Priday, Richard (2018), 'The BBC is ditching its iPlayer Radio app for the podcast age', Wired, 25 June, https://www.wired.co.uk/article/bbc-sounds-iplayer-radio-podcast. Accessed 16 November 2018.

Prix Europa (2016), 'Awards archive', https://static1.squarespace.com/static/5a5f53c9e5dd5bbc01b296f1/t/5aa807f2085229a3e2bac029/1520961525971/PE__2016__Archive.pdf. Accessed 20 July 2018.

Prix Italia Award Archive (2016), http://www.rai.it/dl/siti/html/PRIX-ITALIA-2016-WINNER---RADIO-DRAMA-6e37875e-dbab-4ded-9990-0c05c75c4b82.html. Accessed 20 July 2018.

Prosorov, Valeri V. (2012), 'Lyrical resources of the art of broadcasting and regional radio in Russia', *Journal of Radio & Audio Media,* 19:2, pp. 312–19.

Public Radio Exchange (n.d.), 'About PRX: Making public radio more public', http://www.prx.org/about-us/what-is-prx. Accessed 20 July 2018.

Publishing Trends (2011), 'Keeping up with the new demand for audiobooks', 1 August, http://www.publishingtrends.com/2011/08/keeping-up-with-the-new-demand-for-audiobooks-2/. Accessed 20 July 2018.

Pudovkin, Vsevolod (2006a), 'The film script (the theory of the script) [1926]' (trans. Richard Taylor and Evgeni Filippov), *Selected Essays*, Oxford: Seagull Books, pp. 32–64.

—— (2006b), 'The film director and film material [1926]' (trans. Richard Taylor and Evgeni Filippov), *Selected Essays*, Oxford: Seagull Books, pp. 65–119.

Quinton, M., MacGregor, I. and Benyon, D. (2016), 'Sonifying the solar system', *The 22nd International Conference on Auditory Display (ICAD-2016)*, Canberra, 3–7 July.

Ramsey, Phil (2017), 'BBC radio and public value: The governance of public service radio in the United Kingdom', *The Radio Journal: International Studies in Broadcast & Audio Media*, 15:1, pp. 89–106.

Raphael, Caroline (2014), phone interview by Leslie McMurtry, 18 March.

Rasovsky, Yuri (2001a), 'Directing audiobooks', Yuri Rasovsky, Audio Dramatist, https://web.archive.org/web/20160317112200/http://irasov.com/directing.htm. Accessed 15 July 2018.

—— (2001b) 'Audiobooks or aural art?', Yuri Raovsky, Audio Dramatist, https://web.archive.org/web/20160305011620/http://irasov.com/art.htm. Accessed 15 July 2018.

—— (2001c), 'Audiography', Yuri Rasovsky, Audio Dramatist, https://web.archive.org/web/20170107162223/http://irasov.com/audiography.htm. Accessed 15 July 2018.

—— (2002), 'What exactly does a producer do?', Yuri Rasovsky, Audio Dramatist, https://web.archive.org/web/20160317165024/http://irasov.com/producers.htm. Accessed 15 July 2018.

—— (n.d.a), 'Craven Street: Ben Franklin in London', Yuri Rasovksy, Audio Dramatist, https://web.archive.org/web/20160524052601/http://www.irasov.com:80/craven.htm. Accessed 15 July 2018.

—— (n.d.b), 'To voice or not to voice', Yuri Rasovsky, Audio Dramatist, https://web.archive.org/web/20160317112206/http://irasov.com/voicing.htm. Accessed 15 July 2018,

Rathke, Wade (2013), 'Could community radio drama become our communication organizing tool?' *Social Policy,* 43:1, pp. 62–63.

Rattigan, Dermot (2002), *Theatre of Sound: Radio and the Dramatic Imagination*, Dublin: Carysfort Press.

Raw, Laurence (2011a), e-mail to Leslie McMurtry, 29 July.

—— (2011b), '*The Robber Bridegroom* by Celyn Ebenezer', Radio Drama Reviews, http://www.radiodramareviews.com/id858.html. Accessed 1 March 2014.

—— (2012), '*Father, Son and Holy Ghost* by Kwame Kwei-Armah', Radio Drama Reviews, http://www.radiodramareviews.com/id963.html. Accessed 12 March 2014.

Ray, William B. (1990), *FCC: The Ups and Downs of Radio-TV Regulation,* Ames, IA: Iowa State University Press.

Reddit (2017), 'Is *Serial* 2 worth listening to?', https://www.reddit.com/r/podcasts/comments/5w4wcg/is_serial_season_2_worth_listening_to/. Accessed 5 August 2017.

Reed, Henry (1971), *The Streets of Pompeii and Other Plays for Radio,* London: BBC Books.

Reith, J.C.W. (1924), *Broadcast over Britain,* London: Hodder and Stoughton.

Remonté, Jean-François (1989), *Les Années Radio 1949–1989*, Paris: L'Arpenteur.

Reynolds, Gillian (1996), 'Arts: Review of the year: Changing frequency at the BBC-radio', *The Daily Telegraph*, 28 December, The Daily Telegraph CD-ROM Searchable Database 1996–2000.

Richards, Jeff (2016), 'KZMU to present final installment of *Downtown Abbey* Saturday, March 12 at Star Hall', *The Moab Times-Independent,* http://moabtimes.com/view/full_story/27119435/article-KZMU-to-present-final-installment-of--Downtown-Abbey--Saturday--March-12-at-Star-Hall. Accessed 20 July 2018.

Richardson, David, Spragg, Paul and Griffiths, Jamie (2013), 'CD extras – *Dark Eyes*', *Dark Eyes,* Maidenhead: Big Finish Audio.

Riismandel, Paul (2002), 'Radio by and for the public: The death and resurrection of low-power radio', in M. Hilmes and J. Loviglio (eds), *Radio Reader: Essays in the Cultural History of Radio,* New York: Routledge, pp. 423–50.

Robinson, Sue (ed.) (1997a), *Radio Times,* 11–17 October.

—— (ed.) (1997b), *Radio Times,* 25–31 October.

—— (ed.) (1997c), *Radio Times,* 15–21 November.

—— (ed.) (1997d), *Radio Times,* 22–28 November.

—— (ed.) (1998), *Radio Times,* 26 September–2 October.

Rodero, Emma (2012a), 'Stimulating the imagination in a radio story: The role of presentation structure and the degree of involvement of the listener', *Journal of Radio & Audio Media,* 19:1, pp. 45–60.

—— (2012b), 'See it in a radio story: Sound effects and shots to evoke imagery and attention on audio fiction', *Communication Research,* 39, pp. 458–79.

—— (2014), 'Serial position and attention resources to improve the recall of radio ads', *Revista Latina de Comunicación Social,* 69, pp. 1–11.

Rodero, Emma, Mas, Lluís, Larrea, Olatz and Blanco, María (2014), 'Narrative elements in *The Archers*: An analysis of a long-running radio soap opera', in M. Oliveira, G. Stachyra and G. Starkey (eds), *Radio: The Resilient Medium,* Sunderland: University of Sunderland, pp. 169–78.

Ronish, Marty (2008a), 'KHFM: Disenchantment in the land of enchantment', Scanning the Dial: Marty Ronish and Jack Allen on Classical Music Broadcasting, 10 August, https://www.insidethearts.com/scanningthedial/khfm-disenchantment-in-the-land-of-enchantment/. Accessed 20 July 2018.

—— (2008b), 'Update on KHFM', Scanning the Dial: Marty Ronish and Jack Allen on Classical Music Broadcasting, 14 August, https://www.insidethearts.com/scanningthedial/update-on-khfm/. Accessed 20 July 2018.

Rose, Anthony (2010), 'Introducing the all new BBC iPlayer (this time it's personal)', BBC Internet Blog, 26 May, http://www.bbc.co.uk/blogs/bbcinternet/2010/05/introducing_the_all_new_bbc_ip.html. Accessed 20 July 2018.

Rosenblum, Trudi M. (2010), 'Audio theater on the rise', *Publishers' Weekly,* 248:24, p.42.

Rudin, Richard (2011), *Broadcasting in the 21st Century,* Houndmills: Palgrave Macmillan.

Rudkin, David (1974), *Cries from Casement as His Bones Are Brought to Dublin,* London: BBC Books.

Russo, Alexander (2002), 'A dark(ened) figure on the airwaves: Race, nation, and *The Green Hornet*', in M. Hilmes and J. Loviglio (eds), *Radio Reader: Essays on the Cultural History of Radio,* London: Routledge, pp. 257–76.

—— (2009), 'An American right to an "unannoyed journey"? Transit radio as contested site of public space and private attention, 1949–1952', *Historical Journal of Film, Radio and Television*, 29:1, pp. 1–25.

—— (2012), 'The sound of Radiolab: Exploring the "Corwinesque" in 21st century public radio', Sounding Out! The Sound Studies Blog, 13 August, https://soundstudiesblog.com/2012/08/13/the-sound-of-radiolab-exploring-the-corwinesque-in-21st-century-public-radio/. Accessed 20 July 2018.

—— (2013), 'People with money and go: Locating attention in the human geography of radio reception', in M. Bull (ed.), *Media Sounds*, Sound Studies: Critical Concepts in Media and Cultural Studies, vol. 4, Abingdon: Routledge, pp. 3–9.

Roth, Philip (1998), *I Married a Communist*, London: Jonathan Cape.

Sabbagh, Antoine (1995), *La Radio Rendez-Vous sur les Ondes*, Paris: Gallimard.

Sadoski, Mark and Paivio, Allan (2013), *Imagery and Text: A Dual Coding Theory of Reading and Writing*, 2nd ed., Abingdon: Routledge.

Salcecl, Renata (2010), *The Tyranny of Choice*, London: Profile Books, Ltd.

Sanderson, Ian (2001), *The Archers Anarchists' Ambridge Jubilee: Fifty Years of a Medieval Village*, London: Boxtree.

Santo, Avi (2008), 'Para-television and discourses of distinction: The culture of production at HBO', in M. Leverette, B.L. Ott and C.L. Buckley (eds), *It's Not TV: Watching HBO in the Post-television Era*, London: Routledge, pp. 19–45.

Savage, Maureen E. and Spence, Patric R. (2014), 'Will you listen? An examination of parasocial interaction and credibility on radio', *Journal of Radio & Audio Media*, 21:1, pp. 3–19.

Savage, Roger (1981), 'The radio plays of Henry Reed', in J. Drakakis (ed.), *British Radio Drama*, Cambridge: Cambridge University Press, pp. 158–90.

Scannell, Paddy (1996a), 'Britain: Public service broadcasting, from national culture to multiculturalism', in M. Raboy (ed.), *Public Service Broadcasting for the 21st Century*, Luton: John Libbey Media, pp. 23–41.

—— (1996b), *Radio, Television & Modern Life: A Phenomenological Approach*, Oxford: Blackwell.

—— (2006), 'Broadcasting and time', Ph.D. thesis, London: University of Westminster.

Scannell, Paddy and Cardiff, David (1991), *A Social History of British Broadcasting, vol. 1 1922–1939: Serving the Nation*, Oxford: Blackwell.

Schafer, F. Murray (1994), *The Soundscape: Our Sonic Environment and the Tuning of the World*, Rochester, VT: Destiny Books.

Schneider, Steve (2017), 'Comment: Dear producers of boring audio drama', Audio Drama Production Podcast, Facebook, 26 June, https://www.facebook.com/groups/747178725350066/permalink/1514730398594891/. Accessed 20 July 2018.

Scriven, R.C. (1974), *The Seasons of the Blind and Other Radio Plays in Verse (All Early in the April, The Peacock Screamed One Morning, Dandelion and Parsnip: Vintage 1920, Summer with Flowers that Fell, The Seasons of the Blind)*, London: BBC Books.

Seldes, Gilbert (2001), *The Seven Lively Arts: The Classic Appraisal of the Popular Arts*, Mineola: Dover Publications, Inc.

Seymour, Katharine and Martin, John T.W. (1938), *Practical Radio Writing: The Technique of Writing for Broadcasting Simply and Thoroughly Explained*, New York: Longmans.

SFFaudio (2008), 'About us', http://www.sffaudio.com/?page_id=2. Accessed 20 July 2018.

Shanahan, Morris W. (2006), 'New Zealand Talk Radio: The story', in Broadcasting Standards Authority (ed.), *Freedoms and Fetters: Broadcasting Standards in New Zealand,* Wellington, New Zealand: Dunmore Publishing, pp. 35–45.

Shanahan, Morris W. and Duignan, Gerard (2005), 'The impact of deregulation on the evolution of New Zealand Commercial Radio', in K. Neil and M.W. Shanahan (eds), *The Great New Zealand Radio Experiment,* Victoria, New Zealand: Thomson Learning and Dunmore Press, pp. 17–42.

Shannon, Richard (2014a), 'Impossible radio', *Audio Drama – Histories, Aesthetics, Practices*, University of Copenhagen and the Radiodrama Network, Copenhagen, 20 August.

—— (2014b), '*The Incomplete Recorded Works of a Dead Body* by Ed Hime', *Audio Drama – Histories, Aesthetics, Practices*, University of Copenhagen and the Radiodrama Network, Copenhagen, 20 August.

Shapley, Olive (2001), 'Broadcasting a life', in C. Mitchell (ed.), *Women and Radio,* London: Routledge, pp. 29–40.

Shaw, Bernard Graham (2000), *Voice Overs: A Practical Guide,* London: A&C Black.

Shearman, Robert (n.d.), 'Chain Gang', http://robertshearman.com/chain-gang. Accessed 20 July 2018.

Shepherd, Jean (2000), *In God We Trust, All Others Pay Cash,* New York: Broadway Books.

Shingler, Martin (2000), 'Some recurring features of European avant-garde radio', *Journal of Radio & Audio Media*, 7:1, pp. 196–212.

—— (2006), 'Fasten your seatbelts and prick up your ears: The dramatic human voice in film', *Scope,* 5, pp. 1–12.

Shingler, Martin and Wieringa, Cindy (1998), *On Air: Methods & Meanings of Radio,* London: Arnold.

Sieveking, Lance (1934), *The Stuff of Radio,* London: Castle and Company Limited.

Silvey, Robert (1974), *Who's Listening?: The Story of BBC Audience Research*, London: George Allen & Unwin Ltd.

Singh, Anita (2011), '*The Archers*: Shocked to the core? Fans don't think so', *The Daily Telegraph*, 2 January, http://www.telegraph.co.uk/culture/tvandradio/bbc/8236656/Shocked-to-the-core-Archers-fans-dont-think-so.html. Accessed 20 July 2018.

Skal, David J. (1997), '"His hour upon the stage": Theatrical adaptations of *Dracula*', in N. Auerbach and D.J. Skal (eds), *Dracula: Authoritative Text, Contexts, Reviews and Reactions, Dramatic and Film Adaptations, Criticism,* New York: W.W. Norton & Co., pp. 371–80.

Slattery, Laura (2014), 'Spotify is a hit – But it may be a disposable one', *The Irish Times*, 21 August, http://www.irishtimes.com/business/sectors/media-and-marketing/spotify-is-a-hit-but-it-may-be-a-disposable-one-1.1901565. Accessed 23 August 2014.

Sloan, Anthony J. (2005), 'Anthony J. Sloan, WBAI Arts director emeritus', http://www.ajsloan.name/. Accessed 20 July 2018.

Slotten, Hugh Richard (2009), *Radio's Hidden Voice: The Origins of Public Broadcasting in the United States,* Urbana: University of Illinois Press.

Smethurst, William (1996), The Archers: *The History of Radio Drama's Most Famous Programme,* Bath: Chivers Press.

Smith, Ed (2013), '"The BBC get bashed more than Assad": Chris Patten's mission to restore BBC confidence and moral authority', *The New Statesman,* 15–21 November, pp. 28–34.

Smith, Rebecca (2011), '*Archers* characters more likely to die in accidents', *The Daily Telegraph,* 16 December, http://www.telegraph.co.uk/culture/tvandradio/8958384/Archers-characters-more-likely-to-die-in-accidents.html. Accessed 20 July 2018.

Smith, Reed W. (2014), 'Charles Ferris: Jimmy Carter's FCC innovator', *Journal of Radio & Audio Media,* 21:1, pp. 149–62.

Socolow, Michael (2004), 'Psyche and society: Radio advertising and social psychology in America, 1923–1936', *Historical Journal of Film, Radio, & Television,* 24:4, pp. 517–34.

The Sonic Society (n.d.), 'About', http://sonicsociety.org/about/. Accessed 20 July 2018.

Starkey, Guy (2004), *Radio in Context,* Basingstoke: Palgrave Macmillan.

—— (2013), 'Analogue yet digital', *Radio Conference: A Transnational Forum,* University of Bedfordshire, Luton, 11 July.

—— (2015), 'Cultural policy in the coalition years: Laissez-faire regulation, the public spending squeeze and the drive to digital', *Cultural Trends,* 24:1, pp. 80–84.

Stedman, Michael (2017), 'Understanding the noise of war', What Did World War One Sound Like?, http://www.bbc.co.uk/guides/zwg72hv. Accessed 20 July 2018.

Steffen, Alex (2011), 'Attention philanthropy: Giving reputation a boost', in H. Masum and M. Tovey (eds), *The Reputation Society: How Online Opinions Are Reshaping the Offline World,* Cambridge, MA: MIT Press, pp. 90–96.

Steinbrunner, Chris (1979), 'Preface', in W.B. Gibson, *The Shadow Scrapbook,* New York: Harcourt Brace Jovanovich, pp. i–ii.

Sterling, Christopher H. (2010), 'Podcasts', in C.H. Sterling, C. O'Dell and M.C. Keith (eds), *The Concise Encyclopedia of American Radio,* New York: Routledge, pp. 565–66.

Sterne, Jonathan (2003), *The Audible Past: Cultural Origins of Sound Reproduction,* Durham: Duke University Press.

Sterne, Jonathan and Akiyama, Mitchell (2012), 'The recording that never wanted to be heard and other stories of sonification', in T. Pinch and K. Bijsterveld (eds), *The Oxford Handbook of Sound Studies,* Oxford: Oxford University Press, pp. 554–60.

Sterne, Jonathan, Morris, Jeremy, Baker, Michael Brendan and Moscote Freire, Ariana (2008), 'The politics of podcasting', *The FibreCulture Journal,* 13, http://thirteen.fibreculturejournal.org/fcj-087-the-politics-of-podcasting/. Accessed 20 July 2018.

Stewart, Peter (2006), *Essential Radio Skills: How to Present and Produce a Radio Show,* London: A&C Black.

Stoker, Gill (2004), '*Clare in the Community*: BBC Radio 4 live recording', British Theatre Guide, http://www.britishtheatreguide.info/reviews/clarecommunity-rev. Accessed 20 July 2018.

Stoller, Tony (2012), 'Foresight, fudge or facilitation? The making of United Kingdom digital radio policy 1987–2008', in M. Mollgaard (ed.), *Radio and Society: New Thinking for an Old Medium*, Newcastle: Cambridge Scholars Publishing, pp. 149–65.

Street, Séan (2005), *A Concise History of British Radio 1922–2002*, Tiverton: Kelly Publications.

—— (2006a), *Crossing the Ether: British Public Service Radio and Commercial Competition 1922–1945,* Eastleigh: John Libby Publishing.

―――― (2006b), *A-Z Historical Dictionary of British Radio,* Lanham: The Scarecrow Press, Inc.
―――― (2012), *The Colour of Sound: The Poetry of Radio,* London: Routledge.
Sundaram, Subramaniam S. (2015), 'Audio cues for visually impaired (more than just a research project)', Audio Cues, 13 May, https://audiocues.wordpress.com/author/worksubramaniam/. Accessed 20 July 2018.
Supper, Alexandra (2016), 'Lobbying for the ear, listening with the whole body: The (anti-)visual culture of sonification', *Sound Studies,* 2:1, pp. 69–80.
Svømmekjær, Heidi (2014), 'The sound of a manuscript', *Audio Drama – Histories, Aesthetics, Practices,* University of Copenhagen and the Radiodrama Network, Copenhagen, 20 August.
―――― (2015), 'Radio in proportion: *The Hansen Family* and strategies of relevance in the Danish Broadcasting Corporation 1925–50', Ph.D. thesis, Roskilde, Denmark: Roskilde University.
Tacchi, Jo Ann (1997), 'Radio sound as material culture in the home', Ph.D. thesis, London: University College London.
―――― (1998), 'Radio textures: Between self and others', in D. Miller (ed.), *Material Cultures: Why Some Things Matter,* London: UCL Press, pp. 25–46.
―――― (2001), 'Gender, fantasy and radio consumption: An ethnographic case study', in C. Mitchell (ed.), *Women and Radio,* London: Routledge, pp. 152–66.
―――― (2003), 'Nostalgia and radio sound', in M. Bull and L. Back (eds), *The Auditory Culture Reader,* Oxford: Berg, pp. 281–95.
―――― (2012), 'Radio in the (i)Home: Changing experiences of domestic audio technologies in Britain', in L. Bessire and D. Fisher (eds), *Radio Fields: Anthropology and Wireless Sound in the 21st Century,* New York: New York University Press, pp. 157–67.
Terry, Sharon (2017), e-mail to Leslie McMurtry, 8 August.
This American Life (2014a), 'A brand new series! From the creators of *This American Life!*', 19 September, https://www.thisamericanlife.org/blog/2014/09/a-brand-new-series-from-the-creators-of-this-american-life. Accessed 20 July 2018.
―――― (2014b), 'HOW TO LISTEN TO A PODCAST with Ira and Mary', YouTube, 3 October, https://www.youtube.com/watch?v=8IPV2oSz8m4&feature=youtu.be. Accessed 20 July 2018.
Thomas, Dylan (1995), *The Dylan Thomas Omnibus: Under Milk Wood, Poems, Stories and Broadcasts,* London: Phoenix Giants.
Thompson, Emily (2004), *The Soundscape of Modernity: Architectural Acoustics and the Culture of Listening in America, 1900–1933,* Cambridge, MA: MIT Press.
Thorsen, Einar (2012), 'The second digital wave: BBC news online, embedded video, and the iPlayer', in M. Burns and N. Brügger (eds), *Histories of Public Service Broadcasters on the Web,* New York: Peter Lang, pp. 17–30.
Thraille, Fiona (2013), e-mails to Leslie McMurtry, 22 September and 2 October.
―――― (2014), e-mail to Leslie McMurtry, 13 July.
―――― (2018), 'Comment: I'll admit I've not looked for transcripts', Audio Drama Production Podcast Facebook Group, 13 March, https://www.facebook.com/groups/747178725350066/. Accessed 14 March 2018.
Thynne, Jane (2011), 'This week in radio: Beauty queens save face in a skin-deep study', *The Independent,* 22 September, p. 16,

Touponce, William F. (1998), *Ray Bradbury and the Poetics of Reverie: Gaston Bachelard, Wolfgang Iser, and the Reader's Response to Fantastic Literature,* San Bernadino, CA: The Borgo Press.

Townsend, Sue (1983), *Adrian Mole: From Minor to Major,* London: Methuen.

—— (1992), *The Play of the Secret Diary of Adrian Mole Aged 13 ¾,* Oxford: Heinemann Educational.

Tracey, Michael (1998), *The Decline and Fall of Public Service Broadcasting,* Oxford: Oxford University Press.

Trandafir, Leticia (2013), 'Aural sex: An exploration of sound and female sexualities', https://www.leticia-trandafir.com/aural-sex/. Accessed 20 July 2018.

Truax, Barry (2001), *Acoustic Communications,* 2nd ed, Westport: Ablex Publishing.

Tsakalidou, Ilektra (2013), 'Greece deprived of its public broadcasting service: More than a bad soap opera', Open Democracy.net, 17 June. http://www.opendemocracy.net/ilektra-tsakalidou/greece-deprived-of-its-public-broadcasting-service-more-than-bad-soap-opera. Accessed 20 July 2018.

Tulloch, John (1990), *Television Drama: Agency, Audience, and Myth,* London: Routledge.

Tuomi, Pauliina (2016), 'The twenty-first century television: Interactive, participatory and social', in A. Lugmayr and C. Dal Zotto (eds), *Media Convergence Handbook, vol. 1: Media Business and Innovation,* Berlin: Springer-Verlag, pp. 249–64.

Tusa, John (2011), 'Radio 4 can't please the BBC Trust', *The Daily Telegraph,* 9 February, https://www.telegraph.co.uk/culture/tvandradio/bbc/8314374/Radio-4-cant-please-the-BBC-Trust.html. Accessed 20 July 2018.

UK Department for Digital, Culture, Media, and Sport (2016), 'A BBC for the future: A broadcaster of distinction', 12 May, https://www.gov.uk/government/publications/a-bbc-for-the-future-a-broadcaster-of-distinction. Accessed 20 July 2018.

UK Parliament (2010), 'Early day motion 607. SILVER STREET AND BBC RADIO DRAMA (No.2)', http://www.parliament.uk/edm/2009-10/607. Accessed 20 July 2018.

Vaidhyanathan, Siva (2011), *The Googlization of Everything (And Why We Should Worry),* Berkeley: University of California Press.

Valdez, Charli (2017), '*Serial*'s aspirational aesthetics and racial erasure', in E. McCracken (ed.), *The Serial Podcast and Storytelling in the Digital Age,* London: Routledge, pp. 309–47.

Van der Haak, Kees and Spicer, Joanna (1977), *Broadcasting in the Netherlands,* London: Routledge and Kegan Paul, the International Institute of Communications.

Van der Haak, Kees and van Snippenburg, Leo (2001), 'The Netherlands', in L. d'Haenans and F. Saeys (eds), *Western Broadcasting at the Dawn of the 21st Century,* Berlin: Mouton de Gruyter, pp. 152–66.

Van Voss, Lex Heerma (1995), 'The Netherlands', in S. Berger (ed.), *The Force of Labour: The Western European Labour Movement and the European Working Class in the Twentieth Century,* Oxford: Berg, pp. 39–70.

Verdier, Hannah (2016), '*Homecoming:* A starstudded psychological thriller in podcast form', *The Guardian,* 24 November, https://www.theguardian.com/tv-and-radio/2016/nov/24/homecoming-podcast-catherine-keener-david-schwimmer. Accessed 20 July 2018.

Verma, Neil (2012), *Theater of the Mind: Imagination, Aesthetics, and American Radio Drama,* Chicago: The University of Chicago Press.

Wade, David (1981), 'British radio drama since 1960', in J. Drakakis (ed.), *British Radio Drama*, Cambridge: Cambridge University Press, pp. 218–44.

Wade, Rosalind (1935), 'The bachelor's woman's good-bye to loneliness!', *Radio Pictorial*, 99, 6 December, p.10.

Waldman, Katy (2015), '*Serial* Season 2 is not as riveting as Season 1. That doesn't mean it's worse', Slate, 29 December, http://www.slate.com/blogs/browbeat/2015/12/29/serial_season_2_about_bowe_bergdahl_is_not_as_riveting_as_serial_season.html. Accessed 5 August 2017.

Walker, David Pat (2011), *The BBC in Scotland: The First 50 Years, a Personal Memoir*, Edinburgh: Luaath Press Limited.

Walker, Jesse (2004), *Rebels on the Air: An Alternative History of Radio in America*, New York: New York University Press.

Wallace, Peter (2010), '*This American Life*', in C.H. Sterling, C. O'Dell and M.C. Keith (eds), *The Concise Encyclopedia of American Radio*, New York: Routledge, pp. 767–69.

Walrus Research and AudiGraphics Inc. (2006a), *Reinvigorating Public Radio's Public Service & Public Support: Interim Report 1: Approach*, http://www.rrconline.org/reports/pdf/Audience2010-Approach.pdf. Accessed 20 July 2018.

—— (2006b), *Reinvigorating Public Radio's Public Service & Public Support: Interim Report 2: XM & Sirius*, http://www.rrconline.org/reports/pdf/Audience%202010-XM%20&%20Sirius.pdf. Accessed 20 July 2018.

—— (2006c), *Reinvigorating Public Radio's Public Service & Public Support: Interim Report 3: Reliability & Integrity*, http://www.rrconline.org/reports/pdf/Audience2010-Reliability&Integrity.pdf. Accessed 20 July 2018.

—— (2006d), *Reinvigorating Public Radio's Public Service & Public Support: Interim Report 4: An Historic Loss of Momentum*, http://www.rrconline.org/reports/pdf/Audience2010-AnHistoricLossOfMomentum.pdf. Accessed 20 July 2018.

—— (2006e), *Reinvigorating Public Radio's Public Service & Public Support: Interim Report 5: Historic Sources of Growth*, http://www.rrconline.org/reports/pdf/Audience2010-HistoricSourcesOfGrowth.pdf. Accessed 20 July 2018.

—— (2006f), *Reinvigorating Public Radio's Public Service & Public Support: Interim Report 7: 21st Century Trajectories*, http://www.rrconline.org/reports/pdf/Audience2010-21stCenturyTrajectories.pdf. Accessed 20 July 2018.

Ward, Jack. J. (2017a), 'Dude… Your audio drama lost me', The Writings of Jack J. Ward, 5 August, http://jackjward.com/?p=248. Accessed 28 July 2018.

—— (2017b), '*Slate* magazine and the third wave of modern audio drama', The Sonic Society blog, 21 July, http://sonicsociety.org/slate-magazine-and-the-third-wave-of-modern-audio-drama/. Accessed 20 July 2018.

—— (2017c), 'Comment: *Slate* magazine and the third wave of modern audio drama', The Sonic Society blog, 23 July, http://sonicsociety.org/slate-magazine-and-the-third-wave-of-modern-audio-drama/. Accessed 20 July 2018.

—— (2017d), 'Invisible mode deactivated', The Sonic Society blog, 15 July, http://sonicsociety.org/invisible-mode-deactivated/. Accessed 20 July 2018.

—— (n.d.a), 'Helping you find the best in free dramatized audio', The Audio Drama Directory, http://theaudiodramadirectory.com/index.php. Accessed 22 June 2017.

—— (n.d.b), 'The audio drama ratings system', The Audio Drama Directory, http://theaudiodramadirectory.com/ratings/. Accessed 30 June 2017.

Ward, Lauren (2017), 'Speak up! Why some TV dialogue is so hard to understand', University of Salford News, 27 April, http://www.salford.ac.uk/news/articles/speak-up!-why-some-tv-dialogue-is-so-hard-to-understand. Accessed 20 July 2018.

Wardle, Irving (1968), 'Introduction', in I. Wardle (ed.), *New English Dramatists 12: Radio Plays,* London: Penguin Books, pp. 7–22.

Weiss, Allen S. (1995), *Phantasmic Radio,* Durham: Duke University Press.

—— (2001), 'Erotic nostalgia and the inscription of desire', in A.S. Weiss (ed.), *Experimental Sound and Radio,* Cambridge, MA: MIT Press, pp. 8–21.

West, Samuel (2007), 'Fathers and sons', *The Guardian,* 17 March, http://www.theguardian.com/books/2007/mar/17/featuresreviews.guardianreview13. Accessed 20 July 2018.

Whitby, Alan (n.d.), 'Alan Whitby's ten favourite radio plays', Diversity Radio Plays, http://www.suttonelms.org.uk/articles28.html. Accessed 28 September 2018.

White, Joe (2015), 'How BBC Writersroom 10 led to my first piece for radio', BBC Writersroom, 23 October, http://www.bbc.co.uk/blogs/writersroom/entries/657ac2cd-c9a4-4592-8b0d-ed06a3cff0e3. Accessed 20 July 2018.

Whitehead, Kate (1989), *The Third Programme: A Literary History,* Oxford: Clarendon Press.

Whoriskey, Peter (2008), 'Giant of Internet radio nears its "Last Stand"', *The Washington Post,* 16 August, http://www.washingtonpost.com/wp-dyn/content/article/2008/08/15/AR2008081503367.html?hpid=topnews. Accessed 14 August 2014.

Williams, Raymond (1968), *Drama from Ibsen to Brecht,* New York: Penguin Books Ltd.

—— (1973), *The Country and the City,* Nottingham: Spokesman.

—— (2013), *Culture and Society 1780–1950,* Nottingham: Spokesman.

Winters, Paul E. (2016), *Vinyl Records and Analog Cultures in the Digital Age: Pressing Matters,* Lanham: Lexington Books.

The Wireless Theatre Company (2014), 'The Wireless Theatre Company', 17 April, http://www.wirelesstheatrecompany.co.uk/index.php/our-plays>. Accessed 26 April 2014.

Włodarczyk, A. and Tyminska, M. (2014), 'Cultural differences', *Transformative Works and Cultures,* 19, https://doi.org/https://doi.org/10.3983/twc.2015.0591. Accessed 14 March 2018.

Woal, Michael and Woal, Linda Kowall (1997), 'Forgotten pioneer: Philco's WPTZ', in M.D. Murray and D.G. Godfrey (eds), *Television in America: Local Station History from Across the Nation,* Ames: Iowa State University Press, pp. 39–60.

Wood, Roger (2008), 'Radio drama at the crossroads', Ph.D. thesis, Leicester: DeMonfort University.

Wrather, Kyle (2016), 'Making "Maximum Fun" for fans: Examining podcast listener participation online', *The Radio Journal: International Studies in Broadcast & Audio Media,* 14:1, pp. 43–63.

Young, Andrew (2017), 'Call it *Shit Town:* Because that is its name', The Awl, 6 April, https://theawl.com/call-it-shit-town-8cde2225b742. Accessed 3 August 2017.

Zheng, Lu (2014), 'Narrative transportation in radio advertising: A study of the effects of dispositional traits on mental transportation', *Journal of Radio & Audio Media,* 21:1, pp. 36–50.

Zinik, Zinovy (2011), 'Vasily Grossman's BBC soap opera', *The Times Literary Supplement*, 28 September, http://www.the-tls.co.uk/tls/public/article785746.ece. Accessed 14 August 2014.

Zubernis, Lynn and Larsen, Katherine (2012), *Fandom at the Crossroads: Celebration, Shame and Fan/Producer Relationships,* Newcastle: Cambridge Scholars.

Zurawik, David (2014a), 'A brilliant byproduct of Sarah Koenig's storytelling in *Serial*', *The Baltimore Sun*, http://www.baltimoresun.com/entertainment/tv/z-on-tv-blog/bal-sarah-koenig-storytelling-serial-brilliant-sociology-20141218-story.html. Accessed 18 December 2014.

—— (2014b), 'In the end, *Serial* leaves me disappointed, even annoyed', *The Baltimore Sun*, 18 December, http://www.baltimoresun.com/entertainment/tv/z-on-tv-blog/bal-end-serial-podcast-leave-me-frustrated-annoyed-20141218-story.html. Accessed 18 December 2014.

Radio and Audio Dramas

'10 April 1917' (2017), *Tommies*, BBC Radio 4, UK, 10 April.

19 Nocturne Boulevard (2009–present), Wheeality Productions, http://nineteennocturne.libsyn.com/. Accessed 20 July 2018.

'9 June 1916' (2016), *Tommies*, BBC Radio 4, UK, 9 June.

'A .22 Rifle for Christmas' (1949), *Dragnet*, NBC, 22 December, https://archive.org/details/Dragnet2. Accessed 20 July 2018.

'Abarchuk' (2011), *Life and Fate*, BBC Radio 4, UK, 21 September.

Against the Storm (1940–41), NBC, https://archive.org/details/Against_The_Storm. Accessed 20 July 2018.

Archive 81 (2016–present), http://www.archive81.com/. Accessed 20 July 2018.

Atching Tan (2008), BBC Radio East Anglia, UK, http://www.atchingtan.com/. Accessed 20 July 2018.

'The Bane of Rudyard', (2015), *Wooden Overcoats*, http://www.woodenovercoats.com/press/. Accessed 20 July 2018.

Believe Me (2011), BBC Radio 4, UK, 10 January.

The Big Broadcast (2011), BBC Radio 4, UK, 3 June.

The Black Tapes (2015–present), Pacific North West Stories, http://theblacktapespodcast.com/. Accessed 20 July 2018.

The Bright Sessions (2015–present), http://www.thebrightsessions.com/. Accessed 20 July 2018.

Chain Gang (2004–13), BBC Radio 7 and Radio 4 Extra, UK.

'Chief Tall Horse's Son Is Poisoned' (1954), *Dr Sixgun*, CBS, https://archive.org/details/otr_drsixgun. Accessed 20 July 2018.

Claybourne (1998), NewsTalkZB, https://archive.org/details/OTRR_Claybourne_Singles. Accessed 20 July 2018.

The Clerks (1991), BBC Radio 3, UK, 15 October.

Come Unto These Yellow Sands (1979), BBC Radio 3, UK, 28 March.

Creatures of Beauty (2013), Big Finish Audio, Maidenhead.

Crisp and Even Brightly (1987), BBC Radio 4, UK, 21 December.

Doctor Who: Dark Eyes Series 1 ('The Great War', 'Fugitives', 'Tangled Web', 'X and the Doctor') ([2012] 2013), Big Finish Audio, Maidenhead.
The Dark House (2003), BBC Radio 4, UK, 23 September.
Dracula (1991–92), BBC Radio 4, UK, 26 December–30 January.
Echoes (1970), BBC Radio 3, UK, 1 April.
The Edison Cylinders (2013), BBC Radio 4, UK, 22 March.
Embrace the Darkness (2002), Big Finish Audio, Maidenhead.
An Everyday Story of Afghan Folk (2012), BBC Radio 4, UK, 15–19 April.
'Expand This' (2007), BBC Radio 4, UK, 26 March.
Flip-Flop (2003), Big Finish Audio, Maidenhead.
Frontier Gentleman (1958), CBS, https://archive.org/details/FrontierGentleman-All41Episodes. Accessed 24 August 2017.
A Frozen Stream Called Wounded Knee (1992), BBC Radio 4, UK, 11 May.
Fruits Basket (2013), Furuba Drama, 5 June, http://furubadrama.weebly.com/. Accessed 20 July 2018.
I Count Myself Among Them (2012), Outland Sound, https://soundcloud.com/outland-sound/i-count-myself-among-them-a-northern-indigenous-radio-drama. Accessed 20 July 2018.
In a Manner of Speaking (1987), BBC Radio 3, UK, 6 August.
The Incomplete Recorded Works of a Dead Body (2007), BBC Radio 3, UK, 19 July.
'Indian White' (1955), *Gunsmoke*, CBS, https://archive.org/details/OTRR_Gunsmoke_Singles. Accessed 20 July 2018.
'Journey' (2011), *Life and Fate*, BBC Radio 4, UK, 20 September.
Kafka the Musical! (2011), BBC Radio 3, UK, 24 April.
Lime Town (2015–present), Two Up Productions, https://www.twoupproductions.com/shows/limetown. Accessed 20 July 2018.
The Message (2015–present), General Electric Podcast Theatre, http://themessagepodcast.com/. Accessed 20 July 2018.
'Modesty Blaise' (2014), *15 Minute Drama*, BBC Radio 4, UK, 20 June.
'Moon Graffiti' (2010), *The Truth*, Jonathan Mitchell, http://www.thetruthpodcast.com/story/2015/10/15/moon-graffiti. Accessed 20 July 2018.
My One and Only (2012), BBC Radio 4, UK, 24 April.
The Night Nurse Slept in the Day Room (1976), BBC Radio 3, UK, 5 October.
On a Day in Summer in a Garden (1975), BBC Radio 3, UK, 19 August.
'One by One' (2012), *Darker Musings*, Jack J. Ward, Electric Vicuña Productions, http://www.radiodramarevival.com/category/audio-groups/electric-vicuna/. Accessed 20 July 2018.
Our Fair City (2011–present), Hartlife, http://www.ourfaircity.com/. Accessed 20 July 2018.
Passing Time (1978), BBC Radio 3, UK, 9 November.
'Radio Radio' (1987), *Radio Active*, BBC Radio 4, UK.
The Revenge (1978), BBC Radio 3, UK, 1 June.
Sherlock Holmes vs. Dracula (1981), BBC Radio 4, UK, 19 December.
Silver Street (2004–10), BBC Asian Network.
Snape's Diaries (2008), Misfits Audio, http://misfitsaudio.com/comments/archives/category/snapes-diaries/. Accessed 20 July 2018.

References

Sophia Square (2012–13), Radio Cardiff, https://www.mixcloud.com/discover/sophia-square/. Accessed 20 July 2018.

'Sorry, Wrong Number' (1943), *Suspense*, CBS, https://archive.org/details/itotr-suspense-theradioshow. Accessed 20 July 2018.

Spoonface Steinberg (1997), BBC Radio 4, UK, 27 January.

'The Spy' (2012), *Classic Serial*, BBC Radio 4, UK, 29 January.

Stage Door (n.d.), Gypsy Audio Productions, http://www.gypsyaudio.org/show/classics/. Accessed 20 July 2018.

Star Wars (1981), NPR, 2 March–25 May.

'The Surrender of Sitting Bull' (1949), *You Are There*, CBS, 2 January, https://archive.org/details/You_Are_There_OTR. Accessed 20 July 2018.

TANIS (2015–present), Public Radio Alliance and Minnow Beats Whale, http://www.tanispodcast.com/. Accessed 20 July 2018.

'Tape Delay' (2012), *The Truth*, Jonathan Mitchell, http://www.thetruthpodcast.com/story/2015/10/14/tape-delay. Accessed 24 August 2017.

That Was Then (2018), BBC Radio 4, UK, 16 February.

'The Thing that Cries in the Night' (1949), *I Love a Mystery*, 31 October–18 November, https://archive.org/details/ILoveAMystery. Accessed 20 July 2018.

Turbo Tina, Episode 3 (2009), undistributed audio drama.

The Voyage of the Demeter (2008), BBC Radio 4, UK, 23 February.

War of the Worlds (1938), CBS, 30 October, https://www.youtube.com/watch?v=Xs0K4ApWl4g. Accessed 20 July 2018.

Waves Breaking on a Shore (2010), BBC Radio 4, UK, 28 May.

We're Alive (2009–present), http://www.werealive.com/. Accessed 20 July 2018.

Welcome to Night Vale (2012–present), Night Vale Presents Network, http://www.welcometonightvale.com/listen. Accessed 20 July 2018.

Welcome to Our Village, Please Invade Carefully (2012), BBC Radio 2, UK, 5 July.

'Wuthering Heights' (1946), *Favorite Story*, R U Sitting Comfortably?, 3 December, http://www.rusc.com/old-time-radio/Favorite-Story.aspx?s=682. Accessed 20 July 2018.

Index

A
ABC (American Broadcasting Company) 103–04, 116, 117, 125
acousmatic sound 59, 102
acting 50–53, 63, 67, 136, 182, 184, 191
  casting 60
  rehearsals 52–53, 59
  satellite audio drama 49–51, 184–85
  typecasting 52
adaptation 53, 58, 61, 67, 73, 77–78, 83, 86, 89, 96, 107–08, 135, 144, 158–62, 165–67, 168–70, 172, 182–83, 184, 185, 217, 219, 224, 225, 235, 236–38, 239–40
  Doctor Who 7, 170, 172, 185
  Dracula 57, 162
  Harry Potter 185, 219
  The Spy 61
  Star Trek 143, 185
  Star Wars 143, 219
advertising
  psychology 8, 41–42, 198–203
  on television 116–21
  on US radio 98–106, 109–11, 116, 139, 198–203
Against the Storm 23–26, 128
Allen, Kip 17, 38, 39–40, 139–41, 146, 199–200
Amnèsia (RAI 2) 8, 201
Amos 'n' Andy 30, 101, 107, 121, 230
anthologies
  radio/audio 107–08, 142, 143, 183, 184, 186, 206
  television 118
The Archers 26–29, 87, 88, 133, 136–38, 155, 156, 157, 160, 164, 165, 172, 230, 231
  community 137–38, 161
  education 27
  versimilitude 27–29, 137–38
Arnold, Matthew 81, 90, 118, 177, 218, 230
Audible 54–55, 168, 169, 178, 181, 182, 187, 199, 202, 203, 210–11, 215, 216–19, 221, 222, 224
audio drama 17, 54, 56, 58, 67, 68, 134, 138, 146, 175–78, 181, 183–91
  Archive 81 8, 189
  audiences 4, 175–78
  The Black Tapes 8, 189, 201, 206, 215
  community 182–86
  contemporary British 168–71
  crowdfunding 187, 202–03
  DIY aesthetic 17, 49–50, 185, 211
  fan audio drama 184–85, 215, 218–20
  genre 168, 183–85
  in Germany 220, 221, 238
  interactivity 220–21
  liveness 170, 181–83, 190
  The Message 8, 189
  music 181, 186
  NoSleep 182, 184, 189, 206, 215
  post-*Serial* 4, 8, 187–90, 197–98, 200–12, 216–25, 229–30
  pre-radio 73
  satellite audio drama 5, 48–51, 178, 183–85, 189, 197, 198, 215, 229, 230
  TANIS 8, 189, 190, 201, 206, 236

The Truth 35, 57, 65, 68, 143
audiobooks 54–55, 63, 138, 145–47, 178, 182, 188, 190, 197, 199, 215, 217–19
audiopositioning 63

B
BBC (British Broadcasting Corporation) 5, 7, 8, 9, 17, 22, 48, 51, 52, 53, 60, 63, 66, 77, 81, 104, 105, 111, 115, 116, 119, 127, 131, 134, 136, 143, 144, 146, 147, 153–71, 181, 184, 201, 215, 224, 235–45
   accents 60–62, 81, 84
   audiences 28, 29, 52, 120, 131–32, 136–38, 153–56, 162–63, 165–67, 175, 208, 210, 211, 219, 221
   broadcasting ethos 27, 48, 75, 80, 81–83, 85–90, 106, 122–23, 127, 132, 153, 177, 179, 218, 222, 231
   children's programming 73, 78, 80, 132
   comedy 61, 66, 86–88, 133, 135, 155, 156, 165–66, 172, 225
   criticism of 62, 67, 134, 153–54, 167–68, 180, 225, 231
   early staff members 75–76
   gamechangers 8, 77, 165–67
   gender 17, 81–82, 87, 90
   licence fee 99, 101, 153, 154, 165, 179, 201, 255
   programming 26, 28, 35, 51, 56, 57, 58, 59, 65, 66, 74, 77, 78, 90, 106, 132–33, 135–36, 143, 154–62, 165–67, 172, 190, 217, 224, 230
   Radio Times 78, 81, 85, 90, 135, 136–37, 160, 167, 171, 172, 235–44, 245
   regions 82–85, 132, 155–56
   Royal Charter 81, 154
   structure 73, 97, 101, 116, 106, 131, 132, 153, 154–57, 172
   in wartime 85–86
BBC Asian Network 155, 210–11
BBC iPlayer 163–65, 166–67
BBC Radio 3 6, 58, 89, 90, 132, 133, 135, 154, 156, 158–62, 165, 171, 172, 238
BBC Radio 4 6, 29, 51, 65, 66, 132–33, 135–38, 153, 154–57, 157–62, 163–68, 171, 172, 180, 190, 201, 208, 231, 235
   15 Minute Drama 58, 59, 156, 132, 157, 160, 161, 236, 238
   Afternoon Drama 35, 63, 156–57, 160, 162–63, 166, 236
   audiences 62, 157, 162–63, 208
   Life and Fate 26, 59–60, 65, 66, 165–67
   schedule 133, 156, 164–65, 167–68, 172
BBC Radio 4 Extra (formerly BBC Radio 7) 135, 136, 154, 157, 171, 172, 224, 235
Beck, Alan 42, 51, 52, 53, 60–61, 63, 136
Beckett, Samuel 80, 90, 143
Berkeley, Reginald 79, 81
Big Finish 6, 170, 171, 172, 202, 215, 217
binaural 63, 136, 221
blindness 18–19, 220
Bridson, D.G. 82, 83–85, 87–88, 123, 219
British Broadcasting Company 76–77, 79, 80, 122
Brown, Himan 142–43
Burke, Kenneth 6–7, 9, 15, 20–28, 29, 32, 229

C
Carter, Angela 6, 7, 59–60, 66–67
Cawelti, John G. 15, 29–32, 96–97, 102, 105, 111, 229
CBS (Columbia Broadcasting System) 20, 30, 47, 78, 101–03, 104, 106, 107, 108, 109, 110, 111, 116, 117, 118, 120, 124, 127, 141, 230
censorship
   on radio/audio 65–67, 84, 120, 132–33, 167, 172, 205
   on television 115, 119–26
Chignell, Hugh 3, 9, 15, 16, 18, 21, 22, 23, 35, 39, 89, 90, 209
children's programming 73, 78, 80, 125, 132, 139, 181
   Classic Serial 61, 77–78, 90, 143, 157–58, 160, 165, 166, 236
Claybourne 206–08, 211

The Columbia Workshop 101, 102–03, 107, 230
community radio
   in the UK 76, 133–34, 168, 211
   in the US 97, 138–41, 143, 144–45, 182, 183, 185–86, 190, 211
Cooper, Giles 89, 90, 170, 230
Corwin, Norman 54, 103, 104, 131, 187
Crisell, Andrew 9, 18, 39, 74, 75, 76, 77, 81, 85, 86, 87, 88, 123, 124, 127, 134, 177
Crook, Tim 21, 62, 73, 84, 89, 96, 132, 133, 134, 136, 137, 143, 144, 145, 153, 182, 189, 191, 216, 223
   audio drama aesthetics 6, 16, 18, 26, 38, 78, 79, 135
   audio drama and diversity 210–11
   criticism of the BBC 82–83, 137, 138, 145, 168, 180
   radio drama's critical neglect 3, 17

D
DAB (digital audio broadcasting) 134, 155
dialect 51–53, 60–61
director (role of) 51, 53–54
Douglas, Susan 22, 23, 30, 35, 36, 37, 39–41, 59, 64, 97, 98, 99, 100, 102, 106, 107, 108, 110, 116, 121, 127, 139, 180
Dragnet 95, 108–09, 125
Dubber, Andrew 8, 18, 36–37, 47, 67, 175, 179, 197, 206–07, 215, 229
Dunning, John 18, 97, 101, 102, 108, 109, 121
DXing 74, 97–98

E
earlids 36, 64–66

F
features 18, 83–84, 85, 86, 90, 135, 147, 165, 167, 170, 178, 206, 219
Fibber McGee and Molly (The Johnson Wax Program) 41, 86, 107
first-person shooter (FPS) (video games) 40, 59, 220–21

First World War 25, 40, 54, 64, 66, 68, 73–74, 75, 78, 81, 87, 97, 98, 103, 107, 122
format radio 138–41
found footage 26, 65
framing errors 4, 7–8, 15–16, 26–28, 36, 55, 189
Frankfurt School 19–21

G
Gielgud, Val 15, 21, 39, 59, 73, 77, 78–79, 84, 85, 88, 91, 123, 158, 167, 170, 215, 230
   Caesar's Mistress corruption scandal 82–83
The Goons 41, 88–89, 118
Greenhalgh, Frederick 48–51, 116, 168, 175, 176, 186–87, 216–24
Gruenberg, Axel 23–25
Guthrie, Tyrone 17, 79–80

H
headphone culture 7, 54–46, 75–76, 189, 229
Hendy, David 6, 24, 28, 38, 40, 62, 66, 75, 81, 128, 132, 133, 135, 137, 138, 154, 162, 163, 164, 165–66, 167, 177, 180, 210
Hilmes, Michele 4, 22, 24, 30, 85, 90, 107, 108–09, 119, 142, 144, 209, 220
   podcasting 4, 175, 197, 198, 202, 203, 204, 215, 219
   transnational radio 9, 30, 87, 117, 122, 128
The Hitchhiker's Guide to the Galaxy (HHGTTG) 54, 165–66, 219
hörspiel 8, 16, 83, 143, 144, 221

I
I Love a Mystery 63, 65, 104
imagery (mental) 8, 35–39, 41–43
   delay in sound comprehension 40–41
   experiments 35, 38, 41–42
   memory 42
   sound shots 41–42
Independent Radio Drama Productions Ltd. (IRDP) 134, 147, 168, 171, 211
It's That Man Again (ITMA) 7, 86, 107

J

The Jack Benny Program 22–23, 86, 101, 107, 121, 126

K

Keillor, Garrison 8, 121, 135, 139, 146–47, 184
  A Prairie Home Companion 121, 146–47, 183, 201, 210, 218
KHFM (Albuquerque) 39, 138–41, 144, 199–200
KUNM (Albuquerque) 143, 181
KZMU (Moab) 181, 189–90

L

The Lone Ranger 7, 30–32, 63, 104, 125, 142

M

Maggs, Dirk 135, 182, 224
MBS (Mutual) 102–03, 104–05, 125, 142, 211, 230
media conglomeration 102, 179
media convergence 4, 165–66, 216–18, 220–21

N

nationalism 109
NBC (National Broadcasting Company) 23, 101, 103, 104, 107, 108, 109, 110, 111, 116, 117, 118, 119, 120, 123, 126, 230
Netflix 216–18, 219
nostalgia 26, 98, 121–22, 229
  on radio/audio 28, 115, 121–22, 142–44, 146, 170, 184–86, 197
  technostalgia 189
  on television 115, 209

O

Old Time Radio (OTR) 21, 31, 52, 96, 102, 105, 111, 142–44, 147, 170, 171, 175, 178, 182–83, 184, 185, 186, 188, 197, 209, 211, 222, 231
On a Day in Summer in a Garden 56–57, 62

P

Pacifica network 143–44, 179, 180, 191, 210, 211
Paley, William S. 'Bill' 101, 109–10, 115, 117–27
podcast-makers 17, 60, 176–77, 187–88
podcasts 3–4, 8, 9, 40, 48, 51, 52, 137, 169, 170, 175–79, 180, 183, 185–90, 197–212
  access 5, 6, 177, 179, 197–206
  audiences 35, 175–76, 162, 178–81, 197–206, 220–21
  binge-consumption 4, 179
  iTunes 176, 180, 183, 185, 206, 215
  monetization 50, 197, 198–204, 216–18
  portability 6, 179
PRI (Public Radio International) 144, 179, 181, 204
producer (role of) 53–54
Public Radio Exchange (PRX) 144, 179, 181
public service broadcasting (PSB) 4, 48, 87, 131, 138–42, 146, 153, 168, 176–81, 182, 186, 199–206, 208–12, 216, 218, 219, 221, 223, 225. *See also* BBC
  funding 127–28, 146, 179–80, 190, 197, 200–03
  NPR (National Public Radio) 127–28, 134, 139, 141–42, 143, 144, 145, 146, 153, 163, 168, 178–81, 190, 200–06, 208–12, 218, 224–25
  on US television 127–28, 217

R

radio
  in Canada 83, 89, 184, 229
  definition of 3, 8, 37, 197
  in Denmark (including audio) 219, 221
  deregulation 138–41, 176
  in developing countries 6, 229
  early listening practices 75–76
  as ether 20, 64–65
  in France 19, 79, 163
  gender 75–76, 105, 107, 141

intimacy 37, 39
invasion of personal space 7, 40, 75–76, 110, 116, 120
macro–micro scale 7, 37, 179, 202
music programming 85, 106, 199
in New Zealand 179, 206–08
policy 95, 99, 115, 122, 126, 134, 147, 156, 197, 230
as primary medium 6, 40, 179
propaganda 104–05, 109, 139
race 30, 107, 144, 168, 206–10
regulation 98, 138, 154, 177, 221–22
religion 106, 146–47, 155, 162
in Scotland 76, 87, 155, 156
as secondary/background medium 3, 6, 18, 39, 40, 131, 187
signposting 26
as temporal medium 27, 38
transnational 9, 87, 117, 122–23, 170
in Turkey 17, 25
in Wales 80, 84, 87–88, 134, 155, 156
radio drama
  access 5–6, 206–08
  advertising 99–105, 109–11, 133–35
  aesthetics 6, 7, 15, 16, 26, 47, 53, 73, 76, 95, 99, 81, 182, 183, 185, 186, 189
  audiences 4, 105–06, 137, 165–66
  as auteur medium 48, 108, 125
  awards (including for audio) 88–90, 135, 136, 163–64, 165, 168, 170, 172, 187, 231, 238, 239–45, 246–50
  on British commercial radio 133–34
  canon 15–16, 35, 47
  centripetal 36–37, 47, 179, 189, 207
  close-up 59
  'danger' plays 78–79
  definition of 16
  detective shows 96–97, 102, 108–09, 110–11, 135
  dialogue 19, 36, 56, 57, 59, 61, 62, 80, 219
  as high and low art 15–32, 47, 127–28, 172
  interactivity 135–36, 137

music 17, 56, 58, 59, 76, 77, 135, 155, 184, 210, 219
  predicted demise 4, 112
  sex 28, 65–67
  Shakespeare 77–78, 161, 170
  space 38
  thrillers 48, 65, 86, 105–06, 135
  the uncanny 64–65, 97
  underresearched 3, 15, 16–17, 131, 170–71
  violence 65–67
Radio Drama Revival 48, 186
Radio Luxembourg 27, 73, 80, 81, 84–85, 170
radio reform movement 100–01, 116, 120
radiogenics 7, 29, 41, 66, 73, 78, 87–88, 90, 108, 135, 219
Rasovsky, Yuri 53–54, 143, 145–46, 191, 217
Raw, Laurence 47, 61, 160, 169, 172
recording (of drama)
  on-location 48
  post-production 48
  satellite audio drama 5, 48–51
  in studio 48, 63
Reith, J.C.W. (John) 27, 75, 76, 81–83, 86, 87, 90, 91, 106, 118, 122, 127, 132, 177, 179, 218, 222
Rodero, Emma 8, 35–36, 41, 42, 51, 137, 223

S
S Town 205–06, 210, 212
Sarnoff, David 98, 99, 100, 101, 103, 106, 110, 115, 117–21
Scriven, R.C. 35, 42, 62, 87
Second World War 23–26, 27, 47, 85–86, 103, 106–07, 111, 116, 117, 118, 163
Serial 4, 9, 176, 178–81, 187, 189–90, 197–212, 215–17, 222, 225, 229
serialization 111, 143, 197, 206–08, 215, 230, 231
  in BBC radio drama 78, 138, 160–61, 162, 230
The Shadow 7, 19, 95, 99, 102, 104, 121, 142, 183, 209

Sieveking, Lance 3, 5, 59, 79, 82, 89, 159, 167, 230
　use of montage 83
silence 39, 56, 57, 62, 75, 76, 81, 98, 221, 230
sitcom 112, 119, 124, 125. *See also* BBC comedy
　on radio 88, 96, 106–07, 109, 119, 135, 142, 156, 181–82
　on television 110–11, 125–26
Sloan, Anthony J. 143–44, 191
soap opera 9, 15, 20–29, 87–88, 96, 106–07, 117, 124, 133–34, 138
　criticism of 21–25, 27, 88
　gender 21–26
　as proverbs writ large 20–21,
Sonic Society 49, 186
soundscape 36, 39, 54–67
　sound effects 19, 36, 56–60, 65, 76, 88, 165–66, 220
Spoonface Steinberg 132, 168, 217
Suspense 86, 95, 105, 136, 222

T
talk radio 138–39, 141
techné (of radio) 47, 67, 229
telephone 64–65, 74, 77, 97–98
television 3, 5, 9, 15, 20, 21, 23, 22, 28, 29, 30, 35, 39, 43, 52, 60, 78, 99, 108, 101, 110, 115–28, 132, 133, 138, 140, 141, 143, 147, 154, 164, 165, 166, 167, 168, 177, 179, 187, 201, 205, 209, 217, 219, 220, 223, 225, 230
　acting 52–53
　audiences 43, 118–19, 120, 121
　early British development 38, 116, 123–24
　early US content 30, 108, 110, 118–21, 124–26,
　homogenization of content 120–21, 124–26, 177,
　imagination 43, 124

intimacy 43, 123
liveness 117
social anxiety of cultural decline 43, 121, 124, 168, 180
Third Programme 73, 83, 86, 87, 88–90, 127, 132, 135, 138, 143, 146, 156, 167
This American Life (TAL) 68, 143, 178–81, 189–90, 197–206, 208–12, 215–16
Thomas, Dylan 87, 89, 90, 242
Tommies 66, 73–74
tyranny of choice 164, 177–78, 190, 230

V
Verma, Neil 7, 16, 18–19, 20, 24, 36, 39, 58, 63, 64, 65, 68, 95–96, 97, 103–04, 105, 106, 107, 109, 110, 124, 125, 209

W
Walker, Mike 64, 65, 136, 161
War of the Worlds 26, 36, 37, 47, 104, 112
Ward, Jack J. 49, 56, 186–88, 222
Weaver, Sylvester J. 'Pat' 110, 115, 117–20, 127
Welcome to Night Vale (WTNV) 175, 178, 182, 185–86, 188, 198, 203, 211, 215, 222
Welles, Orson 19, 36, 47, 83, 102–03
westerns 29–32, 96, 125, 143, 145
　Dr Sixgun 31
　Gunsmoke 31, 101, 118
　Native Americans 29–32
　on television 118, 125
Williams, Raymond 20, 27–30, 32, 229
Wireless Theatre Company 168–69, 171, 181, 202, 217
Wood, Roger 37, 75, 76, 77–78, 79, 80, 82, 84, 37, 89, 90, 97, 143, 157, 159, 171

Y
You Are There 31–32, 35
Yours Truly, Johnny Dollar 95, 110–11